The Black Comedy
of John Guare

The Black Comedy
of John Guare

Gene A. Plunka

DELAWARE
Newark: University of Delaware Press
London: Associated University Presses

Associated University Presses
440 Forsgate Drive
Cranbury, NJ 08512

Associated University Presses
16 Barter Street
London WC1A 2AH, England

Associated University Presses
P.O. Box 338, Port Credit
Mississauga, Ontario
Canada L5G 4L8

The paper used in this publication meets the requirements
of the American National Standard for Permanence
of Paper for Printed Library Materials Z39.48-1984.

Library of Congress Cataloging-in-Publication Data

Plunka, Gene A., 1949–
    The black comedy of John Guare / Gene A. Plunka.
      p. cm.
    Includes bibliographical references (p.) and index.
    ISBN 0-87413-763-2 (alk. paper)
    1. Guare, John—Criticism and interpretation.
  2. Black humor (Literature)   3. Comedy.   I. Title.
  PS3557.U2 Z8 2002
  813'.54—dc21   2001036782

PRINTED IN THE UNITED STATES OF AMERICA

Contents

Acknowledgments   7

1. Introduction   11
2. Early Plays, 1966–1969   44
3. *The House of Blue Leaves*   68
4. *Marco Polo Sings a Solo* and *Rich and Famous*   86
5. *Landscape of the Body* and *Bosoms and Neglect*   109
6. *Atlantic City*   134
7. The Tetralogy   144
8. *Six Degrees of Separation*   181
9. The Later Plays   197
10. Conclusion   224

Notes   229
Bibliography   255
Index   271

Acknowledgments

A 1998 University of Memphis Faculty Research Grant enabled me to complete this book. I would like to thank Wayne Key of the University of Memphis Interlibrary Loan Office for his valuable assistance in ordering difficult-to-locate newspapers, magazines, and journals. I am indebted to Judith M. Kass, whose diligent work in the various theater photo collections in New York City enabled her to locate the cover photo for the book. I am also grateful to Stephen Parker, whose eye for detail resulted in the superb editing he did on the manuscript. In addition, I want to thank Dr. Donald C. Mell, Jr., director of the University of Delaware Press and chair of the Board of Editors of Associated University Presses, for his assistance with the external review process.

Finally, I want to express my gratitude to Dr. Christina Murphy, Dr. Naseeb Shaheen, Dr. Jackson R. Bryer, Dr. Robert Feldman, Mark Lapidus, Sally Henderson, Stanley Plunka and his wife Rhona, Harry R. Plunka, and Lillian Siegel for their encouragement and support. By constantly inquiring about the status of my research, my friends, relatives, and colleagues made the book much easier for me to complete.

The Black Comedy
of John Guare

1

Introduction

D URING THE LAST THIRTY YEARS OF THE TWENTIETH CENTURY, JOHN Guare has been lauded as one of the most successful American playwrights. In the late 1960s and early 1970s, Guare was depicted as an aspiring young dramatist whom critics assumed would follow in the footsteps of the masters of American drama: Eugene O'Neill, Arthur Miller, and Tennessee Williams. Indeed, Guare's awards began to accumulate; he has won three Obie Awards, New York Drama Critics' Circle Awards, Antoinette Perry "Tony" Awards, Drama Desk Awards, the New York Film Critics' Award, the Los Angeles Film Critics' Award, the Outer Critics' Circle Award, an Olivier Best Play Award, and an Academy Award nomination for Best Original Screenplay. In the latter part of the twentieth century, Guare, largely due to the universal appeal of his best-known dramas, *The House of Blue Leaves* and *Six Degrees of Separation,* as well as to the commercial success of his adaptation of *Two Gentlemen of Verona* and the fine writing he did for the screenplay of *Atlantic City,* has been placed in the company of Edward Albee, David Mamet, and August Wilson— playwrights who have given renewed life to the contemporary American theater.

However, unlike Albee, Mamet, and Wilson, Guare's plays have been perceived by theater critics and scholars to be much more problematic and paradoxical. Guare is often characterized as a witty playwright who has a good ear for language but one who does little with plot or character development. The form of his plays can range from zany farce to black comedy to theater of the grotesque. In a Guare play, anything can happen and usually does. These surprising twists and turns of the action force critics to assume that his plays are unstructured, chaotic, and therefore undisciplined. Gautam Dasgupta describes what we are likely to encounter in a typical Guare play: "Normal conversations easily give way to song, and characters frequently break away to converse directly with the audience.

11

Rapid changes in mode of presentation are common, with flash-backs, flash forwards, continual cross-cutting, and assorted movie techniques (that urban art form) used to create a stage picture of sometimes dazzling virtuosity. . . ."[1] Others see Guare merely as a prankster with a stinging sense of bizarre humor who fills his theater with wild images of deformity, disease, and mutations of the imagination. These theater reviewers claim that although Guare's plays are lyrical, his juxtapositions of macabre violence with zany comedy suggest a lack of focus. Furthermore, with Guare's propensity to have his characters speak in stream-of-consciousness monologue or to talk to the audience in a metatheatrical manner, he has been accused of writing episodic drama that lacks narrative coherence. Lloyd Rose states, "One can crudely describe the structure of a Guare play as a series of monologues thrown together by a more-or-less arbitrary plot: the monologues bounce against one another until something cracks."[2] At times, the audience is confused about what is occurring or why and therefore may not know how to react. In short, Guare has also been seen as obscure, writing for his own edification rather than for the audience's entertainment.

No one could ever accuse Guare of being a mainstream playwright, despite the fact that he has won his share of awards in the theater. In fact, his unconventional style replete with major reversals of the action and surprises of all sorts, coupled with his bizarre sense of humor, have certainly contributed to the Guare paradox. How is the audience supposed to react to desperate Artie Shaughnessy, who strangles his wife Bananas after his flame, Bunny Flingus, leaves for Hollywood—Artie's fantasyland—with Artie's friend, Billy Einhorn? What is the audience going to think of Stony McBride, the first person in history to have only one parent due to his transsexual mother, who conceived her son through semen saved from before her sex-change operation? What type of playwright has the gall to depict onstage a cancer patient who tries to cure herself by stuffing Kotex into the wound and then waving a statue of Saint Jude into the night air? The plays are comedies yet are permeated with such incidents as children jumping off cliffs to commit suicide, decapitations, strangulation, nuns exploding, lovers shot, a stone lion coming to life and eating a librarian, a man jumping off a Times Square scaffolding to achieve his only chance at fame, an actress lying in the middle of the theater aisle so that the departing audience must step over her, and numerous other elements that seem incongruous with comedy. Despite the fact that Guare is too outrageous to be considered a conventional playwright and that his plays appear to be unstructured, he has become one of the most interesting and provocative, yet misunderstood, playwrights of the twentieth century. This study, the first book written about John Guare, will make this talented yet enigmatic playwright more accessible to the theater-going public and to scholars of the modern stage.

John Guare's wife, Adele Chatfield-Taylor, says her husband is "a man with a mission who believes art can change the world."[3] Guare is essentially an idealist, an optimist who would love to see an end to human misery. Guare continuously writes about utopian communities that fail when reality intervenes. And in Guare's plays, reality always intervenes. During an interview with John L. DiGaetani, Guare admitted, "Who doesn't dream of things being perfect?"[4] When DiGaetani reminded him that conflicts usually occur, Guare responded, "As in life. I don't know anybody whose dreams of a perfect life match up with what they have."[5]

Although Guare rails against human misery, he is excellent at describing it in his plays. Guare's theater exacerbates the dichotomy between mundane reality and one's idealistic vision of the world. He writes about the working class, middle class, upper class—essentially people from all walks of life—whose existence is a Void. The problem, as E. M. Forster stated it, and as Deirdre says to Scooper in *Bosoms and Neglect*, is to "only connect." Guare's protagonists do not connect with themselves or with others because they are too focused on the past or the future rather than being concerned with the present. These characters are imaginative dreamers who often tell colorful stories and drift into long monologues. However, they have trouble connecting with others because they never take time to realize that their personal dreams are all they care about. Moreover, because they spend most of their time in fantasyland dreaming of the future or lamenting the past, their present lives become adversely affected. Guare acknowledged, "I like to write about characters who are not too self-aware. The main source of the cruelty is that these characters mean what they are saying at the moment they speak, but are unaware of the connective tissue between moments. I try to make the audience aware of that connective tissue."[6] Guare's theater depicts people whose lives change only because they age yet who are never able to "connect" because they are oblivious to reality while forever waiting futilely for the promotions and breaks to come.

With regard to depicting characters who cannot function effectively in the present because they are forever preoccupied with the past or the future, Guare has much in common with Chekhov. When

Guare was younger, Chekhov was his favorite writer, and since then, he has expressed his admiration several times for the Russian dramatist.[7] Guare cites Chekhov's *The Three Sisters* as the quintessential drama in which the lives of the characters seem forever wasted because of their dreams of the future. The three sisters are constantly yearning to get to Moscow. The irony is that, with Moscow's present metropolitan growth, these women, in due time, would have realized that they were already in Moscow! Playwright Jon Robin Baitz has noted, "John's specialty—well-intentioned people who long for perfect gestures, for perfectly realized lives, but who can't function at all—is fundamentally Chekhovian."[8] For example, we might examine Chekhov's masterpiece, *The Cherry Orchard.* Each of the major characters in that play lives in the past or dreams of the future. Mme. Ranevsky and her brother, Gayeff, cannot sell the orchard because it represents the past for them—the place where they were raised. Lopakhin cannot prosper as a successful businessman because he is insecure about his former heritage as a serf. Trofimoff is an idealist who represents the new Russia; he sees the phoniness of everyone around him, perceives the truth, but never acts with regard to his present life. Epihodoff, Yasha, and Dunyasha are in a love triangle that goes nowhere, demonstrating Chekhov's favorite motif—unrequited love. Like Chekhov's characters, Guare's protagonists live in a world of illusions, but the reality is that they can never "connect" with anyone or anything occurring in the present.

Chekhov was a physician, and as such, he was able to observe people from all walks of life and record their fears, desires, and anxieties. Guare observes humanity and also records the paradox between people's own obsessions and their concomitant sense of alienation and isolation. Guare and Chekhov see human beings as prisoners of their own dreams and ambitions, trapped in banal existences yet refusing to be humiliated. In the introduction to *The House of Blue Leaves,* Guare explained what appears to be the crux of his theater: "I'm not interested so much in how people survive as in how they avoid humiliation. Chekhov says we must never humiliate one another, and I think avoiding humiliation is the core of tragedy and comedy and probably of our lives."[9] Guare's protagonists are trapped into despising their drab lives, which they can only dream will one day be stupendous and exciting. The longer that these characters ignore reality, the more they are drawn deeper into frustration and despair.

Just as Chekhov acted as a seer who peered into the decline of the Russian aristocracy of the late nineteenth century, Guare, much like a sociologist, examines a troubled contemporary American society.

Harold Clurman has noted, "What motivates him [Guare] is scorn for the fraudulence of our way of life."[10] Guare believes, "Central concerns in all drama are certainly the need to be happy, the inability to face reality, the need not to be humiliated. . . ."[11] Guare's protagonists have failed to come to terms with their unique sense of individuality. Instead, they are lured by the glitz and glitter of the promised American Dream. The little people are inculcated with the notion that success in America is equated with money, beauty, and fame. Dazzled by fantasies of fame and fortune, Guare's heroes try to emulate the rich and famous, but the audience realizes that the adulation is usually to no avail. Dreaming of an idyllic life in the future, these characters have no time for relationships in the present and thus are left with a life that is passionless, love-starved, and devoid of friendship or spirituality. In short, there is no human or spiritual connection; American society has turned individuals into neurotic automatons out of tune with self and others. Samuel J. Bernstein makes the dilemma more universal: "He [Guare] literally touches the ineffable loneliness, doomed frustration, and ultimate failure of his characters, and, thus, of all human beings."[12]

The commercial values and media hype of contemporary American society have channelled its citizens into a worship of celebrities. Guare's wife notes, "John is star struck. He thinks people wanting to be famous for fifteen minutes is the great engine of twentieth-century life."[13] Since our own identities are amorphous and somewhat nebulous, we tend to admire celebrities who have already obtained our dream of material success and everlasting fame. John Harrop summarizes this showbiz mentality of American culture:

> This is seen as representative of a world in which, as Andy Warhol has said: "Everyone will be famous for fifteen minutes"—that lack of real purposes or values which needs to affirm its existence by being seen on television; the desperate desire to be rich and famous (the title of another of Guare's plays); the obsession with being "number one" that was partially responsible for the Vietnam debacle.[14]

Guare laments that the hype to be rich and famous, the need to rely on pop fantasies, has become synonymous with the American Dream. Daryl Chin astutely notes, "Guare's characters approach their lives as if the lyrics of pop songs, the melodramatic extremes of movies, and the complications of television sit-coms were the reality of their lives."[15] Our own individual dreams have been corrupted by an American ethos that has become alarmingly ubiquitous. The "limiting" sobrieties of individual worth, family relationships, friendships, and spiritual connections have been replaced by dangerous cultural norms that force many Americans to live in fantasy.

Guare writes about a crazed, chaotic society of bewildered people out of touch with their individuality yet mesmerized by a media and pop culture hype of fame and fortune. His characters are confused by their insurmountable dilemma, always wondering why they cannot make the most of their lives and why certain people can achieve celebrity status while others, no matter how hard they strive, will never be able to do so. This "invisibility of Anono-Mass," as Ruth Goetz calls it,[16] causes loneliness, bitterness, frustration, and resentment. Louis Malle, who directed Guare's *Atlantic City* and *Lydie Breeze*, writes in his foreword to three of Guare's dramas, "In Guare's plays, characters are forever whirling about, always trying to find out about themselves. They go all the way, exposing their fears, their contradictions, their false identities."[17] James Houghton, the artistic director of the Signature Theatre who staged three of Guare's plays during the 1998–1999 season, noted, "John reveals a wildly vivid imagination and insight into the struggle each of us has to make a difference and feel we belong. All his plays deal with the need for us to matter."[18] Usually, the search for worth and recognition in modern society is often futile or fleeting. The resulting sense of alienation and *angoisse* often leads Guare's protagonists into violence as a means of expressing their frustrations. Life in Guare's world, much of it expressed in New York City as a microcosm for the craziness of contemporary urban life, is synonymous with violence and teeming hostilities. When Guare's characters ultimately realize their unfulfilled dreams, the consequences are often brutal. Guare reminds us through the violence that our wounds never disappear and that this modern neurosis is never pleasant.

Although much of Guare's focus is on individuals who are mesmerized by the cult of celebrity fame and fortune, Guare is also critical of those who cannot learn from the past. In addition, Guare refuses to empathize with those who feel paralyzed by history, trapped in their past. Instead, he believes that we can assimilate something positive from America's heritage. Guare, whose roots are in the Nantucket society of nineteenth-century New England, understands the importance of the strong moral sensibility that once was the backbone behind U.S. culture. However, instead of learning from what has been the moral fiber of our historical heritage, we tend to fictionalize our pasts. Guare realizes "We see it differently from what it really was. That difference can create neuroses and insecurity. To understand ourselves we must reinterpret that past. And each human connection that we can trust helps us."[19] The promise of the future of America, as expressed by the moral optimism of our Founding Fathers and further demonstrated by the rise of utopian communities in the nineteenth century, has degenerated into the pop-art fantasies of frustrated and bewildered little people who find their dreams vanishing. As John Lahr astutely notes, "Guare evokes the central sadness of modern America—a culture groping for a destiny it betrayed: violent and ruthless in its old age."[20]

Despite the overtly pessimistic attitude prevailing in many of Guare's plays, he demonstrates a belief in the natural goodness of humanity. Guare prefers to confront the moral decay and corruption of modern society rather than ignoring our neuroses. He states, "The obligation of plays is to say, 'Oh, that is the worst thing that happened to me, and I want to keep it alive, I don't want to become dead to the great emotional moments in life.' Mental health is not analogous to amnesia."[21] Guare is interested in exploring how we can remain true to the ideals on which American society was originally established. He is convinced that the individual can make a difference in his or her own life and subsequently in the lives of others. The little person can have value. Guare revels in the pioneer spirit of colonial America: "What's important is to honor that revolutionary spirit: 'I can change. I will make a difference.'"[22] The fragmented life of modern urban society may corrupt us and channel us into disingenuous behavior, but the utopian spirit and our personal dreams can still exist. The neuroticism of the modern age must be subsumed by our personal desires, drives, and instincts that will help us create our own unique mythologies free from pop art and commercialized media icons. Our fraudulent way of life must be replaced by a community of lives that touch each other. We must gain the self-understanding and spiritual self-awareness that once defined our greatness and created high culture. Guare thus often allows his protagonists to dream, even if their utopian desires are ultimately dashed by the brutalities of the real world.

As a result of the bizarre, absurd world that Guare depicts onstage, critics have accused him of creating cartoonish characters whose eccentricities bear little resemblance to reality. He admitted, "People ask, 'Where do you get those bizarre ideas, Mr. Guare?' And I want to say, 'Bizarre? That's everyday life.'"[23] In Guare's theater, art imitates life, and as we all know, truth can be stranger than fiction. One may even find the seeds of Guare's "cartoonish eccentricities" on the pages of the *New York Times* or *New York Post*. Guare finds the sources for his "bizarre" material in everyday life. He acknowledged, "I always think that strange things happen in ordinary places. I think everybody's life is strange. If anybody had a dramatist or a hidden movie camera in their apartment recording the event, we would say, God, this is astonishing."[24] Thus, what we find in a Guare play is never far removed from our own very real neuroses that are painful to recognize but easy to dismiss as someone else's distorted nightmarish vision. Guare explained his need to present images onstage that correspond to the reality of modern society:

> Henry James once said you can soar as high as you can, but you've always got to hang onto a string—the string which holds onto that balloon—and that's a very demanding image. I love to anchor things in reality. My current play, *Six Degrees of Separation*, was inspired in part by an actual event reported in the *Times*. *Bosoms and Neglect* is based on a terribly real event that happened to me. I believe that any reality is there to use and explore. We have nothing else but that.[25]

Guare is constantly on the alert for life's amusing, yet terrifying, anecdotes, which he carefully constructs into his bizarre comedy. He revealed, "Mainly, what I do is like listening through a wall. One night in a New Orleans hotel room, I heard someone scratching on a wall next door and crying, 'Help me!' I'm always trying to find out what that is."[26]

Guare believes that much of theater's potential to enrich people's lives is due to its ability to penetrate their unconscious states, the deepest part of their psyches. Guare has taught his playwriting students at Yale University that nightmares are the origins of comedy.[27] Theater is not merely an imitation of reality; it is also a means of shaping and defining our innermost drives, impulses, and desires. Guare has learned "that theater has to get into the deepest part of your dreams, has to show you a mirror you might recoil from, but also show you reality so you might know what to do with it."[28] In short, Guare has also realized that the knowledge he has gained from the theater has prepared him for the greatest experiences in his life.[29]

Depicting how our innermost dreams conflict with the neuroses of modern life, Guare finds comedy to be the most suitable medium to present such ideas onstage. To represent the violence and zany madness of contemporary American life, he uses farce, black humor, and tragicomedy. He writes both to gain insight into the individual's dilemma in a society that worships celebrity and to determine our raison d'êtres in this absurd lifestyle. Guare asserts, "Comedies are traditionally resolved in marriage—that new beginning. I think that, finally, the plays are about how we wed ourselves to life."[30] Guare also finds comedy to be a more suitable medium than serious philosophical drama because "laughter allows you to relax so more doors inside you can open up."[31]

Although Guare is a great innovator of the modern theater, he is not interested in consciously exploring new forms of drama per se. He works with what he knows best—comedy—and while he is interested in extending the limits of that genre, he is not engaged in a theoretical exploration of dramatic structure. Comedy simply allows the audience to participate more fully in the play onstage. The comic characters onstage concomitantly need the laughter of the audience. Guare likes comedy because it has the capacity to liberate the audience from the fourth wall. Guare states, "I think that a play is about making the audience *crazy*. You want to get people off the streets into this dark room and give them that feeling of delight or laughter that makes them crazy. Farce is always being pushed toward hysteria."[32]

Guare is a highly adventurous playwright who tries to push comedy to its limits. In doing so, he has influenced several contemporary American playwrights. Keith Reddin, one of Guare's playwriting students at Yale University, commented, "John didn't set down blueprints for plays. He showed us how you could stop the action, or digress, or take wild turns. He encouraged us to free our imaginations."[33] To Guare, the theater is a venue to liberate our imaginations and return us to a place of poetry, as in the classical Greek drama, where language reigned. Guare prefers the zany antics of farce, in which the audience is enthralled and surprised at what may happen next on stage while at the same time being awed at the wit and verbal virtuosity of the dramatist. Guare expressed the importance of the playwright as a poet-vaudevillian:

> But the theater remains a place for language, a place to be *talked* to. It's as though we lived in a dark room. It's the playwright's job to illuminate and transform that room with all the means at his disposal, and finally to open the door—not to a dead-end, but to yet another room.[34]

Thus, Guare expects a highly educated, sophisticated audience who will be able to appreciate his witty dialogue, his satirical jabs at pop culture, and his ability to keep the action moving at all times. One cannot and will not doze when watching a John Guare play.

Guare sees comedy as a means of opening the door to all of the possibilities of the stage, whereas naturalism, or "kitchen-sink" drama, limits what the playwright can do. Guare learned the fundamentals of playwriting when he took a class from venerable theater critic John Gassner at Yale University. Guare recalls, "Gassner emphasized the word 'wright' in 'playwright,' speaking of it as a craft."[35] Gassner praised Ibsen's realist dramas for adhering to strict formulaic rules of playwriting. Ibsen, he noted, constructed dramas out of iron, whereas Chekhov, much the inferior playwright in Gassner's mind, built plays out of molasses. Although Ibsen is one of his favorite playwrights, Guare nevertheless objected to Gassner's confining definitions of what a play should be. As a child, Guare saw a performance of *Raisin in the Sun*, which became a model for his ideal type of theater and a reaction to Gassner's limited perspective: "The play burst out of its four-walled naturalism. Poetry breathed on that stage. . . . I swore that when I became a playwright I would never settle for a single brief moment of lightning. My plays would live in that lightning. The violent fabric of my dream life would not be forced into any pre-existing mold."[36] Another such model was the theater of Thornton Wilder, which was never constrained by the logic of naturalism. Guare remarked, "Naturalism kills; it's deadly to the theater. I remember the revelation when, as a boy, I read Thornton Wilder's *Our Town*. The Stage Manager says: 'See that boy. He will be killed in the war.' And there's no boy onstage, of course. So I realized you are not bound by four walls."[37]

As Guare began to see more theater in his childhood years, he realized that naturalism was more suited to television and movies; the theater should be a liberating space for the actor as well as the audience. Musicals, in particular, made Guare aware that the theater's range can vary widely.[38] To Guare, the theater must be a place where our unconscious desires, our contemporary sense of rage, can be expressed:

> I love actors who are performers, who are clowns—meaning they are willing to make fools of themselves, to stride that brink of panic. I feel that Stanislavsky—at least the way he's been interpreted through the Method in America—has been the enemy of performance; I'm not interested in that style of naturalism. . . . Theatrical reality happens on a much higher plane. People on a stage are enormous, there to drive us crazy. I love actors who can do that.[39]

Guare recalls seeing a 1952 Tyrone Guthrie production of Marlowe's *Tamburlaine the Great* at the Winter Garden Theater. When Tamburlaine unfurled a huge map of the world onstage and strode across it, Guare was mesmerized. This outrageous gesture was the type of zaniness that Guare sought to exorcise the audience's dreams and desires. Guare admits, "That one image so overwhelmed me that I could no longer watch TV miniatures like the original *Marty* set in living rooms like mine. I despised plays with people sitting at kitchen tables pouring their hearts out and the people in the audience oohing when the people in the play turned on the faucet and real water came out. That kitchen sink. That was what I hated most."[40] Guare, a highly adventurous playwright who tries to extend comedy to its limits, feels confined by kitchen-sink naturalism. During an interview with Anne Cattaneo of *Paris Review*, Guare revealed one of the goals of his type of theater and how it conflicts with naturalism: "It's about finding truth on the large scale with the recognition of the actor as performer. In real life we're all such performers. Naturalism wants to reduce us. Naturalism always seems to be the most unnatural thing."[41] Instead of reducing theater to recognizable boundaries, Guare prefers to liberate our dreams by expanding the parameters of the stage by creating an environment where anything can happen. Surprise is one of his fortes, and the audience watching a Guare play must realize that by keeping the play moving with unexpected twists and turns, he often breaks all rules concerning structure. In this sense, Guare's plays are structured like cinema montage; in particular, the frantic pace Guare sets is similar to the absurdity in a film by the Coen Brothers, such as *Fargo* or *The Big Lebowski*, in which one bizarre event follows another without giving the audience chance of egress. Guare's plays challenge performers to meet his expectations: "I love actors. They're like tubes of paint. All that yellow! All that red! I just want to give them more to do, to push the play as far as it can go!"[42] Thus, Guare wants to dismantle the kitchen sink and take the audience into dangerous terrain, liberate their neuroses, and restore the theater to what he calls "its true nature as a place of poetry, song, joy, a place of darkness where the bright truth is told."[43]

In 1969, at the National Theatre in London, Guare was impressed with Laurence Olivier's performance in August Strindberg's *Dance of Death* and the following evening saw him in Georges Feydeau's *A Flea in Her Ear*. Guare recalls, "The savage intensity of the first blended into the maniacal intensity of the second, and somewhere in my head *Dance of Death* became the same play as *A Flea in Her Ear*. Why shouldn't Strindberg and Feydeau get married, at least live together. . . ."[44] Guare realized that farce was the ideal form of theater that would make the play move faster and liberate the audience from being passive witnesses as they were in naturalistic dramas. Farce's wildly comic nature, as well as its satiric wit and intellectualism mocking social conventions of the day, forces the audience to engage the play in a way that kitchen-sink drama does not. Guare explains, "In most naturalistic plays the characters are living either in the past or in the future, dreaming or remembering. Farce forces people to deal with right now."[45] Despite the reputation that farce has of being associated with low comedy and popular entertainment, Guare gets the audience's immediate attention because his farces often include stakes that are quite high.[46] Guare wants to push people to their limits and force them to recognize that whatever they do may have serious consequences: "I'm only interested in somebody throwing a snowball at the man in the straw hat—who has just had a head operation."[47] Therefore, farce became the ideal medium for Guare's comedy because it breaks down the fourth wall through laughter, takes the play into new directions, liberates the audience from their neuroses, and engages the spectators emotionally and intellectually. In an interview with Patricia Bosworth, Guare discussed how farce is an ideal form of comedy for his plays:

> I chose farce because it's the most abrasive, anxious form and I'm trying to extend its boundaries because I think the chaotic state of the world demands it. Who says I have to be confined and show a guy slipping on a banana peel? Why can't I take him to the next level and show him howling with pain because he's broken his ass?[48]

Farce not only keeps the action moving, it also best reflects the state of the modern world. Guare acknowledges, "I learned that it's better to create panic on the stage because panic is alive."[49]

Critics may claim that Guare's plays are tragicomic: he draws us in with laughter and then sends us away with what he calls "dis-ease," agitation over human frailties.[50] Tragicomedy depicts life as alternately tragic and comic. Guare's theater does not achieve this equal balance. Instead, Guare focuses more on black comedy, which is defined as "humor discovered in pain, despair, horror, or a generally pessimistic view of the world."[51] At times, the audience may have difficulty in knowing how to react: with laughter on the one hand and horror or perhaps disgust on the other. In Guare's theater, humor is often paired with something that, because of revulsion, horror, or fear, is incompatible with laughter. Wolfgang Kayser's book on the grotesque concludes that one particular feature of black comedy is that the artist views the familiar world from a different perspective, rendering it comic and terrifying.[52] In addition, black humor plays half laughingly and half horrifyingly with the deep absurdities of existence. Guare has stated that he deplores the traditional happy endings of comedies: "I think that we have to have endings that say, 'You know what? God doesn't care, and chances are if you win it he'll take it away in about five seconds anyway.'"[53] In short, black comedy goes further than tragicomedy, which depicts the world as once a vale of tears and then as a circus. Philip Thomson, in his book on the grotesque, writes that black comedy is such "that the vale of tears and the circus are one, that tragedy is in some ways comic and all comedy in some way tragic and pathetic."[54] Black comedy is disturbing because it serves to alienate the audience by jolting the spectators out of their accustomed way of perceiving the world and confronting them with a different perspective. However, as Thomson suggests, although the horrifying and disgusting aspects of our existence are brought to the surface, black comedy employs humor to render the resulting alienation less harmful.[55] Thus, we are left with the paradoxical nature of Guare's theater: as black comedy, it both liberates through laughter and creates anxiety at the same time.

Before we can unravel Guare's paradoxical drama, it would be helpful to know the details about his life. John Guare was born in Manhattan on 5 February 1938, the son of Irish parents who were Catholic: John Edward and Helen Clare, née Grady. Guare was born late in his parents' lives. His father once remarked, "You came in at the tail end of everything. You never saw Eddie Cantor in *Whoopee* or Jeanne Eagels in *Rain*."[56] Guare's father's family was from Gloucester, Massachusetts, and Vermont, his mother's relatives from Lynn, Massachusetts. When John was small, the family moved to the Jackson Heights area of Queens, which is essentially where he was raised. Although Guare describes his family relationships as "very passionate" and his dedication of *The House of Blue Leaves* to his parents suggests that Guare and his parents were closely knit, friends of his have told stories of an embittered father and possessive mother who doted on their son.[57] Proud of their son's wit and charm, John's parents constantly showed him off and often exhorted him to entertain their guests.

Guare came from a family that was accustomed to entertaining. He had two great-uncles, Jimmy and Jere Grady, who toured in vaudeville from 1880 to 1925, performing sixteen stock melodramas with titles such as *Pawn Ticket 210, Girl of the Garrison,* and *The Old Toll House.* The plays were bits and pieces of borrowed material that Guare's uncles incorporated into their scripts. The act featured a midget named Billy Rhodes who was brought into the performances after Guare's grandfather, a police officer in Lynn, Massachusetts, raided a cathouse and found the five-year-old who had been left behind by one of the arrested women. Little Billy did well in the vaudeville act because he turned out to be a good singer and an adept dancer. Before John was born, his parents would walk little Billy in their baby carriage. People would stop them on the street and ask to see the darling baby. At that point, Billy, replete with a cigar in his mouth, would exclaim, while flicking an ash, "Get out of here, you son of a bitch." Eventually, he left vaudeville and joined the George M. Cohan Review of 1918. One of his uncles in the vaudeville act, whom Guare calls "Big Bill," later became an agent and was head of casting at Metro-Goldwyn-Mayer from 1934 to 1956, where he discovered Elizabeth Taylor and James Stewart; he represented performers such as W. C. Fields, Al Jolson, and Will Rogers. Guare admits, "I never saw Big Bill much but his presence and power to discover people figured heavily into my dream life."[58] Although Guare's father worked on Wall Street, he was star-struck, having been, as a teenager, George M. Cohan's office boy. Guare believes that his father regretted not going into the theater and wound up disliking what he did for a living. He often urged his son to follow his instincts and work in a profession that he liked. Guare's mother was also inclined to show business and wanted to join the vaudeville troupe, but at that time was denied because only loose women appeared on stage.

John was a pleasant child who was good in school, studied with pleasure, yet learned no sports. He told Patricia Bosworth, "My parents were very bright, very unhappy people. Loners. They lived intensely but separately in their own little worlds. Eventually so did I. I was left alone a lot so I read a great deal—everything from *Madame Bovary* to *Beau Geste* and a lot of mystery novels thrown in."[59] He attended two Catholic schools—St. Joan of Arc Elementary School in Queens and then St. John's Preparatory School in Brooklyn. Guare recalls, "For years I was berated by the priests for reading *Playboy* on the sly. 'John, John,' my confessor would moan, 'have you no consideration for your eternal soul?'"[60]

At an early age, Guare began accompanying his parents to the theater almost weekly. Guare recalls, "At seven, when I entered a theatre, I just felt at home. It was as simple as that. When they say stagestruck, one is struck by a sense of being at home. There is something about walking in that place. There is something about people in masks and make-up. It was more exciting than the movies."[61] In 1949, at age eleven, having witnessed the vivacity of Ethel Merman in *Annie Get*

Your Gun, having listened to the original cast albums of Broadway musicals, and having had the opportunity to sing along with Ray Bolger in *Where's Charley?*, Guare was convinced that he would become a playwright. That summer, when young John and his best friend, Bobby Shlomm, were on vacation in Atlantic Beach, Long Island, they read a story in *Life* about ten-year-olds who made an 8-mm film of *Tom Sawyer* during their hiatus from school.[62] Not wanting to be lazy during his summer vacation, John, who realized he had no camera, wrote three plays instead. The week before the performances of his plays, Guare disguised his voice and telephoned Time-Life, informing the operator that an eleven-year-old had written a drama that was soon to be staged in Atlantic Beach. The operator hung up. After Time-Life showed no interest, Guare called *Newsday* and told them that the proceeds of the plays were going to be donated to the orphans of Atlantic Beach. The trilogy, titled *Universe,* was performed in Bobby's garage for a week; the boys invited people who lived on a different street to see the play each day. On the last day of the performances, a black car drove up and out stepped reporters from *Newsday.* They published a story on the garage performances, giving John his first theatrical review complete with photographs. Guare later recalled that this initial publicity was a dose of elixir for him: "Seeing my name in the paper did something to me. An 11-year old playwright, Mozart as Molière! All I ever wanted to do after that was write for the theater."[63] For John's twelfth birthday, his parents gave him a Royal portable typewriter to pursue his newly chosen career. He still uses it today.

During the early 1950s, Guare often went to see a play a week at the Saturday matinees on Broadway and accompanied his parents, who would take him to the theater on birthdays and holidays. He liked musicals best but also spent time watching various types of drama, including Shakespeare during a 1954 trip to the American Shakespeare Festival in Stratford, Connecticut. He was particularly impressed with Joshua Logan's *The Wisteria Trees,* which took Chekhov's *The Cherry Orchard* and set it in the South. In 1952, he discovered *The Three Sisters,* typed it out on the Royal, substituting New Orleans for every time the three sisters shouted out for Moscow. Guare recalls, "That was the play for me. I could understand those girls being trapped. I was trapped in being fourteen, in hating my life, in wanting life to be splendid which it was not."[64] After seeing a play performed, Guare would often read it and thus was gradually learning about dramatic structure. He also read the record jackets of show albums. He soon recognized that usually the second production number was a "want" song, providing impetus for a character's motivation. Guare acknowledged that, despite what may appear to be a lack of form in his plays, they are grounded in the conventional structure of musicals: "Therefore, beginning a play, what is my 'want'? I came to Stanislavski through record jackets at age twelve, thirteen, fourteen. So I always approach plays in a practical way."[65]

There was a break in John's schooling when his father, who developed angina, took a year off from work. The family moved to Ellenville, in upstate New York, to live with an ailing elderly aunt. The grammar school in Ellenville did not pledge allegiance to the flag, which irked John's father and the nuns at Saint Joan of Arc. They considered it best that John stay enrolled in Saint Joan of Arc and not attend school in Ellenville but instead send his homework to the nuns in Queens. Thus, John had a lot of time to read on his own. He also took his first job. Ellenville was a two-movie town, and the owner of one of those theaters paid John to buy the first and last tickets of the day at his competitor's establishment. He told John, "I want a straight count on what he grosses. No sense me booking in something he lost money on!"[66]

Guare matriculated at Georgetown University in 1956, continuing his education in the Jesuit tradition. At Georgetown, he socialized with people who were interested in theater and were staging new plays. So Guare wrote a new play each year, entering his first contest in 1957; his play, *She Conqs to Stooper,* won second place. *Thirties Girl,* set in Hollywood when the first talkies were making silent films obsolete, was performed at Georgetown in 1959. The play, whose songs were later incorporated into *The House of Blue Leaves,* owed a lot to the musicals Guare enjoyed, particularly *Singing in the Rain. The Toadstool Boy* was staged the following year and dealt with a young rock singer who commits suicide to establish a cult following. Although the latter drama won the Washington One-Act Play Contest in 1960, both plays are no longer extant.

Washington, D.C. was an important tryout town for new plays destined for the New York stage, so Guare was able to see some fine theater during his college career. He wrote a play in emulation of Oscar Wilde after seeing a college production of *The Importance of Being Earnest* and also tried to "assist" Sean O'Casey by composing an additional act for *The Plough and the Stars.* Guare remembers discovering Philip Barry in his junior year and thought that he would follow in Barry's footsteps as an Irish-Catholic playwright wittily observing life, although being somewhat removed from it. Guare states, "But then I did my senior thesis on Barry, I interviewed his sister, and I realized how much he hated sex and life, what the cost of all that glamour was. It was very troubling."[67] Guare also took his first job in the theater when, in 1960, he succeeded Warren Beatty as the assistant to the manager of the National Theatre. Guare enjoyed this job, although it essentially involved selling orange juice and checking coats for the patrons.

During his college years, Guare was editor of the literary magazine, tried out for the glee club (but didn't make it), and tried his hand at writing short stories, most of them Flaubert imitations. In one class, Guare's English teacher knew Katherine Anne Porter, who agreed to pay John $1,500 for the first sentence of one of his short stories: "After Pinky vomited, Ingrid Aldamine sat up in bed." Guare was awed by the fact that a famous writer was impressed with the rhythmic variation of that line. Guare, however, was committed to writing plays rather than other forms of fiction: "I felt I was betraying a higher calling by writing mere short stories or novels. I believed plays to be on a higher and rarer plane. I still do."[68] Guare graduated from Georgetown with a B.A. in English in 1960.[69]

Guare attended graduate school at Yale University in 1960 and obtained his Master of Fine Arts in Playwriting there in 1963. Guare's *The Golden Cherub*, a play in one act whose main character was influenced by Jimmy Porter in John Osborne's *Look Back in Anger*, was performed at the Yale Drama School in 1962, where it was well received. On 10 April 1963, Yale University Theatre staged Guare's three-act drama *Did You Write My Name in the Snow?*, his first whimsical examination of human absurdity. These two early plays have never been published. While Guare acknowledges that the military draft was partly responsible for his stay in graduate school, he did learn from his mentors there. Although John Gassner stressed the logic in constructing plays (and was particularly annoyed when Guare included in one of his dramas a character in the second act who was killed off in the first), Guare learned more from Donald Oenslager and Ernest Bevan, especially about set design, lighting, and costuming. Although he never was any good with set design or with technical production, Guare learned the craft of drama, the work processes, and how important it is for the playwright to assume responsibility for understanding everything on stage, including effective lighting and set design.

New Haven, Connecticut, was also a tryout town for potential Broadway plays, and thus Guare was able to see how plays were rehearsed and rewritten for New York. He ushered at the Shubert Theater in New Haven and worked backstage at summer stock doing jobs that ranged from garbage collector to running light boards to fixing the plumbing in Gloria Swanson's dressing room. One summer, he toured as an advance man for summer stock productions, setting up the show each week in a different theater. This experience taught him the value of going backstage frequently to determine the moods and anxieties of the performers to ensure that the production would run smoothly. Thus, working on shows at Yale, learning from the faculty, talking with his peers about theater, and reading virtually every play in the Yale Library all made Guare's experience in graduate school very rewarding.

Did You Write My Name in the Snow? was seen by promotions people at MCA when it was staged at Yale University. Impressed with Guare's writing, MCA offered him a job as a writing trainee at Universal Studios when he graduated in 1963. At the same time, Uncle Billy, proud of his nephew as a Yale graduate, procured a writing job for him at MGM studios in California. The dilemma of which job to take was solved when Guare received his draft notice. He spent the next six months in the Air Force Reserves (he enlisted five days before receiving his draft notice), a Yale M.F.A. in a squadron with not a single high school graduate. He left the Reserves with the rank he had when he entered—airman, third class (3/C)—the lowest. As Guare was ready to move to California to take a job as a screenwriter, his aunt in San Francisco said she was disappointed that he would forsake his desire to work in the theater in order to write for the movies. Guare recalls, "She had planned to leave me ten thousand dollars. Now, she would give the sum to me if I left California, went back to New York, wrote plays, went to Europe, sent her postcards. If I didn't do this, she would leave the money to a dog charity."[70] All of this sounds like the beginning of a John Guare comedy. Nevertheless, Guare placated her by returning to New York, and while living in a rented room in Brooklyn, he put his chances for success in the hands of off-Broadway producers.

In the early 1960s, off-Broadway theater began flourishing as a training ground for innovative, experimental playwrights who were willing to take risks not afforded by the Broadway stage. Off-Broadway plays could be produced rather quickly and inexpensively, thus providing playwrights with a chance to experiment without having to worry about the scrutiny of theater reviewers picking apart their work. Guare presented two plays to Joe Cino, who ran Caffe Cino on Cornelia Street in Greenwich Village. Cino, a burly Sicilian who worked a day job in a steam laundry, told Guare that Caffe Cino was only doing plays by Aquarians that month. When Guare admitted that he was an Aquarian, Cino checked Guare's driver's license and then, after consulting an astrological chart, told the aspiring young talent that rehearsals started in two weeks, after which his play would run two weeks with the possibility of an extension of a third. Guare reminisced about his first professional production in New York: "I don't know what would have happened to me if I had been a Gemini."[71] Meanwhile, Edward Albee was using the royalties accrued from *Who's Afraid of Virginia Woolf?* to form his own off-Broadway success, the Albee, Barr, Wilder Workshop. Guare's one-act drama, *To Wally Pantoni, We Leave a Credenza,* was staged there in 1965, and although it was produced for NBC Television in 1969, the play has yet to be published. It concerns a childless old couple trying to establish themselves in a new apartment in New York as their old home is about to be demolished. Guare's play laments the demise of the pioneer spirit in favor of the modern sense of technological progress. Shortly afterwards, in 1965, administrators at the O'Neill Theatre Center sent out questionnaires to various theaters and agents to submit names of twenty promising playwrights. Guare's name was selected along with such aspiring talents as Leonard Melfi, Sam Shepard, and Lanford Wilson. These playwrights were brought up to Waterford, Connecticut, where they were questioned about what playwrights want. Guare was assigned a date to have a play finished; under this deadline, he wrote the first act of *The House of Blue Leaves.* Also, for a brief period in 1965, Guare worked as William Inge's assistant for a new pre-Broadway play that Inge had finished. Titled *Where's Daddy?,* the play was panned by a critic in Boston. Inge committed suicide in 1973. Guare thus learned first-hand how thick-skinned a playwright must be to survive.

Suddenly, in 1965, Guare awoke one morning and felt that if he did not go to Europe that day, he would die. Thus, 4:30 that afternoon, Guare got on the *Queen Elizabeth* for a trip to London. After all, he did promise his aunt that he would travel to Europe and then send her postcards. In London, Guare spent some time reading scripts for a publisher. Meanwhile, he was attending the theater, seeing some exceptionally good plays, including Laurence Olivier in *Othello* and the original production of Pinter's *The Homecoming.* In spring 1965, he took the night train to Paris, where he dramatically threw his suitcase in the Seine River. He hitchhiked throughout Europe to Istanbul, on to Cairo, and then to the Sudan, writing constantly yet keeping to himself almost as if he were a loner. Since Guare had virtually no one to talk with, he started writing in pocket-size notebooks. Guare has continued to write in these notebooks and has filled up several dozens of them over the years. Guare began to find himself as well: "I traveled all over Europe and finally began to get a sense of myself. And I started believing in the force of my will and not in the will of God. You can't imagine how important that was because until then I honestly didn't believe I could be responsible for my own destiny."[72]

When Guare was in Cairo at the end of 1965, his parents sent him news clippings about 4 October 1965, the day the Pope, making his first trip overseas, came to New York City. Guare's parents noted that while John was seeing the world, he missed this one magical day that changed the lives of many Catholics. Guare recalls the genesis of *The House of Blue Leaves*:

> Sitting in Cairo, reading what that day meant to them back on Queens Boulevard, I saw my life and all our dreams and where those dreams had taken us, and I realized I had a subject. I started writing *House of Blue Leaves*. I read that letter, and everything that had happened to me in my life became accessible. I heard the sound of my life.[73]

When Guare returned to New York in July 1966, he had part of *The House of Blue Leaves* written. He completed the first act the day his father died, but this traumatic event forced Guare to abandon doing any more writing on the play. Nevertheless, the first act of the drama was given a reading at the Eugene O'Neill Memorial Theatre in Waterford, Connecticut, at the end of summer 1966. At the O'Neill Theatre Center, Guare rubbed shoulders with the likes of Bobby Lewis, Alan Schneider, Jose Quintero, and Lloyd Richards. He enjoyed the receptive audience and learned how to cooperate with actors in trying to understand the rhythms of how a play worked on the boards. As a result of the success of Guare's reading of the play, he received an ABC Television grant to study film writing at Yale University. The grant allowed Guare, Sam Shepard, Kenneth Brown, Barbara Garson, and Megan Terry—aspiring talents of the theater—to adapt their playwriting skills to making movies. Moreover, Guare's staged reading of the first act of *The House of Blue Leaves* caught the attention of Warren Lyons and Betty Ann Besch, two New York producers who immediately optioned the play. Guare, unable to write the second act, withdrew to Yale University to polish his playwriting skills. While he was there, he wrote two short one-act dramas: *Something I'll Tell You Tuesday* and *The Loveliest Afternoon of the Year*. These two plays were first performed later that year on 25 October 1966, at Caffe Cino. Guare recalls the thrill and satisfaction of writing for off-Broadway: "The plays were not reviewed. Audiences just showed up at the theater to see what was there. They were very exciting times. I once wrote a play called *A Day for Surprises* on a Thursday, and it opened the next Monday."[74]

While at Yale, Guare, who was given a deadline for his next play so it could be staged at the Eugene O'Neill Memorial Theatre Playwrights' Conference, wrote *Muzeeka,* inspired by the idealistic undergraduates at the university soon to be faced with the reality of an American society ravaged by the Vietnam War. *Muzeeka* was first staged on 19 July 1967 by the Eugene O'Neill Memorial Foundation Theatre in Waterford, was subsequently part of the first New Theatre for Now Series at the Mark Taper Forum in Los Angeles on 10 October 1967, and then was performed at the Provincetown Playhouse in New York on 28 April 1968. The play, which ran for sixty-five performances, garnered Guare's first major award—an Obie for best play produced off-Broadway in 1968. Guare also won his first Rockefeller grant that year.

In 1968, Guare worked with director Jerome Robbins and lyricist Stephen Sondheim on adapting Brecht's *The Exception and the Rule* into a musical starring Zero Mostel. Leonard Bernstein was to compose the music for this new play, and Guare was to prepare the text, tentatively titled *A Play by Brecht.* The project turned out to be too complicated; the day Jerome Robbins decided he had had enough, Guare was immensely relieved.[75] Meanwhile, in the late 1960s, Guare had been an activist against the war in Vietnam and had participated in virtually every anti-war demonstration held in New York and Washington, D.C. His next play, *Cop-Out,* was based upon one such anti-war demonstration in which Guare experienced the unfortunate mishap of being knocked unconscious after being accidentally kicked in the head by a police officer's horse. *Cop-Out,* which debuted at the Eugene O'Neill Memorial Theatre in July 1968, was subsequently presented on 7 April 1969, on a double bill with Guare's *Home Fires* at the Cort Theatre, his first Broadway premiere. Guare had high hopes for these one-act plays but was devastated by the harsh critical notices in the New York press. The plays closed after only four performances. Depressed by the derisory tone of the reviews, Guare fled the country on the *Queen Elizabeth II,* hoping that the ship would be hit by an iceberg.[76] He stayed away for five months, most of the time hitchhiking in the Arctic Circle, which was warm at that time of the year, but also spent time touring Europe. Actually, *Cop-Out* did not turn out to be the flop that Guare had imagined, for the play later earned him the distinction of being voted Most Promising Playwright in *Variety*'s poll of the New York Drama Critics. Furthermore, while Guare was out of the country, his short play, *Kissing Sweet*, was presented as part of FOUL! on New York Television Theater (Channel 13) in November 1969.

When Guare was in London, he saw Olivier do Strindberg and Feydeau on successive nights, learning about how farce can be an effective form of drama. Upon his return to New York in February 1970, Guare finished *The House of Blue Leaves*, after nearly five years and nine drafts of work on the second act. Guare had all sorts of problems writing the play because he lacked the technical expertise to compose a longer farce that contained nine characters. John Lahr, Guare's friend that he met at the O'Neill Theatre Center, suggested Mel Shapiro, who worked at the Tyrone Guthrie Theater, as a possible director for the play. Guare also came to admire Shapiro's work after seeing a Václav Havel play that he had directed in Lincoln Center. After taking eight months to raise the money for *The House of Blue Leaves*, finding the right theater, and getting Mel Shapiro as the director, the cast, which included Anne Meara, Harold Gould, and Katherine Helmond, went into rehearsals at the end of November 1970. An off-Broadway actors' strike delayed the production for an additional two months. Guare wondered if his play would ever be performed. Finally, *The House of Blue Leaves* had its New York premiere at the Truck and Warehouse Theater on 10 February 1971. The play was a huge success, closing after 337 performances due to a mysterious fire in the theater. The police found the theater vandalized and discovered a body with its throat slashed in an adjoining building. The producers decided not to reopen the show. *The House of Blue Leaves* became Guare's first major breakthrough in the theater: the drama was voted Best American Play of the 1970–71 season by the New York Drama Critics' Circle, received an Obie Award (Guare's second) and an Outer Critics' Circle Award, and earned Guare a cover photo and story in the 12 July 1971 edition of *Saturday Review*, which declared him America's most successful new playwright. Guare was also elected to the Dramatists Guild Council in 1971.

While Guare was busy with *The House of Blue Leaves*, he was asked to help Milos Forman revise the screenplay for his next film, *Taking Off*. Forman began writing the script with Jean-Claude Carrière in March 1968 and finished in October. After Paramount agreed to make the film, Forman and Carrière revised the screenplay. John Klein, a young filmmaker, was brought in to polish the English prose. Executives at Paramount, however, reneged when they read the script, and Forman was obligated to pay $140,000 to be released from his contract. When Universal Studios agreed to take on the project,

Guare was called upon to revise the script because Forman trusted his judgment. The film, which opened in New York on 28 March 1971, starred Lynn Carlin and Buck Henry. Although *Taking Off* did win the Jury Prize at the Cannes Film Festival in 1971, the film is Forman's project, not Guare's, and therefore will not be treated with the same attention that must be accorded to *Atlantic City*.[77]

During the successful run of *The House of Blue Leaves*, Joseph Papp asked Mel Shapiro to direct an adaptation of Shakespeare's *Two Gentlemen of Verona* for a summer Shakespeare festival in Central Park. Shapiro wanted Galt MacDermot, who scored *Hair*, to compose the music and suggested that Guare, fresh from having worked with Shapiro on *Blue Leaves*, write songs and prepare the adaptation. The team rehearsed with an interracial cast—black, Puerto Rican, Caucasian, Chinese—that included Raul Julia, Clifton Davis, Jonelle Allen, Jerry Stiller, Alvin Lum, and Frederic Warriner. The play's love story developed into a metaphor of how the races could possibly live together, much like in a utopian society. Guare kept perhaps half of Shakespeare's dialogue, and although the team began with nine songs, the music in the play proved so popular that they eventually went with twenty-four musical numbers and then added seven more for Broadway. The music was intricate and varied, with one critic describing it as a combination of Caribbean capers, cabaret soul, rock ballad, social commentary song, and early rock-and-roll pastiche.[78] Guare changed the locale of Shakespeare's play from sixteenth-century Italy to modern-day San Juan, Puerto Rico, and New York City. The play opened on 22 July 1971 at the Delacorte Theatre in Central Park and proved to be so successful that it transferred to Broadway's St. James Theater on 1 December 1971, at a cost of $400,000. The critics praised Guare's adaptation, MacDermot's music, Jean Erdman's dance choreography, the polyglot casting, and the madness, cheerfulness, and spontaneity of the play as a New York City block party that was not a spoof of Shakespeare but instead became an updated version of the theme of love and friendship.[79] During summer 1971, *Two Gentlemen* also toured the city's parks and playgrounds with the Festival's Mobile Theater. With *Two Gentlemen* and *The House of Blue Leaves*, Guare thus was to have two plays running simultaneously on Broadway. *Two Gentlemen of Verona* closed 20 May 1973, after 613 Broadway performances. The play was awarded the New York Drama Critics' Circle Award for Best Musical of 1971–72, Drama Desk Awards for Best Book and Best Lyrics, the *Variety* poll award for best lyricist, and two Tony Awards—one for Best Musical Play and the other for Best Book of a Musical. The play was also staged at London's Phoenix Theatre, debuting on 26 April 1973, and receiving mostly positive critical reviews.[80]

Guare's success with *The House of Blue Leaves* and with *Two Gentlemen of Verona* buoyed him in the 1970s to write what would eventually become several of his best-known plays. Guare's next venture was a collaboration with Harold Stone on an adaptation of Voltaire's novel, *Optimism, or the Adventures of Candide,* eventually staged at the Eugene O'Neill Memorial Foundation Theatre in 1973. However, having more notoriety forced Guare to soon question his goals in life. He was fully entrenched as a New York playwright, which presented Guare with mixed blessings. Years later he remarked that life in New York is "a complete addiction. Every day it presents you with something for horror, amusement, despair, and . . . glee."[81] Guare, of course, realizes that New York City is often the source for his inspiration, but also understands how parochial it can be. Guare once remarked, "Oh, if only I could be European or Southern and not cursed with the nothingness of my surroundings!"[82] Feeling that he needed new experiences to sustain him and realizing that some of his family roots were from New England, Guare went to Nantucket to live. He admitted, "It was a joy to discover that I could start all over again, to be able to see things and figure out how we know what it is we learn. It was a lifesaver."[83] Indeed, Guare very much enjoyed working with Mel Shapiro and the Nantucket Stage Company on *Marco Polo Sings a Solo,* which premiered 6 August 1973 at the Cyrus Pierce Theater in Nantucket and ran there for six weeks. *Rich and Famous* also debuted away from New York at the Academy Theater in Lake Forest, Illinois, August 1974, before its premiere in New York at the New York Shakespeare Festival's Estelle Newman Public Theater, on 19 February 1976, eventually running for seventy-eight performances. As the playwright-in-residence at Joseph Papp's New York Shakespeare Festival in 1976 and 1977, Guare was able to get plays produced there.[84] The revised version of *Marco Polo Sings a Solo* was presented at the Public Theater on 6 February 1977. On 12 October 1977, John Pasquin directed Guare's *Landscape of the Body* there after it was tried out earlier that summer at the Academy Festival Theatre. Although the play was well received in Chicago theater circles, the New York critics were not as kind. Even though *Landscape of the Body* went on to win the Joseph Jefferson Award for Playwriting and Sam Spiegel commissioned Guare to write a screenplay for the movie version, Guare was stung by the reviews and wanted his subsequent plays to be spared the New York critical "experience." His next project, *Bosoms and Neglect,* was given a warm reception at the Goodman Theater in Chicago, where it opened on 1 March 1979. However, the play was mauled by the New York press when it made its New York premiere on 3 May 1979, at the Longacre Theatre, closing after only four performances. After the New York productions of four major plays from 1976 to 1979, Guare was able to earn a paltry $24,000 and a small sum of money for winning his second Rockefeller grant in 1977.

Guare was also keeping busy in other ways in the late 1970s. In 1978, he was teaching at Yale University as an adjunct professor of playwriting. His short play, *In Fireworks Lie Secret Codes*, which was commissioned by Jon Jory, opened as part of the Festival of New American Plays staged at the Actors Theatre of Louisville on 26 January 1979. The play was later staged as part of the One-Act Play Festival held at the Lincoln Center Theater Company on 5 March 1981. For these later performances, Guare directed the play himself.

Just when Guare was feeling depressed over the Broadway fiasco of *Bosoms and Neglect*, he received a telephone call on 28 July 1979, from director Louis Malle. The Canadian government was willing to finance Malle's next project, which had to be completed in 1979. Malle turned down the first script that was offered to him and suggested Guare for the screenplay. Malle met Guare in New York, and during their discussion, the latter mentioned that he had relatives in Atlantic City. Guare and Malle rented a car and drove down for the day. Fascinated by this city that was half in the past and half in the future, Malle and Guare knew they had the subject for their film. The next day, Malle flew to France but not before commissioning Guare to write the screenplay for *Atlantic City*. On 10 August, Guare turned the completed scenario over to Malle in Toulouse. Filming began on 31 October; often working around the clock, Malle finished shooting on 31 December. In 1981, Guare's screenplay won the New York Film Critics' Circle Award, the Los Angeles Film Critics' Circle Award, the National Society of Film Critics' Award, the Golden Lion Award at the Venice Film Festival, and was nominated for an Academy Award. The film itself was nominated for five Academy Awards, including Best Director and Best Picture.

Furthermore, in 1981, Guare received the Award of Merit from the American Academy and Institute of Arts and Letters, a prestigious honor, considering that previous winners included Ernest Hemingway, Theodore Dreiser, and W. H. Auden. The following year, Guare won a fellowship from the New York Institute of the Humanities. Furthermore, the amount of money he earned from the screenplay for *Atlantic City* allowed him to buy back the film rights to *The House of Blue Leaves* from Carlo Ponti.

On 20 May 1981, the day he won the Award of Merit, Guare married Adele Chatfield-Taylor and then flew to England for a month-long honeymoon. Guare met Adele six years earlier in 1975, at the home of a mutual friend in Nantucket. During that time, she was living on lower Fifth Avenue while John was on Bank Street in John Lennon's old apartment. Somewhat stupefied by the fan mail and presents that he was receiving with notes such as "We love you, John," Guare was only too glad to move out of Lennon's former residence when the Greenwich Village apartment next door to Adele became available. They soon connected the rooms and added a small space as John's study. Adele is an architect and at the time was director of the New York Landmarks Preservation Foundation and has since then held positions as head of the American Academy in Rome and as director of the design-arts program of the National Endowment of the Arts. As one might expect of an architect, Adele is neat and orderly whereas John prefers clutter, often working on his bed covered with books, looseleaf pages, notebooks, newspapers, the telephone, his Rolodex, scissors, staples, and his pet pugs. An eight-foot service hall keeps their lifestyles separate so their marriage can remain intact. Actually, Adele and John have quite a bit in common. John loves to travel and accompanies his wife to Europe several times each year as part of her duties with the American Academy in Rome. John's mother's death in 1981 left him virtually without any close relatives; thus, John was thankful to adopt his wife's large family as his own. They both share a love of clutter (Adele's clutter is much more organized), like cats and dogs, and appreciate good literature (John spends hours browsing in bookstores such as the Strand).[85]

The marriage seemed to have inspired Guare to take a new direction in his playwriting efforts. After tinkering with a screenplay, *Big Kiss,* that was destined for a Bette Midler film that never got produced, and after directing a playlet for Edward Albee's One-Act Play Series for Lincoln Center, Guare gave serious attention to the writing of his tetralogy, a cycle of four plays set between the Civil War and the end of the nineteenth century. The series of plays is dedicated to his wife and takes place where they initially met and where Guare begins to explore his New England roots: in Nantucket. Guare must have wanted to escape the New York influence. He also tried to explore the world of his parents, who were both born in the 1890s, when part of the tetralogy occurs. Guare states, "I wanted to make sense out of family myths, overheards and recriminations and family legends and half-understood events that happened before I was born in 1938."[86] Most importantly, the tetralogy marks a serious change in the form of Guare's plays. Realizing that black comedy or farce would be inappropriate for this cycle of plays, Guare turned to realism and melodrama, often emulating Ibsen, Strindberg, Chekhov, and O'Neill. Thus, Guare was able to explore his heritage in dramatic literature and learn more about play structure.

In 1978, Guare had written the first act of *Lydie Breeze*, which is chronologically the last play in the cycle. Inspired by a staged reading of the play in a theater workshop during 1979, Guare decided to pursue other plays in the tetralogy. To explain the history of the characters in *Lydie Breeze*, Guare wrote *Gardenia*, which begins on Nantucket in 1875. Guare and Malle so enjoyed their work on *Atlantic City* that Malle agreed to direct *Lydie Breeze*. The play opened at the off-Broadway American Place Theater in New York on 25 February 1982, marking Malle's directorial debut in the theater. A few months later, on 28 April 1982, *Gardenia* was staged at the Manhattan Theater Club with Karel Reisz directing a cast that included Sam Waterston, JoBeth Williams, and James Woods. While in London later that year, Guare wrote *Women and Water*, which is chronologically the first play in the cycle, occurring in 1861 and 1864. As an early draft, *Women and Water* was staged at the Los Angeles Actors' Theater in 1984 and then was produced at the Goodman Theater in Chicago in July 1985. The revised version of the play was given a major production at Arena Stage in Washington, D.C., premiering there on 29 November 1985. Guare has been working for years on the last play of the tetralogy, *Bulfinch's Mythology*, which is to take place a year after the events of *Gardenia*.

In the 1980s, Guare was involved with several theatrical projects. In 1981, he wrote *Moon Over Miami*, the screenplay for a film comedy that Malle was to direct about the ABSCAM scandal during the early part of the Reagan years. Written to feature John Belushi and Dan Ackroyd, the screenplay was abandoned when Belushi died from an overdose of cocaine. Malle suggested to Guare that he revise the script as a play. The revised edition was first presented at the Williamstown Theater Festival in Williamstown, Massachusetts, in August 1987 and then was staged at Yale Repertory Theatre in April 1989. From 23 February to 17 March 1984, *Hey, Stay a While*, a program consisting of *The Loveliest Afternoon of the Year*, *A Day for Surprises*, a few monologues from Guare's plays, and several of his songs that range from musical numbers in *Cop-Out* to *Two Gentlemen of Verona*, was staged in Ingrid's restaurant off the lobby of the Goodman Theater in Chicago. The evening's entertainment also included

House of Love, Guare's mini-opera fantasy about the revenge of Eddie Fisher on Elizabeth Taylor, which he derived from a report in the *New York Post*.[87]

Guare also had two short dramas produced in 1985 and 1986. Guare was asked to compose a play as part of The Show of the Seven Deadly Sins to be staged at the McCarter Theatre, Princeton University. Guare's *Gluttony*, performed in February 1985 as part of Princeton's 1984–85 theater season, was one of seven short plays staged with *Faustus in Hell*, written and adapted by Nagle Jackson from plays by Marlowe, Goethe, and Molière.[88] In Guare's play, gluttony is represented by a modern-day messiah gorging himself with junk food. The second play was commissioned by Anne Cattaneo, dramaturge at the Acting Company. She asked seven playwrights, including Guare, each to adapt one of Chekhov's short stories for the stage. Guare's adaptation of Chekhov's "A Joke" was *The Talking Dog*. These seven short plays were first staged at the Krannert Center in Urbana, Illinois, then were taken on a sixty-city national tour, and finally were presented at New York's Lucille Lortel Theater on 22 April 1986, directed by Robert Falls in a program called *Orchards: A Chekhov Evening*.[89]

Guare's reputation was given another boost with the highly successful 1986 revival of *The House of Blue Leaves*. Director Gregory Mosher at Lincoln Center originally wanted to stage *Gardenia* there, but because the cast that he sought was not available, he decided to do *Blue Leaves* instead for a run of eight weeks. Directed by Jerry Zaks, *The House of Blue Leaves*, which began its run at the Mitzi E. Newhouse Theater on 19 March 1986, with a strong cast that included John Mahoney, Ben Stiller, Stockard Channing, Swoosie Kurtz, and Christopher Walken, proved to be an even bigger hit than it was fifteen years earlier in 1971. Part of its popularity was due to the fact that the audience had changed in those fifteen years, and in 1986, after a pope had already been shot, the pop cultural events of the play came close to being accepted as reality. The huge success of the revival forced the producers to move the play from the 299-seat Mitzi E. Newhouse to the 1,100-seat Vivian Beaumont Theater on 29 April 1986; the play transferred to Broadway's Plymouth Theater on 14 October 1986. By the time *The House of Blue Leaves* closed on 15 March 1987, it had been given 420 performances. The play won four Tony Awards: Best Actress (Swoosie Kurtz), Best Actor (John Mahoney), Best Director (Jerry Zaks), and Best Scenic Design (Tony Walton). Guare went on to become co-editor of the *Lincoln Center New Theater Review*, was elected to the executive board of PEN, in 1986 was elected vice president of Theatre Communications Group (a national organization dedicated to the development of professional theater), won a 1987 New York Institute for the Humanities fellowship, and was elected to the American Academy and Institute of Arts and Letters in 1989.

Invigorated by the success of the revival of *The House of Blue Leaves*, Guare, writing in summer 1989, targeted his new drama, *Six Degrees of Separation*, for possible production at Lincoln Center. The play began performances at the Mitzi E. Newhouse Theater, Lincoln Center, on 19 May 1990, and then had its official opening to rave reviews on 14 June. Jerry Zaks directed a strong ensemble that featured Stockard Channing (Ouisa), John Cunningham (Flan), and James McDaniel (Paul). When Channing left the show briefly to honor a movie commitment, Swoosie Kurtz, who won the Tony Award for Best Actress in the revival of *Blue Leaves*, filled in admirably for her. After the original ten-week limited run of the production had expired, the play opened at the larger Vivian Beaumont Theater at Lincoln Center, with Courtney B. Vance playing Paul and Channing back in her original role as Ouisa. *Six Degrees of Separation* went on a highly successful run of eighty weeks and won the 1990–91 New York Drama Critics' Circle Award for Best Play, an Obie Award, and a Hull Warriner Award. The play also received a highly acclaimed production directed by Phyllida Lloyd in London at the Royal Court Theatre in June 1992, with Stockard Channing the lone holdover from the New York cast. *Six Degrees of Separation* was honored by the British by winning the Olivier Best Play Award in 1993. The original company, including director Jerry Zaks, John Cunningham, and Marlo Thomas as Ouisa, went on a nationwide tour of the play, mounting productions at the Doolittle Theater, Los Angeles, in December 1992, at the National Theatre, Washington, D.C., in March 1993, and in many other cities. On 20 May 1993, after two and a half months of filming in locations around New York City, the movie version of the play wrapped up its shooting. The film, *Six Degrees of Separation*, directed by Fred Schepisi, was released late that year with a stellar cast that featured Donald Sutherland, Will Smith, and Stockard Channing, supported by Ian McKellen, Mary Beth Hurt, and Bruce Davison. The film was particularly praised for Schepisi's fast pace, the strong cast, the ambitious production design by Patrizia von Brandenstein, and Ian Baker's cinematography.

Guare derived the plot of the play from old newspaper clippings, including a report written in the *New York Times* on 18 October 1983, about an African-American teenaged hustler named David Hampton who inveigled his way into four different homes of prosperous

Manhattan couples by pretending to be the son of Sidney Poitier. He also claimed to be a friend of their children—a fellow student at the college they were attending. Guare was particularly intrigued by the scandal because his friends, Osborn Elliott, dean of Columbia University's Graduate School of Journalism, and his wife Inger, were two of the duped hosts. The morning after the Elliotts allowed David Poitier to stay with them, they found him in bed with another man. Guare thought that this young man so obsessed with the creation of celebrity would be the ideal subject for his play.

The trouble began when Hampton, on vacation in Hawaii, was informed by a friend about Guare's play, then running at Lincoln Center.[90] Hampton thought that Guare stole his story without getting permission to use it, even though anyone with a modicum of common sense would realize that Guare's play was fiction and was not defamatory since it did not refer to Hampton's real name anywhere in the drama. Nevertheless, Hampton returned to New York during summer 1990 and began doing interviews with the press. Hampton also telephoned Guare, who refused to talk with him under advice from the press agent for the play, Merle Debuskey, who understood that Hampton was behaving like a sociopath. Hampton began making threats, including this one revealed to Jeanie Kasindorf of *New York*:

> I'm consulting a lawyer right now. I'm going to sue MGM, Pathé, Lincoln Center, I'm going to name names, I'm going to destroy careers. I'm going to blast people if I have to go to *Outweek* and destroy a few of those actors onstage with their closet lives. In other words, if these people don't sit down and talk to me, I'm going to become totally, totally vicious. It is my play, my life that has made John Guare a million. And it is my play, my life that has gotten him all the recognition he's gotten. And I would really advise John to get in touch with me, because if he doesn't, I'm seriously going to wreak havoc, because this has gone on far too long.[91]

Nine days after *Six Degrees of Separation* moved to the Vivian Beaumont Theater, a press party was held at Tavern-on-the-Green. Hampton came to the party uninvited and confronted Guare, who refused to be baited. The show's producer, Bernard Gersten, told Hampton to leave. Hampton obliged, but not before saying, "If it weren't for me, you wouldn't be having a fucking opening night party."[92]

On 10 April 1991, Guare's lawyer, Nicholas Ackerman, filed a complaint against Hampton. In Manhattan Criminal Court on 7 May, Judge Plummer Lott extended a protection order for Guare due to death threats made by Hampton on tape. On one such message to

Guare, Hampton said, "I would truly advise you to give me some money or you can start counting your days."[93] In fall 1991, Hampton filed a $100 million lawsuit claiming civil damages against Guare, Lincoln Center Theater, Random House (Guare's publisher), Bernard Gersten, and MGM-Pathé. Guare, in turn, filed charges of harassment against Hampton. On 30 April 1992, Edward H. Lehner, a State Supreme Court Justice, ruled that Hampton was not entitled to civil damages against Guare, making his case null and void. In Criminal Court in Manhattan on 23 September 1992, Hampton, despite tape-recorded messages of him harassing Guare being introduced as evidence, denied that he ever threatened the playwright. In early October 1992, a jury acquitted Hampton of trying to obtain money from Guare but deadlocked on the issue of harassment. Hampton's lawyer did not deny that his client made telephone calls to Guare in March 1991 but claimed that those messages were not threatening. One such message on 27 March was read in court: "I suggest you count out some cash and allot it to me legally and rightfully like you should do like a gentleman or I am going to do something that you won't be able to walk on stage and accept any awards."[94] Finally, the lawsuits came to closure on 13 July 1993, when five judges of the New York State Appellate Division upheld the 30 April 1992 ruling indicating that Hampton was not due any civil damages.

The David Hampton fiasco probably served to make Guare, previously a private person who despised talking about himself, a bit more tentative in revealing anything about his personal life. However, the success of *Six Degrees of Separation* far outweighed the negative effects of any legal wrangling he had to do in court. In 1991, Guare received an honorary doctorate from his alma mater, Georgetown University. He was a visiting artist at Harvard University in 1990–91, taught frequently at New York University and the City College of New York, was a fellow at the Juilliard Theater Center during 1993–94, and continues to serve as a council member of the Dramatists Guild. Finally, on 17 April 1999, at the Eighteenth Annual William Inge Theatre Festival, Guare was presented with the Distinguished Achievement in the American Theatre Award, an honor previously accorded to playwrights such as Edward Albee, Peter Shaffer, Arthur Miller, and August Wilson, among others.

On 13 December 1994, Guare sat for five hours while artist Chuck Close shot twenty Polaroid portraits of him. Guare's book, *Chuck Close: Life and Work, 1988–1995*, pays homage to this amazing artist who continued his inspired painting after a blood clot in his spinal cord left him partially paralyzed for life. Most recently, Guare has also kept active by editing a 1995 collection of contemporary American experimental drama titled *Conjunctions: 25, The New American Theater,* which includes the first part of his own play, *Moon Under Miami.*

In the early 1990s, Guare continued to expand his theatrical talents. Originally intended as a libretto for Leonard Bernstein, *Four Baboons Adoring the Sun,* Guare's ninety-minute play directed by Sir Peter Hall, premiered at the Vivian Beaumont Theater in Lincoln Center on 18 March 1992. Although its critical reception was mixed, the play, which featured Stockard Channing, James Naughton, and Eugene Perry, received a Tony nomination for Best Play in 1992. Being performed simultaneously with *Four Baboons Adoring the Sun,* Guare's one-act *New York Actor* was initially staged at a benefit of the American Repertory Theater in Cambridge, Massachusetts, in April 1992. André Gregory, Jerry Stiller, and Marion Seldes were among the performers who staged a reading of the play at the New York Public Library on 1 February 1993. Finally, Guare's revised version of *Moon Under Miami* was produced by the Remains Theater in Chicago during April 1995.

In the late 1990s, Kurt Masur commissioned Guare to write the narration for composer César Franck's 1888 symphonic poem, *Psyché.* The five-movement, forty-minute poem, intended for chorus and orchestra, was based on the Psyché and Eros myth. Guare's erotic interpretation of the symphonic poem, with choral interludes, was performed by the New York Philharmonic under Kurt Masur's direction during October 1997. Guare was also one of seven playwrights commissioned by the Acting Company to create an evening's presentation of playlets about love and sex inspired by Shakespeare's sonnets. Guare's contribution was *The General of Hot Desire,* based upon sonnets 153 and 154. These seven plays were initially performed as *Love's Fire* at the Guthrie Theater Lab in Minneapolis on 7 January 1998. Directed by Mark Lamos, *Love's Fire* toured the United States and London (the Barbican Center) in 1998 before being staged at the Joseph Papp Public Theater in New York in June of that year. Guare's latest projects include a screenplay about George and Ira Gershwin that Martin Scorsese has expressed an interest in directing; a musical adaptation of the film classic, *The Sweet Smell of Success,* with Marvin Hamlisch composing the music; a revised edition of part of the musical book and a new song for the updated Broadway version of *Kiss Me, Kate*; and the production of his latest play, *Lake Hollywood* (unpublished at the time of this writing).

Guare considers playwriting to be a privilege. He once stated, "If I hadn't been a playwright, I guess I would have worked in the theater somehow. I wouldn't have cared how. I just love the theater."[95] He feels a serious commitment to a profession that allows him to deal with problems and people on a daily basis without merely dreaming about them. Guare acknowledges the significance of his métier: "I'm very obsessive about work. Work for me is all voyaging, a kind of emotional serendipity. I write to get objectivity on things that have happened. Life is the unconscious, writing the conscious."[96]

Guare's writing method reflects this conscious effort. He is usually writing by 9 A.M. and remains at his work until about 2 P.M. He writes in longhand and then types the material onto a computer or onto the typewriter that his parents gave him when he was twelve. His method is to write prolifically by starting from nothing, without an outline or a plan of organization, and then jotting down speeches and sentences. Only later does he try to discover a central incident to tie it all together and find a suitable character for a speech or a song he has inserted into the play. Guare thus wants to surprise himself during the writing rather than be confined by a preordained plot; he lets the work take its own shape, depending solely on where the material is leading. Guare discussed his writing method with David Savran:

> You have to approach your work in a double way. You have to write it on an unconscious level—just let it come out. Then you have to get a distance from it, and come back to it almost as a collaborator. The hardest thing to do is to listen to your work, putting your ear against it and answering the questions, "What is this material trying to turn into? What is the underlying rhythm in this?" It's always a question of the balance between intuition and conscious choice.[97]

Guare writes a lot and then constantly cuts and revises. At times, he may compose a play quickly, in hours, as he did with *The Loveliest Afternoon of the Year*, or in just a few days, which was the case with *Landscape of the Body*. However, most often, Guare works through several drafts of a play, and in some instances, such as his rewriting on *Marco Polo Sings a Solo*, this may take years. Guare enjoys rewriting because he continues to learn new things about the play and gradually develops the play's sense of rhythm. Also, Guare finds it useful to write in notebooks, scribbling indecipherably. His journal, however, is not confessional: "They're workout books I use every day to keep the buzz going, the buzz that writing gives you, to stop the moss from growing over the brain and blocking that subconscious part, to stop the constant death-desire to self-censor. If I don't have anything to write about that day, I copy passages out of what I'm reading. The papers. A novel."[98] While working on the drafts, Guare discusses them with his wife and friends, even reading them aloud occasionally. Guare also works with the director, the lighting designer, the costumers, and the set designers, often revising the play up until production, for he realizes, "To be a playwright you've got to know about every aspect of what's on that stage—the lighting, the costumes, the set—because that's the visual way in which the audience will enter the world of your play."[99]

The remainder of this book will critically examine Guare's plays, paying particular attention to the unique contributions that his black comedy has made to the contemporary American theater.

2
Early Plays, 1966–1969

F ROM 1966 TO 1969, GUARE WROTE SEVEN PLAYS THAT RANGE FROM ten-minute one-act dramas such as *Kissing Sweet* to the six-scene *Muzeeka*, which is approximately the same length as *Cop-Out*, Guare's long one-act farce. In this early stage of his career, Guare was not primarily interested in exploring the psychology of character, which might normally require a full-length play. Neither was Guare concerned with debate or discussion to probe political, social, or economic ideas, again usually reserved for lengthier plays. Moreover, Guare was not particularly intrigued with developing elaborate plots, which is another reason why his early dramas tended to be more like vignettes than full-length plays. Finally, short one-act plays allowed Guare the opportunity to keep the zany action flowing without sacrificing his point of view and without losing the audience's limited attention. These early plays thus serve as an apprenticeship for Guare to develop his motifs in a somewhat simplistic structure before expanding the elements of the farce, which requires more experience with dramatic structure.

Guare's first two short one-act plays, *Something I'll Tell You Tuesday* and *The Loveliest Afternoon of the Year*, were originally staged at Caffe Cino in New York City on 25 October 1966. Russ Kaiser directed the double bill, and Guare himself was responsible for the scenic design. Although *The Loveliest Afternoon of the Year* was originally written the night before Guare enlisted in the Air Force Reserves in 1963, the play was polished for production when Guare was writing *Something I'll Tell You Tuesday* on a grant to study screenwriting at Yale University in early 1966. The off-Broadway double bill presented at Caffe Cino was not reviewed in the New York press.

Something I'll Tell You Tuesday occurs on West 59th Street between Eighth and Ninth Avenues in Manhattan, New York City being the locale Guare knew best. Although the subject matter ostensibly revolves around the contrast between the old couple—Agnes and Andrew—

45

and their daughter and her husband—Hildegarde and George—
what might be a typical kitchen-sink drama is moved to the vibrant,
cosmopolitan atmosphere of Manhattan. Through the use of separate lighting areas, the locale changes from the old couple's brown-
stone walkup, to the corridor, then to the street, to a lunch counter,
and finally back to the street. Thus, in Guare's first play after his college years, there are indications that he is trying hard not to bore
us with the confinements of the kitchen sink. The bare stage is certainly a contrast to the cluttered set of naturalistic plays. Realism is
also undercut by having the characters pantomime many of their
stage actions.

In *Something I'll Tell You Tuesday*, Guare is much more concerned
with examining the relationships between the two couples than he is
with form or stage devices. In a note to the earliest published edition
of the play, Guare writes, "The play is written to be performed with
the barest minimum of scenery; two chairs are all that are needed."[1]
The one-act format and bare stage thus allow Guare to focus on
content rather than structure or staging.

At the beginning of the play, Agnes and Andrew have just finished
a brief argument before the elderly woman prepares to go to the
hospital for an operation. It's a beautiful April day, prompting Agnes
to want to walk to the hospital with her suitcase in tow. Her husband,
however, insists that they take a taxi. Their daughter, Hildegarde,
soon enters with her husband George, ready to provide encouragement for Agnes's recovery. However, any kind words are soon dimin-
ished by the constant bickering between the young couple. When
Hildegarde and George go to get their car, Agnes and Andrew decide
to walk to the hospital. Although they have not been out together
very much lately and Agnes enjoys the walk, Andrew seems to complain about every little detail. The play ends with Agnes reminding
herself to tell her daughter on Tuesday that the young couple is lucky
that they fight all the time because once you get older, you do not
have the energy to engage in marital warfare.

Something I'll Tell You Tuesday is a metaphor for contemporary urban life. Guare's play is a statement about the vacuity of modern life,
depicted as an alienated existence sadly devoid of any ability "to connect." Instead of any familial or spiritual connection, the two couples
are united in their banal existences by alternate, yet different, forms
of violence. The couples represent two distinct generations whose
ages might suggest fundamental differences, but in reality nothing
has changed in their lives. Guare indicates that the old couple could
be played by youthful actors and "no attempt should be made at

makeup or playing wobbly-old."[2] The subdued behavior of Agnes and Andrew versus the hysteria of Hildegarde and George will be enough to indicate the differences in the ages of the couples. Guare warns, "The trap of the play is playing them as two old sickly sweet people in love with each other. The important thing to remember is that they were Hildegarde and George forty years before."[3]

Hildegarde and George may be wed, but they are certainly not united or connected in any spiritual or humanistic way. From the moment they appear on stage, they are bickering between themselves. Andrew provides us with a preview of what is to come when he acknowledges to Agnes that he refuses to drive with their daughter and son-in-law: "Ah, it hurts me the way they fight."[4] As Hildegarde and George appear onstage for the first time, we notice, "*Hildegarde's hair is askew. George looks like he's on the brink of either murder or an ulcer*" (77). George's first words, admonishing his wife for her inconsiderate behavior, indicates how dysfunctional their marriage really is: "Your mother's sick—for once in your life can't you think of somebody but yourself—yatata yatata—" (77). Agnes urges her husband to refrain from answering the door, hoping that their troubled in-laws may just quietly disappear. Hildegarde complains about the exhausting trip, but George interrupts: "Just shut up, Hildegarde. We got here safe and just shut up" (78). Hildegarde begins weeping and then complains that George is a pitiful driver, having knocked over all of the markers on the George Washington Bridge en route from their home in Newark. George counters by saying, "I do not know where she gets her voice from. She screams and it does something to your ears. (*Leans back disgusted.*) Ah, for God's sake, Hildegarde, let's not wash dirty linen in public" (78). Hildegarde announces that she is fed up with her marriage and with a husband who is trying to drive her insane (79). After George leaves the room, Hildegarde confides to her parents, "He called me the worst names once we got off that bridge. Names you wouldn't call the lowest scum on earth he called me" (79). When George returns, the conversation turns to their daughter Monica; Hildegarde claims that George's gift to Monica, a low-cut dress for her high school junior prom, was inappropriate, especially since Hildegarde is saddled with worn-out lingerie of her own. George, in turn, accuses his wife of being jealous of their daughter. The final straw is drawn when Hildegarde reveals that George punched her recently, cementing the idea that violence permeates their relationship.

Although Andrew and Agnes do not have the energy to fight because of their old age, their quarrels reflect what Hildegarde and

George will be reduced to years in the future. Guare thus intimates that humanity's *angoisse* is cyclical. At the start of the play, Agnes and Andrew are arguing about whether to leave without Hildegarde and George, in what the stage directions indicate is "*the tail end of a fight*" (75). After removing a picture from the wall, revealing a streak underneath, Agnes hints that the elderly couple have inured themselves to a history of bickering:

> The painters had just finished painting this room and the walls were still wet and we were fighting about something and I got mad at you and threw the grapefruit I was eating at you and you ducked and the grapefruit stuck to the wet wall and slid all the way down to the floor. (76)

When Hildegarde and George enter arguing and continue to do so without chance of egress for the older couple, we realize that there is a contrast between their hysteria and the subdued bickering of Agnes and Andrew. However, once the younger couple have left, Agnes and Andrew take a deep sigh of relief and then continue their own life of dissension. Agnes prefers to walk to the hospital, but Andrew, not wanting to be branded a cheapskate, insists on calling a taxi. Agnes gets her wish when Andrew begrudgingly obliges. Behaving curmudgeonly during their trek to the hospital, Andrew, as the stage directions indicate, is "*troubled*" (86) and "*looks morosely ahead*" (86), all the while complaining about his presupposed image as a tightwad (87), the "goddam drivers" (87), the need to be on time (88), and George and Hildegarde (88). During their walk, Agnes and Andrew have realized how much they have aged. In a sarcastic denouement, Guare suggests that despite the fact that Andrew and Agnes have grown old, their life of bickering is merely a subdued version of their former selves. Agnes reveals what she is going to tell her daughter when she visits on Tuesday:

> I'm gonna tell her she's lucky they still fight. That's the worst part of getting old, I decided. You don't miss the love part, the sex part, the not being able to have kids part. You think that's the part you're gonna miss, but you know it's gonna go. No, the one thing I always thought we'd have, you and me, is the fights. God, didn't we toss some beautiful battles. (88–89)

Scott Giantvalley suggests that the elderly couple connect through their constant fighting, much like Scooper and Deirdre in *Bosoms and Neglect*.[5] On the contrary, during this beautiful day in April, Agnes and Andrew, like their counterparts, Hildegarde and George, ironically can have no peace. The audience intuitively realizes that one generation merges into the next, our unimaginative existences framed by inner lives devoid of passion or spirituality. As Gautam Dasgupta astutely notes, "Prone to small talk, the couples in *Something I'll Tell You Tuesday* (one old and resigned, the other young and hysterical) lead banal lives, enlivened only by frequent bouts of family disputes."[6] Guare is exploring how life can pass us by—how people stay trapped in their own fixed identities that can somehow be imputed to be meaningful when they are actually violent, devoid of love and contact. Joy in the present is unattainable—Andrew and Agnes dream of the past and wish they were younger so that they could have the energy to fight again. This early play, then, hints at the sarcastic way Guare's black comedy exposes our sick society that substitutes violence for empathy and viable spiritual connections.

The Loveliest Afternoon of the Year concerns a couple, designated without names as merely He and She, who meet in the park and try to establish a relationship. When He first meets the young woman feeding pigeons in the park "*for want of anything better to do*,"[7] She reveals her loneliness as a midwestern girl in the big city: "I have been in this city eleven months now and you are the first person I've spoken to" (95). The young man tries to ease the tension that She has about meeting a stranger in the park by making humorous comments. She appreciates his wild sense of imagination and his spontaneity. Guare reveals that She is fundamentally isolated and alienated in a cold society: "I'm a young girl and I'm pretty and nobody ever speaks to me—not even to ask directions—and you're the funniest man I've ever met and I thank you in all the languages there are. Thank you for speaking to me" (95). After sharing a long kiss, He and She decide to meet every Sunday in the park. Walking hand and hand each Sunday, the two would-be lovers share dreams about the future. He tells her bizarre stories that reflect the craziness of contemporary urban life. After hearing one such story about his sister who had her arm bitten off by a polar bear at the zoo, only to have it grow back as polar bear hair, requiring her relocation to Alaska, She becomes a little skeptical. He responds, "You're from Ohio. You come from a nice little family. You don't understand the weirdness, the grief that people can spring from—" (97). When She expresses fondness for a merry-go-round's calliope music, He counters with, "They run on steam. My father fell in one and was scalded to death" (98).

Unfortunately, their brief relationship is doomed to failure even though they both need each other. He has a wife, an incredibly obese woman with two fat, ugly children. When He sings a love song to

She, we soon learn that the song's composer was also tainted: "Mario Lanza . . . and right after he sang it, he grew very fat and died" (100). Seeing them together, He's wife takes out a rifle and kills both of them. This is Chekhov's unrequited love, now put into context by Guare's sense of black humor to depict a contemporary society unable to connect in any meaningful way.

The Loveliest Afternoon of the Year is hardly a conventional play. Guare uses flashbacks to disrupt any traditional notion of unity of time. He and She at times speak to the audience directly as narrators; this metatheatrical stage device serves to destroy any sense of the fourth wall. Love songs alternate with morbid, macabre tales that are so exaggerated they must be taken metaphorically rather than melodramatically—serving to disrupt any notion of the verisimilitude of naturalism.

Instead, Guare's imagery, where form more perfectly matches content, suggests the absurdities of modern life, replete with all sorts of neuroses. We witness two desperate people who can only try to survive in a brutal world. In essence, Guare is investigating the nature of our identity in an estranged universe where meaningful contact is fleeting. The young man's comment to She, "You don't understand the weirdness, the grief that people can spring from—" (97), becomes the archetypal lament of humanity's contemporary condition. Moreover, throughout the play, She fails to trust her newly acquired friend because of what seems to be exaggerated stories about the brutalities omnipresent in modern society. Trust is not possible in modern society; we all remain strangers. The only reality is the violence that ensues. Gautam Dasgupta summarizes the plight of the young couple: "Violence, Guare suggests, is a necessary catalyst for the flowering of human relationships."[8] Indeed, at the end of the play, when He and She realize that they are much better off together than each in his own isolated, drab, and banal life, violence intervenes to preclude any affirmation of happiness in the present.

Guare's next play, *A Day for Surprises,* was probably written in 1967, although the date of writing has never been confirmed. In a blurb preceding the play, anthologized in *Four Baboons Adoring the Sun and Other Plays,* the date of the first presentation is listed as August 1967 at Caffe Cino. Since Guare told Anne Cattaneo that he wrote the play on a Thursday and it was presented the following Monday, the date of the writing may presumably be 1967.[9] However, a list of all plays performed at Caffe Cino in 1967 does not include *A Day for Surprises.*[10] John Harrop believes that the play was first performed at Caffe Cino in 1970, and Stanley Richards included it in his collection, *Best Short*

Plays, 1970.[11] In 1971, *A Day for Surprises* was subsequently staged at the Basement Theatre in London.

A Day for Surprises is a short one-act comedy about how people in modern society often live life vicariously while avoiding contact, love, and relationships with others. Guare sets the play in the New York Public Library, which he mocks as a staid, lifeless, and banal milieu. The two characters in the play are simply designated as A and B, reduced by their mundane positions to merely letters: this is particularly apropos since they both work in the library and are bibliophiles. B is actually Mr. Falanzano, in charge of the pasting room, and A, his subordinate, is Miss Jepson, who labors in the overdue fine office. Their daily drudgery is momentarily interrupted when the twenty-eight-thousand-pound stone lion on Forty-Second Street comes to life (the only thing alive in this library) and devours Denise Pringle, B's fiancée, in the ladies' room. Guare gives A and B, two lifeless individuals, exactly what they need: a surprise—something to shock them out of their daily inertia.

Miss Jepson needs some excitement to break the routine of her banal existence. She describes her evening's plans to Mr. Falanzano: "I was going to go home, curl up with a good book, like any other night—look at the phone and welcome even a Sorry Wrong Number. . . . Guiltily turn on my TV and watch re-runs of beautiful domestic comedies—*Father Knows Best*—*Make Room For Daddy*—hi, Lucy, hi, Doris! Then turn them off because it's time to water my geranium."[12] Thus, after being surrounded by books all day long, Miss Jepson does not have enough imagination to do anything else but read. Then she turns to television to provide her with the domestic life that she lacks, interrupting her fantasy life only because the routine of watering her flowers demands it. Attracted to B, she invites him to her place to "start something between the covers" (19), indicating that she might have in mind merely a chat about books or perhaps something more romantic. She admits, "There's a lot of lonely girls in this town, Mr. Falanzano" (19).

Mr. Falanzano's life has also been fairly parochial, with books establishing an identity for him. As a result, the librarian, in frustration, proceeds to tear apart the books in the pasting room. He reveals how he got to know Miss Pringle for the first time. Mr. Falanzano returned to the library one evening when he could not sleep, hoping to find a good book. There he met Miss Pringle, who was totally absorbed in Lewis Carroll, Proust, Camus, and *The Joy of Cooking*. They had known each other earlier after having met during clearance sales at Marboro Books. Pursuing their common interest in reading books at the library, they soon fell in love. During the months that followed, they often would rendezvous in the stacks after the library was closed, strip themselves of their clothes, wrap their bodies around each other, and begin reading. They eventually decided to consummate the relationship: "I bought contraceptives and she bought contraceptives as we had been instructed to do in the New York *Post*'s weekend series: *Stop That Baby*, and we finally felt we were ready. There was a full moon that night. We took a quick gander at *Human Sexual Response* and cleared our throats" (21). Guided by chapter seven of *Ideal Marriage* and a pamphlet from the U.S. Government Printing Office, they had sex together. Despite the precautions taken, Miss Pringle later became pregnant. The result of the pregnancy was their baby: a volume of the complete works of Doctor Spock. Mr. Falanzano laments that the only thing he could father was a set of dull books: "The flour and water of library paste. Not semen at all. My life has been lived in books" (22). A, overcome by this love story, begins pasting herself to B, the only way she can make contact with him.

A Day for Surprises contains several of the motifs Guare works into his more mature dramas. In this early play, Guare focuses on the need to live life fully rather than vicariously through words and images created by others. Guare is suggesting that imagination is the key to establishing an identity for oneself and to making contact with others who might share the same interests. However, being obsessed with anything, including books, television, media hype, or movies, can be distracting and ultimately mundane, leading us away from more imaginative and rewarding real experiences. Those who lead such parochial lives need to invigorate themselves every once in a while with a day for surprises. Similarly, Guare demonstrates that the form of his plays matches the content: what begins as realism is suspended from its inertia by Guare's absurd view of life, in which surprise turns conventional drama into something more creative and imaginative.

In 1967, when Guare was a fellow at Yale University on a grant to study screenwriting, he wrote *Muzeeka*, commissioned by the Eugene O'Neill Playwrights' Conference. At first, he had trouble with its beginning, trying to find something lyrical that had weight. Perusing an old notebook that he had kept when he hitchhiked from Paris to Egypt in 1965, Guare recalled an entry he made when he was in Rome. Trying to escape from a torrential downpour, he ducked into the Etruscan Museum and while there passing the time had written in the notebook about the virtues of being born an Etruscan. Guare now had the image he needed for the beginning of the play. *Muzeeka* was initially staged at the Eugene O'Neill Memorial Foundation Theatre in Waterford, Connecticut, on 19 July 1967. The play was then performed as part of the New Theatre for Now Series at the Mark Taper Forum in Los Angeles on 10 October 1967, because Gordon Davidson, *Muzeeka*'s Los Angeles producer, and Edward Parone, its director, were both interested in showcasing new, experimental drama. Warren Lyons, who wanted to stage *The House of Blue Leaves*, joined Betsy Ann Besch to coproduce *Muzeeka* in New York while Guare tinkered with *Blue Leaves*. After the set designer absconded with his fee and with the sets, as well as after the lead actor was replaced the night before the opening, *Muzeeka* finally had its New York debut on a double bill with Sam Shepard's *Red Cross* at the Provincetown Playhouse on 28 April 1968. Directed by Melvin Bernhardt, *Muzeeka* featured a solid cast that included Sam Waterston (Jack Argue), Marcia Jean Kurtz (Argue's wife), and Peggy Pope (Evelyn Landis). This production marked Guare's professional playwriting debut in New York and his first chance of receiving criticism from the New York press.

Although the off-Broadway production was not heavily reviewed, *Muzeeka* nevertheless drew accolades from the press.[13] Robert F. Shepard, writing in the *New York Times*, believed that Guare's play was stronger than *Red Cross*, praising Guare's craftsmanship as beautifully poetic and always meaningful.[14] While recognizing Guare's humor as pertinent and the writing stimulating, Humm of *Variety* also lauded the stylized staging but questioned whether the "bop the bourgeoisie" mentality would ever be commercially viable.[15] Normally acerbic John Simon, while finding the monologues a bit flat, noted that the ridiculous has its pathos in this play and praised the sketches, which he claimed were quite amusing.[16] The lone dissenting opinion was Edith Oliver's critique in the *New Yorker*, which blasted the play as an insignificant mélange of Brechtian tricks and empty stage pranks.[17] *Muzeeka* won an Obie in 1968 for best off-Broadway play—Guare's first major award in the theater. It was also staged at the Open Space Theatre in London on 23 February 1969, on a double bill with Geoffrey Bush's *The Fun War*.

Muzeeka's structure combines theatrical devices found in Brecht's epic theater, Pinter's plays, and expressionist dramas. The six short scenes of the play, in epic style, follow Jack Argue's travails from domesticity to his involvement in the Vietnam War. Each scene begins with one or more stagehands who function as Brechtian-type narrators carrying banners that announce the events to come, thus reducing the emphasis on Aristotelian plot development or suspense. In addition, the six isolated scenes each represent a parable, similar to Brecht's concept of *gestus* or the German expressionist version of *stationen.* What we see on stage is a reflection of Argue's inner state, much like expressionism (some of which includes early Brechtian drama) and certainly far removed from naturalistic representation. Scott Giantvalley has astutely noted that the play "matches the madness of its content with a free-form style, moving from one isolated incident to another in a method reflective of contemporary fragmentation."[18] Finally, the quick blackouts remind us of Pinter's plays, where the scenery changes with little regard for traditional linear plot development.

Guare explained to Anne Cattaneo the context in which he wrote the play when he was at Yale University: "I wrote *Muzeeka* about all those undergraduates I saw around me, so free and happy but wondering what in adult life would allow them to keep their spirit and freedom? How do we keep any ideals in this particular society?"[19] Guare examines the issue of whether one can establish an identity or find inner peace within a society that turns us into conformists; the influence of pop culture disseminated through the media certainly removes traces of our unique individuality. At that time, the issue was also personal for Guare himself, who was still trying to find himself as an artist. The name of the protagonist of the play, Jack Argue, is an anagram for Guare. Jack suggests a name that is standard fare, a substitute for John, another common distinction. Indeed, the key word in the play seems to be "bland," for Argue's life is without distinction or imagination.

In scene 1, Argue is sitting on a bunkbed, the only prop on an otherwise bare stage, reading the lettering on a penny dated 1965.[20] The inscription, "In God We Trust," is sarcastically paired with "Liberty," which in 1965, with the spectre of Vietnam looming large, often meant that one's freedom might be rather fleeting. Argue makes a choice and flips the coin, which turns up "heads." At this point, we may identify him as the 1960s edition of Forrest Gump, perceiving life to be based upon mere chance.

Scene 2 provides us with a glimpse of Argue's domestic life as we witness the young man in bed with his wife. The scene degenerates from love making to open hostility. In the love making, Argue "*smiles at her and touches her face.*"[21] Contact soon becomes isolation as Argue desperately pleads "I love you" while his wife, ignoring him, furiously turns the pages of a magazine. Argue then gratifies himself with a copy of *Playboy* while his wife sobs. The stage directions indicate that Argue's refrain, "I love you" is stated "*blandly*" (53). At home, then, Argue demonstrates no imagination in his love-making; Guare sarcastically hints that perhaps *Playboy* can inspire him.

Argue, however, is an idealist and aspires to a life other than mediocrity. In scene 3, Argue recites a long monologue about how, if given the opportunity to assume a new identity, he would like to become an Etruscan, emulating a civilization that was wildly imaginative and physically dynamic. However, soon after Argue reveals this ambitious pursuit of a culture that gratified the inner state, he announces that he is going to work for Muzeeka Corporation, "the biggest largest piped-in music company in the whole wide world" (55). As Argue is hired for the job, "*Muzak plays, blandly*" (55). Argue's work for the company consists of piping in the same music into every elevator, office, escalator, toilet, home, airplane, bus, truck, and car in the country. Argue believes that his newly found métier will provide him with the artistic creativity akin to Etruscan civilization. Instead, Muzak will turn the country into insipid conformists:

> I'll wait till all humans are inured to the everpresent, inescapable background ocean blandness of my music, till everyone knows down deep I'll always be there, stroking that cortical overlay till it's as hard and brittle as the clay of an Etruscan pot and then, on a sudden day that is not especially spring, not especially summer, a day when the most exciting thing around is the new issue of *Reader's Digest*, and you read with interest an ad that says Campbell just invented a new-flavor soup, I'll strike. That kind of a day. I'll pipe in my own secret music that I keep hidden here under my cortical overlay and I'll free all the Etruscans in all our brains. (56).

Argue, under the guise of the bland Muzeeka Corporation, will strike by substituting his own unique combination of "Rock and Mozart and Wagnerian Liebestods and Gregorian chants. Eskimo folk songs. African. Greek. Hindoo" (56), destined, in his fantasy, to turn banality into the inner peace experienced by the Etruscans. Planning to demythologize America and bring us out of the stupor of conformity, idealistic Jack Argue, much like the rebellious members of the 1960s counterculture who were upwardly mobile yet distrustful of modern institutions, is a sham. Poor Jack Argue becomes a satire for Everyman who feels guilty about his or her routine existence and feels compelled to change the world instead.

Scene 4 focuses on Argue's pathetic domestic life. Argue momentarily abandons his plain wife, Sally-Jane, for a fling with a whore whose name he picked up from a men's restroom in a bar in Greenwich Village. In an expressionistic transformation, Evelyn Landis, the prostitute, becomes the French whore that Argue expects to see. Argue is out of joint with his society and, as is revealed in this scene, with others as well. His wife is having a baby, but Argue, deciding not to be with her at this very emotional moment, is trying to establish contact with a stranger. He tells Evelyn, "I'm sorry . . . I want to connect in some way" (64). Argue has failed in his quest to establish an identity. The stagehands in scene 4 bring on signs that reveal to the audience that Argue's career plans "TURNED BLAND" (64). Argue, who fails to see the need for personal relationships to establish the spirituality he seeks, tells Evelyn, "I want to connect. Therefore, I must cut. Cut off all the ties just for a while, so I can get back to what I was, am, am down deep. Establish my relation to all the Etruscans, all the animals" (64–65). Argue laments his middle-class life in Greenwich, Connecticut: "It's a nice house. Up to my ass in mortgage. A lawn green as money. At night, a smell of pines. Really. So fresh. Chill. Mist" (66). Thus, Argue has sought out Evelyn so she could give him her patented Chinese Basket Job as a panacea for his quest for contact. However, in a hilariously bizarre dose of black comedy, during the supposedly psychedelic experience offered by Evelyn's Chinese Basket Job, Argue, his body pumping in tune with the sexual rhythms, can only intone platitudes about his mundane life. When Argue receives a telephone call announcing the birth of his child, Evelyn has enough pieces of the puzzle to size up her client: "You phony. You phony. You phony. You phony. You phony" (68). In the next scene, Argue stands speechless before the audience, clearly embarrassed by his plight. The stagehands throw a banner over his head, which reads, "IN WHICH ARGUE IS AT A LOSS" (70). Argue has become a pathetic comic figure.

In the final scene of the play, Argue is in Vietnam. Talking to his Army buddy, the anony-Mass Number Two, Argue tells him that he went to Yale, Harvard, and Princeton. Now he is reduced to trying to enlighten high school dropouts such as Number Two. CBS Television is covering their battle tomorrow. This alarms Number Two, who is under contract with NBC and will lose his rank if NBC finds out that CBS gets the film coverage. He fears the worst: "An educational network unit. I'm not fighting for no Channel Thirteen. I don't want to break contracts" (72). As they put on their makeup to prepare for the television coverage of the next day's killing, Number Two equates his job as a soldier with media celebrity status:

Good thing about NBC—dull days when there's no fighting like Lunar New Year, they rerun our old skirmishes and we get residuals. I see my old buddies and I dream we're all together. Then I watch them get killed all over again and I see me carried off on a stretcher to have my operation photographed for *Saturday Evening Post*. Did you see the spread on me? I love rainy days when we fight only reruns. (74)

American society has become dehumanized, interested more in commercialization of celebrity than in the value of life. Argue and Number Two, both under contract to different television networks, have degenerated into puppets for commercial enterprises fighting not for the salvation of the spirit of democracy, but instead for celebrity status that might increase television ratings. Number Two even boasts to Argue, "I been on the cover of *Look* and that spread in the *Saturday Evening Post*. I been in *The New York Times* and the *L.A. Times* and the *Daily News Sunday Colorado*" (75). Argue's wife enters briefly with her child and reminds us that American society is fueled by the myth of the Great American Dream:

> The baby grew another foot today and I've enrolled her in dancing class already and I've enrolled him already in prep school because it can never be too early and I tell the baby every day his Daddy is a hero and fighting all those dirty Commies in Vietnam so he can come to us and make more money for us so we can move to a bigger house and go to Yale to college and Europe on vacations and take Mommy to dances and plays and the club. (81)

Evelyn Landis enters and, in a takeoff on what might appear to be a Bob Hope special featuring the archetypal songstress entertaining the troops, strips herself of army fatigues to reveal a bikini made of newspaper columns. As she rips clumps of newspaper off her body, Evelyn suggests that the media hype helps America subliminally to associate celebrity with godhead:

> Timothy Leary
> & Jesus Christ
> Bonnie and Clyde
> & Jesus Christ
> Rocky & Romney
> & Jesus Christ
> Johnny Carson
> & Jesus Christ
> Television
> & Jesus Christ
> Eugene McCarthy
> May be Jesus Christ. (82)

In a society that inculcates itself with blandness and superficiality, the media moguls have no trouble manipulating its consciousness.

Argue went to Vietnam to be born again, to find his identity, this last time through violence and killing. He inferred that if one cannot make contact with others, terminating them is the next best thing. However, the commercialization of the war and the numbing effect of killing every day failed to satisfy him. During Argue's dilemma about what to do next, Number Two offers him a job in an atomic-powered cesspool company. Together, Argue and Number Two can rid society of its urban blight. In essence, Number Two is also a dreamer like Argue: his plan to alter America's cesspool mentality is no different from Argue's initial idea to convert the blandness of Muzak into a more imaginative piped-in music that would invigorate a blighted contemporary society with the spirituality of the Etruscans. Argue, realizing the futility of these idealistic visions, stabs himself. The play concludes with a vicious satirical image: the Stagehand pours ketchup, symbolic of Argue's blood, onto a white sheet covering Number Two. In death, Argue, who was forever on a quest for identity, has finally made contact with someone. Argue's idealistic visions are thwarted by a society that molds us into a mass of conformity.

During a 1968 antiwar demonstration in Times Square, Guare was hit in the head when a policeman's horse veered around, accidentally knocking him unconscious. Before he blacked out, Guare noticed that the young police officer looked frightened over the incident. Upon Guare's awakening, the first image that he saw was a Times Square advertisement for Frank Sinatra's new detective movie, *Tony Rome*. Guare also recalls that the demonstrators looked as frightened as the police officers: "Scared decent people on both sides. They might have shared a cup of coffee and a story together in another place, another time."[22] This incident, the bond shared by the police officers and the demonstrators coupled with the movie image of a suave detective, formed the basis for Guare's next play, *Cop-Out*, the title reflecting what happened to Guare during that demonstration.

Guare wrote *Cop-Out* for Ron Leibman and Linda Lavin, two talented comic performers who were at Yale University when Guare was there on a grant fellowship in 1968. *Cop-Out* was initially staged at the Eugene O'Neill Memorial Theatre in Waterford, Connecticut, in July 1968. For Guare's Broadway debut, he wrote *Home Fires* as the curtain raiser for *Cop-Out*. The twin bill of one-acters premiered at the Cort Theatre on 7 April 1969. Melvin Bernhardt, who directed the original production, directed Leibman and Lavin again as they performed all of the roles in *Cop-Out* as they had done earlier in Waterford.

Although the twin bill was not heavily covered by the New York press, the few reviews that were written were harsh and derisory.[23] *Variety*'s reviewer, Hobe, praised the impressive acting by Leibman and Lavin but criticized Guare for writing enigmatic drama.[24] John Chapman of the *Daily News* reduced the twin bill to "feeble exercises in juvenility,"[25] while Richard P. Cooke of the *Wall Street Journal* acknowledged that Guare had a feel for parody and the absurd but wound up writing weak social satire.[26] Martin Gottfried of *Women's Wear Daily* took the plays more seriously and began by recognizing Guare's talent for words and for the "modern pop sensibility." However, he claimed that the plays work better on paper, and because of Guare's inexperience on the boards, the playwright failed to realize that a series of sketches written in vaudeville style could turn bright ideas into listless theater.[27] Even after the twin bill closed, Brendan Gill of the *New Yorker*, who admitted that *Cop-Out* was the more substantial of the two plays as a savage black comedy about the contemporary scene, failed to give credit to Guare because of the "amber trifle," *Home Fires*.[28] The only saving grace was Clive Barnes's neutral review in the *New York Times*. Barnes designated Guare as a "most promising young playwright," a master of "calculated irrelevancy" whose two plays were simultaneously entertaining yet unilluminating, flawed yet not worthless.[29]

The critical response from the reviewers took its toll: the twin bill closed after eight performances. Guare years later expressed his disappointment with his first Broadway experience:

> What I expected from *CopOut* [*sic*] I don't know. The actress—Linda Lavin played the role nobly—had to flee the stage, be shot and fall dead at the theater doors so the audience would have to step guiltily over her corpse in order to leave the theater. She only avoided being trampled on for a few days. I was depressed because the reviews were scathing: "not a review, an obituary" was the tone.[30]

Although Guare fled the country, his reaction may have been premature, for the New York drama critics voted him Most Promising Playwright in a poll conducted by *Variety* in 1969.

On the surface, *Cop-Out* may be confusing, perhaps dense, and the characters may seem cartoonish at first glance. The play, which appears to be haphazardly arranged as mutually exclusive vignettes, is actually carefully constructed in a vein similar to film montage.

There are four realistic documentary-type "scenes" revealing the relationship between the Policeman and a cute peacenik attracted to him. These scenes alternate with three vignettes that trace supersleuth Brett Arrow's search for a murderer. The Arrow scenes are staged with the stylized flair of a "Universal/MGM film" (11), or as Guare indicates in his introductory remarks to the play, "as if every character has been nominated for best performance in a supporting role" (12) in a detective movie. A movie screen at the rear of the stage links the two stories. A flashing strobe light behind the screen indicates the transition from the tale of the Policeman to the fantasy world of Brett Arrow. After a Pinteresque blackout, the scene changes, much in the manner that the Open Theater members and Joseph Chaikin used transformational techniques, particularly effective in Jean-Claude van Itallie's *America Hurrah* trilogy, especially in *Interview*. One actress plays all the female roles in the play, and one actor plays the Policeman and Arrow, which helps us to make the connection between the two men. By alternating these realistic and Hollywood scenes, Guare demonstrates the dichotomy between reality and myth making.

The realistic scenes begin to take shape during an encounter between the unnamed Policeman and a young female antiwar demonstrator. The Policeman seems to relish his role, wishing it were more glamorous. His romantic notions of the job conflict with the harsh realities of routine police activities. The stage directions note, "*He tries to give his billy club a professional swing, but it gets caught up, the leather thong of it gets caught in his thumb*" (21). The Policeman explains to the Girl the dichotomy between the fantasy and the reality: "Look—I became a cop to catch bank robbers. These dreams of breaking up Counterfeiter Rings. God! Delivering babies in taxis. Cats off roofs. Jeez, traffic" (22). At first, the Policeman is so engrossed in his role playing that he refuses to see the Girl as an individual, addressing her as a "Commie dope dupe" (22), "Girl Communist" (21), and "Pinko" (23). However, the cute peacenik persists, and the hardcore officer soon becomes vulnerable to her advances. They wind up making love in his police car on the pamphlets she was passing out as literature.

Several months later, the cop meets the girl at another rally. As usual, she carries her placard, which is blank. As a result of their initial sexual encounter, the girl has had an abortion. Guare satirizes these young antiwar demonstrators who are trying to establish identities for themselves; their goal ideally is only "to connect." The young woman loves to participate, but the blank sign she carries indicates that her commitment is nebulous, apt to change when she finds someone—anyone—who pays attention to her. She admits to the Policeman, "My own parents should've treated me as nice as that abortionist—you and the abortionist—that's the two times I been treated best in my whole life" (30). However, the Policeman's reactions to the Girl are determined by his role as an officer. Claiming that he cannot get promoted if he associates with an antiwar demonstrator, the Policeman, always dreaming of a more attractive life, suggests getting a vasectomy. The operation will put the clamps on what he believes is his virile masculinity.

Running simultaneously with the liaison between the Policeman and the Girl are the Brett Arrow scenes, reflecting the Policeman's fantasy as master detective. Brett Arrow is "the world's toughest superstar" (12), glamorized by the Hollywood media as a Sam Spade-type sleuth or a Mickey Spillane depiction of Mike Hammer. Guare satirizes the Hollywood version of the charismatic, macho detective who parades through a fantasy world of gorgeous women, sleazy underworld characters, and multiple disguises in pursuit of a murderer. Brett Arrow, whose name suggests Waspish roots, is determined to track down and bring to justice Mr. Big, an icon for "Dago / Woppo / Kike-O / Dyke-O / Niggo / Spicko / Faggo / Micko / Mafia" activity (16). Decked out with two guns, the tough, cocky super-sleuth first encounters an old lady covered in blood. Putting her in a half nelson, he forces her to talk about Stockton's death. Arrow is soon on the trail to find Mr. Big—the one who murdered Stockton. Only later does Arrow discover that Stockton was the old lady's cat.

Arrow, as if taking part in a good B movie, begins his detective work by calling on the sultry Larue, who is studded with diamonds. Guare parodies the cliché detective film: *Arrow and Larue meet. Their eyes touch across the stage. Music begins: Lush. Sexy. Ruby. Laura. All of them. He begins that destined-since-the-beginning-of-time cross to her* (25). Larue starts off with the suave approach: "I'm doing my thesis on metaphysical poetry" (25). However, her coyness does not work on hard-nosed Arrow, who assumes the Humphrey Bogart tough-guy role: "Lady, my brains are in my fist and my IQ is in my holster, so kindly dispense with the poetry shit" (25). After Arrow roughs her up, she leads him to Gib, the playwright. Although femme fatale Larue masochistically enjoys being beaten up by Arrow and passionately begs him to continue practicing a little more of that police brutality, he is off to find Stockton's killer, Gib (Mr. Big spelled backwards).

Arrow, snooping around what he refers to as "Green Witch Village," gets a hot tip from a panhandler to take a role in the play that Gib is directing in an off-off Broadway theater. In Gib's play,

Marilyn Monroe is taking turns seducing a bevy of U.S. Presidents from George Washington to Nixon. Arrow ducks under the covers and plays the Presidents in the manner of Groucho Marx and W. C. Fields. Guare is equating political power with celebrity status; politicians can use the perquisites of power to obtain sexual favors. In American society, lust and power reign over any desire for true commitment or spiritual connection. As Arrow is about to save Gib, the old lady arrives. As it turns out, she is actually Gardenia Gertie, who killed Stockton because her cat no longer loved her. Gertie, caught up in the Hollywood myth that old age is synonymous with a loss of power and beauty, took revenge out on a pet that, in Gertie's own mind, personified the horrors of that sense of rejection. When Gertie flees, she is devoured by a horde of insane felines. Stockton has had his revenge. However, Arrow is not satisfied in solving the case so easily and vows to clean up this filthy society: "I'll get you all you Commie Jewo Niggo Dago Woppo Mafio Faggo Russki" (42).

The last segment of the play ties together the Arrow tale with the Policeman's life. After having his vasectomy, the Policeman is now working at a toll booth, hoping to get reassigned to more demanding police work. He blames his demotion on his former girlfriend, who duped him into her radicalism. The Policeman begins to adopt the persona of his mythological hero, Brett Arrow, as he tells the Girl, "Well, your days are numbered. Because there is going to be a White, the Whitest of White on White Revolutions you ever saw and all the people who want this country to be what it can be, well, we are going to win. It's War, you Commie Dope Dupe" (44). When she begins picketing in front of him, he goes berserk, shooting her. He has "copped out" of his role to adopt a fantasy life of celebrity ace detective. The glitz and glamour of the movies has become stronger than reality. The stage directions indicate that once the play ends and the house lights are turned up, "*The actress lies in the middle aisle until the audience goes home*" (45). Forcing the spectators to step over the body before they leave the theater, Guare's denouement engages the audience directly in the action of the play.[31]

Cop-Out depicts the madness of contemporary American society in which myths, fabricated and embellished by the media, tend to overshadow reality. The Policeman, who has a chance to connect with someone who wants to develop a relationship with him, can only fantasize about how his image is played out as celebrity status in the media. Without the ability to develop contact with someone else, the Policeman turns to violence. John Lahr has summed up Guare's achievement in the play: "Guare's fabulous theatrical invention is mixed with a very strong sense of the madness in the social fabric of our lives, where every medium turns into a dream machine to steer us farther from ourselves and from the violence we perpetrate on the world."[32] Although this motif seems to be central to *Cop-Out*, it is often lost among Guare's more truncated jabs at political power, debauchery, and hypocrisy. Also, with not enough signposts, the audience probably has difficulty making the connection between the two worlds of the Policeman and Brett Arrow. Guare's biting sarcasm directed at modern absurdity keeps the play moving, inundating us with the vaudevillian zaniness that prevents the audience from getting bored. However, one may get the feeling that Guare is trying to do too much too quickly in *Cop-Out*. In comparison to *Cop-Out*, *Muzeeka* demonstrates tighter construction, relies less on techniques of film montage, and offers more clearly delineated secondary characters who are not so cartoonishly stereotyped.

Home Fires, the curtain raiser for the twin bill, is at least as powerful as *Cop-Out* and certainly not as confusing to audiences. *Home Fires* is a compact one-act play that exposes the American heritage as being superficially enamored with class consciousness and ethnic identity while hiding under the mask of democratic egalitarianism. Guare set the play in New England, specifically, Swampscott, Massachusetts, close to where America's original Anglo-Saxon ancestors must have landed. In addition, Guare's search for American roots becomes somewhat personal here, for his grandfather was a police officer in Lynn, Massachusetts, where Peter Smith, the protagonist of *Home Fires*, is the local patrolman.

Although *Home Fires* follows the unities and takes place in one setting without a change of scenery, the play's realism is undercut by abrupt changes in lighting, metatheatrical techniques in which the actors try to get the audience to participate in the action, and a wide array of sound effects designed to turn the spectators into a captive audience not mesmerized by fourth-wall conventions. In addition, the dozen musical numbers in the play move the action much closer to the zaniness of vaudeville or musical theater that Guare wants to capture.

The play takes place in what begins as a very solemn setting: Mr. Catchpole's funeral parlor, the night of the day after the signing of the Armistice ending World War I. Expressing his patriotic spirit at the end of the War, Catchpole has reservations about his client, Peter Smith, who speaks with a heavy German accent. Catchpole suspects that Smith's real name is Schmidt. The mortician threatens to throw Smith out of the funeral parlor, even though the latter is there to bury his wife, simply because Catchpole believes that Smith might be German. Despite Mr. Smith's anxiety over his wife's death, Catchpole insists that he might be the instigator of an insidious German plot to capture the United States: "What more ideal place of entry than Swampscott. The gateway to New England! We're right on the ocean" (92). Catchpole is the owner of a posh establishment and therefore must be solicitous about his image and what his other clients might say about him arranging a funeral for a German. Concerned more with image mongering than with providing spiritual comfort and empathy for a family during their time of need, Catchpole is a pathetic example of American patriotism gone to excess.

While the mortician exits to investigate the patrolman's lineage, Mr. Smith's daughter, Nell, enters. She is a U.S. citizen, having been born in Lynn, Massachusetts. However, her birth certificate indicates that her name is Schmidt, the daughter of parents who came to the United States from Hamburg, Germany. In contrast to the somber atmosphere shared by the Schmidt family is the activity of the Sullivan clan, who are attending to funeral rites next door. The Sullivans, decked out in black with red, white, and blue mourning bands on their arms, are the all-American family that can sing and dance. Catchpole praises their patriotic spirit: "They are not letting selfish grief get in the way of joy at the Armistice" (97). The Sullivans have the proper ancestry, which affords them a touch of class; they, unlike the Schmidts, are allowed to celebrate death in peace.

The atmosphere changes for the Schmidts as Peter's son, Rudy, enters with his new wife, Margaret. Rudy and Margaret are class-conscious social climbers. As the doors open upon their entrance, the audience seems to bask in their auras: *All the lights in the room come up a point and you'd swear the couple caused it. He wears a polo coat with a fur collar and a striped suit underneath and a carnation in his lapel and she is in baby blue and ermine and feathers. They glow"* (99). Upon seeing them initially, Peter thinks they are in the wrong funeral parlor and directs them to the Sullivans next door. Rudy is all swagger and style, speaking eloquently in nouveau riche manner: "When your telegram arrived, I tried to hire a bi-plane to fly to your side with the greatest alacrity, but President Wilson has instituted a blackout of the entire Eastern seacoast should the German Armistice prove a ruse" (100). He introduces his father and sister to his wife-to-be, Margaret Ross-Hughes, who is equally proper and elegant. Soon after arriving, Rudy drops cards into the bouquets of flowers sent to the funeral parlor. He then reads aloud to Margaret the names of those who have sent their condolences: "Oh, J. P. Morgan. Ah, Jay Gould.

Ah, Mrs. Astor. Boss Tweed. How nice. Flo Ziegfeld. How sweet"
(101). Margaret, of course, is engrossed in celebrity status. She, too,
tries to impress the family with her wealth and style, epitomized by
the debutante's stilted, pompous, superficial attempt to imitate an
upper-class brogue: "I'm so sorry to meet you when the hands of
Time's clock are draped in black but perhaps the next time we meet
the color of Time will be garlanded with bridal bouquets and the
tears will be tears of joy" (105).

Rudy, after years of trying to find himself by playing baseball with
the Buffalo Buffaloes, working as a hotel desk clerk in San Francisco,
and then panning for gold in the Ohio River, has finally hit paydirt
in show business. Modelled on Guare's Uncle Billy, Rudy is an agent
for the Ben Hur Animal Stables, which Rudy proudly admits, "is now
the fourth biggest account we handle right after Will Rogers, Miss
Fanny Brice and the Creole Fashion Plate" (107). He books camels,
elephants, and palominos that dive into swimming pools. With his
new status as celebrity agent and trying to impress his socialite girlfriend, Rudy has changed his name from the common Schmidt to the
more aristocratic-sounding Smythe. He tells his father, "I'm going to
be King Somebody. Rudyard Smythe. Oh boy, people listen to a Rudyard Smythe" (106). Rudy believes he has climbed the social ladder
since his plans are to marry Margaret, who daily rubs shoulders with
celebrities because she is Anna Held's roommate: "Papa! The famous
Ziegfeld star and ex-wife of same and the Roommate of *my* Margaret
Ross-Hughes" (110).

Rudy and his girlfriend seem to be wearing masks; their lives are
merely facades. Ostensibly, they have returned to Swampscott to attend the funeral. However, they are more interested in gaining pos-
session of Rudy's mother's ruby ring, now remaining on the dead
woman's finger. Margaret even infers that they should go next door
to the Sullivans' funeral reception, which is certainly more lively and
where the food is so much better than chez Smith: "But, Rudy, it's so
gloomy here in the servants' mortuary when Times Square explodes
with excitement right next door" (111). At the end of the play, we
discover that Margaret is actually Anna Held's maid, not a socialite,
and has learned from her wealthy mentor merely how to imitate the
rich and famous. The news does not please Rudy, and Guare's stage
directions indicate that he is being mocked: *"But Rudy has fainted in
his father's arms and the foghorn gives a good healthy raspberry"* (121).

Each member of the Schmidt family is searching for an identity,
never satisfied with the present and always groping for something
intangible in the future. This motif is best realized in the way in which

each family member reacts to the ruby ring that is on the finger of the deceased Mrs. Schmidt. Rudy and his fiancée see the ring as a means to increase their social status. Peter Schmidt, who was forced to change his name to Smith to move up in rank on the police force, believes the ring can help him establish a new identity for himself: "I'm going to hock that ring and buy me a wife that speaks English and I'll invite all the policemen to my house and she'll cook and I'll change my name to Smithereens! To hell with you, Rudy. Your papa's going to be somebody first. Police Chief!!!!!" (114–15). While Peter is trying to assimilate into mainstream American society, his daughter, who is actually a U.S. citizen, has other aspirations. After removing the ring from her mother's finger, she tells the family members, "I have the ring and I'm going to hock it and sail back to Germany and find my name and find my relatives and apologize to them for losing the war and become Nell Schmidt again" (115). The irony of this is that all of their dreams and aspirations, enhanced by the value of a ring, are based upon tainted goods, for Peter Schmidt admits that he stole that ring many years ago to give to his wife.

The final image that we see on stage reflects the sad state of an American society that has lost its heritage: "*The curtain keeps rising and falling revealing frozen tableaux of general confusion*" (121). In modern American society, class matters. One's individual worth is determined by class or celebrity status, not by inner qualities, which are never questioned. Thus, even if a person is not a celebrity or is not a member of society's upper echelon, what matters is to convince others that you are. If the mask fits, wear it; if the facade works, you can be successful. Identity is based merely on convincing others that you can at least hobnob with the rich and famous. The final image in the play is most appropriate, for we are a society confused about what values are important yet willing to accept superficial facades as the only tangible reality.

The last short play of this early flurry of writing in Guare's career is *Kissing Sweet*, a television drama. This one-act play of perhaps ten minutes in duration was composed after Channel 13 in New York commissioned ten American playwrights to write playlets on the threat of pollution on our natural resources. The plays were performed as part of FOUL! on the New York Television Theater, a public television program, on 25 November 1969.

In *Kissing Sweet*, two actors and two actresses play fifteen roles in quick succession as one segment of the play merges into the next, much like the transformational techniques of the Open Theater that Guare employed in *Cop-Out*. The performers "transform" into a series of television commercials played out against a backdrop of one central prop—a table filled with the detritus of our modern wasteland, including lit cigars, loud radios, cans of beer and soda, as well as different varieties of spray cans. During the play, stagehands bring out garbage of all sorts and fill the stage with smoke and noise; by the end of the drama, the actors are inundated.

The play begins with Mister Erg and Mister Ohm singing a commercial tune lauding the value of electricity, "The cleanest power in the land" (7). Then, Actress Two transforms into a matronly lady who complains to her doctor about the smell of her teeth. Next, Jane, an elderly lady, says she plans to leave her husband because of his neck odor. Finally, Actor Two assumes the role of Doctor Theodore Whifman, head research scientist for the President's Commission on Air Pollution, who is interviewed by Actor One, now playing a senator. The senator asks the scientist for the results of a long-term study on air pollution. Doctor Whifman reveals that only 1.9% of the pollution is caused by industry. When asked what causes the other 98.1% of the pollution, Dr. Whifman responds, "People pollute the air. If we didn't have any people, we'd have cleaner air" (101). His solution to the problem seems to be a commercial message:

> More products. More sprays. More pills. More creams. More soaps. We all have to pitch in. Bathe. Spray. Buy. Rid ourselves of our smells and sweats that spew their evil poisons into the skies. Scrub ourselves till nothing is left. (11)

Actor One picks up the cue and becomes the virile voice of the media, subliminally persuading the males in the audience to buy spray deodorant: "Hi, guys, Use *Ball*, the new man's deodorant for those newly discovered hard-to-reach olfactory areas. Help yourself to *Ball*" (11). Actress One is transformed into a super-seductive commercial advertiser targeting a female audience: "Hi, gals, don't offend Mister Right when he comes along. Use newly discovered *Pubia* to make sure the areas that turn on your fella don't turn him off" (11). Meanwhile, the other performers scream "Help Me Help Me Help Me" and perform deep-breathing exercises. As the stage fills with noise, smoke, and garbage, the final irony is a plea for sanity amidst the media hype:

Actor Two.	Keep your blood.
Actor One.	Kissing.
Actress Two.	Sweet. (*The stage hands block them from view with a final volley of newspapers and garbage cans.*)

A Voice.   Ear odor?
All 4 Actors.   (*Shout.*) People! (12)

Kissing Sweet explores the idea that the commercial clichés of a powerful media affect how we perceive ourselves. The play is a representation of Marshall McLuhan's notion that the media can anesthetize the masses into lethargic, passionless individuals. Media advertising can numb people into a sanitized version of Madison Avenue or Hollywood mentality. The individual will is lost, replaced by programmed behavior. Guare is concerned with the media's ability to force us to lose contact with ourselves and with others. The media tell us that we must be socialized according to social mores, and we comply, even if it means destroying ourselves and others in the process. We become homogenized to banal societal norms, forcing us to lose our individuality. Guare suggests that we, as individuals, must think critically for ourselves and use our imaginations to control the influence of Madison Avenue.

These early plays have not received the critical attention they deserve, even though several of them reflect strong writing and play well on stage. Part of the reason why there has been a paucity of critical discussion about these plays is that the characters are not as fully developed as they are in Guare's mature dramas, and their brevity usually precludes widespread performance. One-act plays simply are more problematic for producers to stage and have to be paired with other dramas. At times, when Guare has done the pairing, as is true of *Cop-Out* and *Home Fires*, critics have difficulty making connections between the two plays, where very few links actually exist. However, these early plays provide a preview of Guare's ironic sense of black humor that will blossom into the mature comedies he writes in the 1970s. In addition, the themes Guare examines in these early plays provide the foundation for the development of the social issues he explores more fully in the later plays: our inability to connect with self and others; our need to establish an identity in a society that turns us into conformists; how the media commercialization of celebrities creates myths for us to live by, allowing style to become substance; and how our estrangement in society forces us to gravitate towards violence. Finally, and perhaps most importantly, these early plays allowed Guare to experiment with the stage devices, more fully developed in his mature plays, that make him a uniquely gifted theatrical innovator: flashbacks, quick blackouts, direct address of the audience, songs, and transformational techniques.

3

The House of Blue Leaves

T *HE HOUSE OF BLUE LEAVES*, GUARE'S FIRST FULL-LENGTH PLAY, ESTAB-lished his reputation as one of the finest American dramatists of the latter part of the twentieth century. The seeds of the play had been sown early in Guare's life. When he attended Saint Joan of Arc Grammar School from 1944 to 1952, the nuns there dreamed of visiting the Vatican to be blessed by His Holiness. Touching the Pope would surely mean their salvation. In the "Introduction" to *The House of Blue Leaves,* Guare wrote, "No sisters ever yearned for Moscow the way those sisters and their pupils yearned for Rome."[1] The songs in *The House of Blue Leaves* were taken from lyrics Guare wrote in *The Thirties Girl,* a play he completed in 1960 as an undergraduate at Georgetown University. Ronnie's monologue, which opens the second act of the play, is derived from a childhood encounter Guare had with his uncle, producer Bill Grady. Uncle Billy, casting director at MGM, came to New York to search for the "ideal American boy" to star in a musical version of *Huckleberry Finn* featuring Gene Kelly and Danny Kaye. Only eight years old, John Guare believed that fate would choose him to be Huck and thus to accompany Billy back to Hollywood. Just before John was called out of his room to meet his uncle, suitcase in hand ready to go to Hollywood, it dawned on him that you had to audition for a part in a movie. John went into a wild routine that included singing, dancing, laughing, and standing on his head, finishing the performance with a deep bow. Guare recalls, "My parents were speechless with embarrassment. And then Uncle Billy growled, 'You didn't tell me you had a retarded son.'"[2] Guare was also intrigued by the fact that his uncle drove up to their house in Jackson Heights in a limousine and was decked out in a cashmere suit with a beautiful woman tugging at his sleeve. He wondered how his father, a clerk on Wall Street, and Uncle Billy could be raised in the same environment and end up with such drastically different lifestyles. This eventually became the contrast between Artie and Billy

69

Einhorn. Guare drew the three nuns in the second act of the play from another childhood episode in his life when three nuns called on John's mother to complain about his classwork. Guare reminisces, "My mother was so upset she served them martinis in the living room. Naturally they stayed all afternoon. Finally, mother got rid of them by offering them a thermos of martinis to take back to the convent."[3]

In 1965, when Guare was in Rome, he saw a photograph of the Pope on Queens Boulevard. The Pope was in New York to plead for peace in a speech he was to give at the United Nations on 4 October 1965. En route to Manhattan from Kennedy Airport, the Pope had to travel through Queens. Several weeks later, when Guare was in Egypt, his parents wrote him about the wonderful experience of a lifetime they had seeing the Pope on Queens Boulevard. Guare began writing the play that day in Cairo. Guare later noted, "If I had been in New York, I would have discounted that Papal day and sniffed at my parents' response. Being in Egypt allowed me for the first time to look into my life, into the world of my parents and realize that no life is ordinary."[4]

Guare wrote the first act of *The House of Blue Leaves* rather quickly in 1966. After he returned to New York in 1966, the first act of the play was staged that summer at the Eugene O'Neill Memorial Theatre Playwrights' Conference in Waterford, Connecticut, with Guare performing the role of Artie. However, when Guare's father passed away, the impetus to work on the remainder of the play was lost. Guare wrote eight or nine drafts of the second act but then turned to other projects that were more tenable. He was especially having difficulty writing his first full-length play that included several well-rounded character portraits. Meanwhile, Guare's producer, Warren Lyons, trying to establish a director and a cast for the play, had shown the script to Eli Wallach, Maureen Stapleton, Jason Robards, Gwen Verdon, Anne Bancroft, Geraldine Page, Mickey Rooney, Anne Jackson, Gene Hackman, and José Quintero, all of whom praised it but were unavailable due to previous commitments.[5] The second act finally came together in 1969 when Guare saw Laurence Olivier in London play Strindberg and Feydeau on successive nights and then realized that farce was the ideal medium to make the play work. Guare discussed how the problem of shaping the second act was finally resolved:

> I didn't know how to take hold of the material, because the people in the first act had to tell this vision from California the problems of their life. I said one night to the producer, "I don't know why I have to waste all this time telling them, because nobody listens to anybody else anyway;

she [Corrinna] might as well be deaf." I said, "Oh!" The minute that I knew she was deaf I realized that nobody in the play was paying attention to anybody else anyway. That was the key to it: by making her deaf and not having to say anything, the door opened up and air went through.[6]

Guare, disappointed with the 1969 failure of *Cop-Out* and *Home Fires* on Broadway, abandoned its director, Melvin Bernhardt, who was eager to stage *The House of Blue Leaves* naturalistically, in a manner that Guare rejected. Producers Betty Ann Besch and Warren Lyons signed Mel Shapiro to direct the play off-Broadway; shortly afterwards, the cast was established. Ninety-seven investors, including actors, writers, and directors, raised the money for the production. *The House of Blue Leaves* had been in rehearsals for two weeks when the Actors Equity staged a strike, halting production on 15 November 1970. The performers, unsure of the fate of the strike, dispersed. When the strike ended on 6 December, Anne Meara, who had been rehearsing as Bunny, was still filming a television pilot. To keep the cast intact, an additional $20,000 was raised by the producers. Rehearsals resumed in January 1971, with Guare fine-tuning act 2 a bit more.

The House of Blue Leaves premiered 10 February 1971, at the Truck and Warehouse Theater in New York. The cast featured Harold Gould (Artie), William Atherton (Ronnie), Anne Meara (Bunny), Katherine Helmond (Bananas), and Frank Converse (Billy Einhorn); in April, Glenn Walken replaced William Atherton and Jeremiah Sullivan took over for Frank Converse. Karl Eigsti designed the set, Jane Greenwood was the costumer, and John Tedesco arranged the lighting.

Critical opinion of the 1971 production was mixed, although there were more favorable reviews than negative ones.[7] Both Sege of *Variety* and Clive Barnes in the *New York Times* praised Shapiro's crisp staging, Eigsti's appropriately tacky set, and the macabre zaniness of Guare's text.[8] Writing in the *New Yorker*, Edith Oliver was impressed with the cast and deemed the play to be imaginative, stylish, and quite humorous.[9] James Davis (*Daily News*), Henry Hewes (*Saturday Review*), and Walter Kerr (*New York Times*) agreed that *The House of Blue Leaves* was the most exciting new play of the season.[10]

Catharine Hughes, Richard Watts, and John Simon offered somewhat neutral reviews of the play. Designating Guare as "slick and resourceful" to make the tragic seem humorous, Hughes (*Plays and Players*) was quick to admit that although she did not view the play as the best American drama of the year, she could not fault Shapiro's imaginative production, including the superb cast.[11] Richard Watts of the *New York Post* also was impressed with the performances but had difficulty with what he called Guare's muddled text, which he claimed was "savage, unfeeling and quite literally explosive, and frequently very funny."[12] John Simon, confused about the form of the play as a combination of domestic farce, absurdist comedy, and tragedy, believed that Guare had more work to do on it, acknowledging that it is "a charmingly slapdash play in its better moments, and an exasperatingly undisciplined exercise in its worst ones."[13]

Harold Clurman (*Nation*), Martin Gottfried (*Women's Wear Daily*), Jack Kroll (*Newsweek*), and Julius Novick (*New York Times*) were hostile to the play. Although less critical of Guare for his sense of what he called cruel sorrow, Clurman ultimately wrote an inspired, serious review in which he objected to the realistic set design, the miscasting of Harold Gould as Artie, and Shapiro's direction.[14] Jack Kroll's one-paragraph review in *Newsweek* unfortunately did not do justice to the play. He concluded, "Guare's play suffers from his sordid desire to jam everything in, to show you that not only can he write mordantly funny scenes, but that he also knows exactly everything that's wrong with the world."[15] Martin Gottfried enjoyed the production and noted that Shapiro directed well, but he went on to blame the cast, particularly Meara, and asserted that although half of the play was "fresh, touching, and lyrical," even "rhapsodic," the other half was "crude and forced," making it "one of the most exasperating plays I have ever seen."[16] However, it was Julius Novick's column in the *New York Times* that exacerbated the controversy over the play. Novick, whose review was published after his counterpart, Clive Barnes, had praised the drama as the finest play of the year, called *The House of Blue Leaves* a "long sick joke" because its farce and agony were contradictory.[17] Novick's main point was that he objected to black comedy, which gives credence to pain and frustration, as opposed to comedy, where pain and frustration do not triumph; he therefore accused Guare of laughing at agony. Guare, stung by these comments, shot back at Novick for not understanding the nature of farce:

> I knew Julius at Yale. He had a sour expression on his face then and he has one now. You can quote me on this. Julius has become an aging quiz kid. He lives his life by theories. He thinks every play should sound like Arthur Miller. God denied him a sense of the ridiculous which I pity him for.[18]

On 3 December 1971, the Truck and Warehouse Theater burned down. The firemen who doused the flames found that the sets and costumes had been vandalized. In the tenement next door, a man's throat had been slashed. Investigators later discovered that the fire, vandalism, and murder were three separate incidents. The play was thus forced to close after 337 performances. Guare's compensation was that *The House of Blue Leaves* was well feted, winning an Obie Award for Best Play, the New York Drama Critics' Circle Award for Best American Play, the Los Angeles Drama Critics' Circle Award, and the Outer Critics' Circle Award. The play also began to receive international recognition with its first foreign translation (into French as *Un Pape à New-York*) and subsequent production in Paris, at the Théâtre de la Gaité-Montparnasse, directed by Michel Fagadau, on 4 November 1972. Guare later wrote a screenplay for a film version of the play, but the project did not materialize because Carlo Ponti abandoned it when Sophia Loren was not available to be cast in the movie.

In 1985, director Gregory Mosher and producer Bernard Gersten of Lincoln Center wanted to stage Guare's *Gardenia* following a David Mamet bill. Mosher had directed *Gardenia* at the Goodman Theater in Chicago and sought to use several of the same actors for the New York production. However, when the logistics of gathering the cast became untenable, Mosher and Gersten decided to stage *The House of Blue Leaves*. Guare approached Jerry Zaks to direct the revival. Oddly enough, Zaks told Guare that he had directed the play at Dartmouth ten years earlier and was interested in doing it again. The revival opened 19 March 1986, at the Mitzi E. Newhouse Theater in Lincoln Center. The cast featured John Mahoney (Artie), Ben Stiller (Ronnie), Stockard Channing (Bunny), Swoosie Kurtz (Bananas), and Christopher Walken (Billy). Originally scheduled for an eight-week run, the play proved so popular that it transferred to the larger Vivian Beaumont Theater on 29 April 1986, and finally to the Plymouth Theater on 14 October 1986.

The revival of *The House of Blue Leaves* received quite favorable notices from such critics as Mel Gussow (*New York Times*), William A. Henry (*Time*), Janet Hobhouse (*Vogue*), Jack Kroll (*Newsweek*), Michael Malone (*Nation*), Edith Oliver (*New Yorker*), Frank Rich (*New York Times*), John Simon (*New York*), and Edwin Wilson (*Wall Street Journal*).[19] The general assessment from the press was that the revival was better than the original production staged fifteen years earlier. In particular, critics praised Jerry Zaks's gimmick-free direction, Paul Gallo's imaginative lighting, Tony Walton's set design suggesting urban blight, and the uniformly strong acting, especially the work of Swoosie Kurtz. All of a sudden, Guare's play, which had not changed since 1971 and which was initially thought to be cruel and unfeeling, was now perceived as poignant and compassionate.[20]

The revival of *The House of Blue Leaves* closed after 420 performances, the original eight-week run extending for nearly a year. After witnessing the shooting of Pope John Paul II in 1981, audiences in 1986 were more apt to accept the play as reality rather than as absurdity, and with the ubiquitous blend of satire in popular culture, Guare's sense of humor became less threatening. The revival was nominated for eight Tony Awards, eventually winning four: Best Actress (Swoosie Kurtz), Best Actor (John Mahoney), Best Director, and Best Scenic Design.[21] During the latter part of the twentieth century, the play has been staged worldwide and has become quite popular with college and repertory theater groups.[22]

The House of Blue Leaves is a contemporary version of Chekhovian realism mixed with farce. On the one hand, the play is fully grounded in realism and adheres to the unities. The play occurs in a specific time period (4 October 1965), in a realistic setting (a cold apartment in Sunnyside, Queens), and focuses on a historical event (the Pope's visit to New York to present a speech about international affairs at the United Nations). The two-act structure of the play (act 2 is divided into two scenes) is also conventional. On the other hand, Guare uses farce to fly in the face of such realistic decorum, knocking down the facade of verisimilitude. The bland, placid, and mundane world of the Shaughnessy household is transformed into a vision of the cruelty and sickness in healthy fantasy. Farce enables Guare to act as a surgeon, dissecting the pain and frustration of contemporary urban life, and through laughter, he allows us to acknowledge the often latent agony of our existence. However painful the play may be, Guare reveals the modern neuroses and psychoses that plague us almost daily.

The House of Blue Leaves debunks the American Dream, which contends that hard work will eventually yield fruitful rewards in society. Instead, the American Dream is deceiving, especially when we learn that upward mobility is not possible for many of us. Guare noted, "*House of Blue Leaves* had been a play about limits: people limited by a lack of talent, limited economically, limited emotionally, limited geographically."[23] As a result of these limitations and despite the American Dream enticing us to look to the future, we spend most of our time trying to avoid humiliation. This motif becomes the core for Guare's black comedy. Steven H. Gale astutely realizes that in *The House of Blue Leaves,* Guare " . . . is concerned with how people react when it becomes clear that their publicly announced dreams can never be realized."[24] The reality of our failed dreams is always painful, and thus we perceive it as a blessing when our religious institutions and our popular culture embellish the notion that being rich and famous is within our grasp. Our individual goals and desires are subsumed by a more powerful, glamorized media conception of celebrity. This infatuation with celebrities allows us to dream of fame and fortune while we tend to ignore the reality around us, including what may be meaningful relationships with family and friends, as well as valuable spiritual connections. However, once the superficial and self-deceptive dreams are exposed and we are left with a real world that does not measure up to our fantasies, we are reduced to violent behavior in trying to cope.

Guare set the play in the locale he knew best, Queens, reinforcing the notion that he views New York City as a microcosm of America. To Guare, Queens suggested the magic of the American Dream; it was a residential community, unlike commercial Manhattan, where parents could raise children in peace and aspire towards social mobility. Guare describes how Queens became the ideal setting for his play about vanquished dreams:

> Queens was built in the twenties in that flush of optimism as a bedroom community for people on their way up who worked in Manhattan but wanted to pretend they had the better things in life until the inevitable break came and they could make the official move to the Scarsdales and the Ryes and the Greenwiches of their dreams, the pay-off that was the birthright of every American. Queens named its communities Forest Hills, Kew Gardens, Elmhurst, Woodside, Sunnyside, Jackson Heights, Corona, Astoria (after the Astors, of all people). The builders built the apartment houses in mock Tudor or Gothic or Colonial and then named them The Chateau, The El Dorado, Linsley Hall, the Alhambra. . . . And the lobbies had Chippendale furniture and Aztec fireplaces, and the elevators had roman numerals on the buttons.[25]

Queens, then, was perceived as a pit stop on the path to a more glamorous way of life once the breaks and promotions accrued. It also functions as the ideal setting for black comedy, a place of bitter irony where one's unrealized dreams and fantasies become a constant source of humiliation.

Middle-aged Artie Shaughnessy epitomizes such a life in Queens where reality and fantasy are hopelessly intertwined.[26] Although Artie prefers to fantasize, drab reality weighs heavily upon his life. Artie is a zookeeper by day; at night, he comes home to a different sort of zoo. His shabby apartment is filled with jungle animals, constantly reminding him that his domestic life more closely resembles a zoo than it does Hollywood. The six bolts required to lock the doors and the iron folding gate across the window suggest that Artie is virtually a caged animal, a prisoner in his own home. He laments, "Work all day in a zoo. Come home to a zoo."[27]

Artie's family life is a big disappointment, a bitter pill to swallow for someone who has great aspirations. Much of the zookeeper's domestic menagerie consists of caring for his mentally ill wife, Bananas. When the animals at the zoo get testy, Artie is called in to calm them down. Similarly, when Bananas gets hysterical, and her name implies that she has a tendency to do so, Artie forces tranquilizers down her throat. Artie constantly threatens to have her committed to an insane asylum. At the same time, he is saddled with an alienated and rebellious eighteen-year-old son who is AWOL from the U.S. Army. However, Ronnie's sense of rebellion, demonstrated by his desire to kill the Pope with a homemade bomb, is more than typical adolescent angst. Bananas's insanity and Ronnie's deeply rooted insecurity indicate that the Shaughnessy family is highly dysfunctional.

Artie refuses to recognize the reality of his dismal domestic life and instead dreams of committing his wife to a mental institution while he pursues his fantasy life as a successful songwriter. He admits, "I've become this Dreaming Boy. I make all these Fatimas out of the future. Lourdes and Fatima. All these shrines out of the future and I keep crawling to them" (74). In hopes of fulfilling his dreams, Artie plays the piano on amateur nights at the El Dorado bar. He demands a spotlight and rapt audience attention while he sings such "hits" as "Where Is the Devil in Evelyn?" Artie's tunes often reflect the desperation in his quest for a better life: "I'm looking for Something, / I've searched everywhere . . ." (14). Yet the reality is that, as Artie readily acknowledges, "I'm too old to be a young talent!!!" (85). The brutal truth is that during his search for stardom at the El Dorado, Artie's audience is inattentive and unappreciative, and he is treated rather shabbily, forced to pay for his own beers. Even worse, Artie's Tin Pan Alley-type songs are not original creations, for most of his tunes are plagiarized versions of Irving Berlin's "White Christmas." His talent is part of his fantasy.

Dissatisfied with his drab domestic life, Artie forms a relationship with his downstairs neighbor, Bunny Flingus, whose name suggests that the couple will enjoy a fling together. Although Artie has known Bunny for only two months, she plays upon his fantasy life in a way that Bananas does not. Bunny encourages Artie's dreams and tells Bananas, "I'm taking Artie out of this environment and bringing him to California while Billy can still do him some good. Get Artie's songs—his music—into the movies" (35). Artie met Bunny in the steambath of a local health club. He recalls that upon initially seeing Bunny in the steam room, she appeared to be his mythical savior: "And she was in her sheet like a toga and I was all toga'd up and I swear, Billy, we were gods and goddesses and the steam bubbled up and swirled and it was Mount Olympus" (41). Bunny offers Artie the vivacity and vigorous hope for the future that Bananas cannot provide. The affair they are having, however, is a twisted version of unrequited love. Artie, with his burnt-out sexual desires after years of living with Bananas, only wants Bunny to cook for him. She refuses to prepare any culinary delights for him until they are married; until then, Artie will have to be content with having sex with her. Samuel J. Bernstein explains this strange love affair: "Here, Guare is mocking an American courtship ritual; also, through the food passion, he comments on a lack of spirituality in human relationships."[28] Despite Bunny's shallowness, she reinforces Artie's fantasies of being rich and famous. She insists that his songs are classics and that he has talent that would thrive were he discovered by Hollywood moguls. Whereas Bananas reminds Artie of his drab existence and the reality of dreams gone sour, Bunny keeps the future alive for the aspiring hit songwriter.

Artie is enamored with celebrities and with individuals who have been successful. He has bought into the myth of the American Dream to such a degree that he has become oblivious to people who are not rich and famous, and thus blind to reality. His living room is filled with pictures of movie stars, icons Artie worships. He is forever boasting of rubbing shoulders with the likes of his friend, Billy Einhorn, a big-shot Hollywood producer and director. To Artie, Billy represents everything Artie fantasizes about: wealth, fame, and celebrity status. Upon seeing Billy's friend, Corrinna, Artie says, "You call Billy and he sends stars. Stars!" (55). After Corrinna is killed in the bomb accident, Artie's reaction is predictably, "She could've been one of the big ones. A lady Biggie. Boy. Stardust. Handfuls of it. All over her" (73). Artie's dream is to have his wife committed to an insane asylum, elope with Bunny, and make good in Hollywood like his old friend Billy. Einhorn, the mythical unicorn, is Guare's subliminal hint that the American Dream is merely fantasy.

Artie views Pope Paul's visit to New York City to deliver a speech about peace to the United Nations as his chance to get close to a well-known celebrity. Artie hopes that during the Pope's procession down Queens Boulevard en route to Manhattan, His Holiness will bless his songs; the "superstar" will then provide enough impetus for Artie to make his own luck in Hollywood. Watching the Pope on television, which only serves to reinforce his celebrity status in Artie's mind, the zookeeper pleads, "Help me—help me—Your Holiness" (47). Artie's fantasy penetrates his unconscious when he dreams that his son, Ronnie, becomes the Pope. Pope Ronnie picks Artie up in a limousine yet leaves Bananas behind and takes him to Rome where the songwriter is canonized as "a Saint of the Church and in charge of writing all the hymns for the Church. A hymn couldn't be played unless it was mine and the whole congregation sang "Where Is the Devil in Evelyn? . . ." (28). Thus, when the Pope makes Artie songwriter and saint he bestows upon him fame and fortune—at least in Artie's wildest dreams. As Suzanne Dieckman has indicated, Guare, equating Catholicism with show business, takes a jab at both for promulgating dreams and specious promises.[29]

What makes *The House of Blue Leaves* more poignant than Guare's previous dramas is the depth of Artie's character and the degree to which the audience identifies with his plight. Artie is certainly not cartoonish like Brett Arrow and is much more complex than enigmatic Jack Argue. Although the black comedy is pervasive, Guare is not writing caricature. Like Chekhov, Guare is writing from the heart about the absurdity of humanity's dreams and desires. Jerry Zaks noted, "John has a genuine love for these people. . . . I think one reason the play wears well is because it is an American tragedy, the story of a man who can't appreciate the things he has."[30] During an interview with Guare, John L. DiGaetani accused Bananas of being a neglectful mother, at which point, Guare claimed that Di-Gaetani missed the main idea of the play: "Instead, the father and the boy were so crazy that they completely neglected and ignored her. Their dreams were so great. Their dreams of the future and outside the house were greater than their ability to enjoy what was right there in the house."[31] What was once a loving relationship between Artie and Bananas is now smothered by a tawdry myth that Artie accepts as reality. Artie's neglect of his family is the chief cause of its dysfunction. Bunny realizes, "No man takes a job feeding animals in the Central Park Zoo unless he's afraid to deal with humans" (35). Artie's solution to dealing with his loved ones is to commit his wife to "The House of Blue Leaves," an asylum for the mentally ill. He candidly admits to Billy, " . . . this sounds cruel to say but Bananas is as dead for me as Georgina is for you" (40). He even tries to placate Bananas, assuaging her fears about being reluctant to go to the mental hospital: "You'll like the place . . . a lot of famous people have had crackdowns there, so you'll be running in good company" (33).

The play succeeds because the audience, like Guare, empathizes and pities Artie's plight as our own. The time is exactly right for miracles to occur: the Pope is coming to America, and Billy Einhorn, representing the glitter and glamor of celebrity-ridden California, is Artie's ticket out of the mire of Queens. However, like Everyman, Artie's dreams remain unfulfilled; the myth of fame and happiness leaves us disillusioned. Artie loses Bunny, who selfishly chooses to go to Hollywood with Billy, while the director tells his old "friend" that he is better off staying in Queens. The American Dream has been demythologized, reduced to nothing more than an illusion. At this point, the meaning of the title of the play can be discerned. Near the mental asylum in which Artie plans to have Bananas committed is a tree full of blue birds, which Artie mistakenly assumes are blue leaves. When the birds fly away, the "tree" appears to have lost its leaves and thus becomes visibly barren. The illusion is fleeting; behind it lies the barren reality. As Gautam Dasgupta suggests, "Somewhat like the bluebirds resting on a tree, which Artie mistakenly takes to be a tree with blue leaves, the world is a mirage forever eluding one's grasp."[32] At the end of the play, when the stage is inundated with blue leaves, Artie's mockery is consummated.

During the denouement, Artie receives a telephone call informing him that the animals in the zoo are giving birth. Artie, however, understands that this sign does not suggest rebirth but instead relegates him all over again to the mundane task of zookeeper, called in to care for the animals. Bananas sits on her haunches like a dog and sings, "Back together again, / Back together again" (86). Artie now comprehends that he will interminably be reduced to the temporal role of zookeeper at home and at work. Realizing that his existence has been based on an elusive fantasy and now faced with the grim reality of a life of hopeless dreams that would devastate any idealist such as himself, Artie kisses his wife one last time and then gently strangles her to death. Artie kills Bananas because she is witness to his failure and would serve to reinforce his humiliation for the rest of his life. Again, how we avoid humiliation seems to be the dominant motif in Guare's theater.

As is typical in Guare's plays, protagonists who are increasingly frustrated by their inability to match reality with their dreams ultimately resort to violence. If *The House of Blue Leaves* were a traditional comedy, which is the premise of Julius Novick's argument that the play is a long, sick joke, then the violent ending would be inappropriate.

However, as black comedy, which exposes the cruel hypocrisies of a sick society, the denouement in this play works well. The audience does not laugh at Artie's agony per se; instead, the spectators feel the pathos and bitter amusement that result when we, like Artie, pursue dreams that leave us frustrated, angry, and unfulfilled. Thus, the final image of the play, when Artie, ostensibly smiling, sings, "I'm here with bells on / Ringing out how I feel" (87), followed by the stage filling with blue leaves, becomes the icon for this black comedy. Artie's swan song reflects our own plight in which dreams are touted as real but are actually nothing more than illusions.

Ronnie, like his father, has his own warped dreams of achieving fame and fortune. At age twelve, Ronnie auditioned to win the role of the "Ideal American Boy" to play Huckleberry Finn in a movie Billy Einhorn was producing. Billy's reaction in front of Ronnie's parents, "You never told me you had a mentally retarded child" (53), completely devastated the youngster. From that moment on, Ronnie was seen as a failure: "My father thinks I'm nothing. Billy. My sergeant. They laugh at me. You laughing at me?" (53). Ronnie hopes to gain back his sense of self-respect while simultaneously spiting his father. Again, in Guare's microcosmic view of contemporary American society, frustrated individuals usually resort to violence. Ronnie muses to the audience about his "revenge": "Pop, I'm going to blow up the Pope and when *Time* interviews me tonight, I won't even mention you. I'll say I was an orphan" (67). In this perverse scenario, Ronnie plans to become famous, even if it means being notorious for one of the most heinous crimes of the century. Ronnie boasts that he will soon have celebrity status: "By tonight, I'll be on headlines all over the world. Cover of *Time. Life.* TV specials. *He shows a picture of himself on the wall.* I hope they use this picture of me—I look better with hair—" (53). As the person who assassinates the Pope, Ronnie realizes, "I'll be too big for any of you" (53). However, Guare's black comedy puts star-struck Ronnie in his rightful place. Ronnie's bomb misses the target and instead kills two nuns and Billy Einhorn's deaf girlfriend. As Ruby Cohn observes, Ronnie is as ineffectual as his father, both cut from the same cloth.[33]

Bunny Flingus has much in common with Artie and his son. She is described as "*a pretty, pink, slightly plump, electric woman in her late thirties*" (18). Like Artie and Ronnie, she is shallow and selfish, lacking any spiritual empathy for anyone. As Samuel L. Bernstein reminds us, her name suggests sex and transience.[34] Although she admits that she is "not good in bed" (24), her first name implies that she has had plenty of contact with men but no spiritual relationships with them; they are merely temporal "flings." Sex will always be unsatisfying to her because it is never accompanied by a loving relationship. To Bunny, Artie's marriage is simply an inconvenience, an obstacle to her own personal happiness. Her plans for Artie do not include his wife: "As soon as Bananas here is carted off, we'll step off that plane and Billy and you and I and Corrinna here will eat and dance and drink and love until the middle of the next full moon" (65). Bunny actually wishes that Bananas will die, allowing her to escape with Artie to Hollywood. Her selfishness is also revealed in what she plans to say to the Pope when he passes in his limousine: "'Your Holiness, marry us—the hell with peace to the world—bring peace to us'" (21). This comment is particularly unnerving when one realizes that the purpose of the Pope's visit is to plead for world peace at the United Nations while the Vietnam War rages on and while Artie's son is about to be sent to fight in that war. At the end of the play, when Bunny gets her chance to go to California with Billy, she cruelly and selfishly leaves Artie behind. Moreover, Bunny's transience, her lack of identity, is reflected in the numerous flighty jobs that she has held. She has worked for a telephone company, Con Edison, a movie theater, a law office, a lending library, a theatrical furniture store, a travel agency, a ski lodge, and the music department at Macy's—and this list includes only the jobs that she has informed us about and does not include perhaps many others.

Bunny's values have been formed through gossip columns, television, and movie magazines. In short, the media have cultivated her belief that human beings are worthless unless they possess the glamor of celebrities. She is more concerned about Sandra Dee losing her hair curlers the evening before her film debut than she is about establishing a purposeful spiritual connection with others. Like mainstream America, she has become "narcotized" to *Reader's Digest* values.

Bunny has become mesmerized by the notion of celebrity to such an extent that it is of paramount importance in her life. Her dream is to marry Artie and live in Hollywood, the place where celebrity status is fully appreciated. She sells the hype to Artie: "You'll be out there with the big shots—out where you belong—not in any amateur nights in bars on Queens Boulevard. Billy will get your songs in movies" (21–22). Her vision for Artie is winning the Oscar for Best Song and being presented with the award by none other than Greer Garson herself. Bunny treats Billy with reverence as if he were the savior with the capacity to discover ordinary individuals for the movies, thus enshrining and ennobling them for eternity. When Artie hesitates calling his friend at two o'clock in the morning, Bunny indicates that she sees Billy not as an individual with feelings, but as an icon of fame and fortune who could never be bothered by such a minor intrusion as a telephone call: "In Hollywood! Come off it, he's probably not even in yet—they're out there frigging and frugging and swinging and eating and dancing. Since Georgina died, he's probably got a brace of nude starlets splashing in the pool" (36–37). In addition, deaf movie starlet Corrinna Stroller, whose only claim to fame was the one B movie that she made, is perceived by Bunny to be emulated as a success story: "Corrinna Stroller! Limos in the streets. Oh, Miss Stroller, I only saw your one movie, *Warmonger*, but it is permanently enshrined in the Loew's of my heart" (55).

Bunny, decked out in binoculars and wearing two Brownie cameras on cords, wants to get a good spot on Queens Boulevard so she can get a glimpse of the ultimate celebrity, the Pope himself. Bunny equates the Pope's procession to a movie premiere: "They're stretched out in the gutter waiting for the sun to come out so they can start snapping pictures. I haven't seen so many people, Artie, so excited since the premiere of *Cleopatra*. It's that big" (18–19). To Bunny, the Pope is equated with such "big" show business celebrities as Sandra Dee (34), Annette Funicello (35), Doris Day (38), Rock Hudson (38), Marlon Brando (39), and Mitzi Gaynor (39). Wearing an "I Love Paul" button on her coat, Bunny explains, "They ran out of 'Welcome Pope' buttons so I ran downstairs and got my leftover from when the Beatles were here!" (48). The Pope and the Beatles are synonymous to Bunny as charismatic popular culture icons. When the Pope is seen on television delivering a speech from Yankee Stadium later that day, he becomes further enshrined as a media celebrity. In Bunny's distorted parochial view equating religion and star status, if Artie gets his songs blessed by the Pope, through this momentary contact with such an eminent celebrity, the aspiring songwriter will take the first step to fame and fortune. The Pope's message is transmitted from Yankee Stadium:

> We feel, too, that the entire American people is here present with its noblest and most characteristic traits: a people basing its conception of life on spiritual values, on a religious sense, on freedom, on loyalty, on work, on the respect of duty, on family affection, on generosity and courage—(71).

The irony is that for Bunny and for millions of Americans like her who are awestruck more by the Pope's temporal majesty than by his plea for spiritual connection, his message falls on deaf ears.

Guare reveals that those who supposedly dedicate their lives to spiritual attainment also succumb to the lure of fame and fortune. Three nuns who failed to see the Pope because the crowds were so huge browbeat Artie into letting them share the experience on television. The nuns act more like spoiled celebrities enamored with materialistic concerns rather than with spiritual comforting. They grumble about the fact that the beers Artie gives them are not imported and that his television is not a color set. Fighting for the best viewing position by the television set, they behave like teenagers watching their favorite soap operas rather than as spiritual leaders. The head nun vies with her two cohorts to have her photo taken with celebrities: "There's Jackie Kennedy!!! Get me with Jackie Kennedy!!! *She puts her arm around the TV*" (59). The second nun exclaims, "There's Mayor Lindsay! Get me with him! Mayor Lindsay dreamboat!" (60). The awe of the fantasy of celebrity is so potent that it overwhelms our real lives, even ones that already have some semblance of spiritual significance. When the nuns become too rambunctious, Artie asks them to leave the room. Forced to abandon the almighty television and thus relinquish their fantasies about media personalities, the second nun tells Artie, "I'm going to start picking who I pray for" (60). The nuns later accost Ronnie for Corrinna's tickets for the Pope's mass at Yankee Stadium. Hoping to be in the presence of the biggest star of all, the nuns, like Bunny and Artie, believe that the Pope's aura will shine on them, turning their drab lives into glitter and glamor.

While staying briefly in Artie's apartment, the nuns have a chance to partake in material pleasures and commercial ventures not otherwise available in the convent. They have the opportunity to snack on peanut butter, drink beer, try on dresses, watch television, and get autographs from real celebrities such as Corrinna Stroller. Upon meeting Corrinna for the first time, the little nun runs to her side and proudly announces, "I saw *The Sound of Music* thirty-one times. It changed my entire life" (59). The implication is that Catholicism, for which the nun took her vows, is equated with show business. The nuns even quarrel about the right to pray for such a distinguished personality. After Billy gives the little nun some money to care for Bananas, she comprehends that the virtues of celebrity far outweigh drab life in the convent and thus decides to stay and live in Bunny's apartment, abandoning her vows. After all, she candidly realizes, "The convent was very depressing. Pray a while. Scream a while" (77).

Throwing her habit down, the little nun rejects her calling and goes with the advice from a celebrity who, through past experience, can best show her the way to fame and fortune. Kissing the television and calling it a shrine, the little nun states, "I wanted to be a Bride of Christ but I guess now I'm a young divorcee" (85). Using the popular culture terminology of "young divorcee," the little nun demonstrates how the spiritual values associated with organized religion can become tainted by increased commercialization.

Bananas is the result of a society that worships big names but neglects the little person. Once happily married to Artie, Bananas, in her forties, is now prancing around half dazed in her nightgown, crying continuously, never leaving the apartment, and trying to maintain the dignity that she enjoyed earlier in life before her husband began to ignore her in favor of the younger Bunny Flingus. Bananas is suffering because her husband has been cruel and uncaring to her. She confronts Artie: "Are you leaving to get away from me? Tell me? The truth? You hate me. You hate my looks—my face—my clothes— you hate me" (26). Her lament, "Why can't they love me?" (46), is the quintessential question so many of us are compelled to ask in a society in which values are distorted, making spiritual and familial communication unattainable. Artie, forced to give his wife tranquilizers to calm her violent spasms, wants Bananas committed to a mental asylum, but Bunny prefers to see her dead. A few months earlier, Bananas tried to slash her wrists with spoons, suggesting that she is so pitifully demented that she cannot even commit suicide properly. Once, she wandered out in a snowstorm wearing only her nightgown, only to be found in the blizzard twenty-four hours later.

Bananas is having recurrent nightmares as well: "I dream I'm just waking up and I roam around the house all day crying because of the way my life turned out" (29). One such dream had her driving a taxi, picking up Cardinal Spellman, Jackie Kennedy, Bob Hope, and President Lyndon Johnson at the intersection of Broadway and Forty-Second Street. With stars in her cab, what might be construed as rubbing shoulders with the elite ends in disaster. The taxi gets four flat tires, and then the celebrities each hail separate cabs, abandoning Bananas. That evening, Cardinal Spellman and Bob Hope joke about the experience on the *Tonight Show* with Johnny Carson. Bananas thus dreams that she is mocked before a nation of viewers—all of America shares in the vision of Bananas as a sham.

Unable to obtain love from her family, Bananas becomes incorrigible. In a futile and pathetic attempt to scald Bunny in her apartment downstairs, Bananas floods her own bathroom with hot water. She winds up cooking Brillo pads as hamburgers for dinner. Given the chance both to catch a glimpse of the Pope on Queens Boulevard and to have the opportunity to get out of the apartment on a rare occasion, Bananas claims she cannot face the crowd because her fingernails are different lengths. Meanwhile, she further exacerbates the pain by imagining a more idyllic existence in the past, exhorting her husband to play "I Love You So I Keep Dreaming."

Starved for love and victimized by her selfish husband, Bananas, a battered mutt, reaches out to touch the stars. Her conversations are replete with almost pathological adulation for the celebrities she occasionally mentions: Bob Hope, Cardinal Spellman, Jackie Kennedy, Johnny Carson, and Kate Smith. To Bananas, the Pope has the same type of eminence, and she dreamily admits, "I'd like to jump out right in front of the Pope's car" (36). The Pope can possibly provide the love, nurturance, and compassion that is missing in her life: "He'd take me in his arms and bless me" (36). In a pathetic scenario, Bananas runs to the television screen to kiss the Pope's garments, hoping to come into contact with His Holiness so that her own life can be changed for the better. Unfortunately, Bananas can only sigh, "The screen is so cold . . ." (47). This image suggests that the meretricious media hype intended to make religious leaders as well as popular culture icons into celebrities is alluring yet essentially cold and disingenuous.

Artie calls on his old friend, Billy, to provide the salvation he seeks. Upon first glance, Billy would seem to be the logical choice to help Artie, for he has made his fortune and commands a certain amount of respect as a filmmaker in California, the place where fantasies are realized. However, when the veneer of celebrity is ultimately examined more closely, we find that underneath lies artificiality. Billy's first film, *Conduct of Life*, was an artistic success and still is shown regularly in museums. In contrast, at the height of his success, Billy sells out his talent in favor of making sugar-coated commercial movies with Doris Day and Rock Hudson. Billy, modeled after Guare's uncle, but also a name suggesting the immaturity of adolescence, has reneged on a chance to be a mature talent and opts instead for appealing to the frivolous and mundane tastes of the starry-eyed masses, including Artie himself. Billy's latest project is to move to Australia and make a film, which is unimaginatively to be titled *Kangaroo*. Artie views this film as another success story similar to Billy's previous epic production, *Warmonger*, another mundane effort created with a title that would likely attract mass audiences. As Harold Clurman has mentioned, Guare suggests that even the mediocre can possess glamor if sufficiently publicized and perceived that way by the half-wits who buy into the Hollywood hype.[35]

Instead, Billy, the celebrity, not only is shallow and superficial, but also is incapable of helping Artie. Billy demythologizes the notion of the American Dream of fame and fortune. Supposedly playing the role of a genuine success story for Artie, Billy instead argues that the songwriter has the best of all possible worlds at home in Queens with Bananas. Billy views his life as a sham compared to Artie's "success story": "You were always healthy. You married a wonderful little Italian girl. You have a son. Where am I?" (80). Proving that "the grass is always greener on the other side of the fence," Billy says that he envies Artie's domestic life and reminds Artie of a happier time when Bananas was mentally healthy and a loving wife. Rather than acting as a role model, Billy instead selfishly perceives his chance to replace his dead wife, Georgina, with the lively Bunny Flingus, who jumps at the opportunity to go to Australia with the movie producer and abandon Artie. Billy justifies the need for Artie to remain in Queens, deflating his friend's dreams:

> If ever I thought you and Bananas weren't here in Sunnyside, seeing my work, loving my work, I could never work again. You're my touch with reality. *He goes to Bananas.* Bananas, do you know what the greatest talent in the world is? To be an audience. Anybody can create. But to be an audience . . . be an audience. . . . (84)

Artie believed that Queens was unreal and that Hollywood was the ultimate reality. Billy demythologizes the dream by insisting that Queens is real and that the identity of the rich and famous depends on middle-class Americans who pay to see the stars. Thus, Artie, who tried to use Billy to enhance his dreams of success, much in the same manner that he tried to avail himself to the Pope, realizes that his fantasies have been naive.

Billy brings with him Corrinna Stroller, supposedly the personification of the type of star success Artie emulates. Samuel J. Bernstein notes the irony that Guare presents when the Shaughnessy household discovers that Corrinna, the embodiment of a Hollywood dream world in which the elite can undo the ravages of time and fate, is actually stone deaf.[36] When Bananas swallows Corrinna's transistors, thinking that they are her tranquilizers, Miss Stroller's glamorous image is deflated, and she instead is unmasked as a clownish figure. When Artie auditions his songs for the movie star, the implication is that California dreaming is futile; Artie's tunes fall on deaf ears.

The House of Blue Leaves was a major breakthrough for Guare because, for the first time, we see fully developed characters with which
the audience can empathize. Guare's play touches an American conscience that dreams of a more perfect life yet refuses to realize the
intrinsic value of relationships based on shared experiences. Lured
by the power of media suggestion, conditioning, and advertising that
manipulates our idealistic visions, we become helplessly immersed
in artificial values. Guare, like his mentor, Chekhov, unmasks the
hypocrisy of the comic nightmares we lead. Guare demonstrates that
friendship and marriage, based upon emotional communion, are
subsumed in favor of prefabricated fantasies. By constantly yearning
to touch the stars, we often forget to connect with friends and family
around us. The irony is that when we do not connect with our loved
ones and yet still get the chance to obtain celebrity status, we realize
that it is a sham, and then we may, like Corrinna, wind up deaf to
those around us.

4

Marco Polo Sings a Solo and *Rich and Famous*

WITHIN A TWO-YEAR PERIOD, FROM 1972 TO 1974, GUARE WROTE *Marco Polo Sings a Solo* and *Rich and Famous*. The former play is one of Guare's least successful dramas while the latter reflects Guare's ability to craft black comedy. This chapter examines both plays and seeks to explain how *Marco Polo Sings a Solo* invites many of the stereotyped critical opinions about Guare's theater and how *Rich and Famous* dispels those myths.

Marco Polo Sings a Solo appears to be Guare's bête noire. Guare began writing the play in 1972 on a return airplane trip from London, where he saw *Two Gentlemen of Verona* performed. Fearing that he had no new project in the works, Guare, in a panic, wrote the first act of the play before he arrived at Kennedy Airport in New York.[1] The ninety-minute first act of the drama is approximately twice as long as the second act. For years, Guare experimented with the play, writing at least fifteen drafts. Most of the writing occurred over a four-year period, during which time Guare lost touch with the original impetus that spawned the project. With Guare's imagination running wild, many of the scenes kept getting rearranged. Even one of the most recent versions of the play in 1996, printed in Guare's collected works, indicates several changes from the 1977 edition published by Dramatists Play Service; however, most of these emendations are in the stage directions rather than in the dialogue. During an interview with Lloyd Rose, Guare was asked to enlighten the critic about *Marco Polo Sings a Solo* and responded, "I can't even enlighten myself about it!"[2] Guare went on to admit, "There are so many layers of the play for me, so many versions of the play, that I see it and I sort of can't see it clearly. It was personally, in a growing way, one of those plays I learned an extraordinary amount from."[3] Guare probably learned a lot about audience analysis, for what was clear to him in writing the play was obscure for most spectators, and his later plays do not reflect this paradox.

Marco Polo Sings a Solo premiered at the small Cyrus Pierce Theater of the Nantucket Stage Company in Nantucket, Massachusetts, on 6 August 1973.[4] John Wulp, the producer for the Nantucket Stage Company, underwrote the play, perceived as a work in progress, for six weeks of performances and asked critics not to review the production. Mel Shapiro, fresh from his success with *The House of Blue Leaves*, directed a cast that included Piper Laurie (Diane), Beeson Carroll (Stony), James Woods (Larry), and Paul Benedict (Frank).

The first major production of the finished version of the play went into rehearsals in early December 1976 and debuted at Joseph Papp's Newman Theater of the New York Shakespeare Festival's Public Theater on 6 February 1977, while Guare was serving there as a playwright in residence; although public presentations began on 12 January, those performances were not reviewed. Mel Shapiro directed a promising cast that featured Madeline Kahn (Diane), Joel Grey (Stony), Anne Jackson (Mrs. McBride), and Sigourney Weaver (Freydis). John Wulp created an immaculate set of a glacierlike fjord, and Theoni V. Aldredge designed fancy costumes for the eight performers. Although there were several positive reviews of this production,[5] most of the criticism was negative.[6] The play closed in early March after a limited run of approximately one month.

A few critics attempted to make sense of the confusing play. Richard Eder, writing in the *New York Times*, compared the drama to a series of images depicting humanity's ability to endure, calling it "a brilliantly absurdist comedy of ideas."[7] Praising the play as science fiction comedy replete with jokes and surprises, Edith Oliver (*New Yorker*) argued that Guare had one of the most fertile imaginations in the theater today.[8] Perhaps the most creative response to *Marco Polo Sings a Solo* was Michael Feingold's review in the *Village Voice* in which he conducted a mock interview with Ibsen (frequently mentioned in Guare's play), who provides his own commentary on Guare's work: "Well, he takes conventionalized versions of people from the old theatre—you know, the one I got rid of—and twists them into odd, comic shapes. It's a crazy world, he seems to be saying, so the people and the situations are going to be crazy, too."[9] Jack Kroll's review in *Newsweek* was neutral; he praised the beautiful production, the acting of Joel Grey and Madeline Kahn, and the clever set by John Wulp, but he claimed that Mel Shapiro could not shape these fragments into a play.[10]

Most of the critics lauded the distinguished cast and the elegant production while refusing to lay the blame on Mel Shapiro for not being able to shape a baffling play into a coherent whole. Clive

Barnes (*New York Times*) claimed that Guare's "miasmic playwriting" left him numb and puzzled, Gerald Clarke (*Time*) referred to the drama as imaginative disorder, and Alan Rich (*New York*), confused about the *Mad* magazine type of science fiction spoofery, labelled it "uninspired lunacy."[11] Howard Kissel (*Women's Wear Daily*) agreed that Guare's play contains flashes of humor and inklings of deeper meanings, but the result is a lot of one-liners and some comic monologues that do not add up to anything significant.[12] Douglas Watt (*Daily News*) also focused his attention and anger on Guare's writing, claiming that it was "extravagantly self-indulgent and flatulent," "drivel," and "an abomination."[13] Ross Wetzsteon (*Plays and Players*) described Guare's writing as vivid, hilarious, imaginative, and insightful, but noted both that the play was unstructured to such an extent that the speeches could be read in random order and that the ideas were unrelated.[14] Martin Gottfried (*New York Post*), on the other hand, complained that Guare's talents were in decline from an offbeat sense of humor and an original style expressed in his previous plays to what is now an "otherwise glib and strident comedy" depicted as "an impertinent, mean spirited, thinly veiled and dirty little snipe at figures in New York show business."[15]

During 1998–1999, the Signature Theatre Company dedicated its season to Guare; its first production was *Marco Polo Sings a Solo*, directed by Mel Shapiro. The cast included Bruce Norris (Stony), Beeson Carroll (Lusty), Judith Hawking (Diane McBride), Polly Holliday (Mrs. McBride), Opal Alladin (Freydis), and Jack Koenig (Tom Wintermouth). The critics ravaged this production as well. Donald Lyons, writing in the *Wall Street Journal*, making a half-hearted attempt to characterize *Marco Polo* as similar to Wilder's apocalyptic doom in *The Skin of Our Teeth*, updated by a John Waters sense of weirdness with a touch of Monty Python, resigned himself to admitting that neither the play nor the production achieved consistency.[16] Peter Marks (*New York Times*) lauded the concerted efforts of the appealing cast but lamented that the play had not aged well and was essentially two unplayable acts of "free-floating wit without foundation," a hyperbolic satire that the audience could not relate to because the characters were interchangeable.[17] John Simon (*New York*) argued that Shapiro, who directed the 1977 production, provided no new take on the dated play, which he characterized as part vaudeville, part sophomoric social satire, and part attenuated bedroom farce full of "sporadic cleverness and much immature self-indulgence."[18] The only serious attempt at criticism of this production was John Lahr's review in the *New Yorker*; in particular, Lahr seemed to grasp

Guare's main point in this ostensibly obscure play: "Guare's characters are victims of the envy and humiliation that Veblen called 'invidious comparison'; they dream of wanting, and most of what they want is worthless."[19]

Guare may have miscalculated the abilities of his audience when writing *Marco Polo Sings a Solo*. Although the play is quite witty at times and contains some lyrical, elegant writing, too much of it is obscure for most audiences to follow. First, Guare is working with too many cardboard characters whose identities are not fully developed; thus, the audience has difficulty empathizing with anyone and inevitably loses interest. Second, setting the play in a science fiction atmosphere in 1999 on an iceberg off the coast of Norway can only create further confusion for most spectators; the play can also become quickly dated and thus unintentionally absurd. Having part of the play take place in outer space also makes the material seem cartoonish. Third, the quick exits and entrances of the characters create vignettes that do not allow for sustained character development that would be possible in lengthier scenes; thus, the structure of the play needs further work. Fourth, too much of the play is suggestive rather than cohesive, including the humorous dialogue consisting largely of in-jokes that Guare did not realize would be difficult for most audiences to grasp, especially when they would be absorbed in trying to determine where the plot was leading. Clarity is sacrificed in favor of philosophy, forcing the audience to determine how much of what is said is actually metaphorical rather than literal; the science fiction setting only exacerbates this confusion. Finally, the intertwining strands of the narrative are also too complex for effective dramatization; admittedly, the play works better on paper than it does on stage. When we add Guare's zany comedy to the mix, as well as long monologues that tell us about the action rather than having the actors show us what is happening, the audience can become thoroughly distracted and confused.

In contrast to *The House of Blue Leaves*, which focused on people who were controlled by their environments, *Marco Polo Sings a Solo* is concerned with a utopianlike society in which the characters are all rich or famous and therefore have no limits to mitigate their dreams and desires. In his "Author's Note" to the play, Guare discussed the principal motif he was trying to convey:

> What do you hang onto in a limitless world? The answer seemed to be obvious: yourself. Each character in *Marco Polo Sings a Solo* is yearning for an even greater glory, an ever greater beauty, a greater power, a greater

love, a greater truth, and moving into such intense territory by yourself, that very same self becomes all the more important.[20]

Each person in the play is searching for some type of structure that solidifies his or her life, allowing the individual to flourish. The quest to create a legacy in their lives leads to a dependence on self. Guare concludes, "The 'Notice Me' becomes as powerful in a world without limits as it did in a world walled only with limits."[21]

Marco Polo Sings a Solo occurs in spring 1999, on the eve of the turn of the century. Traditionally, the turn of the century meant a time of soul searching to look back on the past and anticipate the future. Isolated from the rest of the world on an iceberg in the Norwegian sea (Guare decided to make use of his remembrances of his 1969 trip to Norway), the characters in the play are in the ideal environment remote enough for serious contemplation of how humanity will evolve in the twenty-first century. The implication is that humanity's fate is approaching chaos and destruction. There are many images in the play that suggest impending doom and the fact that history is changing. An earthquake in Italy has destroyed its boot, leaving twenty million people dead. Earlier, Hawaii faded into the sea. New Zealand, in anger, is bombing Toronto, and the Gulf Stream has been diverted to Norway. Mrs. McBride acknowledges, "I don't know much about symbols, but I'd say when frozen flamingoes fall out of the sky, good times are not in store."[22]

A new day is dawning, a time to make important, soul-searching decisions. The play occurs on the fifth wedding anniversary of Stony McBride and his wife Diane, suggesting a time of contemplation about the past and the future, especially for Diane, who is seriously in love with Tom Wintermouth. During this time, Stony is winding up the filming of a movie about Marco Polo, an explorer who serves as a metaphor for the search for new worlds that ultimately initiated many important changes in Western history. Marco Polo, the great adventurer, is the epitome of the quest for change. Stony explains the significance of his film at the turn of the century:

> Marco Polo has been sidestepping death. Wandering through all these new worlds. He's seen so much. He's witnessed so much. But he has nothing of his own. He wants to change his life. Twenty-four years have gone by. Marco Polo comes home to Venice. To be recognized. (49)

Marco Polo represents change made through enrichment, not destruction and chaos. Set out to conquer new worlds without the imposition of limits or structures, Marco Polo changed history for the better. In addition, Ibsen is evoked in much the same manner. His drama, *A Doll House*, is mentioned at least six different times in the play. Mrs. McBride has seen forty-one different productions of it. Nora's slamming of the door on her husband and children represents the penultimate change, which is, as Tom notes, personal as well as historical: "Nora slammed the door behind her and Modern Drama was born" (70). Thus, the wedding anniversary, the completion of the film about Marco Polo, and the Norwegian productions of *A Doll House* all suggest that the time is ripe for change. Tom, observing the sun rising in the sky, notes that a new day is dawning: "Diane! See that! That yellow! That blue! That gold! That red! The winter's over. The summer can begin. And change is coming into our lives as surely as the light gathering strength to appear" (60). Although the elements for change are rather ubiquitous, the characters in the play are egoists too frightened to abandon their pasts or their dreams for the future and thus are unable to learn and grow.

Stony McBride's parents drift aimlessly because they hopelessly cling to their pasts, ignoring the reality of the present. Although they are rich and famous and thus ostensibly without limits, their microcosms are actually confined rooms, like Nora's prison with Torvald, her husband. Lusty McBride, née Philip McBride, is a former Hollywood movie star now in his sixties.[23] He is starring in his son's movie in order to have one last chance to obtain "heroic stature" in the film world and thus create his own legacy. Lusty is a supreme egoist who insists on being photographed from the left side only. He sees himself as a legend in his own mind: "Well, I'm going to be an original postage stamp. The United States Post Office has picked me to be a commemorative stamp for the end of the twentieth century. I got the six-cent slot. Beat out Paul Newman. Beat out Gary Cooper" (62). Lusty, as his name implies, was sexually promiscuous; he became notorious with groupies who were fond of his musicals that featured nudity. Lusty, however, preferred the company of men, many of whom he solicited on the street. Locked into the image he created of himself as a sexually promiscuous celebrity, Lusty is unable to grow and thus dies when the lightning bolts strike down. Guare wrote, "The bolts from heaven come down to wake these people up, to purify them, to restore nature to some kind of balance before this new century comes into being."[24] Lusty apparently is beyond salvation.

Mrs. McBride is a comic character thoroughly absorbed in her own little world and oblivious to her changing environment. The stage directions indicate that she "wanders" in and out of the play, almost as if in a daze. She was the original flower child of the 1960s, and at the end of the century, she sees no impetus for her to change. "She" was once a man named Elliot whose passion for movie star Lusty was so great that he had a sex change operation and became Debbie Lisa in order to marry her idol. Lusty, as it ironically turns out, married her because she could get him in contact with his true love, Elliot. Before Elliot had his sex-change operation, he deposited his semen in a sperm bank. Transsexual Debbie Lisa received the first artificial womb and then impregnated herself with his/her own semen deposited before the operation, making Stony the first child to have an androgynous person as both of his parents. If Mrs. McBride is the first flower child, Stony is the first love child, a product of Mrs. McBride's love for herself. Mrs. McBride is lost in her own little world of the 1960s, fully engaged in getting high on drugs, prognosticating about the end of the Age of Pisces, and spouting clichés from the Vietnam War era: "Hey Hey LBJ How Many Kids Did You Kill Today" (78), "Ho Ho Ho Chi Minh. NLF Is Gonna Win" (78), and "LBJ pull down your pants! All we are saying is give peace a chance" (79). If Mrs. McBride were to abandon her egotistical dreams of what she believes was a once-idyllic world (thirty-five years ago), she would have nothing for which to live. She is hopelessly out of touch with the potential growth endemic to the portents at the end of the century.

Tom Wintermouth, in his late thirties, is a dreamer who seeks a greater glory for himself and is obsessed with his self-image. He has already won the Nobel Prize, primarily for his settlement of peace in the Middle East by creating the new state of Saudi-Israel. The diplomat is on his way to the United Nations to deliver the only known cure for cancer. He will have established his own legacy: "Already hospitals are closing entire wings. Patients who were considering suicide are signing up for dancing lessons. Pain is about to be stopped. The world will be at peace" (60). When President Adalbert has a stroke and the Vice President commits suicide, the government goes into chaos, and Tom is selected to be President. He admits, "The cure for cancer makes me a very powerful man" (73). When the lightning bolts destroy his cure for cancer, he is devastated. The structure that he sought for his life is now gone, so Tom is unable to adapt. He is too obsessed with himself and therefore too frightened when he must stop listening to his "solo." Oblivious to the signs suggesting change and perhaps even apocalypse at the end of the century, Tom's selfish nature is concerned only with his intense passion for Diane McBride. When Stony asks him to explain the world of politics in which New

Zealand is bombing the hell out of Toronto, Tom responds, "Let me explain negotiations. *I. Want. Your. Wife*" (58). When he becomes the newly appointed President, he hopes to send for Diane within three months. However, with the cure for cancer lost, he may not be able to follow through with his plans for Diane. In desperation, he begs Stony for a job on the film, hoping that his reputation can be resurrected. He is terrified of seeing his dreams dissipate:

> I am a laughingstock, Stony. I heard on the radio that my name has passed in the vocabulary. Not since Wrong Way Corrigan. As sure as Benedict Arnold is a synonym for traitor so will Tom Wintermouth pass into everyday speech as a byword for asshole. For one who promises and cannot deliver. For one who has a smugness and a self-pleasure. (86)

Tom's desperate plea, "Look, Stony, your wife sleeps with me and that gives me some rights around here" (87), falls on deaf ears. Tom, in frustration, hurls himself through a giant map of the world, an ironic gesture of how one's dreams of greater glory can become so obsessive that other viable choices become negligible. Tom, who had the world in his hands by having unlimited talent, is consumed by his self-image. Constantly reinforcing that image by congratulating himself on his accomplishments, he has no life ahead of him after the lightning bolts strike.

Diane McBride is the ideal representation of a person without limits looking to the future, never remaining content with having everything. Diane was a child prodigy who matured into a world-renowned concert pianist. Her recordings have sold worldwide, and she has won numerous, prestigious awards for her artistry. One record jacket noted, "Diane de la Nova has reached a pinnacle of perfection" (70). Described as a "*lush, indolent beauty in her thirties*" (46), she is attractive to men. She has been married to Stony for five years, has a child, and is pregnant. However, like the other egoists who find themselves in a limitless world, she wants more. Fully immersed in the "Notice Me" syndrome, Diane McBride claims that she does not receive enough attention from her husband: "You're up here filming over on that other iceberg all the time. No sunshine. I don't even cast a shadow. Who needs me? I wanted something in me so I wouldn't float away" (75). She is so frustrated with her life that she uses her unborn child as a weapon against her husband:

> Let its eyes develop so it can see you for the fool you are. Let its sex develop into a man so you can see the man you should be. Let its ears develop so

it can hear the shit I have to contend with. Let his feet form so he can run away from you. Let his spine develop so he can stand up straight. He'll be born in the year 2000. He's due to be born in the last week of December 1999, but I'm holding him in. I don't want this kid born in any century that contained you. (75)

Diane is in love with Tom Wintermouth, who, as a future occupant of the White House, represents her ticket out of what she perceives to be a bland marriage. Tom also is passionate about Diane, exclaiming, "Sex with you is lurid and gaudy and hot and brazen . . ." (56). He knows how to make Diane happy: on her wedding anniversary, Tom presents her with Edvard Grieg's piano. Diane projects an idyllic existence for herself and Tom. The impetus for the change is Nora in *A Doll House*, a play Diane has seen many times. Diane views Nora's decision to slam the door on her family as enlightening, providing a paragon for her own behavior: "I closed one door. Opened another. Now I close that door and open yet another" (70). While watching a video of Ibsen's play performed on trampolines, Diane, observing Nora leap, says, "Oh, God, to be that free" (69). Tom encourages Diane to learn from Nora: "And in leaving that life, find a better life. A truer life" (67).

However, as the bolts from heaven strike down and hit the piano and Diane's baby carriage, the destruction brings Diane back to reality. She almost loses her baby and the piano, her most cherished possessions. Tom, with his new moral status as President, cannot be perceived as a home-breaker and thus will be unable to send for Diane. Unfortunately, Diane cannot relinquish her ego and still holds out for a change in the future. She is merely fooling herself when she tells her baby, "But we'll keep the promise of change. Let's just hold each other and heal our wounds and call that growing" (88). Out of frustration, she repeatedly slams the piano lid on her hands until she bleeds. Tom, using the parable of Chekhov's *The Three Sisters*, gives her some good advice, encouraging her to stop dreaming of an idyllic future and start focusing on present reality:

Those poor girls, all the time trying to get to Moscow. I looked at this map before I went through it. The town they lived in was only forty-eight miles from Moscow. In 1999 that town is probably part of Greater Downtown Moscow. They were in Moscow all the time. Those three dumb broads. There all the time. We spend all this time talking about the future. We're here. Baby, we are the future. (90)

Astronaut Frank Schaeffer is the Marco Polo of 1999. Just as Marco Polo journeyed to conquer unknown territories, Schaeffer, only in his thirties, embarked five years ago to discover a new planet and thus become a legend. Stony admires his spirit: "Frank Schaeffer lands on the new planet. The earth will never go hungry again. He is elated. Immortality guaranteed. He toasts the plants that live on this planet with powdered champagne" (58). Frank names the planet Skippy to coincide with his wife's spirit.

Frank's wife has changed her name to Freydis and is now working as a servant in the McBride household. She is unaware that Frank is using her to explore his own technological prowess. Skippy was kidnapped and taken to the White House, where a metal disc was inserted into her body. Frank is now sending semen via nuclear bolts through space to impregnate Skippy. Frank plans to arrive back home in time to get in the record books for producing the first baby of the twenty-first century. He reveals his scheme to Freydis: "The child was supposed to be born in the White House. You're so goddam selfish. I'd splash down New Year's Eve as 1999 becomes 2000. You'd present me with the perfect child. Give the world a new legend" (61). When Skippy, alias Freydis, refuses to cooperate, Frank becomes arrogant and indicates that he is more concerned with his legacy than with his future offspring: "Okay, Skippy. Deny the world dreams. Deny the world legends. I'm sorry, but my kid is going to be born in the White House or not at all" (62).

Frank Schaeffer's technological experiment goes awry when the bolts strike everything in sight, including Freydis. Rather than the semen hitting its mark and initiating life, the destruction instead suggests the apocalypse. As the flamingoes fall, Frank realizes that he has missed his mark: "Hawaii fell into the sea. The entire pineapple industry lost. I negotiated for Norway to buy the rights to the Gulf Stream before I left for space. The Gulf Stream is on its way up here now. Nuclear re-routing. I guess the bolts made it all happen sooner. Oh God" (80–81). Furthermore, Skippy's child is dead because, upon birth, he followed the lemmings who leaped off the cliff. Frank has learned nothing from the shock of the bolts from the sky; he refuses to change, unable to let go of his ego. Instead, Frank Schaeffer, alone on stage, sings a solo: "Now let me see, what are my choices? Should I go back into space and become a hero or stay here and try to win Skippy back? The world on one hand. Me on the other. (*Frank takes a burned flower from the bouquet and begins plucking the singed petals to make his choice.*) The world. Me. The world. Me" (85).

Ostensibly, Stony McBride would appear to be in the same mold as the other egocentrics in the play. Initially, Stony fantasizes about fame and fortune, which could become his reality once he completes the movie about Marco Polo. He tells Diane, "My father and I finish this picture. My life begins" (74). Stony assumes that making a film about a great explorer will ennoble the world and thus concomitantly will feed his ego as he moves into the new century. His idol is astronaut Frank Schaeffer, who is already exploring new technologies and discovering new worlds. Diane realizes, "Stony projects his life onto the life of Frank Schaeffer the way you would project a film onto a screen to give himself size. To give himself shape" (59). In other words, Stony, a successful film director and in love with Diane, a person who would seem to have everything, must fantasize about even greater glory. As John Lahr, suggests, Stony's need to invent himself as Frank Schaeffer becomes a bulwark for his own inadequacy.[25] Stony insists on donning Frank's spacesuit for a trip to outer space. While comets, asteroids, and novas swirl by, Stony explains his need to explore this final frontier:

This is the world I want! A world populated by only me. I hear a scream. One me hits another me. Is that rape? One of the mes rapes another me? More mes now march out of more petals. Mes fill the horizon. Downtown India is a ghost town compared to all the mes screaming in fear. Me! Me! Notice me! Each me is screaming to be heard. Me! Me! Each one moaning, whining Me! (83)

Stony, however, distinguishes himself from the others in the play by abandoning his fantasies and choosing to accept himself as he is rather than what he might become in the future. Guare writes, "One of them makes it. The others are too frightened to let go of themselves ultimately, in spite of the massacres and demolition."[26] Stony's desire in life is to be an artist/scientist, a calling that he has, yet one that has little to do with personal glory and fame. In particular, Stony, who equates plant life with human nature, would like to be a vegetable researcher. As a film director, he can only philosophize about his most intimate desires: "Man is a plant. We may look like meat, but we're not meat. We can never escape. Nor change. We are firmly planted in the ground. We are what we grow out of. My plant nature. I celebrate that" (58). Stony tries to rationalize why change is so difficult:

Why is it that all the things that should hold us together, help us change—love, creativity, sex, talent, dreams—those are the very elements that drive us apart and the things that you think would separate us—hate, fear, meanness—those are the very things that bind us together and keep us from growing. Keep us from changing. (85)

While in outer space searching for his true self by trying to imitate Frank Schaeffer, Stony abandons his "solo," his ego, and begins to develop a more viable identity. He conquers his fear and takes the risk: "Is the fear out of me? I am so quiet. I have killed me. I want no more solos. I crave duets. The joy of a trio. The harmony of a quartet. The totality of an orchestra. Home. I head for home! . . . I descend on my garden. I am home" (84). At the end of the play, Stony laments the fact that his colleagues at the end of the century wait for a rebirth that will never materialize. Stony chooses to live in the present rather than fantasize about a utopia in the future. He reveals his plans: "Go out into the now. Out there where you live. Into the present. Out there where you are. Grow. Change. My plant nature. Our plant nature. To celebrate that" (91). He discards the spacesuit he is holding; in his hands now are two green plants. By taking risks, overcoming fear, and refusing to allow ego to push us into establishing ourselves as legends, Stony finds instead a viable structure for his life.

Rich and Famous, written in three days, premiered at the Academy Festival Theater in Lake Forest, Illinois, during late July 1974. Guare again worked with Mel Shapiro, the director, and the husband-wife duo of Ron Leibman and Linda Lavin, who met Guare in 1966 at Yale University and later performed in *Cop-Out* during 1969; Guare wrote *Rich and Famous* as a vehicle for Leibman and Lavin. Ron Leibman assumed multiple male roles in this version of the play, Linda Lavin played most of the female roles, and Charles Kimbrough starred as Bing. Although this production was not heavily reviewed, the critics praised the actors, Mel Shapiro, and Guare, the young playwright whose promise, they believed, had yet to be fulfilled.[27] However, two out of the three critics who reviewed the play thought that it would be ill-suited for New York.[28] Michael Feingold provided the most effective caveat: "*Rich and Famous* is expected to come to New York in the fall, where it is likely to offend more than a few people dedicated to the survival of the commercial theatre."[29]

In 1976, Guare continued to revise the play for its first New York production. Again, Guare faced the same problem that occurred when he returned to *Marco Polo Sings a Solo* after several years had elapsed since the initial writing: he had lost touch with the original impulse for the play's creation. Unable to rewrite the play because of time constraints, Guare merely made editorial changes. However, in the rehearsals, Guare realized that the denouement of the play in which Bing throws away his cufflinks, representing his shabby dreams, just did not fit. In this revised version, Bing cannot get the second cufflink off, suggesting, as Guare noted, "it's too hard to get rid of those dreams."[30]

Rich and Famous, after its opening was postponed three times, finally debuted in New York at Joseph Papp's Estelle Newman Public Theater on 19 February 1976. Mel Shapiro directed, Arden Fingerhut designed the lighting, Dan Snyder created the sets, and Theoni V. Aldredge was the costumer. The cast featured William Atherton as Bing, Ron Leibman assuming all of the male roles, and Anita Gillette playing the various female characters. Although the critical opinions of this production of *Rich and Famous* were divided, with more negative reviews than positive ones, the play weathered some harsh attacks to run for seventy-eight performances.

Four critics provided favorable responses to the play: Clive Barnes (*New York Times*), Catharine Hughes (*America*), Jack Kroll (*Newsweek*), and Edith Oliver (*New Yorker*).[31] Barnes commended Guare for writing an "unusually frank apologia for a play," noted that the acting was inspired, and praised Shapiro's sensible direction that moved the play along quickly, "as if it were a cross between a jet plane and a hurdy-gurdy. . . ."[32] Oliver, one of Guare's most consistent supporters, deemed the play "buoyant and original"; Kroll found Guare to be witty and the production snappy, while Hughes singled out Shapiro's direction, Dan Snyder's set, and Guare's trenchant humor representing his best seriocomic talents.[33] Michael Feingold, whose critique appeared in the *New York Times* nine days after Barnes's review was published, offered a neutral assessment of the production; he commended Leibman and Gillette for exploiting a play that he claimed merely rambled from one episode to the next.[34] Christopher Sharp (*Women's Wear Daily*) credited Shapiro's dazzling direction and Snyder's rotating sets but argued that Guare must clarify the denouement if the play expected to have a run on Broadway.[35]

Although many of the critics spared their harsh attacks on the performers or the production crew, they did not exempt Guare from their vicious comments. Stanley Kauffmann (*New Republic*) admitted that Guare's dialogue was sharp and his songs were clever, but he claimed that there was no discerning thematic issue to tie things together; Alan Rich (*New York*) and Ross Wetzsteon (*Plays and Players*) agreed, stating that the play merely consists of a series of satirical sketches or what Rich referred to as "pure *shtik*-writing, on a level far below Mr. Guare's proven talent. . . ."[36] R. Z. Sheppard, writing in *Time*, was confused about Guare's intentions in putting Bing through these torments and labelled the script a cross between bittersweet sentimentality and soft-core cynicism.[37] Martin Gottfried (*New York Post*) complained about the play's lack of structure, its cartoonish style, an overabundance of dialogue, and caricature that is often funny yet at times becomes "ill-mannered and boorish gutter sniping."[38] Finally, Michael Feingold's 1974 warning about the play possibly being offensive to theater aficionados became a reality.[39] Douglas Watt (*Daily News*), who said he was bored, make it a point to note that Guare included lots of Schubert Alley quips, and Harold Clurman, in his review for the *Nation*, wrote, "But the whole matter in *Rich and Famous* is reduced to the tricky evasion of local chitchat, grist to the columnists' mills."[40]

Rich and Famous is structured as a fast-paced musical comedy, a style that has become Guare's trademark. In the "Production Notes" to the 1977 edition of the drama, Guare discussed his ideas for staging: "Keep it bright and brilliantly high-spirited so the audience won't know where to look next. The play is about the theatre; keep it theatrical."[41] Guare wrote the lyrics and the music for the five musical numbers in the play. Originally, Guare structured the drama into seven scenes and two interludes, one each preceding scenes six and seven. However, when he revised the play for inclusion in his collected works, Guare kept the same structure but did not designate scenes or interludes. The revised version of *Rich and Famous* is quite close to the originally published edition, with only slight editorial changes that do not affect the content or structure of the play.

Guare intended for three performers to assume all of the roles in the play. One actor would take the role of Bing; a female would play Leanara, Veronica Gulpp-Vestige, Allison, Bing's mother, and the Actress while another actor would perform all of the other male roles. Thus, during Bing's quest for identity, he encounters various "doubles," each manifesting an aspect of the ego or superego of his dreams. Bing's conflict at every turn in the play is with his own perception of himself and with how he confronts his own dreams and desires. The play proceeds in picaresque fashion as each vignette suggests Bing's increasing alienation and his concomitant failure to learn about his own identity.

Bing Ringling, the protagonist of the play, is a confused young man with a consuming desire to be rich and famous. His infatuation with celebrity status is his sole motivation and defines his identity for him. His name suggests the legacy that he assumed from his parents: his first name reminds us of Bing Crosby who, in one national poll, was the most popular person in the United States during the early 1940s; Ringling intimates the circus as icon for popular entertainment. The alliterative name also indicates a somewhat cartoonish figure. Indeed, when we first see Bing on stage, he appears to be rather clownish, wearing a rented tuxedo and clutching the script of his play destined, he hopes, for Broadway. He tells his friend Leanara, who has a role in Bing's play, that his life will be immortalized in musicals one day and enshrined in bookstores: "I went into that little all-night bookstore over there on the corner to see where I'll fit in and I'll be between Rimbaud and Rin Tin Tin."[42]

Somewhere between Rimbaud and Rin Tin Tin is exactly where his talents lie. His cultural taste seems to be rather parochial. He admonishes Leanara for criticizing Chekhov because, despite the Russian playwright's attempts at drama, Bing says, "He tried" (153). Bing, who fears being stereotyped as the World's Oldest Living Promising Young Playwright, believes he has outdone Aeschylus, Brecht, Chekhov, Molière, Feydeau, and Racine by writing 843 plays. However, his latest play, a musical version of *Dante's Inferno*, appropriately titled *Spreaded Thin*, now playing on Lower Death Street off-Broadway, is, he swears, his ticket to success. He is so confident about his talents that he bought a pair of cufflinks in a magic store; they are imprinted with the letters "R" and "F," for "rich" and "famous." However, when Bing recites his favorite lines from his play, we realize that his dreams may be premature: "I ran down into the subway. In a panic. I'll go anywhere. Trains rush past me. E trains. F Trains. As. GGs. RRs. Cs. Pursued by the entire alphabet" (154). Bing can be compared to Artie Shaughnessy, another dreamer who wants to "make it big" in the world of show business but cannot seem to escape the reality of his lack of talent.

Leanara serves as Bing's alter ego, reinforcing his hyperbolic statements about his play and fueling his cravings for fame. She is superb at telling Bing exactly what he wants to hear. The suggestion is that Bing has hardly formed a relationship with her; instead, Bing loves her because she massages his ego, giving his dreams credibility. Bing seems to have problems connecting with someone other than himself.

As Bing and Leanara chat, an ominous chord is heard, indicating a change of pace. Bing notices the face of his childhood friend, Tybalt Dunleavy, on a billboard overlooking Times Square. Tybalt has gone on to become a successful actor who is now starring in a new movie,

Gangland, advertised on the billboard. The name Tybalt Dunleavy suggests everything Bing would like to be: rich and famous; after all, children from the lower and working classes are rarely named Tybalt. The billboard dominates the stage action throughout the play, offering the subliminal message that Bing's alter ego overshadows everything the aspiring playwright does.

Backstage during opening night of Bing's play, Aphro, whom we later learn is a black transvestite call girl, is donning his costume to play Dante Alighieri. Obviously, the casting done for Bing's play leaves something to be desired. While marching through the audience during the play, Aphro is handed a note from Tybalt to give to Bing. Apparently, Tybalt was so impressed with the opening night that he wants to star in his old friend's play. Tybalt's note in part reads, "God, *Gangland* played to five hundred million people in movie theaters and I envy you tonight playing to ninety-nine live ones" (157). Just as Billy Einhorn, the celebrity who had it all, craved to be in his friend Artie's shoes, Tybalt is not happy with his existence and fantasizes about adopting Bing's persona. The implication is that our fantasies force us to anticipate the future, and even those who have reached the pinnacle of success must have their dreams.

Bing's producer, the venerable Veronica Gulpp-Vestige, enters, giving Guare the chance to satirize the show business of Broadway. Ms. Gulpp-Vestige has been a highly successful producer who has staged the world's greatest musicals, such as *South Pacific, Carousel,* and *The Sound of Music,* without the music. She has also catered to popular tastes by presenting a musical version of the *Encyclopedia Britannica* and a nude version of *Hamlet* on ice, with Aphro skating the role of Ophelia. However, for Bing's play, she has made an exception by keeping the music intact. We learn that she is staging Bing's play for the sole reason of having a comeback from a highly successful career. She reasons that she cannot have a comeback if she continues to produce hits, so she needs a flop. Thus, we have a situation in which the producer uses Bing for her own vanity, which is ironic because Bing believes that he is using Ms. Gulpp-Vestige to enhance *his* chances for success. Bing, supreme egoist that he is, virtually ignores what his producer is telling him about the worth of his art. Instead, Bing is lost in his dream world in which he is the center of attention:

Veronica, only this afternoon I had this dream where the whole world died except for me. Only it wasn't their bodies that died, but their minds. But luckily I had stored up in my shopping bags all the great books and paintings and music the world had ever produced. The world was lost and confused and there I am with my shopping bags, doling out the art, dealing out the magic, parcelling out the joy. (159)

Rich and Famous gets stronger as the play progresses, and a perceptive audience should realize that Guare's black comedy becomes simultaneously more pathetic and hilarious with each new scene. In his drive for glory, Bing next seeks out Tybalt at the Algonquin Hotel, hoping that the star's presence in his play will make the difference between failure and success. Bing meets Aphro, the hooker, who came to the Algonquin to ask Tybalt for a role in his next masterpiece. Bing and Aphro get a chance to read the opening night reviews of *Spreaded Thin*. Their hopes of becoming rich and famous are dashed when they realize the reviews are disastrous. Aphro, like Bing, is worried about his own reputation: "I can't even find my own damn name. Oh, here's a mention. Sheeee, they spell it all wrong again. I ain't no hairdo" (161). To make matters worse, Bing learns that Tybalt checked out of his hotel room and muses that the reason for his departure was that he read the pitiful reviews and thus wanted no part of Bing's play. Veronica Gulpp-Vestige wanders by, depressed by the derisory notices in the press. The revered producer climbs into a garbage can, and with her legs dangling over the edge of the trashbin, sings a song about the comfort of Valium and Librium.

In the next scene, Bing seeks solace in the home of his collaborator, Anatol Torah, a sadomasochistic Jewish bisexual composer. This segment of the play reflects some of Guare's best writing in which his dark sense of humor prevails. Anatol Torah is a has-been, and for all we know, perhaps a never-was, but Bing recognizes him as an inspiration. Torah has proof that he once rubbed shoulders with celebrities, for in his apartment are signed photographs of Greta Garbo, Charlie Chaplin, Indira Gandhi, and Harry Truman. Bing is enthralled with Torah's music, admitting that he grew up listening to it. He is also encouraged by the fact that Anatol has told him that reviews are meaningless—it is the work that counts; thus, Bing can ignore the harsh critical responses to his play. When we hear Torah sing his songs, we realize that they are all absurdly repetitive of Yiddish double talk: "Moloch Mosai, Mallaca Mazoy" (164). Like Artie Shaughnessy's songs, Anatol Torah's tunes all sound alike. He has no discernible taste, which is perhaps why he can praise Bing's work, especially his acolyte's latest endeavor, *The Odiad*, a musical version of *The Iliad* and *The Odyssey*.

Gradually, we realize that Anatol Torah fawns over Bing's work, not because he has any artistic interest in it but because he is sexually attracted to Bing. In short, his motives are all selfish. Bing provides the over-the-hill composer with hits of marijuana and sexual stimulation. Torah admits, "Bing, I kiss those evil, wicked reviews. I wanted your play to close. I can now tell truths. I resented your play for taking you away from me" (166). Torah urges Bing to quit his job in the restaurant, not because it inhibits his artistic career, but because he will get dishpan hands. He even makes a call to the Board of Health to complain about the "ferkachte restaurant": "The Ristorante Rigoletto in Greenwich Village. Dirty. Filthy. Bugs!!!! Close them down! Bugs right now crawling all over my lasagna" (167). In good faith, he gives Bing money as an advance for the musical on which they plan to collaborate. Bing responds, "I sure could use a few bucks. I can't get a grant because I haven't had a hit, but if I had a hit, I wouldn't need a grant" (167). Bing is so impressed with Torah that he calls Leanara so the composer can sing one of his famous songs for her. During this telephone conversation, Bing learns that Leanara has just received a job offer to do a television series and thus is leaving town. There is no spiritual connection between Bing and his girlfriend; when she receives a better offer, particularly one that might lead to fame and fortune, she takes it. In this sick society, relationships are abandoned in favor of hope that springs eternal. Torah's response to Leanara's departure is also selfish, for now he can have Bing for himself without competition: "Good! Get rid of the baggage. Artists and revolutionaries should never have families. Never have connections" (168).

Anatol Torah has plans for his collaboration with Bing. To make *The Odiad* successful, Torah insists on casting Tybalt Dunleavy to play Ulysses. Apparently, Torah became attracted to Tybalt when he saw him one evening in Studio 21. Torah had his curiosity piqued and asks Bing about the types of bars Tybalt might frequent. When Bing professes his ignorance about such "scenes," Torah enlightens him:

> There are bars for everything. Bars where boys go to meet girls. Where boys go to meet boys. Where dwarves go to meet dwarves. Firemen to meet other firemen. I even heard there's a bar in the East Eighties . . . where they prop up dead people on stools in booths. Where you can go to meet dead people, which is a very hard thing to do socially. Drink with them. Talk with them. Dead people can be very cheery, if you happen to be frightened, as some people are, of living people. Kiss them if you're shy. Try out the latest or the oldest dance steps. One nifty thing about dead folks, they can't say no. (168)

Torah then reveals to Bing that his fantasy is to go to Hamburg to visit one of these specialty bars where sadistic and masochistic charades are the norm. Torah's particular fetish is sadomasochistic: "And when my vague double enters, I buy him a drink and then take him into the back room specially provided and I take a length of piano wire and turn that man's throat into a Steinway, a Knabe, a Yamaha, and I squeeze a symphony out of that man's body and I pretend it's my own body . . ." (171). Torah justifies his behavior: "Bing, there's nothing illegal in this. Death between consenting adults is hardly illegal" (171).

Torah also must have Tybalt in the play because the former worships celebrity, and, in his mind, it is Tybalt's star status that would determine the success of the Bing-Torah collaborative effort. Torah admits, "Tybalt Dunleavy wouldn't be too big for me, but he thinks he's bigger than me and that's what I want! That's what I need! Someone bigger than me!!!" (170). Torah well understands that Bing is impressed by superstar status, and so he baits his young sycophant: "Anatol Torah, legend that is he, doesn't frighten you?" (170). Bing instead admits that Torah's fame thrills him. Torah now has Bing in the palm of his hand and thus tries to impress him with the story of how he met the penultimate celebrity:

> Jesus appeared in my room. In the dark. All lit up. Inner light. Looking great. I said, Jesus, what are you doing here? He said, I hope I haven't bothered you, but I just wanted to meet you once before you died. He, Jesus, wanted to meet me. I'm not even Christian. His light shown up the dark. Now that's big! (170)

Torah implies that if he fraternizes with Jesus, then he certainly is good enough for Tybalt Dunleavy. Torah produces a contract that reveals that when Bing delivers Tybalt to him, his working relationship with Bing is over, and Tybalt becomes the new collaborator. In short, just as Leanara abandoned her friend once she had a better offer, Torah will do the same.

The scene shifts to an art gallery opening where Bing meets Allison de Mears, a former school chum with whom he once had sex. Allison has heard about Bing's new musical and admires his talents. She admits that Bing seems to inspire her: "I'll never be rich and famous like you are, but I can have a life. I'm so frightened. Give me courage. I want to thank you. What a wonderful bump-into" (175). Bing has provided the impetus for Allison to divorce her rude husband, perhaps get a job working with emotionally disturbed children, or go to night school to advance. Her idyllic, utopian vision of the future is projected onto Bing:

I've got all these dreams. You're so lucky. You're doing what you want to do. Talent. A place to put your dreams. You must be raking in the cash, Bing. All the wonderful things you can do for people. Your parents must be crazy with joy. A passport to freedom. Dreams. Money. (175)

Thus, the absurdity continues as we see that Allison idolizes Bing, who worships Anatol Torah, who fantasizes about Tybalt Dunleavy; this concept of the double will be made clearer by the end of the play. Guare ultimately reveals that each link in the chain is nebulous, phony, and superficial.

Bing, on his way to visit his parents, is accosted by a Hare Krishna disciple. The young Krishna reads a passage from the *Bhagavad Gita*: "When the mind leaves behind the dark forest of delusion, you shall go beyond time past and time that is to come" (176). Guare's protagonists cannot escape their delusions about the past or fantasies about the future. However, Bing fails to heed these words of wisdom, reducing the intrusion to "some Westchester kid on vacation" (176).

Bing's visit to his parents is another hilarious scene in which Guare's black comedy is most effective. Bing's parents have inculcated him with the idea that life is worth living only if one is rich and famous. Bing's father, in particular, is so enamored with celebrity status that he rhythmically inundates his conversations with the names of famous people so as to make his son aware, perhaps subliminally, of successful people:

Mom.	Why don't you write?
Dad.	Orville Wright! Wilbur Wright!
Mom.	Call anytime of the day or night.
Dad.	Dennis Day. Fuzzy McKnight.
Mom.	Either one of us is always here in case you want to come home. Twenty-four hour devotions at the phone in case you want to call.
Dad.	Alexander Graham Bell. (176)

Bing's parents expect that the budding playwright is proceeding up the ladder to the top of the show business world. They wonder if Bing will get too "big" for his relatives. Bing interrupts their fantasies to bring them back to reality: "Mom. Dad. I'm so unhappy. Believe it or not, I came home to be somewhere familiar. I don't have a nickel to my name" (177).

Bing complains that his parents imbued him with an ideology based upon their own fantasies. He admits, "I want life to begin for me and I think maybe I picked the wrong profession. The wrong dreams got tattooed on me. I'm dreaming somebody else's dreams" (177). Bing recalls that as a child, his parents would wake him in the middle of the night, disturbing his own dreams with their vision of his future, insisting, "Don't be like us" (178). Therefore, *Rich and Famous* is partly autobiographical: it is Guare's search for an identity as a successful, rather than as a promising, playwright, one who aspires to his parents' fantasies. Suzanne Dieckman astutely notes, "As in *The House of Blue Leaves*, Guare portrays the influence of the parents who demand that their son succeed in order to fulfill their dreams. . . ."[43]

Bing, however, is trying to find himself and returned to his parents' house in order to connect with relatives. Bing seeks to establish an identity free from the fantasies of his parents. He tells them, "All this grappling after me me me. Don't you ever want to rub a big eraser over yourself? I do. Don't you ever dream that you don't want anything? I do. Don't you ever dream that you don't dream? I do. What went so wrong in your lives that you have to take it out on my life?" (179).

Bing's words fall on deaf ears. His parents are only concerned about the success of their son's play and how it will lead to his immortalization. Bing hints that his play may flop: "The man playing the lead is terrible. The producer is crazy. And it might not be very good" (181). He then whips out the reviews so his parents can read the truth. Bing's father is so upset at his son's ineptitude that he pulls out a gun and shoots at Bing. Bing's parents surmise that if Tybalt had been their son, their fantasies would have materialized. The stage directions indicate, *"Mom and Dad turn their couch into a pull-out bed. They ignore Bing"* (182). Seeking only "to connect" with someone, Bing is now rejected by his own parents. Similar to the way Leanara abandoned Bing when she received a better offer and much like Anatol Torah's rejection of Bing when he had a chance to collaborate with Tybalt, Bing's parents desert him for Bing's childhood friend. Bing, in desperation, rebels against his parents by taking out a gun and shooting at them. Guare again demonstrates that the refusal to connect with others results in violence. In Guare's zany comedy, however, the violence is symbolic rather than literal. Bing cannot destroy the vision that his parents have for their son: it is larger than life. Instead, the fantasies are only exacerbated as Bing's parents project their dreams onto Tybalt:

> *Dad.*   Under normal circumstances, we would die, but you know why we won't.

Mom.	They don't give Pulitzer Prizes to boys who kill their parents.
Dad.	Your play is going to be wonderful, Tybalt.
Bing.	I'm not Tybalt.
Dad.	Yes, you are. You're our success. (182)

The last segment of the play, Bing's encounter with Tybalt, his alter ego, is a tour de force. The scene takes place on top of Tybalt's billboard advertising *Gangland* in Times Square. Tybalt, clinging to his own image atop a scaffolding, tells Bing that a consortium headed by Norman Mailer has bought the rights to his death; he plans to jump off the billboard, committing suicide right in the middle of Times Square. Tybalt believes that his suicide will make him immortal, enshrining him forever in fame. He explains, "I'm a legend now. I don't want to do any parts that'll hurt my legend. Protect myself. Lucky Jimmy Dean. Lucky Marilyn. Lucky people like that. Jesus. Lucky Jesus. Never get old. No work. No sweat. No reality getting in the way of my immortality" (185). Tybalt assumes that after he leaps to his death, a book will be made about his life, then a play followed by a movie, a stage musical, and ultimately a film musical. Tybalt hopes to reach the pinnacle of perfection in his profession: "I'll be bigger in death than I ever was in life . . ." (186). Through Tybalt, Bing begins to see how artificial his dreams have been; Tybalt, the envy of everyone in the play, is nothing more than vain and shallow. When Tybalt asks Bing to write about him after he commits suicide, Bing states, "No. I'm going to write about a guy. A fella. A boy really. Who keeps seeing life through everyone else's eyes" (187). After Tybalt pitches himself off the scaffolding, the stage directions read, "*And Bing digs his hands into his eyes as if to dig out these old eyes. Tybalt is like the amputation of some terrible part of himself*" (187). Bing realizes that at times you may get what you wish for; but if being rich and famous means divorcing yourself from any sort of connection with others in order to enhance your status as legend, then the dream must have been superficial in the first place. In short, in a society where the dream to be rich and famous is paramount, we are often led down the wrong path, ignoring personal relationships in favor of fantasies. Neither can those who wind up rich and famous ever be satisfied, for they still continue to fantasize about bigger dreams.

The actor and actress who played the other roles confront Bing dressed exactly as he is; Bing is thus faced with his double, his mirror image. The actress sings a song about broken promises, and as Bing's alter ego, she laments, "When will life be / The way I want it to be????????" (188). Bing realizes that his fantasies, instilled in him by others, have misdirected him into pursuing wasted dreams. In his original production notes to the play, Guare suggested a slight alternative to the denouement: "And if I want to show Bing's confrontation with himself and his dreams at the end of the play, I can think of nothing more horrifying than a stage full of actors dressed as Bing's doubles singing the final moment of the piece."[44] Bing proudly removes one of his "R" and "F" cufflinks and tosses it away as his alter egos imitate his actions. Guare writes, *"Bing tries to undo the other cufflink. It won't come loose. It's a struggle. It won't come out. He does not want to give it up. He can't give up that final cufflink. He lowers his hands in dismay"* (188). Bing, who, through the example of Tybalt's fate, has realized that the desire to be rich and famous may literally and figuratively lead to the death of the artist, has trouble abandoning his dreams. Guare is suggesting that for an individual to relinquish the energy that fuels our society is not a simple task but is instead more profound than we might realize.

The comparison between *Marco Polo Sings a Solo* and *Rich and Famous* tells us a lot about John Guare's theater. Mel Shapiro, who directed the New York production of *Rich and Famous* in 1976, explains the universality of the play: "Bing Ringling wants to be rich and famous, and we can all identify with that. He wants a meaningful relationship, we know what that is all about. He has parents he cannot connect with, and that is something many of us have unfortunately experienced."[45] Why does *Rich and Famous* work so well with such universal appeal while *Marco Polo Sings a Solo*, written during the same time period, falls short? First, Guare's best writing is heavily grounded in a strong sense of place, the milieux that he knows best, namely New York City or New England. Setting *Marco Polo* on an iceberg near Norway obviously was a mistake. Second, Guare seems to flourish when he probes characters who cannot connect with others in modern society. He therefore does well in exploring Bing's eccentricities but fails when the characters in *Marco Polo* become cardboard figures without the depth necessary for psychological examination. Guare is superb at picking apart our frailties exacerbated by the neuroses of modern urban life; exploring the subtleties of science fiction characters is not his forte. Third, and probably most important, Guare has developed his unique brand of theater through the use of black comedy to examine, expose, and make us laugh at the cruelties of contemporary life in the United States. In *Marco Polo Sings a Solo*, what little black comedy exists in the play is lost because of weak character development, an obscure plot, and a lack of a coherent and consistent point of view. Guare without black comedy is simply Guare denuded. Finally, in *Rich and Famous*, Guare, through the acid test of laughter, was in touch with his audience. In *Marco Polo*, Guare seemed to lose touch with the audience and wrote a play that was more like closet drama filled with lengthy monologues, unusually lyrical passages that might function better as poetry than as theater, and "in" jokes that did not work well because Guare lost the original impetus for the play; thus, there was a dichotomy between what Guare knew about the play and what the audience actually knew when seeing it for the first time. In the next chapter, we will see Guare returning to secure ground with *Landscape of the Body* and *Bosoms and Neglect*.

5

Landscape of the Body and *Bosoms and Neglect*

G UARE'S NEXT TWO PLAYS, *LANDSCAPE OF THE BODY* AND *BOSOMS AND Neglect*, represent his darkest black comedy and concomitantly his most effective theater. These two dramas must be analyzed carefully, for audiences unfamiliar with Guare's intentions can easily misinterpret the plays as brutal and caustic rather than as comedies that mix the grotesque with pathos.

After *Marco Polo Sings a Solo* opened in New York during February 1977, Guare was depressed by the harsh critical notices and, as usual when one of his plays flops, began to search for material for his next drama. He recalls, "One of the things that pissed me off a lot after *Marco Polo* was people saying they didn't understand where they were in the play, they didn't understand the literal action on stage. So I wrote a play where the narrative was totally clear, where an audience couldn't be confused about the overall structure."[1] The impetus for *Landscape of the Body* occurred one day in spring 1977 while Guare was living on Bank Street in Greenwich Village. Guare woke up one morning and discovered that the water in his building had been cut off, so he went to a coffee shop on Hudson Street to get something to eat and drink. While at the luncheonette, Guare noticed four toughs—two girls and two boys—aged eleven or twelve sitting in a booth. He described the scene: "The boys had their sleeves rolled up to show the enrapt girls their forearms covered with an awful lot of gold wrist-watches. They leaned forward like conspirators, whispering, giggling, bragging. I couldn't get close enough to hear the words. I went home and wrote down what I imagined they were saying."[2] Guare wrote *Landscape of the Body* in two days after the closing of *Marco Polo* in March 1977. William Gardner, the producer at the Academy Festival Theatre in Chicago, was in New York and stopped by to see Guare as he was finishing the play. After Guare allowed Gardner to read the script, the producer was so impressed that he agreed to stage it; thus, *Landscape of the Body* was optioned merely forty minutes after Guare had finished typing the manuscript.

Landscape of the Body premiered at the Academy Festival Theatre in Lake Forest, Illinois, in July 1977, directed by John Pasquin. The cast featured Shirley Knight (Betty), F. Murray Abraham (Captain Hola-han), Paul McCrane (Bert), and Richard Bauer (Raulito). The production staff included John Wulp (scenic design), Jennifer Tipton (lighting), and Laura Crow (costumes). With intermission, the play ran three hours. In the only major review of this production, Linda Winer, writing in the *Chicago Tribune*, offered a neutral appraisal; she claimed that the play was confusing yet clever, praised the cast and crew, yet was disturbed by the unevenness of the songs, the length of the play, and Pasquin's somewhat "ragged" direction.[3]

Joseph Papp read the script and offered to stage the play in New York. With virtually the same cast and director intact from the Lake Forest production, *Landscape of the Body* made its New York debut at the Public Theater of the New York Shakespeare Festival on 12 October 1977. Santo Loquasto designed the set and the costumes, Jennifer Tipton again was responsible for the lighting, and Wally Harper arranged the music. The critical response was mixed, but the play ran for sixty-four performances.

Edith Oliver, writing in the *New Yorker*, although confused about the plot of the play, nevertheless commended Guare for his imaginative vision and resourcefulness in what she perceived to be a drama about the unpredictability of life.[4] Alvin Klein (*New York Theatre Review*), admitting that the play could use a bit more sharper definition, still argued that despite its blemishes, *Landscape of the Body*'s dazzling predilection for normalizing the offbeat aspects of humanity made it Guare's most successful play since *The House of Blue Leaves*.[5] Walter Kerr (*New York Times*) agreed with Oliver in stating that the play was weak because it needed firmer anchoring yet admitted that Guare's writing was inventive and the script was skillfully deployed.[6] Jack Kroll's review in *Newsweek* was also neutral, with Kroll acknowledging that *Landscape* contained a lot of brilliant comedy but complaining that he was uncertain whether Guare's focus was absurdist or realist.[7] Finally, Harold Clurman (*Nation*) was divided in his response to the play, arguing that the production was well mounted, the cast performed admirably, and Guare was capable of good comic writing but could not solve "his aesthetic problem" of making his ideas understood by the audience.[8]

Two of the most negative opinions were expressed by John Simon and Richard Eder. Simon's review in *New York* focused on the lack of a clear purpose in the script, the undeveloped content of the play, and what he designated as "an imaginary landscape overrich in second-rate imagination and grievously undernourished in body."[9] Although Eder, writing in the *New York Times*, admitted that the play had some authentically moving moments, he believed that the incidents Guare depicted were too crude and facile while the melodrama itself was often banal and grisly.[10]

In May 1984, artistic directors Robyn Goodman and Carole Rothman of Second Stage, a company whose purpose is to give deserving plays a second chance, produced *Landscape of the Body* at their new Walter McGinn/John Cazale Theater on upper Broadway. Gary Sinise directed a cast that included Christine Lahti (Betty), Dann Florek (Captain Holahan), Mary Copple (Rosalie), and Christian Slater (Bert). This production was not as heavily reviewed as the 1977 New York performances. Mel Gussow's favorable review in the *New York Times* was the only serious discussion of the play. Gussow, whose only caveat was that the first act was still too long, described the play as "a cross between a metaphysical mystery and an absurdist musical" and, as such, one of Guare's most compelling dramas.[11] Clive Barnes (*New York Post*), who did not review the 1977 production, praised Sinise's direction and the balanced acting and admitted that the play "won't go away in my mind," even though he found the writing to be poorly organized, facetious, pretentious, and, at times, boring.[12] Edith Oliver (*New Yorker*) and John Simon (*New York*), both of whom had reviewed the original New York production, again offered their assessments. Oliver, who had been one of Guare's most consistent supporters, now changed her mind about the play, finding it "pretty depressing."[13] Simon, however, who had been one of Guare's major detractors, virtually repeated what he wrote in his earlier review in 1977, maintaining that the play was pointless, odious, and humorless, with the songs inept and irrelevant.[14]

Guare has had moderate success with *Landscape of the Body*. Since its 1977 premiere, the play has been one of the favorites for stagings by repertory groups throughout the United States.[15] Movie producer Sam Spiegel was so impressed with the drama that he commissioned Guare to write a screenplay adapted from the original script. Guare spent considerable time with Spiegel working on the project. However, although the Hollywood mogul was inspired by Guare's screenplay, he realized that the subject was too esoteric and probably too depressing for mass consumption. The project was abandoned as Spiegel prepared for his next film, working with David Lean and Robert Bolt in the South Seas.

As a result of the audience misunderstanding his intentions in *Marco Polo Sings a Solo,* Guare was determined to clarify the narrative events of his next play. Guare recalls the genesis of *Landscape of the Body*: "So I said, 'What I'm going to do is write a play with a narrative line, so that the event will in no way be indecipherable. I'm even going to have a narrator to say exactly what is going to happen.'"[16] Rosalie, Betty Yearn's sister and now deceased, acts as the omniscient narrator who traces Betty's history from her New England departure to the unsolved mystery of her son Bert's death. The play is divided into two acts without scenes, with the first act at least twice as long as the second. Fade-ins and fade-outs move us from one interlude to the other similar to the way montage works in film; Rosalie simply fades into a dark area after announcing each of the various flashbacks to the audience. Rosalie, formerly a pornographic film star who moves with the grace of a striptease artist, makes for an ideal cabaret-type hostess, allowing Guare to use her as a vamp for several catchy songs in the vaudeville tradition. The overall effect is similar to Brecht's theater, particularly the early plays that were written in cabaret style.

Much of the play takes place in Greenwich Village, except for the interrogation scenes that occur on a ferry boat sailing from Hyannisport to Nantucket. The settings allow Guare, for the first time in his canon, to make implications about the two microcosms he uses to represent the American heritage: New York City and New England; when most of a Guare play occurs in New York, one can guarantee chaos on the horizon. The dichotomy between the two locales reflects Guare's vision of the gap between the real and the ideal. After Betty leaves Bangor, Maine, to visit Rosalie in New York City, attempting to bring her sibling back to the safe haven of New England, she decides to stay when her sister is killed in a bicycle accident. Although New England represents the idyllic in Guare's world, New York is the dream fantasyland, much in the manner that Manhattan became Nirvana for the suburbanites who viewed Queens as a pit stop on the way to success. However, the reality is that New York represents the insane, crippling, and devastating effects of modern life. Gautam Dasgupta describes the importance of Guare's setting in *Landscape of the Body*: "A far more despairing play than his earlier works, Guare's Dickensian portrait of life in New York is indeed bleary—characters are left with no other alternatives but to search out the ignoble as a way of life."[17] A ferryboat ride to Nantucket, however, suggests freedom from the oppressive reality of America's urban landscape.

Marco Polo Sings a Solo was concerned with the dreams and aspirations of people who had achieved success and were rich and famous. In contrast, *Landscape of the Body* explores the way in which people who have nothing, certainly no dreams or imaginative vision, try to connect in a society that is onerous, violent, and destructive. Guare has always been intrigued, amused, and terrified by how we tend to cope with the imperfections and irrationality of an unpredictable world in which truth is often stranger than fiction. Guare commented, "*Landscape* is about people trying to deal with all the chaos inside and trying to find some form for it so that they're not overwhelmed."[18] The dominant image in the play, the one that begins the drama and serves as the focal point in the present where the flashbacks originate, is Betty onboard the ferry, stuffing notes in bottles that she throws overboard. Betty states, "My life is a triumph of all the things I don't know. I don't have to know everything. I read Agatha Christies and throw them away when the detective says 'And the murderer is . . .' The mystery's always greater than the solution."[19] In Guare's most philosophical play, he delves into life as an enigma, painful yet inexplicable, with truth based largely upon chance. John Harrop provides an overview of this philosophy: "This play develops the earlier theme of life's unknowable purposes—messages cast upon the ocean—and uses the metaphor of the ship of fate or fools, also introducing the theme of retiring to an island both to avoid life's corruptions and to seek solutions."[20] People living life without any reason, devoid of imagination and dreams that seemingly fuel the vitality of middle and upper class citizens, seem to be more susceptible to the violence, disorder, and chaos of modern society. *Landscape of the Body* thus provides Guare with a chance to employ black comedy to its greatest effect as an ironic device to indicate how tenuous many of our lives are; but the play works only because its viciousness is tempered by Guare's compassion and pathos for the plights of his protagonists in a cruel world.

Landscape of the Body begins on the ferryboat headed for Nantucket where Betty Yearn, née Mandible, aged thirty-six, is casting bottled notes into the ocean. She is being pursued by Captain Marvin Holahan, a New York City homicide detective, who questions her about the decapitation of her son, Bert. Betty admits that she has been estranged from her husband, whom she has not seen in years. Alienated and frustrated, Betty is in dire need of a physical relationship and more importantly, a spiritual connection. She seeks empathy from the ever-pursuant detective: "What is my motive? I cannot believe I am a suspect in my own son's death. I am supposed to be comforted. I am supposed to be held and allowed to cry and not made to feel . . . there's no insurance" (102).

Through flashbacks, the audience learns more about Betty's painful life. She left the husband she once revered as a god when he stuck her son's head down the toilet and flushed it after having done the same thing to her. Betty laments, "I don't want anybody giving me presents. I don't want to be reminded what I missed out on. We should've had a family. We could've had a family" (126). She is also grieved about the slow, agonizing death of her former best friend, Mavis Brennan, who had to have her breasts amputated due to cancer. While Bert is giving Betty a shampoo, the latter reveals how her friend's radiation therapy forced her to lose all of her hair and emaciated her body. During the summer before Mavis died, Betty visited her in the hospital every day to read from *The Sensuous Woman* because Mavis wanted to learn how to be attractive, sensuous, and have orgasms. Guare's black humor, however, is also tinged with sympathy for Betty's suffering. As Bert continues washing her hair, Betty's words take on symbolic value expressing her frustration: "I hated life. I hated Mavis. I hated. Rub the hair. Wash it out. More hot water. More bubbles. More soap. Get it all out of my head all the bad into a bubble and fly it away and pop it. Get it out" (141).[21] Without dreams or imaginative vision, Betty lives life on a day-to-day basis, which only serves to exacerbate an existence filled with pain and brutality. She desperately needs to connect with someone and even admits to her son, "I wish sometimes you were a girl. I wish sometimes I had a friend" (139).

Betty and Bert left Bangor, Maine, two years earlier and went to New York to escort Rosalie, Betty's younger sister, back to the wholesome life they once led in New England. Rosalie, however, was firmly entrenched in the wonders of New York City life, starring in pornographic films part-time and working full-time in a sleazy travel agency. Excited about life in the fast lane in Greenwich Village, Rosalie had no desire to return to her mother and the mundane lifestyle of New England. Six months later, Rosalie is killed on Hudson Street, right in front of the Ristorante Rigoletto (Bing Ringling's employer) when a ten-speed yellow Raleigh bike hits her. The cyclist's reaction is indicative of brutal, impersonal life in the big city: "I don't give a shit if she's dead! Who's gonna fix my bike? The chain is off my bike! Who's gonna pay for that?" (116).[22] The incident implies that in Guare's world, take one wrong step and your life can come to an abrupt halt. Guare recognizes that there is a fine line between life and death; our existences are tenuous, often based upon chance. With this premise running throughout the play, Guare becomes intrigued and perplexed by the types of lives led by people without imagination or dreams where chance can intervene and send us to our deaths at any moment. For these individuals, the ultimate question to be asked is, as Mel Gussow has perceptively noted, "Is there life before death?"[23]

After Rosalie's death, Betty stays on in her sister's apartment in Greenwich Village, and, in order to pay off her sibling's debts to the Mafia and settle the estate, she becomes a pornographic film star in Mafia-made movies. Betty thus makes plenty of contact, but it is not the lasting type of committed love relationship that she needs. She also follows in her sister's footsteps by taking a job selling honeymoon holidays at Dawn's Promising Star Travel Agency. Thus, Betty Yearn, as her last name suggests, is searching for an identity haphazardly without any distinguishable purpose in life. Her decision to make pornographic films is probably the closest she will come to stardom and will vicariously satisfy her desire "to connect" with someone, albeit momentarily. Furthermore, Dawn's Promising Star Travel Agency is only suggestive of glitter and glamor but in actuality is just another sham in a life of aimless existence.

The travel agency where Betty works is owned by a con man named Raulito, a suave Latino with a pompadour who flashes diamond rings on his fingers. He wears a gold lamé 1940s Rita Hayworth evening gown over his business suit because it makes him feel wealthy. Raised in poverty in Cuba, Raulito understands, "The dreams we have as kids, they're the dreams we never get over" (122). As a child in Cuba, he watched American films, and now living the American Dream complete with his lamé dress, he plans to fulfill his childhood fantasies. He created Honeymoon Holidays to prey upon other people's dreams and fantasies. Raulito and Betty take the engagement section in the Sunday newspapers, and from the wedding notices, they glean enough information about the newlyweds to get their telephone numbers. Then, Raulito or Betty makes a call, congratulating the bride and groom on the all-expense paid honeymoon that they have won. However, they must stop into the travel agency and sign some forms to make final arrangements for what turns out to be a fake honeymoon. Raulito's pitch to the newlyweds preys upon humanity's desire to dream of a future idyllic existence:

> The past shows us the mistakes we made. The future's the place where we won't make them again. Dreams are the fuel for reality. A new family is coming into the world! Oh God! Grab the Now! The Now is all quicksilver and mercury. The Now is diamonds. Can I make an appointment for you? (120)

Betty, who is resigned to a life of disorder without committed dreams and desires, also falls under Raulito's spell. Raulito has a strong sexual presence and can intimidate women, particularly those who are pliable, such as Betty. He is an egoist whose fantasy is to tell his life's story while being interviewed by Johnny Carson on the *Tonight Show*. At first, Betty is meek and humbled in his presence: "I'm a Betty. That's all I am. I have no story. I'm no guest on any talk show. No story. I am a middle-aged woman. I'm a young girl. I'm regular. Quiet. Normal. Human person" (123). A year and a half later, Betty has followed in his sister's footsteps by having an affair with Raulito. The stage directions indicate, *"Betty is quite snappily dressed and a lot more sure of herself in the last months since we've seen her"* (125). Unfortunately, there is no serious love relationship or spiritual connection between the two. Raulito, who is married and has plenty of children, is merely using Betty as an object of his desires. In having the same type of affair with Rosalie, Raulito seems to use women for selfish reasons. Meanwhile, Betty, who is still making pornographic movies with titles such as *Do Me Do Me Do Me Till It Falls Off* and *Leather Sheets*, even starring in "golden showers" films, now simultaneously becomes an object of desire for voyeurs and an object for Raulito.

Betty's "family life" deteriorated after she moved to New York. Her son, Bert, age fourteen, hangs out with a depraved group of teenagers. Guare's portrait of them brings out the best of his black comedy in which the modern urban landscape is depicted as frightening and grotesque. Bert's girlfriend, Joanne, has an affinity for telling morbid stories about healthy people who suddenly experience gruesome deaths. She has a knack for always interrupting the conversation with something that is grisly and hideous: "Papers I read a German shepherd ate a newborn baby" (153). In one such tale, a woman with a beautiful beehive hairdo wound up with black widow spiders nesting there. Because she used hairspray, the spiders became trapped within her hair. She died after the black widows ate their way through her skull in order to escape. Joanne recalls another episode in which a woman bought a dress from India at Korvette's Department Store. Cobra eggs got woven into mirrors on the dress where it was made in India; when the eggs hatched from the heat when the dress was mailed to Korvette's, a cobra emerged from the drawer in which the dresses were kept. The lady was bitten when the eggs also hatched in her home.[24]

Bert and his friend, Donny, commit felonies when their mother is away from the apartment. They pick up gay men on the street, bring them back to Bert's residence, and then Donny, unseen behind the shower curtain, hits them with a monkey wrench. Bert and Donny steal their watches and wallets, roll them out the door, urinate on them, spill wine on them to make it seem as if they are drunk, and then inform one of the neighbors, who proceeds to call the police. The victims never report the incident because they would have to admit to picking up a minor. Bert has a warped sense of humor. Joanne tells Donny about the passion she shares with Bert: "Putting razor blades in frisbees and then when we see somebody we don't like from Elizabeth Irwin High School, we toss it at them and say 'Hey, grab!'" (152–53). In addition, Bert and Donny are indirectly responsible for a murder. One of their jokes is to go to a bank and write on the back of a deposit slip, "Hand over all your money or I blow your brains on the wall" (152). Then the unsuspecting customer depositing money becomes a bank robber unknowingly. One day, when Raulito is depositing money in the bank, the joke goes awry. The teller pushes a button summoning the police; when they arrive, they shoot Raulito dead. Guare implies that there is a fine line between life and death. Raulito, innocently depositing a check, winds up like Rosalie, killed by a cyclist while she walked nonchalantly down the street. Life in contemporary society can be violent, terrifying, and enigmatic.

Betty, who lacks a strong identity of her own, realizes that her son is incorrigible, yet she is in no position to provide adequate solutions for her son's delinquency. Betty and Bert share a strange love-hate relationship. Betty did leave her husband after he put his son's head down the toilet, and Bert insists, "I have dreams sometimes of water rushing by me" (128), musing, "I think I'll join the Navy when I can. The submarine service" (128). Betty at times may even share a joint with her son, although he tries to hide the drugs from her because he selfishly wants to keep his supply for himself. Betty viciously teases her son about following a filthy old man in Bangor and calls him a "little faggot" (130). She even suspects he may be involved with the recent murders on the docks. Bert, in turn, riles his mother about her age, calling Betty an "old hag" and "old crone" (129). Bert spars with her verbally, trying to hurt her: "I hate you. You're going to die. You know what I want for Christmas? You in a coffin under a Christmas tree" (129). This particular verbal abuse ends in physical warfare, as Bert hits his mother, and Betty retaliates in turn. When Betty receives a better offer and goes off to live with Durwood Peach, she leaves Bert with a thousand dollars and tells him to fend for himself.

Unable to establish an identity for herself or to connect with anyone, being treated like an object by her son and her employers,

Betty, as might be expected, jumps at the opportunity to develop a meaningful love relationship. Durwood Peach, who sold Good Humor ice cream to Betty nineteen years earlier when she was living in Bangor, tracked down her new address, and winds up visiting Betty in Greenwich Village. Durwood, although he has never even dated Betty, claims that he loves her and proposes marriage. He admits that he will never forget how infatuated he was when he overheard a conversation between Betty and her sister on their porch in Bangor nineteen years ago. When Betty realizes that Durwood is a wealthy farmowner in South Carolina, the offer looks attractive. Durwood lures her with an appeal to the imagination, something she is hardly familiar with but is nevertheless enticing: "But if I had to choose between where I live and you, I'd rip up everything I own because the only landscape worth looking at is the landscape of the human body" (142–43). Durwood begins to wax eloquent, and this lyrical onslaught sweeps Betty off her feet. Just as she is beginning to dream of an idyllic existence with Durwood, reality reenters the picture: Bert will not be allowed to accompany her. In order to experience love, Betty must abandon her son. As is often true of Guare's black comedy, the audience does not know how to react.

When Betty arrives in South Carolina, she meets Durwood's family, including his wife. Durwood has been placed in a mental asylum, and the doctors thought that a trip to New York might do him some good. The family extends their thanks to Betty and puts her on a bus to Wheeling, West Virginia, where she can make connections back to New York. Thus, Betty deserted her son to run off with a madman. Meanwhile, back home, Donny, upset because Bert hugged him out of desperation from being abandoned, picked up the monkey wrench and accidentally killed his friend; then Donny stole the thousand dollars. Joanne, with her warped ideology, helps Donny decapitate Bert, put him in a bag, and then leave him by the docks so the police will think the murder is merely one more in a series of trademark killings that have occurred in the city. Donny seems to rationalize the crime as a death of just another guttersnipe: "My uncle saw a dirty movie and he told me Bert's mother was in it" (158). Joanne asserts, "Bert wasn't from here. Bert never belonged here" (158). The price of Betty's aimless meanderings is now clear: her son is decapitated, and she is now the chief murder suspect in his death. Guare has commented about the tie between Betty's banal lifestyle and Bert's strange fate: "The play is about a decapitation, a loss of head, about people living life without any reflective powers, without their reason, without their imagination."[25] In short, Betty, without a strong sense of identity, a person who fails to know herself, is unable both to connect with others or to nurture her family.

Betty's chance to connect with the Other comes in the form of Captain Marvin Holahan, who has known her for the past five months when his investigation of her son's decapitation began. With Betty as the chief suspect in the murder, Holahan pries into her past, and, by doing so, he begins to take an interest in her private life. As a movie buff, Holahan has something in common with Betty: he watches films and she stars in them. In addition, Holahan was fascinated by Betty's perseverance in denying that she was the murderer. Holahan reveals that he was on probation from the police force, and solving Bert's murder would have been his ticket to reinstatement. Thus, after being released from his duties as a police officer, Holahan, intrigued by Betty's wiles and will power, continued to follow her when she left New York for Nantucket.

When we first see Holahan, which is at the beginning of the play, he is in a Groucho Marx type of disguise as he pursues Betty on board the ferry heading for Nantucket. Holahan, who has no one and now has no job, has been honest in confiding with Betty over the last several months. While uncovering Betty's past and during his one-on-one conversations with her, Holahan feels as if he has made contact that has otherwise been absent in his life. He remarks to her, "I begin talking and you pick right up on it. We could have a marriage made in heaven. We can talk. I think that's why marriages fail. People can't talk. People fight to have something to talk about" (97).

At first, one might imagine that resigned and deflated Betty and boorish and brusque Marvin Holahan would have nothing in common. However, they share the fact that they are two desperate people trying to connect with someone for once in their lives. Betty admits, "My confidence is in bad disrepair and needs all the propping up it can beg, borrow, or infer" (97). Holahan, in his role as police officer, daily views the underlying violence and rage of contemporary urban life; Betty has witnessed its repercussions firsthand. Holahan has lost his job, his profession; Betty has lost her son, her only offspring. They both could use a fresh start; as Betty realizes, "It's amazing how a little tomorrow can make up for a whole lot of yesterday" (134).

Betty's epiphany comes after she remembers years ago in Bangor the conversation she was having with Rosalie, the intensity of which had such a profound effect on Durwood Peach that he fell in love with her. Rosalie was explaining to Betty how our spirits float in space and are eventually pulled into the earth, as if we were baited by fishing hooks. Waxing philosophical, Rosalie implies that our existence on Earth is transient and short-lived:

> Wait for that one day we can bite free and get back out there in space where we belong, sail back over water, over skies, into space, the hook finally out of our mouths and we wander back out there in space spawning to other planets never to return hurrah to earth and we'll look back and can't even see these lives here anymore. Only the taste of blood to remind us we ever existed. The earth is small. We're gone. We're dead. We're safe. (166)

Despite Betty's search for some order in her life, she learns that life is a mystery, an enigma that can never be solved. She begins to accept the idea that life is a triumph of many things we cannot explain. Perhaps it is best to throw away the Agatha Christie mystery when the murderer is to be revealed. In the murder mystery she has just lived through, Betty realizes that she will never know the motive for her son's death or the identity of the murderer. Cyclists on ten-speed bicycles can end our lives in an instant, and picking up the wrong deposit slip in the bank can be fatal. In this horrendously violent society that we live in, death can come at any moment; the absurdity of our lives precludes any rational explanation.

Understanding that life is enigmatic and that as spirits we are on Earth only a short period of time, Betty finally realizes that life is painful but is also worth living. Guare perceives this only too well; his purpose in writing the play was to explore what this concept means to individuals who do not have dreams of being rich and famous. How does a person develop a sense of dignity without an idyllic vision of life as a means to pursue goals for the future? The key is in the title of the play. Individuals who are disassociated from themselves and who merely meander aimlessly from one incident to another without desires of fame and fortune can connect through the body. If the spirit is eternal, the body is what gives us purpose on Earth. Having lost everything, Betty only has the body left to provide her with a sense of dignity. The body represented the spiritual connection that Durwood Peach intuitively understood as the means to connect with Betty and thus spark his eternal passion for life. Guare ends the written text with a quotation from Wallace Stevens's *Esthétique du Mal*: "The greatest poverty is not to live / In a physical world, to feel that one's desire / Is too difficult to tell from despair" (167). Betty and Captain Holahan understand the despair. The stage directions read, "*Betty looks at Holahan. A long pause. She moves toward him*" (167).

The violence in their lives has reduced their cynicism and despair to enigmas that will best be left unresolved. The key to their survival will be how they can connect with each other emotionally and search for a passion that they can celebrate together.

Guare began writing *Bosoms and Neglect* during summer 1977 when *Landscape of the Body* was playing in Lake Forest, Illinois, before its New York premiere. The Prologue of *Bosoms and Neglect,* Henny's revelation of breast cancer to her son, occurred almost exactly as Guare wrote the scene, decimated and in a stupor, on the subway immediately after the traumatic disclosure happened. During January 1979, Guare, who was doing research on the nineteenth century to prepare for his writing of *Lydie Breeze,* needed a respite from historical material and thus turned to something closer to reality. The remainder of the play came quickly to him over a two-week period in early 1979.

As a result of the hostile critical reception of *Landscape of the Body* by the New York media, Guare was determined that *Bosoms and Neglect* should be spared such unwarranted treatment. He commented, "I was going to protect myself and my play from that kind of commotion. You need all the energy you possess just to get the play onstage; you shouldn't be diverted or drained with other things that can be avoided."[26] Furthermore, Joseph Papp's Public Theater, Guare's favorite venue for the New York debut of his plays, was no longer a viable option because Bernard Gersten, Guare's colleague and the Public Theater's associate producer, was no longer there. Gregory Mosher, the artistic director at the Goodman Theater in Chicago, was enthused about Guare's script and scheduled the play for the 1979 season as a last-minute replacement for a cancelled production of Ibsen's *Ghosts. Bosoms and Neglect* opened at the Goodman Theater on 1 March 1979. The cast included Paul Rudd (Scooper), Kate Reid (Henny), and Marian Mercer (Deirdre) in a production directed by Mel Shapiro with sets designed by John Wulp. Chicago's theater critics, proud to have a major contemporary playwright stage the world premiere of one of his plays in their city, gave it positive reviews. Richard Christiansen, the influential critic for the *Chicago Tribune,* deemed Guare a poet, "perhaps the most supremely gifted playwright of our time," yet conceded that *Bosoms and Neglect*'s timing needed work before its Broadway debut.[27]

After doing brisk business in Chicago, *Bosoms and Neglect* premiered on Broadway at the Longacre Theatre, 3 May 1979, despite the fact that the play was more suited to the experimental confines of off-Broadway. The cast and crew of the Chicago production remained essentially the same for the Broadway transfer. *Bosoms and Neglect* made it to Broadway when a last-minute scheduling change allowed the play to be slotted in when *Faith Healer* closed. The cast and crew were familiar with the play from the Chicago production, but they had only four days to rehearse for New York. Although the play received its share of favorable notices, the majority of the reviewers, with an eye toward the ubiquitous commercial appeal needed for Broadway, panned the production. With negative reviews from the major dailies (*New York Times, New York Post,* and *Daily News*), the producers felt that the odds were against mounting a successful promotional campaign for the play. *Bosoms and Neglect* closed after four performances.

Terry Curtis Fox (*Village Voice*), Martin Gottfried (*Saturday Review*), Howard Kissel (*Women's Wear Daily*), and Jack Kroll (*Newsweek*) were the biggest supporters of the play; Edwin Wilson (*Wall Street Journal*) was lukewarm in his assessment. Many of the critics praised John Wulp's set design of Deirdre's book-cluttered apartment and Kate Reid's performance as Henny, but several complained that Paul Rudd was miscast as forty-year-old Scooper. Kissel was impressed with the range of Guare's humor that displayed a combination of various effects: wild, erotic, sick, witty, and endearing.[28] Gottfried argued that *Bosoms and Neglect* did not deserve abusive reviews, and although he acknowledged that it was too abstract for the commercial theater, he insisted that the play was inventive, energetic, and significant.[29] Fox and Kissel offered the most thought-provoking critical responses to the play. Fox agreed that the structure of Guare's drama needed revision, especially the Prologue, which seemed pretentious and unsatisfying, but he concluded that it was an intelligent and deeply felt play expressing how the attachments people make to each other often lead to pain.[30] Kroll realized that Guare's black humor imbues us with compassion for the bizarre lives we lead: "Now, in his wildly, sorrowfully funny new play, Guare has begun to find the secret form hidden within our chaos."[31] Wilson's review was ambivalent; he recognized Guare's cleverness and imaginative vision but understood how an audience could be confused about whether to laugh or sit in baffled silence in reaction to the play.[32]

However, most of the critical reaction to the Broadway debut of *Bosoms and Neglect* was certainly somewhat less than effusive. Hobe, *Variety*'s critic, found Kate Reid's performance to be "distressingly squirming" and the humor too imbecilic for Broadway.[33] Douglas Watt (*Daily News*) claimed that Shapiro's direction could not save what was otherwise a "static" play, tedious when Henny is not onstage, while Richard Eder (*New York Times*) agreed, claiming that the dialogue was dull and the performances were exaggerated and campy.[34]

Walter Kerr, Eder's colleague also covering Broadway for the *New York Times*, complained that the play was wordy, heartless, anchorless, yet clever at times.[35] Brendan Gill, writing in the *New Yorker*, described Guare as a mischievously self-delighted artist good at writing humorous one-liners yet one who failed to realize that his play was too perplexing for audiences.[36] Clive Barnes (*New York Post*) also noted that the play had little structure, less development, was confusing, yet featured "sophisticated humor that owes something to the Marx Brothers, T*he National Lampoon, Mad Magazine*, the cartoons from the *New Yorker*, and Jules Feiffer."[37] Finally, John Simon's review in *New York* echoed several of the remarks of his fellow critics as he admitted that the play was sporadically humorous, unevenly structured, immiscible, and often fluctuated from the absurd to the naturalistic.[38]

Almost immediately after *Bosoms and Neglect* was accorded shabby treatment by the Broadway reviewers, the play became a cause célèbre among sympathetic producers and critics. Reminding the press that *Bosoms and Neglect* did good business in Chicago, where it received favorable notices and sold out for its six-week run, Guare acknowledged that in New York, "During the first week of production, $75,000 in investments came from people who had seen it."[39] Bernard Gersten and John Wulp, the producers of the Broadway version of *Bosoms and Neglect*, ran a full-page ad in *Variety* the week following the disastrous reviews in which they included excerpts from several of the favorable comments written about the play. Shortly thereafter, *Bosoms and Neglect* began to develop somewhat of a cult following among regional theater groups throughout the United States.

In fall 1979, *Bosoms and Neglect* was chosen to open the season of Providence's Trinity Square Repertory Company; it was directed by Larry Arrick and staged at the Downstairs Theater. Kevin Kelly's rave review in the *Boston Globe* suggested that the play may be bitter and bruising but was not too cynical and could be brilliant with a superior cast and crew.[40] This production then transferred for a five-week run at Boston's Charles Playhouse beginning 21 November. Meanwhile, Lloyd Richards, director of the Yale Repertory Theatre, chose the play to inaugurate Yale University's 1979–80 theater season to make a statement about the viability of new experimental drama that might otherwise be smothered by the commercial pressures of Broadway. *Bosoms and Neglect* opened at Yale on 5 October 1979, in a twin bill with Peter Handke's *They Are Dying Out*, directed by Steven Robman. Guare made a few revisions for this version of the play, and Mel Gussow, although admitting that Guare needed to tighten a bit more, believed that this production was an improvement and offered a clearer picture of the playwright's intentions.[41] The West Coast premiere of the play was staged shortly thereafter during February and early March 1980 at the Berkeley Stage Company under the direction of David Walker.[42]

Bosoms and Neglect was included in August 1980 as one of the sixteen plays performed during the six-month-long Stratford Festival in Ontario, Canada. This highly successful production was directed by Mel Shapiro and featured Kate Reid's polished performance as Henny; Guare was now receiving recognition for his imaginative text, which Dan Sullivan in the *Los Angeles Times* described as his finest play since *The House of Blue Leaves*.[43] *Bosoms and Neglect* was also staged at the Imaginary Theatre in Atlanta during January and February 1981 and at Los Angeles's Odyssey Theatre during February 1986 before its return to the New York stage.[44] The New York revival of the play began its brief run on 26 March 1986, at off-Broadway's New York Theatre Workshop at the Perry Street Theatre. For this production, directed by Larry Arrick and starring Richard Kavanaugh (Scooper), Anne Meara (Henny), and April Shawhan (Deirdre), Guare added several lines to the conversation between Scooper and Deirdre in act 1. Although this production was not heavily reviewed, the consensus among the critics was that the play was still baffling and seemed like two separate one-act dramas sewn together but was superior to the original Broadway version.[45] Finally, *Bosoms and Neglect* was the second play to be staged in repertory during the Signature Theatre's 1998–99 season featuring plays by Guare. Directed by Nicholas Martin and featuring Mary Louise Wilson (Henny), David Aaron Baker (Scooper), and Katie Finneran (Deirdre), *Bosoms and Neglect* ran from 13 December 1998 to 10 January 1999 and was perceived by theater critics to be a much better selection than the Signature Theatre's initial production, *Marco Polo Sings a Solo*.[46]

Bosoms and Neglect consists of a brief Prologue followed by two acts. Most of the play takes place in Henny's apartment in Queens and in Deirdre's Manhattan residence, so one might expect that the New York locale provides Guare with a license to employ his bizarre brand of mordant comedy that is full of surprises. Strangely enough, *Bosoms and Neglect* is the most realistically staged black comedy in Guare's canon. There are no songs, musical interludes, asides, pyrotechnics, fade-outs, nor flashbacks. The contemporary settings are realistic rather than stylized. Moreover, Guare's black comedy is a bit more subtle, even subdued, and certainly not as pervasive as in the earlier plays. We can speculate that one reason for the change of structure is that Guare, fully immersed in the realist tradition while writing *Lydie*

Breeze during this period, attempted to apply that form to contemporary black comedy as well. In addition, Guare, accused of being obscure in his recent plays, may have been overly conscious of aiming for simplicity to make *Bosoms and Neglect* more accessible. Finally, Guare probably realized that writing a comedy about cancer, a gruesome subject with which most members of the audience have had contact through its effects on friends or relatives, borders on a violation of common decency, and thus he chose to subdue the heavily satirical tone.

Bosoms and Neglect is Guare's most autobiographical play. Guare's mother was the model for Henny; when Guare wrote the play, his mother was blind and rarely left the house. John Wulp, who designed the set for the Chicago and Broadway productions, crafted Henny's residence at least partially from a description of Guare's mother's apartment. Guare is similar to Scooper—both were born late in their parents' lives, both are voracious readers, and both frequent New York City bookstores regularly. One may speculate that Deirdre is perhaps partially modelled on Adele Chatfield-Taylor, Guare's close friend who was later to become his wife. The play can be read as a rationalization of Guare's guilt over the revelation of his mother's cancer, or, in other words, Guare's catharsis about the neglect of his mother during a period when he was spending more time with his friend. In any event, Guare began the play with the discovery of his mother's cancer, a personal tragedy that forced him to come to terms with his own turmoil:

> An event happened to me, and I came out and wrote it down because I didn't know what to do with it, it was so shocking to me. It was incredibly personal, and it was shocking. I was not emotionally prepared for it, and I said, "Here is something I don't know what to do with—it terrifies me, it scares me, it challenges me. I don't know what to do with this event." And so I said, "I'm going to write a play about it."[47]

Guare is always searching for a metaphor to make his black comedy more universal, an image that is so engrossing and disturbing that it can wake him up shaking in the middle of the night. His mother's cancer became the perfect image to portray a sick contemporary urban society.

Bosoms and Neglect is primarily concerned with how individuals in contemporary American society can connect with each other in some meaningful or spiritual way despite the fact that neglect, indifference, and alienation reflect the norm in human relationships.

Guare's play probes the human psyche to explain why individual relationships become superficial rather than spiritually satisfying. *Bosoms
and Neglect* examines how we seek refuge from reality and from our
guilt by immersing ourselves in fantasy lives. Guare commented on
this motif in his play: "A lot of times 'the answer' is right there under
our noses, but we're so obsessed with our own needs that we don't
see it. I hope the play makes people ask themselves, 'What secrets are
there lurking in our lives that we're not noticing?'"[48] Guare implies
that we need to connect by taking risks as we become emotionally
and spiritually involved with a person we love, rather than hiding
behind self-centered intellectual fantasies that mask our fear of the
reality of the modern malaise. He noted that *Bosoms and Neglect* reflects the notion that "we operate more with the angers of neglect
than the passions of acceptance."[49]As is typical in one of his plays,
Guare demonstrates that lack of compassion and spiritual connection may lead to insanity, violence, decay, and disease so prevalent in
contemporary urban life.

The Prologue sets the tone for this black comedy. The setting
is eighty-three-year-old Henny's apartment in Queens, New York,
where she is talking with Scooper, her forty-year-old son. Although
Henny's spirit is strong, she is blind and physically deteriorating. She
complains to her son that she is in pain when urinating, her uterus
has fallen out, and she has been bleeding from the breast, symptoms
that began two years ago. To treat the wound in her breast, which
later is revealed to be cancer, Henny has been praying to Saint Jude,
Patron Saint of Lost Causes. She describes her unique cure for the
disease: "It bleeds and bleeds and I put Kotex over it and stand in
front of the window all night in the dark looking up waving a statue
of Saint Jude over it so it'll dry by the morning. But it never dries.
It never stops bleeding. I sent out for more Kotex."[50] The neglected
cancerous breast, a grotesque and brutal sight, becomes the dominant image in a play where the word "neglect" is repeated several
times to create a resounding effect. Scooper says to Deirdre, "She
had so neglected herself that the disease was sick of not being noticed. The disease finally burst through her skin" (181). Henny has
obviously neglected her body, but Scooper, shocked when Henny reveals her cancerous condition, has also failed to connect with his
mother. He has been too busy with his own emotional problems
to pay appropriate attention to his mother's physical health. Guare
told Frances Herridge of the *New York Post* that the play is "about
the connections we all try to make and what we neglect in the process. The breast, obviously, is the first connection."[51] The implication

is that the deterioration of the diseased breast that once nourished Scooper, his first "connection," is a result of the neglect that Scooper shows his parent and his concomitant inability to return nurture to his mother. John Harrop explains it well: "The visible decaying of the source of our nurture shows the evident results of the neglect of human relationships for fear of accepting responsibility for their inevitable pain."[52]

Henny's life has been one big tale of neglect. Henny maintained her virginity until she was married, at the age of forty-two, rather late in life. After her father passed away, Henny was lonely and frequented bars, where she eventually met her future husband, Jack. She also ventured to Boston before she was married and met a wonderful Amish fellow named Don Walker. Unfortunately, Don's mother would not permit her son to wed an Irish-Catholic girl. Henny recalls how she was spurned: "But only a Quaker girl was good enough for her son. He buckled under. Stopped calling me. Neglected to keep dates. I got the message" (247). Although she loved Jack, their marriage did not involve the sharing of intimate, personal information, including details about income or age. She was frequently confined to hospitals to alleviate her disturbed mental condition, but the only effect that she can recall was that the electroshock therapy administered to her caused blackouts. Jack's alcoholism eventually killed him, and while he was confined to the hospital, Henny attempted suicide by swallowing an overdose of pills. Henny tries to rationalize her suicide, claiming, "I reached for the wrong pills. I couldn't see. I thought they were breath fresheners. Life Savers" (226), but Scooper intervenes: "Nobody takes eighty-six Life Savers. Nobody's breath is that bad" (226). We later learn that Henny went through ten years of suicide attempts. Henny has been a ravaged and abused woman searching to connect with someone, and now the ramifications of her life history of neglect is that the mental abuse leads to physical deterioration: cancer takes its toll. Through Scooper's recounting of his mother's terminal illness, Deirdre understands Henny's plight: "Poor tragic lady. Outliving her friends. Standing all night at a window. Not trusting any human being enough to reach out" (182).

Henny, in trying to live somewhat vicariously through her son, ends up neglecting him as well. In an unusual gesture, Henny gave her son the same name as her husband—Jack—yet he later preferred the nickname Scooper. Signs of Scooper's insecurity developed early in his life when at age eight, he began wearing his mother's makeup and dresses. He is haunted by a dream in which his mother picked him up and used him as a weapon. This incident occurred when

Scooper was a child and Henny took him to Boston to confront her old beau, Don Walker. Her plan was to act as if she accidentally bumped into him and then show off her child to indicate what a beautiful life Don was missing. Henny describes to Scooper what became a traumatic experience for her son during their encounter with Henny's former love:

> And after we said hellos and fancy meeting yous and acted surprised, I picked you up to show him what he missed and instead I hit him with you. Because he wasn't your father. Because he hadn't trusted me. Because I hadn't meant enough to him. I kept hitting him with you, pushing your face into his, till I realized your nose was bleeding. He was so shocked. I kept saying "You neglected me." (248)

The result of this trauma is that the most fundamental human relationship, the bond between mother and child, is badly damaged. Henny had cancer for two years and did not even trust her son enough to confide the details of her illness to him. Instead of communicating with each other, Scooper and Henny exist in their own little worlds and fail to pay attention to each other:

Scooper.	Why don't you ever tell me the truth?
Henny.	Why don't you ever ask me the truth?
Scooper.	Why did you try to kill yourself ten years ago?
Henny.	Why aren't you married?
Scooper.	Why did you get married so late? (227)

Henny's neglect of her son has led to Scooper's inability to connect with anyone else in a meaningful way. He castigates his mother for contributing to his social and spiritual alienation: "I feel you holding my feet and my face so close to this strange man and my head is hitting his. My friendships with men are all fucked up. My friendships with women are all fucked up. The doctors say you can't live alone anymore" (236).

To cope on a daily basis, Scooper has spent six years in psychotherapy with Doctor Virgil James. Six years ago, Scooper had a nervous breakdown that began when he was walking barefoot down Fifth Avenue in the middle of winter carrying a red plastic machine gun. He followed a young woman for five blocks, posing as James Bond to protect her from vicious aliens. The woman screamed when Scooper pulled her into a side street, and after a passerby tried to intervene, Scooper smashed his lit cigarette in the Good Samaritan's face. This led to Scooper's confinement in the psychiatric hospital. The fact that James, alias Scooper, whose father's name was also James, now seeks solace from Doctor James suggests an almost Freudian need to mitigate modern neuroses through contact with a father figure who is now represented as psychotherapist. The joke is that Scooper, who is a computer analyst, seeks help from a psychotherapist: the analyst needs analysis. However, when Dr. James decides to go on vacation to Haiti for four weeks, Scooper is left virtually defenseless. With the surrogate father figure leaving town and with the news of his mother's cancer, Scooper desperately needed someone to connect with, so he decided to pick up Deirdre.

Scooper had seen Deirdre in Doctor James's office during the past eleven months while she was in therapy, but now, almost on the spur of the moment, Scooper becomes attracted to her. Part of the reason for Scooper's newfound love is that Deirdre replaces Henny, the mother figure that Scooper cannot connect with, a mother-son relationship that has grown further apart since the revelation of Henny's cancer. Another reason for Scooper's attraction to Deirdre is that they both share a passion for books, especially those written by neglected authors. Scooper loves to browse in bookstores so as to create different personae for himself in order to hide behind fantasy and evade the painful reality of modern life. Scooper reveals to Henny how books provide him with refuge from the harsh reality of life and from the guilt he has about being unable to relate to people:

> I need my life structured, enclosed. I pick up a book. The page's rectangular shape, obvious but important, *constant* from book to book, dependable, the passion, wisdom, excitement captured in the center of the page tamed by the white margin. I lie on the rectangular couch of Doctor James and yes I become the words on the page. I can face my dreams. (236)

Scooper may be a success at business, but he is otherwise neurotic—a failure at making connections with others. He is also quite egocentric and has no guilt about the fact that the affairs in which he is engaged may stroke his ego but concomitantly often hurt others. While he is pursuing a relationship with Deirdre, he has also been having an affair for the past five years with Valerie, a woman who has sought psychological counseling for most of her life. Valerie is married to Ted, who had been Scooper's college roommate and then his business partner for years, and they have three children. In front of Deirdre, Scooper describes Valerie as "My lady. My girl. My mistress. My blood. My brain. My heart. My wonder" (194). Scooper reveals to Deirdre that his relationship with Valerie is not Platonic: "She had Bradley and Kim and Sophie by Caesarean so she is still tight like a young girl and you come into her so firm and then suddenly it's like coming into St. Peter's in Rome, the way you round a small corner and the entire basilica is wide open in front of you" (194–95). Valerie was so unhappy and felt so guilty about her affair with Scooper that she wound up in group therapy; naturally, that did not deter self-centered Scooper. Moreover, since Scooper's source of pain relief, Doctor James, is on vacation, he decides that he must temporarily have a surrogate comforter, so, during the psychotherapist's hiatus, Scooper selfishly plans to fly with Valerie to Haiti. Scooper does not care that his affair with Valerie has forced her to neglect her children. He plans to inform Ted of their vacation trip while Ted is at his own group therapy session during the evening of their departure. When they return from Haiti, Scooper and Valerie will move to Maine, where they will operate a bookstore open twenty-four hours a day. However, Scooper has to cancel the trip because of his mother's cancer. He is so self-centered that he blames the cancelled trip on his mother: "She did it on purpose. She knew I was leaving. That's why she waited till yesterday. This operation. This cancer caper. All designed to keep me from going. I don't know how she knew but she knew. Mystic connection" (196–97). Guare's sense of humor develops into the darkest black comedy, and the audience does not know how to react to Scooper's castigation of his mother: "She's been saving that breast to whip out just at an instant like this" (200).

Deirdre, a very beautiful, intense woman in her thirties, cannot provide the spiritual connection that Scooper seeks, for she is also neurotic herself. Scooper first became personally acquainted with Deirdre in a Fifth Avenue bookstore. Deirdre is a bibliophile whose drab life becomes enchanting only through the fantasy world of books. She has been in therapy for eight years with Doctor James and suffered a nervous breakdown last October. Like Scooper, she has had an affair with a married person. Initially, the breakup of Deirdre's affair occurred when her partner decided to return to his mate; Deirdre's reaction was to crown her lover with an ashtray, the violence leading her to seek counseling from Doctor James. Furthermore, Deirdre is a compulsive liar to the extent that the audience has difficulty sorting out the reality from the fiction. She informs Scooper that she is married to a man named Raymond but later, once she warms to him, admits that Raymond is fictitious. She wears a wedding ring because her friend advised her, "It avoids hassles" (204). At first, she tells Scooper that her parents were killed in a car accident when she was very young, then claims that she turned in her father to the authorities because of his illicit activities in the New Jersey Mafia; only much later does she admit that he is a librarian. Although she indicates to Scooper that she connected with her father and would like to accept this notion, the truth reveals a story of neglect.

Deirdre ostensibly has much in common with Scooper. Deirdre, who buys and sells first editions of books, fell immediately in love with Scooper when he admitted to reading Rilke. Deirdre's apartment is lined with books, and, like Scooper, she has a fetish for neglected authors who provide the peace necessary to avoid contact with the painful reality of their neurotic lives. They both share the same psychiatrist and are completely dependent upon him as a comforting father figure; Deirdre even describes analysis as "Brothers and sisters sent in for a private loving audience with our father" (188). Furthermore, Scooper and Deirdre have both had unsatisfying affairs with married persons. Finally, they have both been obsessed over, and consequently neglected by, a parent: Scooper by his mother and Deirdre by her father. Deirdre admits to Scooper, "We both share a guilt about the way we neglected a parent" (212). Thus, Deirdre, like Scooper, realizes that the solution to their dilemmas is, as E. M. Forster writes, "Connect. Only connect" (211).

Much of what makes Guare's black comedy so effective occurs in Deirdre's apartment during act 1, where the witty banter between Deirdre and Scooper indicates that the two bibliophiles can never connect. Their verbal sparring about neglected writers and literary allusions serves to mask the deeply rooted terror and absurdity of contemporary urban life. The reality is that Deirdre is using Scooper for her own purposes in much the same manner as Scooper uses her. Scooper becomes Deirdre's temporary panacea for her neurosis while Doctor James is on vacation. She is terrified of having to live one month without psychotherapy: "How am I going to get through this goddam month?" (243). Deirdre, who admits that she once became a nun, is searching for the spiritual connection in a world where her reality is based upon rejection and neglect by family and friends.

Unfortunately, Deirdre's relationship with Scooper is also characterized by neglect. While in analysis, Deirdre shared the same waiting room with Scooper, who failed to even notice her. Deirdre thus stereotyped Scooper as just another individual who exacerbated her feelings of alienation, isolation, and, in particular, neglect. She tells Scooper, "You became my father. My lovers. My teachers. My uncles.

My bosses. Every man who's ever gone out of his way to ignore me" (205). Her life has become a search for an identity, a quest for a committed relationship that would establish her dignity as a human being. Deirdre has even written a book, the fate of which is synonymous with her life of rejection: "Talk about neglected. It never took off the way they hoped. Out of print. No copies" (212). She has truly become the namesake her father gave her: Deirdre of the Sorrows.

The result is that there is no viable connection between Scooper and Deirdre; instead, they neglect each other. Scooper begins to understand the truth about their lives: "We spend all our time babbling to Herr Doktor across the street about ourselves and we don't figure in anyone's life. I bring my life to Doctor James and we turn my life into a lullaby until I am as fictional to myself as any one of these books are to me" (217). Scooper and Deirdre can have no relationship because neither of them has a viable life; they each live in a fantasy world of books that masks a fear of the reality of incessant neglect. The idyllic connection between Scooper and Deirdre culminates not in romance or erotic embrace but in violence. As is typical in Guare's plays, the frustration of being unable to connect in any spiritual way because our fantasies or our egoism interfere usually results in violence. Scooper begins ripping apart Deirdre's first editions in her book collection, screaming "I wish I were blind! And illiterate!" (217). Deirdre picks up the paper knife and stabs him with the weapon. Out of desperation they, in turn, each yell, "Doctor James, come back!" (218). They proceed to punch, stab, and attack each other, stopping only when they realize that Scooper is bleeding.

In act 2, Guare ties together the lives of Henny, Scooper, and Deirdre. The setting shifts to a hospital room where all three characters are maimed or injured: Henny recovering from mastectomy, Scooper bandaged and in a wheelchair from his encounter with Deirdre, and the latter on crutches. All three have been ravaged by neglect and are in need of some sort of spiritual healing to recover from their wounds. Scooper has returned to his mother's breast, his first connection, to attempt to make some sense out of his confused life. He is in Henny's room, not so much to comfort his mother, but rather due to personal reasons. He admits to Henny, "I'm having trouble with women" (220). Scooper believes that if he can connect with his mother, he will be able to establish relationships with other women, which thus far have gone awry. He acknowledges to Henny, "If I can straighten things out with you, maybe I can do it with all women—" (230). Scooper's reasoning is warped: he somehow is convinced that by making amends for the fact that he was not close to his dying mother, he will be able to connect with other women.

However, during their conversation, Scooper and Henny talk around each other rather than to each other. Scooper is chiefly concerned about resolving his personal problems and talks with his mother only to get information about his past, not to comfort her. After revealing that the mastectomy was only a temporary solution to the cancer that has probably spread into the lymph glands and may take years to ravage her body, Scooper offers Henny sleeping pills so she can commit suicide. Scooper would like to be rid of the guilt that he feels because of the way he neglected his mother; her death will allow him to start over with women. Henny, however, refuses to co-operate and flings the pills across the room, screaming, "You rotten little shit, do you think they're going to let me bring killer pills in here? These are for my gas. You'd have done it? You'd have let me die?" (239–40). Scooper's response is selfish: "I want you dead" (240); he is an egoist, the center of the universe, and can only commiserate about the aborted suicide attempt in which "Nothing's working out for me" (240).

At the end of the play, Henny reveals to Scooper the story behind the dream that has been plaguing her son for years. The blind woman does not realize that Scooper and Deirdre have left the room, embarking for Haiti to seek comfort from their surrogate father figure, Doctor James. Henny's confession ends with the need to touch her son: "This was my prayer. A better life for you" (248). She asks Scooper to take her hand and reaches out for him, but her effort to connect is in vain. The same image was present at the end of *Landscape of the Body* where Betty, in moving towards Captain Holahan, makes a lasting connection; in *Bosoms and Neglect*, however, the hands do not touch. Scooper and Deirdre are fully immersed in a facade, an artificial veneer that masks a spiritual connection that could lead to a physical relationship; they are so dependent on an illusory world of games that painful reality must be assuaged in therapy. Desperate to seek help from his psychiatrist and only concerned about his personal welfare, Scooper ignores his mother's attempt to connect while she is trying to recover from a ravenous illness. *Bosoms and Neglect* becomes a painful yet poignant indictment of a sick modern urban society where individuals prefer to take refuge behind fantasies that reinforce their egos rather than risk establishing committed spiritual relationships that take time and effort.

Landscape of the Body and *Bosoms and Neglect* reflect Guare's maturity as a dramatist. These two plays allow Guare to employ his most caustic black comedy to demonstrate the neuroses of the modern psyche. On the one hand, these dramas depict life in contemporary urban society as a nightmarish and grotesque groping for a deeper meaning behind the superficial facade of the dreams and illusions that sustain us daily. On the other hand, Guare demonstrates a comical pathos for the many individuals who are wounded by their inability to connect with someone because of values we cherish even when they can be harmful.

6

Atlantic City

O N 28 JULY 1979, FRENCH FILM DIRECTOR LOUIS MALLE TELE-
phoned Guare to solicit his help on his latest project. Malle, whose
film ventures included *Murmur of the Heart, The Fire Within, Lacombe,
Lucien, My Dinner With Andre, Au revoir les enfants,* and the controver-
sial *Pretty Baby,* admired Guare's plays, which he had seen in Paris
and at the Public Theater (where *Landscape of the Body* was being
produced in 1977), and thought that he would be ideal to work on
the screenplay for his next film. The project was being financed by
Canadian producers who were anxious to take advantage of a one
hundred percent tax write-off that the Canadian government was
offering to promote filmmaking in Canada. The producers, including a Winnipeg rabbi, had already raised $7.5 million for Malle to
direct a thriller that would star Susan Sarandon, Malle's girlfriend,
and an unnamed bankable male lead; to take advantage of the tax
break, the film had to be completed by the end of 1979. Malle had
already rejected one script when he suggested that the producers
consider Guare to write the screenplay. After doing some research
on Guare, the producers waivered about employing the talents of a
black humorist to work in an art form that appealed to a much wider
audience than the theater to which Guare had been accustomed.
Nevertheless, Malle defended his choice: "But I wanted him because
I liked his sense of the baroque, his feel for dialogue, his insight into
the relationships between people."[1]

Malle and Guare met in New York City to discuss the project.
Guare, mentioning relatives who told him about the renovations occurring in Atlantic City, suggested to Malle that the city might serve
as the ideal locale for shooting. Guare was particularly fascinated by
the transformation in Atlantic City from an old resort town to a gambling mecca controlled by the Las Vegas mob. He also had a contact
there: Anthony Raye, a friend of the family, years ago worked at the
Waldorf when Uncle Billy's wife stayed there to recuperate from her

Hollywood flings; Tony Raye was now manager of Resorts International, the first hotel to bring gambling to Atlantic City. Guare and Malle drove down to Atlantic City the next day where Tony Raye led them on a tour of this quickly changing vacation town. Guare was impressed and immediately recognized Atlantic City as a place where dreams were being envisioned. Guare remarked, "He showed us a city with no present. It's all future and all past."[2]

At the entrance to Resorts International, Guare and Malle noticed a perky woman working at an oyster bar, one of many hopeful blackjack dealers who first had to climb her way up the ladder before getting one of the more lucrative casino jobs; they both realized that she could be the model for the role Susan Sarandon was to play in the film. In an old photo album about Atlantic City, Guare came across a shot of a 1920s gangster convention; in the photo, Al Capone and his associates were on the boardwalk while the bodyguards lingered in the background. Guare focused on one young thug in particular. Guare thought that today this now elderly man would be the ideal choice to fall in love with the girl who worked in the oyster bar. All at once, the screenplay was forming in Guare's mind. The young woman, originally from Saskatchewan (the film is, after all, a Canadian production) moves into the building where the old gangster resides, and he soon begins to ogle her, envisioning her as a goddess.[3] The Betty Grable beauties who came to bond rallies in Atlantic City during World War II became the model for Grace, played by Kate Reid in the film. Guare admitted, "It was so fascinating, so puzzling, this strange city, half in the past, half in the future, these people with all their dreams . . . yesterday . . . tomorrow."[4] During the return trip to New York City, Guare and Malle agreed that they both shared a fascination for Atlantic City as the ideal locale for the movie, and by the time they arrived in Manhattan, they had worked out the characters for the film.

Malle returned to France the next day. On 10 August, Guare met Malle in Toulouse, carrying the first draft of the script with him. They spent one week hammering out the completed screenplay. When the producers arrived, Guare and Malle acted the script out for them. Now the rush was on to deliver the movie by the end of the year, which was the deadline that would have to be met in order to take advantage of the tax break. The script was sent to Burt Lancaster, who agreed to play Lou, the old gangster. Filming began on 31 October— only twelve weeks after Guare received the initial telephone call from Malle—and finished New Year's Eve. The interior scenes, although they appear to be shot in a dilapidated roominghouse near the Atlantic City boardwalk, were actually filmed in Montreal. At first, the producers objected to Guare's presence on the set, especially since the script was already completed. However, Malle placated them with the now-classic response: "If you have someone here for the hair, why not somebody for the words?"[5] The cast included Burt Lancaster, Susan Sarandon (who starred in Malle's *Pretty Baby*), Kate Reid (who played Henny in the original Chicago and New York productions of *Bosoms and Neglect*), Hollis McLaren, Michel Piccoli, and Robert Joy; Robert Goulet was featured in a cameo appearance.[6] During the shooting, Malle and Guare went with the cameraman to act out the scene at the next location before the actors played it for filming. Each evening, Guare would watch the rushes with Suzanne Baron, the film's editor. Guare made any necessary adjustments of the screenplay during the filming, since he was on the set all the time.[7]

Atlantic City matured into one of Guare's major successes. Guare told Anne Cattaneo that his collaboration with Louis Malle resulted into a wonderful working relationship: "When *Atlantic City* was finished, we looked at each other and said, that's exactly what we meant."[8] The film, originally titled *Atlantic City, U.S.A.*, was screened at the Venice Film Festival on 2 September 1980, with a running time of 104 minutes.[9] *Atlantic City* was then released 3 April 1981, in New York City, opening to critical acclaim that paid particular attention to Guare's impressive screenwriting. In 1981, Guare's achievement earned him the Best Screenplay Award from the National Society of Film Critics, the New York Film Critics' Circle Award, the Los Angeles Film Critics' Circle Award, the New Generation Prize for best screenwriting, as well as an Academy Award nomination. The film accrued other awards as well. Burt Lancaster, in probably the finest performance of his career, won the New York Film Critics' Circle Award, a British Academy Award, the Los Angeles Film Critics' Circle Award, and the National Society of Film Critics Award for best actor; Susan Sarandon, perfect as the young, googly-eyed Sally, was voted best actress by the Canadian equivalent of the Academy Awards. The film also won the Golden Lion Award at the Venice Film Festival. *Atlantic City* received five Academy Award nominations, including Best Director, Best Actor, Best Actress, Best Screenplay, and Best Picture. The *New York Times* voted it one of the ten best films of the year.

The dominant image that defines *Atlantic City* as a film that could not be transformed into a play is the city itself. Guare acknowledged, "*Atlantic City* could not have been done on stage because the documentary reality of the setting was absolutely necessary. The film's poetry was in that reality."[10] After the credits roll, we see one of Atlantic City's elegant buildings, the once-stately Marlborough-Blenheim Hotel, being dynamited; the movie concludes with the image of the wrecking ball destroying the old to make way for a new Las Vegas-type casino. Once a resort that catered to East Coast racketeers during Prohibition, a paradise for middle-class vacationers, characterized as Sin City in Thornton Wilder's depiction as a pleasure-going retreat in act 2 of his Pulitzer Prize-winning 1942 play, *The Skin of Our Teeth*, Atlantic City is now stripped of its former glamor in its quest to become Las Vegas with a beach, a trend that began when casino gambling was legalized there in 1976.[11]

The eradication of Atlantic City's grandiloquence, demonstrated through the demolition of its grand hotels and pleasure palaces, sets the stage for a tale about crumbling myths juxtaposed with dreams of the future. Atlantic City, a place where legends were immortalized and myths were created, now becomes the high-tech world where the future beckons. The romanticized view of the city gives way to the Las Vegas-type glamor of fantasy fulfillment. Through the sounds of the jackhammer and shovel that weave their way throughout the film, Guare and Malle constantly remind us, consciously and subliminally, that the passage of time is the central motif of the film. The setting becomes the perfect locale for a Chekhovian tale, similar to *The Cherry Orchard*, about the passing of the old order and its concomitant replacement by a new way of life; Firs dies, but Lopakhin prospers. Guare immediately recognized the Chekhovian parallels while filming on location: "Suddenly, we had a very Chekhovian story about all these different people, different styles, in one place. It was everything. Slick, stripped down, grotesque, bare, gaudy, baroque: that's what was so nourishing about the movie."[12] Vincent Canby, writing in the *New York Times*, described the film as a fine, perverse ghost story.[13] In this sense, *Atlantic City* recalls Ibsen's *Ghosts* in which the characters, particularly Mrs. Alving and her son Oswald, are defined by the past and cannot escape it, much like Lou; Captain Alving's reckless life as a seaman resulted in Oswald's syphilitic condition and defined Mrs. Alving's life for her. On the other hand, Regine, like Sally, looks to the future as they both share some of that Ibsenite "joy of life" and seek to escape the past rather than be affected by the "sins of the fathers." In her critique of *Atlantic City* for the *New Yorker*, Pauline Kael astutely noted the importance of the setting to produce the Chekhovian-Ibsenite effect Guare sought: "The whole city seems to be in deep focus; you're sharply aware of old and new, age and youth."[14]

Lou Pasco (Burt Lancaster) epitomizes the plight of Atlantic City, where myths and dreams are being demolished in favor of a homogenized venue that lacks the style and flair of the legends that inhabited this gambling mecca forty years earlier. Lou, like Artie Shaughnessy, is faced with a drab reality but dreams of a better life; whereas Artie hopes for a future in show business, Lou fantasizes about the past, which to him means an idyllic vision of a utopian society full of excitement and adventure where tough guys like him could admirably serve legendary gangsters.[15] Lou, modelled in part upon Guare's father, tries to maintain his sense of dignity in a world where the shallow and artificial have replaced legend and glamor. Pauline Kael suggests that this dichotomy between the real and the ideal epitomizes the bizarre fabric of Guare's black comedy: "This spa that became a racketeers' paradise during Prohibition and is now on its chaotic way to becoming Vegas with a beach is an improbable place; it gives a hallucinatory texture to the characters' lives."[16]

Lou seems to be be doing his share of hallucinating, especially since his drab life contrasts so sharply with his idyllic view of the past. During the grand era when the gangsters ran Atlantic City forty years earlier, Lou was nothing more than a glorified errand boy. Although he envisions himself as a bodyguard and former hit man for the mob, Lou was actually at the bottom of the hierarchy. Lou evokes a sense of pathos and dignity as he dresses in a suit and irons his only decent silk tie in order to make his daily rounds as a numbers runner collecting fifty-cent or dollar bets from Atlantic City's slum dwellers. He lives in a modest apartment in a dilapidated rooming house about to be demolished to make way for another new casino.

Lou's days are largely spent taking care of Grace (Kate Reid), his downstairs neighbor and formerly the wife of mobster Cookie Pinza, who had hired Lou as his flunky. Grace, a fading moll who is now mostly bedridden, depends on Lou to make breakfast for her, walk her dog and make sure the poodle receives its proper grooming, and run errands for her, just as he did for the gangsters years ago; Lou occasionally even services her sexually. Although Grace's health is fading almost as quickly as is the city's once-vibrant energy, Lou is attracted to her in the same way that he romanticizes about his fantasy-filled past. Grace initially came to Atlantic City as a teenager during World War II to compete in a Betty Grable lookalike contest.[17] After her husband Cookie died, she stayed in Atlantic City, maintaining her sense of dignity as the wife of an important gangster, a princess in her own mind. Lou views her as a link to the past where legends were immortalized and women were treated with gallantry.

Grace, as her name implies, believes she was close to royalty and now spends her days in a pink-walled room with a mirrored bed and a box of chocolates, dreaming of the days when molls drank champagne and pranced around in lucite heels filled with live goldfish. Meanwhile, Grace brings Lou back to reality when she reminds him that the racketeers referred to him as "Numb Nuts" and considered him too soft to be a hoodlum. Indeed, as Grace constantly reminds him, when the going got tough, Lou tended to run away from trouble and leave town.

Evading the reality of his cowardice, Lou envisions himself as a tough hoodlum who rubbed shoulders with the likes of Bugsy Siegel, Lucky Luciano, Dutch Schultz, and Meyer Lansky, all of whom "took a shine" to him. Michel Legrand's "Atlantic City: My Old Friend," sung by Paul Anka, becomes the perfect accompaniment to represent Lou's reminiscence of a idyllic past that was exhilarating when the city was immersed in style, panache, glory, and dignity. Lou reminds Grace that in those days he was on the Ten Most-Wanted List. Atlantic City years ago was an exciting resort town, the "lungs of Philadelphia," a place where gangsters could escape the big city and breathe freely as kings of all they surveyed. Lou tells Sally's husband Dave (Robert Joy) that in those days a person could dance to "real" songs, such as "Flat Foot Floogie With the Floy Floy." Trying to impress Dave, a young street punk, Lou reveals that he killed a few people in his glory days with the mob, and then, to wash away the stench and blood, he would dive into the Atlantic Ocean. Once refreshed, he was cleansed and ready to kill again. Lou's fixation on the idyllic world of the past is best represented in his conversation with Dave in which Lou delivers the most memorable lines in the film: "The Atlantic Ocean was something then. Yes, you should have seen the Atlantic Ocean in those days."[18]

What was exciting to Lou about illegal activity in Atlantic City years ago has been replaced by legalized gambling with Howard Johnson Hotels running a lily-pure, homogenized operation. Lou admits, "It's all shit now." Lou's numbers-running operation, considered an illegal activity that coincides with mobster machismo, has now been replaced by the sanctioned, controlled, innocuous activity of casino gambling. He prefers to reminisce with Buddy O'Brien, an old friend from the Prohibition era who has now become a washroom attendant and has descended on hard times like Lou but still remembers the glory years. The wholesome nature of the casinos, which cater to what Lou refers to as "nickel and dime stuff," has removed the glamor from the city, turning the exotic and adventurous Baghdad by the sea into

fun for the whole family. As the wrecking ball tears down the relics of
years past, we realize that the myths and dreams of Lou are echoed
by the changing shape of the city itself.

Lou gravitates to Sally Matthews (Susan Sarandon), a young, starry-
eyed opportunist. When we first see Lou as the credits roll during the
beginning of the film, he is playing the role of voyeur, watching his
next door neighbor as she performs the nightly ritual of rubbing
herself with lemons to remove the smell of seafood acquired during her evening's work at the oyster bar in the Resorts International
Casino and Hotel. Sally plays a tape cassette recording of the aria
"Casta diva" from Italian composer Vincenzo Bellini's opera, *Norma*,
as her immersion in lemons becomes a modern variation of Bellini's
mistletoe-cutting scene.[19] Once Lou meets Sally, he intuitively understands that they have something in common: they are both dreamers whose lives are based on healthy, yet all-too-consuming, myths.
Whereas Lou dreams of the mythical existence he never had as a
big-time racketeer years ago, Sally looks to the future for her hope
of a more fulfilling and rewarding life. She, like many of Guare's
protagonists, sees stars in her eyes and dreams of an exotic, idyllic
existence free from her drab reality. Sally married Dave (Robert Joy)
in order to escape the daily drudgery of Moose Jaw, Saskatchewan.
When Dave ran off with Chrissie (Hollis McLaren), Sally's younger
sister, and got her pregnant, Sally ventured to Atlantic City, hoping
to begin a new career as a card dealer, never looking back to return to parochial Moose Jaw. Sally believes that her days working as
a waitress in rural Moose Jaw are behind her; her goal is to travel
throughout the world, earning her living as a dealer in the European casinos. She is even listening to cassettes to learn French, which
she believes is the language of international diplomacy, and plays
educational tapes that teach her about French culture. Eventually,
she would like to become the first female croupier in Monte Carlo
and has taken a second job learning to deal blackjack in order to
achieve her lofty goals. She is in the right locale—Atlantic City, a
place where wealthy casino owners pitch fame and fortune to tourists
and to those who visit the city as a respite from the daily grind. Indeed, if Lou represents the old Atlantic City, Sally is like the new gambling town—forging ahead, destroying the old while looking towards
the future.

Lou understands that he has much in common with Sally and perhaps views her as the type of aspiring social climber that he himself
was forty years ago. Lou also realizes that Sally has class and dignity,
despite the fact that her life, like Lou's, reflects the drab reality of a

loser. Sally, after all, although an eager learner, is not a very adept blackjack dealer and is harassed by the Frenchman (Michel Piccoli) who is providing tutelage for her. She seems to have more success as a waitress at the oyster bar, a position similar to the one she had in Moose Jaw. Nevertheless, Lou recognizes a lot of himself in Sally, and, as a seasoned man of the world, he can offer her valuable advice. Sally views Lou as a successful, cultured person who can show her the way to succeed in the world of glitter and glamor. She implores Lou to "teach me stuff." Like Artie Shaughnessy, Lou is caught between two women. Grace, with her constant harangues belittling Lou about his failure to achieve his fantasies, is much like Bananas, whose physical and mental deterioration remind Artie, on a daily basis, that his life is closer to a zoo than to heaven in Hollywood. Sally reinforces Lou's fantasies in much the same way that Bunny represents a means of escape from Artie's family life; both Sally and Bunny look to the future and suggest to Lou and Artie, respectively, a more idyllic scenario. When Lou reveals that he watches her at night during her ablutions, Sally is not incensed but is instead moved by Lou's passion and honesty. Pauline Kael describes this emotional moment: "He pushes her blouse down from her shoulders and looks at her ripe young flesh, and his watery eyes are full of reverence and regret."[20] They make love together because they intrinsically share a deeply rooted passion for dreams, which they can see in each other's eyes.

Lou and Sally wind up sharing their dreams through a bizarre series of events similar to the farcelike quality of Guare's plays. At the beginning of the film, Dave and Chrissie seek out Sally at the Resorts International after hitchhiking ostensibly all the way from Canada. They both need a place to stay since Chrissie is pregnant and in need of a rest and Dave must hide out from mobsters who are after the cocaine he stole from them in Philadelphia. Sally, associating her sister and husband with her past life and thus disconnected from the idyllic future she has planned for herself, wants nothing to do with the two scoundrels. Lou takes a liking to Dave, who flatters the would-be racketeer by telling him that he is well known in Las Vegas among the mobsters there. Lou even assists Dave in selling some of the cocaine. When the two Philadelphia mobsters kill Dave in order to recover their drugs, Lou, left holding the stash, manages to make a profit by selling it to Dave's friends. With newfound prosperity in hand, Lou is able to play the role of sport and usher Sally around town, treating her to an elaborate lunch at an expensive restaurant and paying for Dave's funeral expenses, including flowers so Sally can make a good impression on her relatives. Initially, when the mobsters rough up Sally on the street while looking for the cocaine that her husband stole from them, Lou is helpless to thwart the assault. Later, when the racketeers threaten Sally at the casino, Lou ignores the diversion, fleeing from trouble as usual. However, when the two hoodlums corner Sally and Lou on the street a second time, demanding that Lou turn over the money earned by selling the cocaine, he pulls out a handgun, killing both of them. This allows Lou and Sally to flee, bonding together as co-conspirators on the lam from local authorities.

With their newly acclaimed status as murderers eluding the police, Lou and Sally spend the night on the outskirts of Atlantic City. Seizing the opportunity for the first time to make it "big" in underworld circles, Lou, now playing his role to the hilt, ditches the murder weapon and then hides out from the law as well as from the racketeers. He proudly reveals that this is the first time he has been out of Atlantic City in twenty years, a definite change in his persona. Lou at last has the chance to live out his dreams as a big-time hoodlum who now has gained notoriety. Drinking champagne together, Lou and Sally watch the evening news, where they discover that Atlantic City police are on the lookout for the dangerous murderer who has disrupted the normal complacency of their resort town. A composite sketch of the murderer is flashed across the television screen and is printed the following day in the newspapers. Lou is so enamored with his newly gained status that he envisions taking Sally to Florida to showcase his success for his former cronies.

During their evening of glory in the motel on the outskirts of the city, Lou reveals to Sally that he never murdered anyone in his life until that day. Lou admits that his only contact with Bugsy Siegel was when the former was in jail for a drunk and disorderly offense and met the notorious hoodlum during his ten-minute stopover on the way to Leavenworth. The following morning, when Sally takes Lou's money in order to flee for France, Lou willingly lets her go. He has seen her fired after six weeks of training to become a dealer and has watched her get thrown out of the casino, her place of dreams. Yet Lou realizes that he shares a strong bond with Sally: they are the working class, the forgotten "little people" whose dreams fuel their otherwise drab lives, filled almost daily with disappointment and frustration. When Sally leaves, Lou probably realizes that he will never see her again. Instead of disappointment, Lou is flattered when Sally reminds him, "You saved my life." Lou can now bask forever in the glory of knowing that he asserted his manhood while defending the honor of a young, beautiful woman. He reminds her to ditch the car, implying that he knows that she is abandoning him but that he has decided to let go of the reins in order to allow her to pursue her idyllic dreams.

Unlike Guare's plays in which the black comedy underscores the ongoing search for meaning in a world where our dreams and idyllic visions are constantly shattered, *Atlantic City* winds up closer to a Feydeau farce where everything that originally went awry eventually, through a strange turn of events, winds up righted. Rather than having their dreams humiliate them into a pathetic condition, Lou and Sally have their dreams confirmed. Lloyd Rose notes, "Violent, funny, and amoral, *Atlantic City* affirms the strength of the American dream, which rises in all its acquisitiveness and hopefulness, along with the new casinos, from the rubble of buildings torn down and days gone by."[21] Sally is all smiles as she leaves Lou behind and listens to an educational radio program discussing the wines of France. Monte Carlo awaits, and Lou, a relic of the past, has no place in her future plans. In turn, Lou returns to Atlantic City, where he will now have a firmer conviction of himself as a mobster living in the glory days of yesteryear. As Lou and Grace stroll the boardwalk, arm in arm, we grasp that the prince and princess have virtually reached Nirvana. *Atlantic City*, one of Guare's finest black comedies, ends as most classical comedies do—with a sense of reconciliation. The protagonists survive largely because their dreams have provided them with the type of vitality and energy that Guare so much admires.

7

The Tetralogy

IN THE LATE 1970S, WHEN GUARE'S CAREER WAS PROSPERING AS HE mastered the fine art of black comedy, he began exploring how the modern *angoisse* developed out of nineteenth-century American history. Guare sensed that the loss of spirituality in contemporary American society could be traced to the moral decay omnipresent after the Civil War. Guare saw himself becoming typecast as a New York writer and wanted to explore not only a more ubiquitous American persona but also a part of his own past as well. Living in Nantucket, with his father's family originally from Gloucester, Massachusetts, and Montpelier, Vermont, and his mother's ancestors from not-too-distant Lynn, Massachusetts, Guare became interested in re-creating the roots of American history through his New England genealogy. Guare explained to Robert Berkvist his reasons for venturing into the past in search of new material for his theater: "I wanted to invent my own world. I wanted to write about material that belonged only to me. I mean, when you're living in America, in New York City, in 1982, you find there are a lot of people reeling out of the same shocks of experience."[1] Guare is suggesting that he tried to use his art as a means to find out more about himself and his ancestry.

Guare had the idea of the Lydie Breeze tetralogy since the mid-1970s, but the impetus for the writing derived from an incident that occurred when he was living in Nantucket. He recalled a Polish woman for a long time in exile from her home intently instructing her niece on the beach. Guare wondered what this Polish woman was teaching the young lady:

> And that image of this woman and this girl made me think, where do we get our information about life? We all have to live our lives based on these little shards of knowledge. Half the time we have to make up our information as we go along, but I thought, how do we learn how to live? That's what the plays came out of—just that question.[2]

Thus, as is often true for Guare, he began with an image and tried to explore the story behind the event. He stated, "In writing the *Lydie Breeze* plays, I wanted to go into a world where I didn't know anything, where I would be lost."[3] Guare thus abandoned the familiar world of New York City and contemporary urban life to venture into New England in the 1860s—when his grandparents were born. By replacing the point of departure from New York City to Nantucket, Guare admitted that he invented a world that would live up to his dreams while forsaking a microcosm that had become "pretty thin gruel for playwrights."[4] He began by trying to determine how America developed from its utopian dreams in the nineteenth century to our modern neuroses: "What is the Puritan truth, the Calvinist punishment that affected us? It's more than just a personal interest when I see how willed consciousness is passing into willed unconsciousness, a fast-food life."[5] Living in Nantucket provided Guare with the incentive to come to terms with the roots of our modern malaise as well as with the underpinnings of family myths and legends—personal stories that he overheard but would now have the chance to unravel through his imagination.

Guare obviously also realized that farce and black comedy would no longer be suitable as forms to represent nineteenth-century American history and culture. This gave Guare the opportunity to explore his dramatic heritage in the nineteenth century. Guare admitted, "the movies had taken over what the stage used to do. And what the stage used to do has always haunted me."[6] Guare has always been fascinated by nineteenth-century plays, particularly Ibsen. Moreover, Guare read many nineteenth-century novels, especially those written by Wilkie Collins, Henry James, and George Eliot; his interest in the subject peaked with Leon Edel's massive five-volume study of Henry James. Guare also began reading James's own writings and became intrigued by his fascination with the past: "He traveled back to Europe like some mysterious *wounded ship*, trying to make sense of the past. So there's that pull, that tension between where we've been and where we're going, that I wanted to explore. I wanted to make that time come alive—there was so much juice in it."[7] Guare's goal was to make nineteenth-century American history come alive on stage through a form that was closer to the nineteenth-century realism of the novel. Due mainly to the epic quality of the tale needed to be told and the aesthetic enjoyment Guare received from the genre itself and not for reasons of nostalgia, he tried to mesh the nineteenth-century novel with the drama. Guare acknowledged, "I realized that I was not trying to put a novel on stage, but was drawing on 19th-century techniques to remove the squalor from the word that now lies there splat in the modern gutter: melodrama. To find the emotional truth behind 19th-century melodrama."[8] Guare was also interested in exploring nineteenth-century theatrical techniques because he felt that contemporary drama was becoming too minimalist, merely a theater of images that a strong director could shape according to his or her whims.[9] Rather than conceiving of one of his plays as an unshaped libretto, Guare, seeking the nineteenth-century novel's thrust to keep long threads of narrative alive, sought to explore the conventions of realism and melodrama.

In attempting to move away from farce and black comedy and into nineteenth-century realism, Guare became more familiar with the masters of the modern theater, particularly Ibsen, Strindberg, Chekhov, and O'Neill. In order to transform the nineteenth-century novel onto the stage, Guare had to learn a different ear for dialogue and for stage rhythms. By delving into his own imaginative vision of life in New England and by concomitantly working with a different form of drama, Guare, while exploring his literary and historical heritage, was expanding his talents as he experimented with dramatic structure to learn more about what works on stage. In June 1982, Guare realized that in writing the tetralogy, "I'm trying to find a different form, a different use for language. I'm trying to be more rigorous with myself."[10] Earlier that year, in February, Guare had elaborated on how writing *Lydie Breeze* expanded his horizons as a playwright:

> I wanted to use historical events to find a different response. I also wanted to create a world where I could write in a heightened language, a world where I could create the rules, where I was responsible—and a world where the past had shaped the present. It was a way of making greater demands on myself, a way to pull myself into deeper waters.[11]

Guare finished writing the first act of *Lydie Breeze* in 1978 and then returned to it on 4 May 1979, the morning after *Bosoms and Neglect* was vilified by the critics during its Broadway debut; this is consistent with Guare's need to have a play in the works once his latest drama is being dissected by reviewers. Within four months, Guare had completed the play; *Lydie* was then given a staged reading by three performers at Michael Bennett's studio in Manhattan. This workshop was quite a success and gave Guare the idea to develop a tetralogy that would cover thirty years of American history from the 1860s to the 1890s. The tetralogy would be Guare's version of the fall of American utopianism, on a similar order to Faulkner's saga of Yoknapatawpha County. *Lydie Breeze*, the first play of the tetralogy, is chronologically the last, occurring in Nantucket in 1895, years after the commune had been dismantled. *Gardenia*, the second play of the tetralogy, was finished in 1982 and describes the events occurring twenty years earlier (in the commune during 1875) and in 1884 at Charlestown Prison, where Joshua Hickman is serving time for the murder of Dan Grady. *Women and Water*, written in draft form in 1984, was the third part of the tetralogy; the audience is now taken back to 1861 and 1864 during the Civil War to learn the events leading up to the creation of Lydie's utopian dream. *Bulfinch's Mythology*, the last segment of the tetralogy to be completed, occurring one year after the events of *Gardenia* and thus the third in chronological order, was begun in 1984.[12] Guare admitted having difficulty writing the last play in the tetralogy: "One thing though: Moncur, the boy who holds the key to it, dies in *Women and Water*. And after I lost him, I realized that he must be alive. It was a mistake. He is a key for *Bulfinch's Mythology*. I couldn't carry the plot without him. So I had to go back and unravel that. But generally the characters were all very clear in my head."[13] When Guare revised *Women and Water*, he changed the ending to allow Moncure to escape to Canada, presumably to build his own utopia there; but it seems clear that Guare was not quite sure how to fit the pieces of the puzzle together to make this last play work. As of this writing, *Bulfinch's Mythology* has not been staged or published.

Although Guare began *Lydie Breeze* in 1978, he started seriously rewriting the draft in late 1979. By late November 1979, the play was pared from its three-and-a-half-hour's length and reduced from "lots of characters" to merely seven; in addition, a chorus of six actors was deleted.[14] At this point, the play was being rewritten for Jason Robards and Frank Langella, with Meryl Streep supposedly waiting in the wings to play young Lydie. *Lydie Breeze* premiered on 25 February 1982 at the off-Broadway American Place Theater in a production by Roger S. Berlind and John Wulp, the latter having created the sets for *Marco Polo Sings a Solo* and having co-produced *Bosoms and Neglect*. Louis Malle marked his directing debut for the New York theater with this production, after having successfully collaborated with Guare on *Atlantic City*. The cast, which did not feature Robards, Langella, or Streep, included Cynthia Nixon (Lydie), Roberta Maxwell (Beaty), Josef Somer (Joshua), Robert Joy (Jude), Madeleine Potter (Gussie), and Ben Cross (Jeremiah). Willa Kim designed the costumes, Glen Roven composed the music, and Jennifer Tipton arranged the lighting effects.

Lydie Breeze's run at the American Place Theater received favorable notices from only three critics: Howard Kissel (*Women's Wear Daily*), Jack Kroll (*Newsweek*), and Edith Oliver (*New Yorker*).[15] Oliver claimed that the first act was mystifying but seemed placated that the confusion was resolved in the latter part of the play—a trifle she was willing to tolerate as one of Guare's theatrical innovations.[16] Describing Guare's vision as poignant as well as nightmarish, Kissel praised the play as complex, rich, imaginative, and mesmerizing, superbly staged by Malle.[17] Kroll claimed that the play was Guare's most ambitious to date—lyrical, elegiac, melodramatic, humorous, and sorrowful—and was glad to see Malle contain Guare's "anarchic energy" in an ensemble that he described as beautifully organic.[18] On the whole, these three critics praised the cast and the overall quality of the production.

The majority of the critics gave *Lydie Breeze* harsh reviews. Several critics put the blame squarely on Guare's script. T. E. Kalem, writing for a wide audience in *Time*, described the play as consisting of vivid imagery, gnarled symbolism, "gothic dry rot," and sporadically placed humor, all of which combined to create an implausible drama.[19] Clive Barnes (*New York Post*) and Rex Reed (*Daily News*) admitted that they were stymied by the play: the former acknowledged that *Lydie Breeze* "might be symbolic," although the lack of a clear purpose undermined any poignancy[20]; the latter called the drama "pretentious idiocy," preposterous and confusing to the point that he thought it might be one of Guare's comedies.[21] Richard Gilman's review in the *Nation* criticized the play as "a lurid tale" of false lyricism without substance.[22] Robert Brustein (*New Republic*) accused Guare of writing a clumsy, implausible plot and creating unconvincing characters, all of which made him believe that Guare's play was more like a rough sketch or a draft awaiting another rewrite.[23] Douglas Watt (*Daily News*), agreeing with his colleague, Rex Reed, lamented that the play, stylish and abstruse but also verging on balderdash, can be reduced to nothing more than imagery and atmosphere.[24] Allan Wallach (*Newsday*) placed some of the blame (and praise) squarely on Guare for his "mad mix of elements" while suggesting that Malle had not "found a way to give the play's overabundance a shape and unified style."[25] Humm (*Variety*) explained that this "murky opus" was the result of the characters representing attitudes rather than dimensioned people and that most of the action is indirect—either offstage or descriptions of past events, thus precluding the play from a Broadway run.[26] In his usual harsh diatribe, John Simon (*New York*), acknowledging that even Glen Roven's music was out of place, stated that nothing could save *Lydie Breeze*, which he characterized as "a murky, turgid, implausible, melodramatic tale," essentially reduced to "disjointed, garish, and vacuous claptrap."[27] Several of the critics commended John Wulp for his impressionistic scenic design. However, they were divided about the quality of the acting; although most critics praised the cast's performances as impeccable, Simon and Brustein called the acting uneven while Reed complained that the performers appeared akin to mental patients roaming the halls of Bedlam.[28] The result was that *Lydie Breeze* closed a few days before *Gardenia* opened at the Manhattan Theater Club in late April 1982.

Despite the harsh criticism from the New York reviewers, *Lydie Breeze* has been somewhat successfully staged by college and repertory theater troupes. One of its most notable productions was at the New Playwrights Theatre in Washington, D.C., where it was performed on alternate nights with *Gardenia* from late May 1984 until 8 July.[29] James Nicola and Lloyd Rose directed a fine cast that seemed to make the melodramatic elements work in a way that the New York production failed to do. Clarity was also probably the forte of Rondi Reed's production of *Lydie Breeze* at the Steppenwolf Theatre Company in Chicago, opening on 18 May 1986.[30] The overall high quality of the acting and directing in this production accentuated Guare's intense lyricism and made his complex narrative structure less problematic for the audience.

The first draft of the play was based upon an adaptation of Ibsen's *The Lady From the Sea*, with Lydie Breeze in the role of Ellida, Ibsen's "Lady." The original title was *Annie Breeze*, but as Guare explains, "Annie Breeze was my great-grandmother, but there're so many Annies around, I changed it to Lydie, a great-aunt."[31] Guare soon abandoned the idea of adapting Ibsen and began to focus on re-creating, and thus discovering, his family ancestry through his imaginative vision. He began with images that he had of his family, mythologizing the statements that he overheard at funerals and as part of the family's lore. Guare explains how he combined fact and fiction: "It's a way of using things overheard. It's a way of using things that one could never put together, that no one ever questioned, facts that were just there. . . . But there are certain events that are as happened and others that are inventions."[32]

Despite Guare's intentions to abandon an adaptation of Ibsen's *The Lady From the Sea*, Ibsenite elements inundate *Lydie Breeze*. The dominant motif of failed utopian dreams demonstrated by the syphilitic condition that has spread throughout the commune and the concomitant legacy of a maimed generation of offspring is derived from

Ibsen's *Ghosts*. Although syphilis was the inferred but never mentioned result of the "sins of the fathers" in Ibsen's play, Guare, unlike his nineteenth-century mentor, explicitly uses the world a couple of times in *Lydie Breeze*. Moreover, just as Mrs. Alving, in choosing to remain with her husband, Captain Alving, inadvertently passed syphilis on to her son, Lydie, infected by Dan Grady, passed the disease on to his son, Jeremiah; now, Jeremiah, like Oswald Alving, has returned home to come to terms with his tainted ancestry. Finally, the mood of the play, with its evocative imagery, symbolic language, and emphasis on suggestion rather than didacticism, serves to move the play away from an exploration of sociological issues that marked naturalist drama of the nineteenth century but is much closer to the impressionism of Ibsen's late plays, especially *The Lady From the Sea, Rosmersholm, Little Eyolf,* and *John Gabriel Borkman*. In this respect and with no clear-cut resolution of the action in the denouement, *Lydie Breeze* can also be conceived of as modelled on Chekhov's mature impressionist plays, which are structured more as mood pieces rather than being plot-driven.[33]

Ibsen and Chekhov seem to be Guare's models for the form, language, and mood of *Lydie Breeze*, while various segments of the play also have a European legacy. The curse on the family/commune seems to be taken from the fatelike force that runs throughout much of Greek tragedy; the blight on the land in *Oedipus the King*, to use one example, is now the poisoned dream of a diseased utopia. Protagonists in classical Greek drama who tried to defy their fate rather than seek forgiveness eventually wound up spiritually maimed, much like the characters in *Lydie Breeze*. Following in the tradition of classical Greek drama, much of the action and gory details occur offstage. Guare's play also evokes Shakespeare, particularly *The Tempest*. Nantucket becomes an idyllic island kingdom where Prospero, now in the role of Joshua Hickman, has thrown down his mantle, his manuscript, *Prolegomena to Duty*.[34] This is a significant image in the tetralogy because the idea of recording narrative events in a journal occurs throughout these plays but is abandoned in *Lydie Breeze*, where no one is keeping a written record of the events. Furthermore, as Lloyd Rose has noted, the notion of forgiveness, and in particular, the reconciliation of fathers and daughters, is manifested in Shakespeare's late comedies, especially *The Tempest*.[35] Guare also drew inspiration from Mary Shelley's *Frankenstein*. Jeremiah Grady is actually modelled on Shelley's Monster, a divided creature with his own feelings yet a product of the whims of others who have shaped him and made him into a surrogate of their dreams and desires. Understanding the dynamics of the image of the Monster enhances and exacerbates the gothic atmosphere that permeates the play.

Although the European legacy plays a major part in *Lydie Breeze*, most of the play's antecedents are derived from American literature. Throughout the play, the gothic overtones on Nantucket echo Nathaniel Hawthorne's New England; the curse on Lydie's utopia seems to parallel the decline of the Pyncheons in Hawthorne's *The House of the Seven Gables*. *Lydie Breeze* begins with Lydie's daughter, blind from an accident and thus dead to the external world, seeking to communicate with her mother's corpse, evoking the short stories of Edgar Allan Poe. Indeed, Guare's tale of the destruction of utopian dreams has much in common with Poe's melancholic gothic saga of the fall of the House of Usher. However, although Poe's sensibility impregnates much of *Lydie Breeze*, the play clearly ends with the sentiments of Walt Whitman near the turn of the century. Joshua persuades his daughter to read Whitman's short poem, "On the Beach at Night Alone," from *Leaves of Grass*. The cynical and foreboding start of a play that echoes Poe with images of shutters banging in the wind where no breeze is present wind up as Whitman's optimistic message in which "a vast similitude interlocks all," including all souls, living and dead.[36] Progressing from the gothic to Whitman (which parallels American literary history in the nineteenth century), Joshua teaches his daughter to read, which opens her sensibilities to something other than just oral history. Finally, Guare's play owes a debt to Eugene O'Neill. Guare's sense of "the haunted" and how the ubiquitous nature of death and destruction after the Civil War worked in a fatelike way is quite similar to the New England saga of the Mannon family in *Mourning Becomes Electra*. One may also recall that by setting thē mythical tone for *Desire Under the Elms* in nineteenth-century New England, O'Neill conveyed the sin and brutality that became the unconscious collective impulse for modern American history. And Guare's use of the fatelike force behind the destruction of nineteenth-century American utopianism, although ostensibly derived from Greek tragedy, may be seen in O'Neill's *Anna Christie*, where the sea's omniscience determines the fate of star-crossed lovers and doomed families.

Melodrama seems to be the genre that ties together the British and American antecedents of the tetralogy. Melodrama is certainly apropos as a starting point for Guare, who is using Ibsen and O'Neill as his models, especially when one recalls that Ibsen often began with melodramatic conventions and turned them into serious dramas, and O'Neill's early and middle dramas, certainly through *Beyond the*

Horizon to *Anna Christie* and continuing with *Mourning Becomes Electra* and *Strange Interlude,* contained elements typically found in that tradition. The tetralogy is based on the conventions of melodrama—a series of misfortunes, implausible coincidences, mistaken identities, and the gothic sensationalism of murder, disease, mutilation, poisoned sex, suicide, madness, and long-lost secrets that made the genre so much of a cliché.

Guare's starting point in *Lydie Breeze* is a nuclear family that becomes a metaphor for an extended American family. Guare began with his personal exploration of family lore passed down through generations of whisperings and recriminations. He characterized *Lydie Breeze* as "a play dealing with the shambling remnants of a dream and how children survive their parents' disasters."[37] The dominant image of disaster in the play is syphilis, suggesting that the past is like an infection, a social disease ravaging our present and future lives. Thus, Guare, writing about idealists who seek to form a much better life for themselves, finds them compromised by a past that traps and haunts them. *Lydie Breeze* is essentially Guare's *Ghosts*: like the Alvings who are spiritually and, in the case of Oswald, physically *vermoulu,* the members of the commune are spiritually and physically maimed in 1895 Nantucket. The characters in *Lydie Breeze* meet again to exorcise the past that keeps haunting them in the present. Louis Malle, who directed the play off-Broadway, told Ross Wetzsteon, "The play's about finding peace, about dealing with the past, facing it, getting rid of it"; Guare added, "It's about wounds and healing."[38] After all, the title of the play suggests that the focus is on a dead character from the past whose spirit lingers interminably in the present.

Guare's forte is his ability to extend the nuclear family into a metaphor for the failure of the American Dream. Guare's search for connection in a spiritually maimed modern society, the dominant motif of his black comedy, is now transformed as the search for the soul that America lost at the end of the nineteenth century. The chronology that Guare creates becomes the key to understanding the parallels between the nineteenth and twentieth centuries. The utopian community of the tetralogy was founded near the end of the Civil War, but by the turn of the century, the idealistic dreams petered out and became nothing more than the fantasies of the young. This parallels the commune ideal of the 1960s that failed shortly after the Vietnam War era. Guare wants to explore the poisonous effects that infected American society after the Civil War and how they parallel the dissipation of the American Dream after Vietnam. What was the ravaging effect in our history that caused the sense of alienation and isolation in contemporary society? Guare views the turn of the century as the ideal time to rectify this apocalyptic slide toward the moral decay of our nation and a chance to come to terms with a past that was once full of dreams and idealism but is now much more consistent with broken promises.[39]

Lydie Breeze is set on Nantucket, the site of a once-prosperous commune named Aipotu (Utopia spelled backwards), which was created near the end of the Civil War by nurse Lydie Breeze, Joshua Hickman, Dan Grady, and Amos Mason.[40] Now, years later, in 1895, this utopian society seems to have fallen victim to a curse that has withered the family and virtually devastated the land. The foreboding signs suggest that near the turn of the century, the modern Wasteland awaits; the American Dream of the nineteenth century has been eroded. Lydie Breeze, initially viewed as "a saint,"[41] has committed suicide by hanging herself as a result of Joshua's murder of Dan Grady, who, in the free spirit of communal living, was also Lydie's lover. The result of the grand dream of a perfect society expressed in Lydie's utopian experiment has been the spread of social disease: Dan infected Lydie with syphilis, who knowingly passed it on to Jeremiah, Dan's thirteen-year-old son; Jeremiah, in turn, gives the disease to Beaty, the Irish serving girl living with the Hickmans. Thus, as in *Ghosts*, the syphilis represents the albatross of the past but also suggests that the free love of the utopian spirit, the American Dream associated with the establishment of the commune, has been tainted. Joshua laments to Jeremiah this sense of loss: "No love. No love at all. We used to read here. We used to have knowledge here. We used to dream here. America could have been great, my Jeremiah, but we never trusted our dreams" (36). The creation of the commune was once synonymous with the moral spirit of Emerson embodying the nineteenth-century notion that individual regeneration must precede social or political development. Joshua, talking to himself, remembers the idyllic past: "You thought Walden was a dream? Walden was a Buffalo Bill Wild West Show compared to the austere moral splendor of our model community" (38). The dream has now degenerated into corruption and moral turpitude, a spiritual loss. The corruption and devastation is physical as well: Aipotu has been hit by a hurricane, leaving it isolated. Lydie explains to Jeremiah the physical devastation: "The waves were so high we thought the whole island would go. This house is the only house out here now and soon this land will go too" (24).

The commune is now tainted, almost as if the utopian dream is diseased or infected from within. Instead of being ingratiated by the spirit of Emerson, Aipotu more closely resembles the legacy of Poe.

Referred to as "The House of Usher" (41), Aipotu is now reduced to the gothic sensibilities concerned with exorcising ghosts from the past and neurotic obsessions with the dead. Robert F. Gross describes what appears to be a curse on the house: "Originally the site of an experiment in communal living, 'Aipotu,' the house has degenerated into a dilapidated hulk that echoes with memories of violence and loss."[42] Aipotu, which originally was begun as the promise of an enlightened future, a means of eradicating the past, has now ironically sunk to an obsession with the past. The commune now consists of isolated individuals whose sense of mourning replaces the spiritual vitality that once formed the focal point of their ancestors' idealism.

Fifteen-year-old Lydie Hickman, supposedly the daughter of Lydie Breeze, has certainly been adversely affected by the curse on the household.[43] Whereas her mother was a nurse, a caregiver who healed others, Lydie Hickman is now the one in need of spiritual and physical comfort. Traumatized by her father's murder of Dan Grady, his subsequent imprisonment, and the suicide of her mother as a result of Joshua's violence, Lydie is living a burnt-out existence, virtually isolated and ostracized on Nantucket. In contrast to her mother's grace and savoir-faire, which included an imaginative vision partly accrued from her love of the great tradition in American literature, Lydie is semi-literate. Rather than reading Whitman's poetry, Lydie is learning at the feet of Beaty, a servant herself tainted with syphilis, the family curse. Instead of Lydie going to school, Beaty, in a perverse sort of way, provides Lydie with her education. In the gothic spirit of Poe, Beaty inculcates Lydie with ritualistic chants similar to those found in the Mass in order to resurrect the spirit of Lydie Breeze's ghost: "Hoc Est Enim Corpus. Hoc Est Enim. And the priest eats the flesh of Christ and Christ is alive for one more day. We must keep your mother alive" (6). Moreover, Beaty's instruction is primarily oral, and although she has taught her the alphabet, Lydie's writing skills are inadequate. Guare views this as the disastrous effects of the curse: "The key image in each play is a journal. The cycle is all about books, about the printed word."[44] In *Lydie Breeze*, the oral tradition has replaced the printed word until Joshua reads Whitman to Lydie at the end of the play.

Lydie has been spiritually maimed. After the murder of Dan Grady tore the commune apart, she had been haunted by the past. Unsure about whether her father was Dan Grady, Joshua Hickman, or even Amos Mason, Lydie is confused about her origins. Joshua, supposedly her father, is perceived as a traitor by Beaty, who constantly reinforces Lydie with this notion: "And those men betrayed you. Your father betrayed her" (8). Lydie has taken the past personally and believes she is partly responsible for her fate. She tells her elder sister Gussie, "Ma killed herself. Maybe over something I did" (16). The result is that Lydie is deeply disturbed and has tried to emulate her mother's suicide. Lydie describes to Jeremiah how her mother hanged herself: "Her own hand. Bought the rope. Tied the rope. Put her neck into the rope. I've done that. Put my head in a noose to see what it feels like" (24). This deeply rooted family tragedy has caused Lydie to become distrustful of others and deeply resentful. She does not even trust her own father, whom she describes as "an evil man" (24). When Joshua inadvertently puts nosedrops in Lydie's eyes instead of eyedrops, she accuses him of malice: "My father tried to make me blind because I might see him for the evil that put him in prison" (24).

Lydie Hickman's physical degeneration coincides with her spiritual maiming. The result of her mother's legacy is a syphilitic infection; instead of being at ease, she is constantly dis-eased. Furthermore, Lydie was blinded on the Fourth of July when several boys exploded fireworks and the glass flew into her eyes. Thus, even on a day ostensibly reserved for celebration, Lydie is cursed with bad luck. Lydie, however, accepts this temporary loss of sight merely as a sign, a means for her to come to terms with her ghosts. The blindness causes her to turn inward; rather than find her self, she becomes more introspective. She tells Beaty, "I am safe. I am my mother. Losing my sight is a present from her. Dead to the world so she can come in me" (8). The play, then, becomes the struggle for Lydie to find herself despite the overwhelming stigma of the past (the title suggests that it is her mother's spirit that pervades the play, not Lydie's) that has turned her into a social outcast, as well as a physical and psychological wreck.

Lydie Hickman has come to rely on Beaty, the servant girl who nurtures her and has single-handedly raised her; Beaty proves to be a feeble role model, for she is virtually mentally ill herself. If Lydie's life is defined in the past by her mother's absence, in turn, Beaty's existence is distinguished by one particular traumatic experience. Years ago, thirteen-year-old Jeremiah Grady impregnated Beaty on the beach, the latter acquiescing to the sexual encounter because she fantasized that her lover was Amos Mason. Beaty, reduced to the role of a servant having sex with the master (Amos), much like Strindberg's Jean in *Miss Julie,* used young Jeremiah to fulfill her fantasy (45). Jeremiah, not realizing that he was infected with syphilis, had sex with Beaty on the beach. Beaty makes it clear to Lydie that this traumatic experience haunts her and makes her present life intolerable:

A little sore came on me. Like a red jewel. This man had given me a red jewel. The jewel grew in size. Another red jewel appeared. My body made fluids that were like poison. The sores moved onto my lips. My face was distorted. That man on this beach had put poison in me. (26)

Beaty, like Lydie Hickman, is cursed with an affliction from the past, which becomes so overbearing that past and present become merged as one big nightmare. During the second encounter on the beach with Jeremiah, which occurs years later, Beaty, obviously demented, still confuses Jeremiah with Amos. She longs to merge into eternity with her fantasy lover, suggesting that they tip the boat over in the ocean. Beaty entices Jeremiah: "You'll be home. Let the earth forget its dreamers. Take me to the sea. Wash away all the pain. I forgive you. Take me to the sea" (46). The expiation of guilt leads them to a double suicide—death by drowning.

Joshua Hickman, the only original surviving member of the commune still living on Nantucket, is the third beleaguered member of the troika. Describing himself as "a man who ached for a utopia" (55), Joshua is now reduced to an embittered alcoholic, a shell of his former self. His albatross is history gone awry. Joshua's optimistic American Dream of a utopian community has been completely shattered with little chance of its reemergence. Joshua, after killing his best friend and serving time in prison, watched as his wife committed suicide because of the murder, thus marking the destruction of Aipotu, his dream. Joshua's idealism has now turned to apathy and cynicism. Once a forceful man who survived the battle scars of the Civil War, Joshua, after his dreams have dissipated, is now disenfranchised from the America he so loved. Robert F. Gross astutely suggests that Joshua is "the Fisher King in Guare's Waste Land."[45] Certainly, Joshua's guilt is overwhelming; for example, he admits to Jeremiah, "I've done time for what I did to your Pa. He was my closest friend. I do time every day missing him. I'm paying prices" (29). Suffering from many sleepless nights, Joshua cannot escape the curse of the ghosts from the past. The day Joshua found Lydie's body after she hanged herself, he tried to cleanse himself of the guilt by swimming out to sea; every day, he completes the same ritual, almost as if he were compelled to fight the curse on a daily basis. Acknowledging that he has virtually gone to the grave with Lydie, Joshua's bereavement has extended beyond the normal time of mourning and has degenerated into a curmudgeonly disengagement from life.

Once a promising writer, Joshua has abandoned any plans for artistic creation. After the commune disintegrated, Joshua seemed to relinquish his dream of a literary vocation as well. However, this Prospero drowning his book is a sign of degeneration, not renewal. If, as Guare mentions, "The cycle is all about books, about the printed word,"[46] then Joshua's abdication of his vocation and his writing skills becomes seminal: not only is no journal kept, but also Joshua's daughter, barely able to read, will be unable to record historical events. In short, Joshua's embitterment has allowed him to abdicate the most fundamental responsibilities—the education of his daughter. Lydie, in turn, views her father as evil, and rather than forgive him for his past transgressions, she reinforces the blame for virtually everything he does. Joshua, then, is a pariah even in the eyes of his own daughter.

Rather than allow the destruction of Aipotu to degenerate into a family's personal tragedy, Guare's play implies that the loss of idealism moves from the nuclear to an extended family—the decline of American social consciousness at the end of the nineteenth century. The idealistic sense of community sharing propagated by the creators of Aipotu has been superseded in the Gilded Age by a culture defined by power and materialism. The new century will be dominated by the wealthiest individuals and ultimately by the most powerful countries. Gussie argues that the utopian dream is over: "Pa, the curtain is about to go up on a new century. The United States of America is not playing a bit part anymore" (12). Power and greed reflect the new America; the commune that was formed near the end of the Civil War as a spiritual alternative to the magnates of the Industrial Revolution is now relegated to the past. The icon of the new America is William Randolph Hearst; his yacht, mentioned throughout the play, is the omnipresent representation of the power and materialism replacing the spiritualism of the commune. Hearst can plan the Spanish-American War and then, because he controls newspapers as part of his vast empire, can be the first to make history by reporting it. Hearst has become the voice and conscience of America. Gussie admits, "Mr. Hearst decides what all the folks in America should think and then they think it" (11). Amos Mason, one of the founding members of the utopian community, is the man Hearst is touting as the next President of the United States. Joshua sees Amos as nothing more than a role player: "The actor who found the role. It's what Amos Mason is preaching for America. Find the role. Find the power. The peace of the proper role" (30). Amos's loss of idealism coincides with what Guare believes to be the demise of American spirituality and the concomitant push towards the consumer culture of the twentieth century, fueled by materialism, greed, and power.

Gussie Hickman represents the new American society driven by its Carnegies and Hearsts. Gussie, Lydie's twenty-two-year-old sister, is now the mistress/private secretary of Senator Amos Mason who, although he carries the syphilitic seed of the past with him, now looks toward the future where he can sow only the seeds of power. Nantucket's spirituality is not for her; instead, Gussie has been living in Washington, D.C., surrounded by the prophets of power that she so admires and being at the center of the political action. To Gussie, being around politicians and businessmen is stimulating. She prides herself on the fact that she has penetrated the inner circles of the most powerful men in America: "I thank God for my shorthand and my typing. It's let me meet people like William Randolph Hearst" (11). As mistress to Senator Mason, who, through the political clout of Hearst may soon be President, Gussie will be socializing with the elite. She boasts to her sister, "I'm in love with the future. The next King. The next President" (27). Gussie has abandoned the past, which includes her mother's utopian vision, and instead opts for a life of conspicuous consumption, even if it means going "into bed with everybody" (17), as Lydie concludes, to get what she wants. To Gussie, the past, reflected in her former home, is nothing more than "Goddamn Nantucket. Damp Damp. Damp [*sic*]" (39). Seeing the monstrous performed in *Frankenstein* on the London stage forces her to recall the hideous and ghastly in her past. She tells Lydie, "Every evil ugly thing that ever happened woke up inside me. Ma killing herself. Pa going to prison. I got asthma worse than ever" (15–16). Gussie is an opportunist who looks to the future and hopes to ignore the past. She claims, "It's almost 1900. I'm American, by God. It's about to be my century" (53). Throughout the play, Gussie is primarily concerned with material possessions: her silk dress (14), her perfume bottles (39), and Mr. Hearst's yacht (10). The yacht, in particular, reflects her greed:

> I'm staying on the biggest damn yacht you ever saw. A yacht the size of the Oklahoma Territory. No, I mustn't exaggerate. But I know for a fact Mr. Hearst's yacht is one foot smaller than the entire state of Rhode Island. And that's the truth. It's got a mahogany ballroom with a grand piano. And a map of the world in different colored marble on the floor. I been on it before. Not my first time. Not my first yacht either. (10–11)

The implication is that if Gussie represents the future and a rejection of the past, the American consciousness has moved from the spiritual to the material, the latter fully realized through power.

The impetus for the exorcism of the past and a new vision for the future comes as a result of Jeremiah Grady's return to the United States. The purpose for his trip is twofold: to kill Lydie Breeze and to avenge the death of his father, murdered at the hands of Joshua Hickman. Lydie was responsible for passing the syphilis on to Jeremiah when she had sex with his father, Dan Grady.

Jeremiah is a terribly insecure young man in his late twenties. The stage directions indicate that his demeanor is feminized: "*He affects the pose of a dandy, a ragged Byronic mien. . . . His whole manner is histrionic, except—that anguish, that pain—that is authentic*" (21). Joshua mocks Jeremiah's gender marginality in a reference to Oscar Wilde's homosexuality: "You wearing black because of Oscar Wilde? Is he one of your chums?" (32).[47] Jeremiah is depicted as a marginal man—part dandy and part authentic sufferer.

As an actor playing Frankenstein's Monster for the past five years in the theatrical version of Mary Shelley's novel dramatized on the London stage, Jeremiah is the epitome of a dandy. Joshua reveals Jeremiah's living conditions in London: "I saw pictures in a magazine of your flat in London. Windows sealed in blue silk" (28). Joshua remembers him as "Little Lord Fauntleroy" (33) with "this frigging Oliver Twist more porridge voice" (33), a boy in a man's world. Moreover, Joshua recalls Jeremiah's father as a real man because together they dodged bullets during the Civil War. Meanwhile, Jeremiah has become an actor, an effeminate profession in Joshua's eyes. Joshua mocks Jeremiah's threat of revenge: "This man has come back to avenge his father's death? Is that it? Hell no! He's come back to avenge his front tooth. I love actors. Is that what you're stewing over in your London parlor with the Russian silk sky?" (31).

The other side of Jeremiah the marginal man is the authentic sufferer. Jeremiah, like the former denizens of Aipotu, is haunted by guilt. When Jeremiah was fifteen years old, a fight between his father and Joshua erupted when the latter ripped the bottle of stolen Moxie out of Jeremiah's mouth, causing him to chip his tooth. Ostensibly, this initiated the fight that resulted in Dan's death at the hands of Joshua. Eventually, Joshua was sent to jail, and the commune disintegrated from then on. Jeremiah internalized the guilt as "two men fighting over my honor" (33), even though the widespread perception, expressed for example by Gussie, is that Joshua murdered Dan because of his love for Lydie. The quarrel put an end to his father's dreams of a utopia, and the only legacy Jeremiah was left with was the syphilis inherited from Lydie after she seduced his father. The doctors revealed to Jeremiah much later that because of his syphilitic condition, he could never have sex with another woman; he had become, like the others surviving Aipotu, infected by the curse. His return is sparked by anger—a need to dissolve the past by taking revenge on Joshua and Lydie, the latter, of course, now dead.

By returning to seek revenge, Jeremiah provides authenticity to a life that has thus far been an evasion of responsibility. As an actor playing Frankenstein's Monster on stage every evening, Jeremiah has become a role in which he can lose himself. As a marginal man, he fits right into the role of the divided Monster in the play. Robert F. Gross writes, "Jeremiah is fatally ill and ontologically incomplete. His choice of an actor's life is portrayed as an act of cowardice, a flight from an anxious self."[48] Jeremiah can identify with his role as a monster, an outcast of society. In addition, the Monster is created and controlled by Frankenstein and is never whole unto himself; although the Monster may express his own feelings, he is fundamentally at the mercy of his creator. Jeremiah also is at the mercy of the curse precipitated by his ancestry and family history. Gussie admits that in the London production of the play, the Monster was controlled by "other people's dreams. Other people's nightmares" (15). Jeremiah, like the Monster, has lost his own sense of volition and has become a victim of the effect the Other has had on him. Thus, by playing the Monster every evening, his guilt has been exacerbated while his self remains divided; the role therefore increases his alienation, further preventing him from connecting with others. It is this very spirit of the divided self that forced Jeremiah to adopt the persona of the Other and become Amos during his relationship with Beaty. While they engaged in sex on the beach, Jeremiah realized that he "loved being someone else" (44). Jeremiah has returned to the scene of the Original Sin to slough off the curse. He is aware of how tainted his life has been and now seeks to cast off his monstrousness and connect with his heritage. He confesses to Joshua, "I don't want to be this monster. I am sick of playing this monster and if I am asked to play it for the rest of my life I have to have a whole human being to come back to when the curtain comes down. A human being!" (35).

In coming to grips with the past, Joshua forgives those he wanted to take revenge upon and thus provides the impetus for the curse to be lifted. After being taunted by Joshua and forced to relive that terrible moment that defined his fate years ago when he was thirteen, Jeremiah extends his hand and says, "Joshua, I forgive you" (36). Although he did not knowingly infect Beaty with syphilis, Jeremiah feels guilty about doing his share to pass the curse along to her as part of the ill-fated household. Jeremiah expiates his pent-up hostilities that have divided his self, preventing him from achieving ontological wholeness. He repents: "Beaty, I have to find some kind of forgiveness . . . to make up for the pain I know I've given you" (45). Jeremiah forgives and then submits to the inevitability of the curse upon him. By forgiving those he sought to take revenge upon, Jeremiah's death becomes a martyrdom. Jeremiah moves from divided selfhood to ontological security and wholeness by first acting as a role model seeking forgiveness and then by ridding himself of the curse that infected others.

When Jeremiah first suggests forgiveness, Joshua mocks him. He becomes defensive about his role as murderer: "Forgive me? I'm no monster who kills who he wants night after night and then turns to his audience and is applauded into innocence. Killing your father is the only true moment in my life" (36). Then Joshua changes his tune, asserting the Lydie Breeze was so noble and pure that she does not warrant forgiveness: "And you'll forgive her? The arrogance! If there's anyone you have to forgive, it's your father. He picked up a dose of syph from one of his Boston whores" (36). Joshua, in effect, shifts the blame to Dan, attempting to put doubts in Jeremiah's mind by revealing something about his father's secret past. However, it is obvious that Jeremiah's gesture of forgiveness has confused and agitated Joshua. As a dominant male, the patriarch of the commune, Joshua feels that he must take control rather than show a sign of weakness. His best recourse is to insult Jeremiah: "The War Between the States was our finest hour, us as we truly are. Forgiveness from another human being? You'll never get it. Syphilis. That's all you'll ever get from another human being. Syphilis and suicide notes" (36). Joshua's final gesture of denial, which closes act 2, suggests that the curse will continue as long as the violence reigns and no forgiveness is forthcoming for past regresses. Joshua reacts to Jeremiah's quest for revenge with his own threat of vengeance: "I loved your father. He was my friend. He took my wife. He wasn't clean. Forgiveness? (*Joshua raises his fist.*) I could kill you all over again" (37). By phrasing his comments in the past tense, Joshua demonstrates at this point in the play that he has not been able to come to grips with history and is not ready for forgiveness.

The double suicides of Jeremiah and Beaty gradually teach Joshua the lesson that forgiveness is the means to heal the wounds of the past. Guare apparently finds it significant that Joshua, the only surviving original member of the commune who still maintains the burning passion for idealism, must reconcile himself with the past through forgiveness. Near the denouement, Joshua is talking with his daughter Gussie while she is spinning a Ouija board. Gussie is looking for a spiritual sign to help determine her fate:

Gussie.	Washington smells. All those swamps . . . I'm trying to get this damned spirit board to spell out H.E.R.E. Stay here. But it keeps coming back to F.O.R.G.
Joshua.	F.O.R.G. Forget here. Forget your father. Forget Nantucket.
Gussie.	I beg your pardon, Pa. It's spelling out forge ahead. For Gussie. Forget me not. Forego any bad thoughts. For God's sake, don't despair. All for Gussie! (51)

During this scene, Joshua realizes that neither forging ahead, foregoing bad thoughts, nor forgetting the past will allow people to connect their lives in a rewarding way. By reconciling with Gussie, Joshua begins to learn that forgiveness is the best way to connect with people. Joshua appears ready to reconcile with Lydie; this, he realizes, will be a much more arduous task since he feels guilty that he raised her as a daughter he never really accepted as his own because he felt that she may very well be Dan Grady's child.

Joshua's reconciliation with his daughter Lydie occurs during the last scene of the play. Lydie, approaching menstruation, grows up as her father decides to bury the past, make peace, and forgive. In fact, Lydie has just received a sign, via secret code, that her friend Irene Durban had recently experienced her first period; Lydie's maturation is also about to occur. Joshua recites to Lydie Whitman's "On the Beach at Night Alone," which he reveals was the poem his wife read to him the first night they spent on the island together years ago. The poem is special to him, for Lydie read it to Joshua exclusively, not to Amos nor Dan. The poem reinforces the spiritual connection that has been missing from their lives: "A vast similitude interlocks all. / All spheres, grown, ungrown, small, large, suns, moons, planets, / All distances of time. All souls—" (55–56). Father and daughter now bond through the faith reinforced by Whitmanesque transcendentalism; Poe's gothic spirit in which the ghosts of the past weigh heavily on one's fate is now superseded by a new reality near the turn of the century. Joshua is teaching his daughter to read and write— she will now be able to follow in the footsteps of her mother, not through sin and by passing on disease, but by reinforcing and continuing her mother's cultural heritage. Lydie, in a critical point of her life, will be able to accept her own womanhood in a positive manner. Joshua's forgiveness thus allows his daughter to heal her wounds, be reborn, and, like her mother, the nurse after the Civil War, perhaps begin to heal others after the crises she has experienced. Whitman's poem suggests sanctuary under a benevolent spirit that offers the opportunity for connection in the modern world. Robert F. Gross summarizes the importance of Joshua's choice of verse: "Guare finds in Whitman's poem an image of non-coercive order that might provide a sanctuary from monstrous violence."[49] Furthermore, Joshua exhorts Lydie to recite the poem herself, although her poor reading skills force her to do so with difficulty. By accepting his paternal role, Joshua seeks Lydie's forgiveness as he rejects the monstrous violence to which he has been accustomed. He acknowledges, "Oh yes, I'm her father" (55), and Lydie responds by calling him "pa" several times (55) throughout the scene.

In contrast, forgiveness is not part of the credo of the Gilded Age. Beaty has persuaded Lydie to bring a message to Hearst indicating that Amos Mason infected her with syphilis. Hearst's response is quick and decisive. He abandons his support for Mason's bid for the presidency and, assuming that Gussie is also infected and that her father is nothing more than a murderer, breaks up any marriage plans that the two may have had. Hearst, a powerful force of absence (like Lydie Breeze once was) in the play, represents the new curse awaiting the twentieth century. Forgiveness is replaced by power, and connections are destroyed, not made. With power-hungry men like Hearst at the helm, Guare suggests that a new curse will bring increased alienation and isolation rather than shared connectedness through spirituality.

Guare introduces two minor male characters, Jude Emerson and Lucian Rock, who "connect" with the two women, Lydie and Gussie, respectively, to induce the healing process. Jude Emerson provides Lydie with solace after she learns of the double suicides of Beaty and Jeremiah. Drowned together, the hands of Beaty and Jeremiah tied with rope, their deaths force Lydie to recall her mother's suicide in which she hanged herself with rope. Lydie interprets this as a sign that her mother and Beaty exhort her to commit suicide and join them in death. At this point, Jude Emerson intervenes. His name suggests the Roman Catholic patron saint of lost causes (Jude) and the icon of American transcendentalism (Emerson); he represents the spirit of her mother, whom Lydie described as "a saint," in combination with her father's transformation through Whitmanesque transcendentalism, espoused here through Emerson as a kindred spirit in defiance of the haunting gothic of Poe. Jude comforts Lydie, who now, for the first time in the play, begins to accept mourning and bereavement as natural occurrences rather than ritualistic obsessions

that are part of a curse. Lydie sloughs off suicide and becomes reconciled to forging ahead. At the end of the scene, when Jude asks
her if she is frightened, she says, "I don't think I am. No" (48). During the play's denouement, Jude asks Joshua for permission to court
Lydie. When Joshua wonders why he needs to give his permission,
Jude responds, "You're her father" (54). At this point, Joshua reads
Whitman's poem to Lydie. Faith has been restored in the future
where father and daughter have been reconciled and where Lydie,
through Jude's optimistic belief in humanity, can forgive and forget
and thus begin life anew. The dead have been exorcised, and the
power-hungry Hearsts are noticeably absent. Perhaps the dream of a
utopia can also be renewed.

Near the end of the play, Guare introduces inventor Lucian Rock
as a sort of deus ex machina straight out of the melodramatic tradition. Lucian has been looking for Lydie, whom he claims is the
girl of his dreams, comparing her to Aphrodite (51), Dido (52), and
Persephone (52). He is about to depart for Europe to sell high-speed
sewing machines that he has adapted for industrial use. Just as Jude
asks Joshua for permission to court Lydie, Lucian goes one step further by offering to marry her. Lucian, however, mistakes Gussie for
Lydie. On the spur of the moment, Gussie, realizing that her oppor-
tunistic dreams have been shattered when her ties to Amos Mason
were severed by Hearst, grabs the chance to see the world and have
a better life in the future by deciding to go to Europe with Lucian.
Gussie breaks the curse by following her own intuition, thus taking
her chances with Lucian in hopes of fame and fortune by embracing
someone who will at least demonstrate entrepreneurship in what to
her may be exotic, far-off places.[50] Gussie, like many of Guare's protagonists, is a dreamer, and Guare seems to admire her spontaneity as
an alternative to the re-creation of order established by Lydie, Jude,
and Joshua at the end of the play.[51] Gussie, appearing to be Lydie
to Lucian, is willing to relinquish her identity in order to have the
chance for a better life. She will never mourn over the past, admitting
to her father, "Pa, I'm starting from scratch. Lucian Rock might hear
me wheeze, but he'll never hear me cry" (53). Gussie, whom Lucian
sees as someone who "ran out the dark back door into the bright light
of mythology" (52), will now have the opportunity to create her own
myths through dreams enhanced by travel and serendipity.

Lydie Breeze is Guare's paradigmatic search for the soul of the American consciousness. The play attempts to come to grips with the loss of
idealism in the nineteenth century and how we must learn from the
past, forgive our mistakes, exorcise the violent monster in ourselves,

and forge ahead. However, Guare intentionally leaves the ending ambiguous, refusing to be didactic by providing any sort of panacea. The harmonious peace of Lydie, Joshua, and Jude becomes just as viable as the creative venture into the mythology of chance and adventure Gussie pursues.

After Guare completed *Lydie Breeze*, he must have realized that the play, powerful in its attempt to come to grips with the modern malaise by exploring the decline of American idealism, relied heavily on characters talking about the past or action taking place offstage rather than on the more dramatic effect of direct stage action. He thus obviously felt a need to flesh out the details that led to the events occurring in *Lydie Breeze*; in any event, critics of that play also reinforced Guare's intentions when they claimed that the action, relying on murky past events, was not sufficiently dramatized on stage. Guare was thus writing *Gardenia* while he was revising *Lydie Breeze*. *Gardenia* was first staged on 28 April 1982 at the Manhattan Theater Club, virtually two months after the off-Broadway premiere of *Lydie Breeze*. Karel Reisz directed the production, Ann Roth designed the costumes, Glen Roven composed the music, Craig Miller supervised the lighting, and Santo Loquasto created the sets. The cast included Sam Waterston (Joshua Hickman), JoBeth Williams (Lydie Breeze), Edward Herrmann (Amos Mason), James Woods (Dan Grady), R. J. Burke (Jeremiah Grady), and Jarlath Conroy (O'Malley).

The critics were divided in their appraisal of the play. Clive Barnes (*New York Post*), Howard Kissel (*Women's Wear Daily*), Jack Kroll (*Newsweek*), Edith Oliver (*New Yorker*), and Douglas Watt (*Daily News*) were impressed with the production.[52] The consensus among these critics was that the cast was quite strong, the text was not as dense or outrageous as *Lydie Breeze*, and the production was enhanced by Loquasto's evocative sets and Roven's haunting score. Several critics commented that film director Karel Reisz, in his theatrical debut, helped bring the script to life brilliantly.

A group of dissenting critics made their voices heard. In his review for the Sunday edition of the *New York Times*, Walter Kerr complained primarily that *Gardenia* was undramatic because the audience learns things secondhand since much of the action occurs offstage and the audience is not close enough to grasp it and thus could care little about Lydie; he suggested that this technique made for dull theater and that Guare should have considered writing a novel instead.[53] Robert Brustein (*New Republic*) agreed with Kerr's assessment of the play, calling it an undramatized, "disunified sketch in search of another draft" and arguing that Guare's intent was more impressive than his execution.[54] Frank Rich, Kerr's colleague writing the week-day theater reviews at the *New York Times*, echoed Brustein's remarks when he complained that although Guare's intentions were worth-while, they were undramatic, at times self-indulgent, and characteri-zation was underdeveloped.[55] John Simon (*New York*) seemed to sum up the negative press when he described the best parts of the writing occurring offstage or between the acts but the rest confined to mostly prologues or epilogues to missing epiphanies in which the action is often removed from the characters.[56]

The next staging of *Gardenia* occurred two years later when the New Playwrights Theatre performed the play on alternate nights in repertory with *Lydie Breeze* from late May to 8 July 1984, in Washing-ton, D.C. Despite the magnitude of the theatrical undertaking, this production was quite successful.[57] On 20 October 1984, *Women and Water*, which was playing at the Los Angeles Actors' Theater since September, was now joined in repertory by *Gardenia*. A wonderful cast led by Laurie O'Brien (Lydie) and David Huffman (Joshua) could not seem to breathe much life into the play to make it work well enough onstage.[58]

Guare varied the structure and form of *Gardenia* so as not to match what he did with *Lydie Breeze*. The former play was structured as nine scenes in four acts; *Gardenia* consists of only two acts, with act 1 broken into four scenes. *Lydie Breeze* is similar to the late symbol-ist plays of Ibsen and includes many conventions associated with nineteenth-century melodrama. In contrast, act 1 of *Gardenia* seems to evoke Chekhov's impressionism, and although there are melodra-matic conventions (the recovery of a Gladstone bag containing a for-tune, the return of the prodigal son at a most opportune time, the misfortune of an idealist reduced to charwoman, the duel between two men over the love of a woman, etc.), the passions are not as over-stated as in the former play. The form of act 2 of *Gardenia*, written in the tradition of realism, however, is distinctly different from the first act and from the style of *Lydie Breeze*.

The major motif expressed in *Gardenia*, a play that is not as com-plex with regard to psychological machinations as the first part of the tetralogy, concerns the loss of idealism and the failure to live up to the American Dream. In *Gardenia*, we learn that Lydie Breeze was a hospital nurse who took care of wounded veterans Joshua Hickman, Amos Mason, and Dan Grady during the Civil War. Disgusted with corrupt antebellum politics that led to what Amos describes as "a war fought against false and cruel principles,"[59] Lydie and the three men decide to pool their resources to buy land on Nantucket. Their goal was to create a utopian society or, as William Dean Howells noted, "a community dedicated to living out higher ideals since the conclusion of that tragic war" (7). Designed to show the world contempt for their institutions, Aipotu, thirty miles off the U.S. coast, was to be a model community where, as Joshua hoped, "We'll write manifestoes and develop a society that will shine as a beacon to the world. A paradise of the mind. A garden of Eden" (11). Aipotu was dedicated to a "life of the mind" (12) through spirituality that would transcend corrupt politics and the materialism of the emerging Gilded Age. The idea was to share equally rather than raise money to support a lifestyle that was dedicated to expanding the mind. Pure in intent and devoid of the moral corruption inundating postbellum society, the founders of Aipotu came to the island to lead exemplary lives, unlike most of the masses who, as Lydie explains, "find their perfect God in presidents like Ulysses S. Grant" (21) or in idolization of entrepreneurs such as "Carnegie and Rockefeller and Jay Gould" (21). Lydie, the nurse, wanted to heal the wounds of a society broken by the spirit of war; she convinced Amos, Dan, and Joshua that on the island paradise they would seek "perfection" (55). The island kingdom becomes modelled on the idyllic community in *The Tempest* (37) where one can commune with nature, enjoy spiritual solace, and reign as Prospero, the role model for all of the men of the commune (38).

Gardenia begins where *Lydie Breeze* ended, with Joshua reading from Whitman's "On the Beach at Night Alone" on Nantucket in 1875, twenty years earlier. The beginning is quite an appropriate choice on Guare's part, for the poem conflates the spiritual purpose of the commune with the learning process. However, the Whitmanesque transcendentalism in which "a vast similitude interlocks all" (5) soon degenerates into a discussion of a withered gardenia, the image that gives the play its title. Joshua was charged with taking care of the plant while Lydie helped Doctor Paynter unsuccessfully deliver a child on the mainland. Lydie, ever the idealist, castigated the baby's father for his proud display of a picture of President Grant: "You support Grant's third term in office? You support strengthening the military? You support graft and corruption? No wonder your baby died!" (9). Lydie's comments, coupled with the image of the fading gardenia that Joshua failed to tend, indicate that the idealistic society has begun to decline. *Gardenia* was also the name of Lydie's father's whaling ship, which once represented the staple of the island; the fishing industry has withered away, no longer reflecting the life of the local economy. The plant obviously has symbolic value for Lydie.

She explains that her mother gave her father a gardenia for their wedding "so he'd always have roots on this island" (6). The gardenia also reflects the legacy that Lydie hopes to pass on to her daughter, and she reminds Joshua, "I've had this gardenia longer than I've had you. I wanted this plant by Gussie's bed. I've planned telling her all the stories around this gardenia so she'd have a sense of her past in this corrupt universe" (6). Lydie, however, trying to keep the dream alive while refusing to see the signs of decline in her utopian paradise, rationalizes the accident: "(*Kicking the plant.*) The gardenia. Throw it away. Not worth a snap. Just a plant. Almost a weed. The human spirit. That's the real show" (13).

In act 1 of *Gardenia,* we see that the utopian dream is gradually crumbling. Although Aipotu was originally designed as a free-thinking community that would liberate the mind, Joshua was forced to marry Lydie to legitimize the commune and therefore allow the authorities to sell the land to them. Thus, Lydie loves Dan but is forced into a marriage of convenience with Joshua. To make matters worse, Lydie has miscarried Dan's child but had a daughter (Gussie) by Joshua. If the island was founded upon freedom, it seems that the only remaining principle based on this concept has been reduced to free sex, thus leaving doubts about who Gussie's real father may be. The tension between Dan and Joshua has forced the former to take a brief hiatus as a railroad conductor. When Dan returns, he tries to entice Joshua to take William Dean Howells's advice and go to Europe to experience his roots. The conversation degenerates to which of the two men will selfishly possess Lydie:

Joshua.	I don't want you staying here with her.
Dan.	I thought we were above all that.
Joshua.	(*Vehement.*) She's my wife.
Dan.	She's an equal member of the community. (33)

The idealistic dream of sharing has faded, and in its place has become almost an obsession to possess another human being. Ironically, what is being shared is syphilis; in short, the original noble principle of sharing ultimately produces only disease and infection. Guare's black humor is evident when one looks closely enough.

Act 1 of *Gardenia* also explores how humanity's idealism can be countered by self-destructiveness. What began as a sanguine belief in the mind and the spirit is now replaced by the needs of the body and egotistical concerns. Joshua, who has been working seven years on his magnum opus, *Prolegomena to Duty,* has had the manuscript rejected by Howells, who exhorts him to discover his past by travelling to Europe. Joshua is willing to forego his dreams of an idyllic society founded upon intellectual pursuit and freedom of the mind in order to pursue his egotistical personal goal of getting his book published. Amos is also fed up with idealistic visions that have yet to be achieved. A life dedicated to the mind has ironically become so taxing to the body that he can no longer function intellectually. He complains to Lydie and Joshua, "I'll tell you what's ironic. Me peeling potatoes to the music of your pen scrawling away after our immortality. I'm so exhausted trying to keep this meagre farm alive. My labor produces no music. I can't think" (16). Amos is considering selling out his comrades by going to law school as a means to get into politics, which the founders of the commune unanimously once agreed was anathema to the spirit of their very existence. Dan's once lofty aspirations have been superseded by his intense desire to become, of all things, a conductor on the railroad. As their spirituality is displaced by more benign desires related to self-protective interests, the commune begins to disintegrate. Instead of a life dedicated to the spiritual and to intellectual freedom, the men stay up all night drinking (35). What began as a unified microcosm has become a divided community, especially when Dan urges Joshua to travel to Europe so he can selfishly spend time alone with Lydie while her husband is out of the picture. The island paradise has turned the prospective Prosperos into monsters; Lydie exclaims, "Caliban. You'll all read Caliban. You're all a pack of Calibans" (41). Amos characterizes the commune as a desert wasteland, nothing more than a boardinghouse: "Sahara. That would be the proper name for this—what? rooming house? That's what we've become?" (20).

The most damaging seed of corruption infecting this idyllic society, much like the temptation of the serpent in the Garden of Eden, is the lure of materialism. Working as a train conductor, Dan overheard two rival business tycoons in an argument that eventually led to a double murder. Seizing the opportunity, Dan stole their bag of money destined to be used by the two lobbyists to bribe Congress and President Grant. Now Dan has brought this graft to Aipotu as if it were manna from heaven (29). This bag of money, headed for the corrupt hands of President Grant, now taints the spirit of Aipotu, originally created as an alternative to political greed. At first, Lydie is petrified, but Dan can only think of the opportunity to purchase some soft-shell crabs and whether his son will demand paprika on all his food (25). Dan promises that the illicit money can be used to send Amos to Harvard Law School, thus allowing Amos's personal ambitions to interfere with communal sharing. The money can also be the means for Joshua's European voyage to gain experience to write his book and at the same time allow Dan to eliminate the competition so he can be alone with Lydie. Joshua relishes the opportunity to have to depend on Dan's cash: "I looked at a map of the world. I've drawn out lines going this way and that way. If it's too hard to get from Italy to Switzerland, I can pay to remove an Alp" (39). Dan even suggests that Joshua buy off William Dean Howells: "Perhaps we could pay him money to change his opinion of your book? Do you want me to do that?" (33). When Joshua altruistically wonders whether Dan should give the money to charity, or at least half of it as Lydie implies, Dan emphatically states, "Not a kopek. Not a rubel. Not a peso. Not a franc. Nada" (37). Joshua even has the gall to tell Lydie that her shattered dreams, represented by the withered gardenia, can be replaced by commercial interests: "With Dan's money, we can buy forests of gardenias" (31).

Act 2 occurs in Charlestown Prison near Boston nine years later, in 1884, where Joshua is serving a sentence of life imprisonment for the murder of his rival, Dan, during a fit of jealous rage. Guare demonstrates that the once-held utopian dreams of the commune have gone awry. Joshua, formerly a budding writer, now is reduced to working in the prison's printing room and teaching criminals how to read by piquing their interests with famous tales of prison escapes. Amos sarcastically notes, "Mr. Hickman still has his knack of instilling people with ideals" (45). After touring Europe as Howells recommended to acquire knowledge of his heritage, Joshua now has the pleasure of rubbing shoulders with the likes of the Brighton Mauler, who is about to be executed for murdering immigrants. Lydie has also fallen on hard times. She has been banished from Nantucket—from the utopia she created—after she tried to kill her children there; Gussie and young Lydie are now being cared for by Beaty. Lydie has abandoned nursing, the healing profession, and is now reduced to working as a charwoman ravaged by the effects of the syphilis. Her dream of freedom of the mind has been replaced by cleaning dirty rooms of the undergraduates at Harvard. The result is that even idealistic Lydie has become disillusioned, especially by the fact that the concept of sharing became nothing more than mere ideology when Joshua killed Dan for personal reasons: the fear of losing her to Dan (59).

Amos has also been adversely affected by the capital gains accrued from the money Dan stole. With a law degree from Harvard, Amos has entered politics and is now ready to run for the Senate seat in New York; the seeds of corruption have been sown. He now has high ambitions and is worried about his personal reputation. While in prison, Joshua has written his second book, *Aipotu: A Nantucket Memory*, which has been praised by Howells as a masterpiece. Amos has come to visit Joshua in prison to persuade him not to publish these memoirs, for if this book about free love and socialism goes to print, his reputation would be impugned, precluding any chance for a successful run at the Senate and thus extinguishing his political aspirations. Amos has brought Lydie with him to get Joshua to listen to reason and accept a deal: using his political power and the last of Dan's money as a bribe, Amos will get the governor of Massachusetts to grant Joshua a pardon if he destroys his manuscript. If Joshua accepts this bribe, Lydie's banishment from Nantucket will also be lifted, and thus Joshua will be reunited with his wife and daughters.

The consensus among critics is that *Gardenia* is not nearly as complex or interesting as *Lydie Breeze*, and until the middle of act 2 of *Gardenia*, this may be true. For much of the play, Guare was confined by the parameters set in *Lydie Breeze* and was primarily concerned only with fleshing out the details of the decline of the commune. However, by the middle of act 2, we begin to see that Joshua's dilemma reflects the choices America has near the beginning of the modern age. The freedom of the island paradise versus the constriction of Charlestown Prison, which, as Jack Kroll mentions, was superbly manifested by Santo Loquasto's design of the openness of the beach in contrast to the confining detritus of the print shop in the original production, suggests a diptych of nineteenth-century America.[60] The choice is between America's salvation through the Whitmanesque spirituality and freedom of the mind practiced in the commune or acquiescing to the greed, ambition, and materialism endemic of the Gilded Age.

Joshua tells Amos, "You don't understand. I'm very happy here" (53). In prison, Joshua is at peace with himself and, strangely enough, views the murder of Dan as his liberation. During Joshua's conversation with Lydie in prison, he reveals that he allowed his emotions, especially power and ambition, to affect his attitude towards communal sharing when he destroyed her gardenia: "You were away. The letter of rejection came. I wanted to hurt something. Inflict a wound. Power over something. The book was rejected. You were away. There was this healthy blooming thing that you loved" (58). Lydie responds, "If I'd known that fact, Dan Grady would be alive today. I would have left you. I would not have stayed in a house with a murderer" (58). Despite Lydie's disappointment with Joshua, she urges him to allow Howells to publish his manuscript rather than destroy it.

In the denouement, Joshua learns more about himself and comes to terms with the truth about any aspirations he may have had with regard to the creation of a utopia. Joshua, like all of Guare's protagonists, was searching for a spiritual connection and realizes in Charlestown Prison that he found it in Lydie. He tells her, "You connected me and I could dream—go anywhere I wanted and never lose myself because I was connected to the earth. By this. By your gravity" (60). However, Joshua, intuitively understanding that Lydie probably loved Dan more than she loved him, kept searching for his spiritual foundation. He travelled to Europe but admits to Lydie, "And all I saw was you. You were my voyage. You were my Europe. You were my mythology" (59–60). Joshua begins to understand that the original noble yet false idealistic goals of the commune masked his personal desires for individual freedom and ambition (reflected through the publication of his *Prolegomena*). He admits to Lydie how the personal outweighed the group's sense of idealism: "There was no noble motive. There was no great passion. The same petty furies that made me kill the gardenia, those same petty furies made me kill Dan. Rage over losing you" (59). Joshua concludes that ego far outweighed the dreams and aspirations of the commune as a whole: "Oh, Christ—in all our dreaming we never allowed for the squalid, petty furies. We lived on a beach in a vast landscape. We mistook the size of the ocean, the size of the sky for the size of our souls" (59).

Joshua's decision is to shred his manuscript rather than allow Howells to publish it. This ending is somewhat ambiguous. On the one hand, Joshua, in refusing Lydie's advice but yet finally coming to terms with his ambitious desires during his conversation with her in prison, may be understood to have developed the requisite peace to discover the truth within himself. His lambaste of false idealism would suggest that this is so. However, as Dennis Carroll indicates, an important caveat marks the end of the play: "Yet he [Joshua] is forced to compromise by destroying his revised manuscript, a document that authenticates his pain and could give shape and meaning to his odyssey of crime and redemption."[61] Joshua's compromise is no different from the lure of materialism for Dan and Amos; he has sold out to win his freedom—nothing less. If, as Guare stated, the key image of the flourishing utopia is found through the transmission of the written word that inspires freedom, then Joshua's destruction of his manuscript is similar to Prospero's laying down his mantle and thus dissolving the dream of an island paradise. The monsters have indeed won out, and Joshua is part of that capitulation. Guare acknowledged, "*Gardenia* is about the destruction of two manuscripts."[62] This would conform to the structure of the play in which act 1 presents the budding writer forced to destroy his *Prolegomena*, and then act 2 parallels this action with the shredding of *Aipotu*. Robert F. Gross makes the connection clear: "Thus, Aipotu is destroyed twice in *Gardenia*; both as commune and as its literary re-creation."[63] The result is that Joshua's selfish destruction of the book, a gesture indicating the renunciation of the mind, is a portent of the disaster to come. Lydie eventually commits suicide. The Whitmanesque spirit that began the play now will give way to the decline of the utopian vision and a reemergence of the gothic spirit that will years later haunt Lydie's husband and daughters. A sanguine tale of faith in the American Dream has deteriorated into a perverse type of fall of the House of Usher replete with moral decay caused by greed, ambition, and perverted dreams.

Women and Water, the third play Guare wrote for the tetralogy and the one that occurs first chronologically, was staged in draft form at the Los Angeles Actors' Theater, opening 12 October 1984 under direction by Bill Bushnell; on 20 October, *Women and Water* went into repertory with *Gardenia* until December. The four-hour production had a cast of twenty-five that included Laurie O'Brien (Lydie), David Huffman (Joshua), Tom Everett (Amos), Jason Oliver (Moncure), Christopher Allport (Dan), and Thomas Newman (Captain Breeze). This version of the play, which was not heavily reviewed, was believed to be a bit too ambitious and required editing.[64]

Guare condensed the three-act play into two acts by eliminating several characters and reducing the number of subplots. He showed the script to Jim Nicola and Lloyd Rose, who had codirected *Gardenia* and *Lydie Breeze* in 1984 when they were staged in repertory at the New Playwrights Theatre in Washington, D.C. Soon after *Women and Water* closed in Los Angeles, Arena Stage actors read Guare's revised version of the play on the Kreeger stage in January 1985. After a second reading of the text by the Arena players in August at Colorado College in Colorado Springs, Guare tightened the play even further.

Women and Water opened at Arena Stage in Washington, D.C., on 5 December 1985, where it ran until 5 January 1986. Even with Guare's editing of a play that at one time contained thirty-five scenes, the production ran for three hours and included a cast of twenty-nine performers. Douglas C. Wager directed, Tony Straiges designed the sets, Allen Lee Hughes arranged the lighting, John McKinney composed the music, and Julie Taymor and Robert Flanagan devised the puppets, including a unique buzzard that looked frighteningly real. The cast featured Cary Ann Spear (Lydie), John Gegenhuber (Amos), Tom Hewitt (Cabell), John Leonard (Joshua), Casey Biggs (Dan), and Mark Hammer (Captain Breeze).

Unlike New York productions, *Women and Water* at Arena Stage was not heavily reviewed but received more critical attention than did the Los Angeles premiere of the play. Richard Christiansen of the *Chicago Tribune* and Edwin Wilson of the *Wall Street Journal* were the play's biggest supporters. In his brief two-paragraph review, Wilson was impressed with the play's rich texture, with its versatile and effective staging, and with Wager's vigorous and forceful direction.[65] Although he acknowledged that the play had some technical problems and that Guare never explained the spiritual alliance that drew Lydie close to Joshua, Amos, and Dan, Christiansen praised Guare's bold theatrical inventiveness.[66] David Richards and Joe Brown, both writing in different sections of the same edition of the *Washington Post*, offered neutral reviews. Richards described the play as containing moments of sharp intelligence, stunning theatricality, and mordant irony yet lacking a simple human connection and often devoid of logic.[67] Joe Brown lauded the production work of the Arena Stage company but argued that the acting was uneven; with regard to the writing, he found the text to be ambitious yet composed of fragmented images and stilted conversations that resulted in a play that was whimsical, maudlin, preachy, and too long.[68] Finally, Mel Gussow's review in the *New York Times* characterized the play as "tumultuous," unenlightening, and subject to rhetorical excess; he claimed that although Wager made several of the battle and sea scenes visually and aurally arresting even with a cast that seemed out of their element, the play contained too much material for even three hours.[69]

Guare continued revising the play, including eliminating a mythical confrontation between Ulysses S. Grant and Robert E. Lee, into its present format of two acts and a running time of two hours and forty minutes with intermission. In its final version, the play was directed by Stephen Schacter during summer 1988 in a production staged by the Atlantic Theater Company in Montpelier, Vermont. A few months later, in October 1988, *Women and Water* was broadcast by BBC Radio under direction by Ned Chaillet.

Of all Guare's dramas, *Women and Water* is the most demanding and difficult to stage. The play consists of over two dozen performers, and although some minor roles may be doubled, the major ones cannot. Guare discussed the evolution of his epic saga:

After I saw Louis Malle's terrific *My Dinner With Andre* (Malle, by the way, being the original director of *Lydie Breeze*), I thought if two people having a meal can be a movie, then it's time to bring Cecil B. De Mille back to the boards. But our version of De Mille. I had this vision of Cecil B. and Samuel Beckett wrestling it out stage center. Are they shaking hands? Is it a draw? Is this a new union? Bring on the Red Sea! Paging Ben Hur! The fresh air of doing a play with no offstage action.[70]

Guare, accused of relegating the action to the past or to offstage events when the critics reviewed the first two plays in the tetralogy, now returns with all of the action reserved for the stage. Although Guare claims that *Women and Water* could be produced on a bare stage,[71] certainly the battle scenes during the Civil War, the mutiny at sea, and the steamboat journey would all be less effective if they were given the minimalist staging of a Beckett play. A director would have a particular dilemma with the wild pig, which could be done with a puppet, with an actor (as was the case in the Los Angeles and Arena Stage productions), or with lighting and sound effects (used in the Atlantic Theater Company's staging). Guare, aware that the difficulties of performing the play might scare directors and thus preclude any chance of production, wrote notes to placate skeptics. He assures us, "It's not a play about scenery nor the authenticity of props that will give it its truth; it's the actors' belief in those props. Don't worry about not having authentic Civil War guns or costumes. Children at play believe in the authenticity of their props."[72] The play need not be staged with realistic props, costumes, or sound effects, for Guare considers it to be a melodrama, and thus its heightened emotions can be stylized. Above all, Guare views *Women and Water* as having the same sort of frenetic energy found in his comedies: "The play must have no break in its action. Keep it alive and present and active. And simple. Let each scene flow into the next" (6).

Whereas *Lydie Breeze* contained flourishes of Ibsen's late plays and *Gardenia* recalled Chekhov in act 1 and realism in act 2, *Women and Water*'s antecedents are nineteenth-century American and European melodramas. Replete with episodes of heightened emotions, suspense derived from the perils of an adventure story, a plot held together by several portentous secrets, and sensationalism presented via dramatic artifice such as daring rescues and escapes, *Women and Water*'s form is substantially different from its predecessors in the tetralogy. The dialogue, much less lyrical in the latter play than in the two earlier dramas, also is much closer to the diction in melodrama, including the early O'Neill period through *Beyond the Horizon,* than it is to the language of Ibsen or Chekhov.

As critics reminded Guare, much of the action of *Lydie Breeze* and *Gardenia* occurred offstage or in the past. Guare's objective in *Women and Water* was thus to see the characters in action in the present when the past, because of their youth, was inconsequential. Guare acknowledged, "I wondered what the lives of these people had been before they found each other—before their lives blended into a golden time that would become their life's central experience."[73] In short, melodrama became the ideal form of drama to use for *Women and Water* rather than the more lyrical style of late nineteenth-century symbolism or impressionism. Guare explains his intentions in the "Author's Notes" preceding the play:

> WOMEN AND WATER would be an adventure play where the people are moving too rapidly to remember, people so young they don't have anything to remember, to write a play where the poetry lies not in the language but in the events themselves. To write not about the memory of a golden time but to write the golden time itself. What you're seeing is what they'll be remembering, albeit each in his or her own way. (3)

One of Guare's primary intentions in writing the tetralogy was to discover how one can learn from the past and explain how our decisions are based upon historical events. However, what happens when the past is ambiguous or dependent upon subjective interpretation? *Women and Water* is partially concerned with the need for keeping a journal to provide an accurate written record of historical developments so that decisions in the present can always be more carefully nurtured. Throughout most of the play, Lydie is unaware of the importance of keeping a journal and thus must pass history on to us orally. Guare realizes that what Lydie says is the key to future decisions: "The actress playing Lydie must not put formal quotation marks around these addresses out front, but rather trust that we are there for her to confide in. We are her journal. We are her children-to-be. We are her future" (7) Lydie's search for truth during the Civil War, like Guare's search for the utopian paradise that remains elusive after Vietnam, is dependent on an accurate assessment of historical events. Lydie learns that her father, who passed on his values to his daughter, could be a murderer, yet only Captain Breeze's logbook will unravel the truth. Guare states, "The key image in *Women and Water* is the father's journal, and the lies told in that, and then Lydie writing a journal."[74] Lydie's epiphany is realizing the value of the written, rather than the oral, transmission of history as a means for future generations to discover the truth. Keeping a record in her journal will allow future generations to come to grips with the past and therefore take the first step in making connections with self and others. Lydie eventually learns how the truth can be shared: "One day I must have children and they must read what the world was. I must record what I see" (28).

Women and Water focuses primarily on Lydie Breeze's search for the past in order to establish a value system in a world where events in the present seem uncontrollable. Lydie is clearly the heroine of this melodrama, and, like most plays in that tradition, the other protagonists are either stock characters or are woefully underdeveloped. Amos, Dan, and Joshua seem to act more like a chorus of men disenchanted with the war and concomitantly in need of spiritual belonging, and although there is a clear-cut dichotomy between Lydie's attraction to Dan's competent worldliness and her mothering spirit towards Amos and Joshua, the men are not nearly as clearly delineated as they are in *Gardenia*.

Women and Water begins as the Civil War rages at Cold Harbor, Virginia, in 1864. Lydie Breeze is a nurse in her early twenties tending Union soldiers during the battle, where she meets Captain Joshua Hickman, working as a photographer, and Amos Mason, a private fighting under the Union banner. In the heat of the battle, men are being sent to the front lines as fodder when the sergeant randomly calls their names to enter into the fray, enticing them with the carrot that across the lines there will be women and water available. The dying men entrust Lydie with their valuables rather than allowing the Confederates to gain access to them. Lydie feels helpless as a healer, for without adequate supplies, the men will die no matter how much she tries to assist them. Her first encounter with Joshua occurs when he is shot in the shoulder for asking the sergeant to arrange a truce so supplies can be distributed. Joshua's idealism is revealed when he tells Lydie that he rebelled against his father's parochial attitude toward slavery, and as a southerner from North Carolina, he abandoned the Confederate cause: "I hear my father saying: 'Don't fight slavery. Slavery is a beautiful thing. Slavery is a gift from God. Fight for slavery.' And I ran further and further away. Till I'm here. Now" (19). Joshua decides to lead Lydie to the waterfront to catch a steamer travelling up the Pamunkey River to bring back supplies for the war-ravaged men. She enlists the aid of Sergeant Dan Grady, who accompanies her on the journey up the river. On board the steamer, Lydie helps Joshua recover from malaria by obtaining quinine for him and soothing his spirit by reading Whitman's "On the Beach at Night Alone" to him.

The Civil War is the impetus for the search that Lydie and her spiritual brethren undertake to salvage the truth from the madness surrounding them. Lydie, Joshua, and Dan search for enlightenment in a world that they are unable to control. Joshua poses the question of identity in a society devoid of spiritualism replaced instead by a sense of selfishness personified by the image of the buzzard: "What happened to Jesus? What happened to Jehovah and Buddha and Mohammed and Allah? All the gods packed up their tents. They now all work for the Buzzard god" (20). The solution does not lie with the will of the government, which usually results in war or corruption. Joshua extols the virtue of the human spirit over the will of the government: "Revolution is David and Goliath. This is the only rule I believe in. That the people together are David. And governments are Goliath. And the Davids always win" (76–77). Lydie, the epitome of the healing spirit, has had her faith destroyed by the will of the government:

> Two years in this war and I'm still drifting. I look at the blood spreading out on a soldier's bandage. I study the point where the blood begins to blur. There I am. This blur. Drifting. Without purpose. Day to day. I had a purpose. It's all turned into a blur. (21)

Joshua understands Lydie's *angoisse* in a world that is absurd because she has no control over it. He reminds Lydie why she sought supplies for the men: "You gave away your soul to this war. You're trying to get back your soul" (23). When Lydie tells Dan that he must choose the path that provides the greatest good, he questions her: "For yourself?," to which she responds, "For mankind" (26). In order to achieve this spiritual connection with self and others, Lydie must first learn to come to grips with her past. Dan reads what she has written in her journal: "'I must always tell the truth and find the truth and know the truth at any price'" (38). Lydie begins to unravel the past, which becomes the stepping stone for her spiritual enlightenment and for the means to understand her role in a corrupt society that she is helpless to control.

En route to seek supplies on board the *Pamunkey Queen*, Lydie reads to Joshua, Dan, and Amos from her journal, which began on 30 October 1861. Lydie reveals that her journal was a means to discover the past for herself and for future generations: "I dreamed one day I'd have children and present this journal to them. They would see their mother as a woman who challenged the universe! What is man's role in determining history and not becoming a victim of history?" (40). As Lydie talks to the audience, a flashback takes us to Nantucket where Captain Breeze's whaling ship is finally returning home after four years at sea. Cabell, Lydie's brother, recounts how twenty-six hundred barrels of whale oil were lost when the ship went up in flames. Captain Breeze was allegedly shot in the back when the blacks on board the ship mutinied, and the shock of these events gave him a stroke that rendered him mute. Lydie's father's log book is revealed to have been lost at sea. During the hearing to determine whether the insurance company would pay for the losses, Cabell testifies that the blacks mutinied for fear of sailing past Confederate waters on the way home to Nantucket. The only worthwhile item salvageable from the ship is a gardenia, which, as we have seen earlier, has symbolic value for Lydie years later as a link to her past.

The insurance company settled in favor of Captain Breeze's family, and soon afterwards, he began a slow recovery from his stroke. Once he could talk again, he asked to see Moncure, the black cabin boy. Inexplicably, Captain Breeze committed suicide by shooting himself and taking his secrets with him, and Lydie, convinced that Moncure held the key to her father's death, set off in search of him. Lydie spent the next two and a half years attempting to find Moncure, the pain easing a bit as she became preoccupied with her duties as a nurse during the war.

The flashback ends act 1, and act 2 begins with Lydie returning to the battlefield with the supplies. In a stroke of luck befitting any good melodrama, Lydie miraculously runs into Moncure, who is fighting as a soldier for the Union Army. Moncure claims that he fled from Captain Breeze because "The police find a colored boy there, they put him in jail" (66). Lydie and Moncure team up to rescue Joshua and Amos, who have been held captive in cages as prisoners of war. Lydie, now the heroine of the day, even kills a wild pig that earlier tormented Joshua and Amos when the animal occupied the cage next to them.

Moncure reveals that the truth of what happened on board Captain Breeze's whaling ship lies in Lydie's father's log book, which can be found in his coffin. Lydie's return to Nantucket is thus inevitable, but she now sees no reason for the men to engage in an absurd war any longer. She encourages them to return to her paradise island: "Singly we are nothing. But pasted together we're—David—doing battle with all the Goliaths of the world. I see the design less darkly. It began in Nantucket. It shall end in Nantucket" (80). With visible proof that

Lydie is a leader and a healer, Dan, Amos, and Joshua follow her back to Nantucket to create a utopian community.

Upon her return to Nantucket, Lydie is surprised to find that her brother has been using the island as a waystation for former slaves en route to Canada. The log book is soon unearthed from Captain Breeze's coffin. As Lydie reads from the log, we flash back to events occuring on board the *Gardenia* in 1861. Captain Breeze describes how Cabell, in an argument with a black man, slashed the sailor's throat. Cabell was taken off to be incarcerated as Captain Breeze records, "I will no longer write the words My Son" (90–91). A few days later, Cabell and the white sailors of the crew mutinied against Captain Breeze, during which time Cabell shot his father in the back. During the mutiny, the men took turns murdering the blacks on board, but Moncure was somehow spared. The log book reveals that Captain Breeze shared with Lydie many of the same aspirations: "Lydie will understand. I'll get back to Nantucket. We shall invent a new world. A hunt, a chase, a gamble. But above all, the truth. The truth. Any cost. The truth" (93). Cabell lied to Lydie, claiming that her father's log was lost in the fire and that the blacks mutinied and then fled the ship to build a new world; however, he argues that he holds the key to the truth, not Moncure, who is nothing more than a black cabin boy. Moncure, in a fit of rage over Cabell's lying, draws a pistol and shoots him in front of Lydie. Cabell insists that his version, sworn to during the trial, is the truth and if the story is not corroborated, Lydie would have to return the insurance money. Cabell is buried with Captain Breeze, and together they hold the key to the truth; the gothic atmosphere of secrets buried with the ghosts is about to surface. If Moncure's story is true, we still do not know why a blameless man would want to commit suicide. Joshua realizes, "The truth is in that grave somewhere" (101).

By coming to grips with the skeletons in her closet—by unravelling the truth through her father's logs—Lydie is able to forge ahead and look to the future. She exhorts her comrades to burn her father's old log books as a rite of passage, for Lydie is now convinced of her father's righteousness, and what others may think is moot; Lydie, in coming to terms with her past, is free to follow her idealistic dreams. Lydie explains to Joshua, Amos, and Dan how the past is linked to the future: "We have achieved experience. We are transformed by experience. Not I. Not you or you or you. But us. On this beach. Right now. Together we're a great soul capable of doing extraordinary things" (103). And Lydie, with an eye towards the future in which her children will learn from the past, vows to pass history along by starting her own journal. She says, "We will sign our own truce. I take my book. My journal. My testament to my children to be. (*Lydie writes.*) As my father would terminate his log at the conclusion of a voyage, so I hereby terminate the recording of my involvement in the War of the Rebellion and announce the commencement of a new life" (105). *Women and Water*, then, is far removed from the modern vision Guare usually represents in his theater; the play lacks the subtle irony of Guare's black comedies, for Lydie is a passionate seer, too young to be jaded by life's bitter realities. In that respect, *Women and Water* is not as interesting as the other two plays in the tetralogy: the realistic representation of the golden time is not as intriguing as the gothic effect it has on Lydie's family and friends years later.

The question that remains to be answered is whether the tetralogy enhanced Guare's reputation as a playwright and made him a better dramatist. Guare would probably argue that unearthing the past was personally rewarding for him. There is also no doubt that any contemporary playwright would learn more about the dramatic tradition and about dramatic structure by seriously studying the form and language of the modern masters such as Ibsen, Chekhov, and O'Neill. Moreover, the individual plays in the tetralogy can stand on their own merit since they are often quite lyrical, poignant, and carefully crafted. However, in working with this nineteenth-century melodramatic style, Guare's forte, his black comedy, is lost. The result is that Guare did an excellent job of imitating the masters of the modern drama, but the zany sarcastic comedy, the element that distinguishes Guare as a creative genius from other contemporary playwrights, is virtually nonexistent. Writing the tetralogy, nevertheless, seemed to have been a useful exercise for him because Guare was able to exorcise his demons and thus return to the type of innovative caustic comedy that has become his trademark.

Six Degrees of Separation

SIX DEGREES OF SEPARATION MARKS GUARE'S FINEST THEATRICAL achievement, in which the idea of a spiritually dysfunctional society in need of viable connections with self and others is best illustrated through farce and black comedy. Guare wrote the play relatively quickly in 1989 with the intent of staging it at Lincoln Center. He passed it on to Lincoln Center's director, Gregory Mosher, and its executive producer, Bernard Gersten, who had successfully produced the revival of *The House of Blue Leaves* there in 1986. They were so impressed with Guare's script that they began plans for production without benefit of readings or workshops, with Jerry Zaks to direct, as he did for the 1986 revival of *Blue Leaves*, and essentially the same production team that worked with Zaks earlier. Auditions for the seventeen roles in the play began in October 1989.

Six Degrees of Separation opened at the Mitzi E. Newhouse Theater at Lincoln Center on 19 May 1990. The cast featured Stockard Channing (Ouisa), John Cunningham (Flan), James McDaniel (Paul), and Sam Stoneburner (Geoffrey); Channing, nominated for a Tony Award for Best Actress during the revival of *The House of Blue Leaves*, was fast becoming a staple in Guare's theater. The production crew included Tony Walton (sets), Paul Gallo (lighting), and William Ivey Long (costumes). Guare wanted the ninety-minute play performed rapidly and without an intermission. Guare later stated he originally told Tony Walton, "All I know is, it's got to move fast, because I just did a production of a play at Yale and the scenery looked pretty as a picture, but it took thirty seconds or a minute to change each scene, and in a farce, that's an eternity."[1] Zaks astutely realized that much of the play involves narration, similar to stories told at a campsite. Guare recalls, "He [Zaks] and Tony Walton devised a production scheme whereby the actors (except Paul, the Hustler, and the Doorman) sit in the front row for the course of the performance, appearing and vanishing, handing up, holding up, and receiving props and costumes as needed."[2] The Newhouse Theater's thrust stage, in which the audience sat three-quarters of the way around the performance space, worked well for the intimate contact that the actors must have with the audience in this type of play.

After Stockard Channing took a hiatus from the production to honor a movie commitment on 1 August, Kelly Bishop and then Swoosie Kurtz filled in for her in the role of Ouisa. During this time, James McDaniel left to do a television series, so Courtney Vance stepped into Paul's role (Gregory Simmons also filled in briefly). On 8 November 1990, the production transferred to the larger Vivian Beaumont Theater at Lincoln Center, with Vance continuing as Paul and Channing returning to play Ouisa again. Originally scheduled for a ten-week run, *Six Degrees of Separation* was so popular that it continued for nearly twenty months at Lincoln Center, closing on 5 January 1992.

Six Degrees of Separation was heavily reviewed by the press. Although most of the critics wrote about the original production, several of them, apparently thinking that the performances at the Newhouse Theater were trial runs, waited until the play transferred to the Vivian Beaumont before they made their assessments. Rarely since World War II has any play received such unanimous raves and accolades as did *Six Degrees of Separation*. The play was called "provocative" (*USA Today* and *America*),[3] disturbing yet poignant (*New York*),[4] "absorbing" (*Christian Science Monitor*),[5] "inspiring and uplifting" (*Wall Street Journal*),[6] "insightful," the best play in several seasons (*Variety*),[7] and a "hilarious and searing" panorama of modern urban life (*New York Times*).[8] Zaks was praised for his snappy direction, and the cast, particularly Channing, who had to transform from benign hostess to a sympathetic woman of unexpected pathos, was lauded as a strong ensemble. Paik, writing in *Variety*, credited Tony Walton's set design for enhancing the invigorating rhythm of the play and for providing its visceral impact.[9] *Six Degrees of Separation* also received favorable notices in the *New York Post, New Republic, Time, Daily News, New Yorker, Newsweek*, and the *Washington Post*.[10] There were only two major dissenting views. Gerald Weales (*Commentary*) had no quibble with the play's message but claimed that the fragmented presentation, including Zaks's direction resulting in "noisy nervousness," never allowed the characters to develop.[11] In contrast, Thomas M. Disch (*Nation*) praised Zaks and the cast but disliked the play because he claimed it pandered to a liberal upper-middle-class audience.[12] *Six Degrees of Separation* went on to win the New York Drama Critics' Circle Award for best play of the 1990–91 season, giving Guare his third such award.[13]

On 18 June 1992, *Six Degrees of Separation* had its European premiere at the Royal Court Theatre in London. British director Phyllida Lloyd's production featured Stockard Channing, the only holdover from the New York cast, Adrian Lester as Paul, and Paul Shelley playing Flan. The British press were just as ecstatic about the play as were their American counterparts.[14] The result was that on 18 April 1993, the play garnered the Olivier Best Play Award for the 1992 season.

Beginning in October 1992, Jerry Zaks took the play on tour throughout the United States, winding up the road trip in Boston during May 1993.[15] Although the production team was the same as in New York and John Cunningham continued in the role of Flan, the cast now included Marlo Thomas (Ouisa) and Ntare Mwine (Paul). Cunningham and Mwine did well, and Thomas, forever compared to her predecessor, Channing, was tender, self-mocking, and funny but appeared to lack Channing's "emotional shimmer."[16] During the next few years of the 1990s, *Six Degrees of Separation* had extraordinary success playing worldwide from Washington, D.C., to Los Angeles and from Tokyo to Istanbul.[17]

With the international success of *Six Degrees of Separation*, various directors, producers, and performers had plans to turn the play into a film. Norman Jewison, Barbra Streisand, Quincy Jones, and Jessica Lange expressed interest in the project. However, Australian director Fred Schepisi, who seemed to have a rapport with Guare and understood his intentions, was chosen. Schepisi had worked with plays and playwrights before: he had collaborated with Tom Stoppard in shaping his screenplay into *The Russia House,* had filmed David Hare's *Plenty,* and had turned *Cyrano de Bergerac* into the successful Steve Martin comedy, *Roxanne.* MGM financed Schepisi's venture with a budget of $15 million. Guare insisted on Stockard Channing to continue in the role of Ouisa, and MGM, seeing her as a bankable star, agreed. Schepisi, believing that John Cunningham was too old to play Flan, persuaded Donald Sutherland to take the role, even though the latter was amazed at the meager fee he was offered. Will Smith was cast as Paul, and to prepare him for the part, Schepisi took him to London during fall 1992 to see the stage version playing at Royal Court. The supporting cast featured Ian McKellen (Geoffrey), Mary Beth Hurt, and Bruce Davison.

The challenge for Schepisi was to make a film that would be as emotionally rousing as the play while maintaining its poignancy. Schepisi acknowledged, "On the surface, it's a work that's terribly witty and great fun. But when you left the theater, you left deeply touched."[18] Preproduction was scheduled for Toronto, which would have saved the producers money rather than having to undertake the more expensive filming in New York City. However, Guare received a telephone call from a friend who told him about the availability of newly renovated condominiums in New York City. The film's executive producer then struck a deal to pay $200,000 for two floors of the condo to serve as the set for the Kittredges' Fifth Avenue apartment. Schepisi was thus able to film in New York City during a two-and-a-half-month shoot that finished on 20 May 1993. Guare was on the set daily—the filming became just the elixir he needed after the disappointing 1992 reviews for *Four Baboons Adoring the Sun* (see chapter 9) and the soon-to-be termination of the touring version of *Six Degrees of Separation*.[19] The film version was true to the play but with the added glamor that the New York City locales provided and with what seemed to be a larger role for Flan than he had originally. In the play, Paul's con artistry was revealed through flashbacks. In the movie, the tale is recounted at the Gotham Bar and Grill and at the Metropolitan Museum of Art, among other locales. The rest of the shooting, which featured filming at the Strand bookstore, the Cathedral of St. John the Divine, Central Park, the Rainbow Room, and Manhattan College (substituting for Harvard), included several of Guare's favorite stomping grounds.[20] The film finished shooting on schedule, and Schepisi, whose work is meticulous, did a fine job and did not compromise his standards to get the product he envisioned.

The movie premiered in New York City on 6 December 1993. Always a bit leery about transforming a successful play onto the screen, the critics instead agreed that this was the rare exception that worked well.[21] Schepisi's film maintained the fast pace of the play through his superb job of supervising the editing of the scenes. The critics acknowledged that the cast was uniformly excellent, perhaps with Will Smith the weakest of the lot. Patrizia von Brandenstein's sets were immaculate, and costume designer Judianna Makovsky did a wonderful job of giving Paul the preppy look while fitting the flamboyant Flan with Hermès, Sulka, and Armani suits. Ian Baker's crisp cinematography enhanced the film's sophisticated quality. Overall, the film captured the play's dark comedy while maintaining its poignancy.

The structure of *Six Degrees of Separation* is congruent with Guare's attempt to dismantle the realism of kitchen-sink drama. The theater-in-the-round staging works perfectly for this type of play that relies on metatheatrical techniques that assist the actors in addressing the audience in an intimate way. The Brechtian alienation effect of having the actors sit closely to the stage to appear and vanish at will, reinforcing the notion that the tale is being narrated as performance art, also serves to raze fourth-wall conventions. Changes in milieux and times are perceived through different lighting effects. By not dividing the play into acts or scenes and by keeping the ninety-minute running time constant without an intermission, Guare kept the energy of the play at a high pace usually found in his black comedies, reinforcing the panic he wants to associate with our modern neuroses. The form of the play thus meshed well with the ideas Guare was trying to convey.

Six Degrees of Separation begins as a flashback in the plush New York apartment of waspy Upper-East-siders Flanders (Flan) and Louisa (Ouisa) Kittredge.[22] The wealthy, middle-aged couple are recovering from their previous evening's encounter with a young black man named Paul they invited to stay overnight in their son's bedroom; Paul took advantage of them by picking up a male prostitute on the street and bringing him back to the bedroom. When Ouisa and Flan pull off their bedtime attire to reveal dinner dress, we are flashed back to the previous evening. Flan reveals that he is an art dealer who specializes in buying from friends and then selling the paintings for much higher prices, even for millions of dollars, overseas. Tonight they are entertaining their friend, Geoffrey, a British South African businessman and art dealer who has made his fortune in gold mines. The Kittredges hope to wine and dine Geoffrey to get him to contribute two million dollars to their purchase of a Cezanne, which will eventually be sold to Japanese collectors for ten million dollars.

Geoffrey is well liked by the Kittredges despite his pomposity. Asked why he remains in South Africa, Geoffrey replies, "One has to stay there to educate the black workers and we'll know we've been successful when they kill us" (10). To repay the favor of such a quaint evening's entertainment, Geoffrey invites the Kittredges to South Africa to show them the sights: "I'll take you on my plane into the Okavango Swamps—" (12). Yet Flan and Ouisa are willing to tolerate Geoffrey's excesses because of his wealth. Ouisa describes Geoffrey as "King Midas rich. Literally. Gold mines" (7). Although they mock Geoffrey for not having the price of a dinner, they realize that his two million dollars is what counts. Ouisa acknowledges, "Rich people can do something for you even if you're not sure what it is you want them to do" (9). While they laugh at his jokes, Ouisa muses, "We weren't auditioning but I kept thinking Two million dollars two million dollars" (13). Flan and Ouisa seem to be more concerned with the art of the deal than they are with the art. They are willing to prostitute themselves in order to get Geoffrey to commit to two million dollars. Money is equated with value, but values are lost in the transaction.

As John Peter suggested in his review of the London production of the play at the Royal Court Theatre, the artwork of the transaction becomes more significant than buying the art itself, distinguishing value from values.[23] The monetary value of the art outweighs its aesthetic or artistic value. Flan and Ouisa are essentially con artists—upper-class hustlers. Through elegance and erudition, Flan and Ouisa have mastered the art of the deal but have no idea of their hypocrisy; instead, they see themselves as charming and sophisticated socialites, but underneath there is a shallowness at the core of their lives.

The art dealings are interrupted when Paul, a preppy, young African-American male in his early twenties, is ushered into the apartment by the doorman. Paul claims that he was mugged in nearby Central Park, with the robbers stealing his money and briefcase containing his thesis. Paul tells the Kittredges that he is a school chum of their sons, Talbot and Woody, at Harvard. After the mugging, he remembered that the Kittredges' sons had given him their parents' address, and realizing that their apartment was across from Central Park, he sought solace there. The Kittredges bathe him, administer First Aid, and then try to learn more about Paul. He tells them that his father is actor Sidney Poitier, currently coming to New York to conduct auditions for a movie version of *Cats* that he plans to direct. To legitimize his story, Paul intimately recounts the details of Poitier's life, including the exact titles and dates of nine of his forty-two films. Flan and Ouisa, like Guare, somewhat haunted by celebrity status, are now intrigued by having the son of a movie star in their home.[24] Flan woos Paul: "Tell us stories of movie stars tying up their children and being cruel" (25). Paul, dressed in a Brooks Brothers shirt that makes him look preppy and demonstrating a cosmopolitan, worldly air of wisdom, is invited to stay for dinner, even though the original plans were to treat Geoffrey, with his limited time in New York, to a fine restaurant. Paul turns out to be a surprisingly good cook, and during dinner, he displays more of his charming wit and personality. Flan and Ouisa are mesmerized by Paul's account of his childhood in Switzerland and his overall literacy level, including well-placed references to T.S. Eliot (20), Freud (29, 30), Salinger's *The Catcher in the Rye* (31–33), Chekhov (33), Beckett (33), and *Lord of the Rings* (33). Paul admits that he is also an international traveller: "I really don't know New York. I know Rome and Paris and Los Angeles a lot better" (23). In a perverse sort of parody of Poitier's own *Guess Who's Coming to Dinner*, Ouisa and Flan do more than just invite Paul to dinner. Ouisa admits, "I just loved the kid so much. I wanted to reach out to him" (31). They insist that Paul stay overnight and even give him fifty dollars in spending money upon agreement that he will maneuver to get them roles as extras in *Cats*. Geoffrey is so enamored with Paul that he envisions plans for a Black American Film Festival in South Africa, juried, of course, by Sidney Poitier. Flan and Ouisa go to bed thrilled that they have saved money by eating at home, have taken Geoffrey's two million dollars, and have brushed shoulders that evening with a celebrity. Flan and Ouisa equate money and celebrity with godhead:

Flan.	There is a God.
Ouisa.	And his name is—
Flan.	Geoffrey?
Ouisa.	Sidney. (44)

In this respect, as James Campbell suggests, by helping Paul, Ouisa and Flan initially may be trying to make a good impression on Geoffrey, who has revealed that Sidney Poitier "means a great deal in South Africa" (25).[25]

When Paul is discovered the next morning with a hustler in his bed, compliments of the fifty dollars the Kittredges gave him, things turn sour. The original stage version depicted fellatio at this point in the play.[26] Flan exclaims, "You brought this thing into our house! Thing! Thing! Get out! Get out of my house!" (49).[27] Paul is asked to leave, and after he does, Flan can only hope that his silver Victorian inkwell has not been stolen.[28] Somewhat later, Kitty and Larkin, friends of the Kittredges whose son is at Harvard also, recount their tale in which Paul, claiming to be Sidney Poitier's son, also became a guest in their house. Kitty and Larkin had an engagement, so they left Paul alone in their house; upon returning, they found him chasing a blonde boy that the couple assumed was a thief. Kitty and Larkin learned the truth when they shared their stories with the Kittredges. Paul, however, stole nothing from either household. He even sent the Kittredges a flower arrangement, a pot of jam, and a thank-you note.

The con game continues as Dr. Fine, an obstetrician at New York Hospital, treats Paul, who had come to the doctor's office with wounds that we later learn were self-inflicted. Dr. Fine, believing that Paul is his son's colleague at Dartmouth, gave Paul the keys to his house. When Dr. Fine calls his son to confirm the story, the latter bawls his father out for being naive enough to give a stranger house keys. Meanwhile, Ouisa's detective work has paid off—she has discovered that Sidney Poitier has four daughters but no sons. Ouisa, Flan,

Kitty, Larkin, and Dr. Fine urge their children to unearth the facts and explain how this impostor could be using their names to gain access to various homes.

The conversation with the children of these affluent parents reveals quite a bit about the lack of connection in, and the neuroses of, modern society. The first contact with these adolescents is when Doug, Dr. Fine's son, lambastes his father for being "a real cretin" (65). The discussion centers on alienation and isolation where no spiritual connection exists. Doug even defends his mother's divorce: "Dad, sometimes it is so obvious to me why Mom left. I am so embarrassed to know you" (65). Doug then accuses his father of being an alcoholic, a wife beater, and a rotten lover (65). Guare makes it clear that Doug is not doing well when he wonders to his father, "Why you had to bring me into the world!" (65). Tess, the daughter of Ouisa and Flan, is obviously troubled and plans to escape to Afghanistan and climb mountains to find herself (71). When Flan counters by unequivocally stating that he has not invested time and money in her so she can scale K-2, she responds, "Is that all I am? An investment?" (71). Later in the play, she openly rebels against her parents, promising them, "I'm going to ruin my life and get married and throw away everything you want me to be because it's the only way to hurt you!" (102). Woody, the youngest son of Ouisa and Flan, is amazed that his parents let a stranger wear one of his favorite shirts, which was a Christmas present he cherished. He tells Flan and Ouisa, "I can't believe it. I hate it here. I hate this house. I hate you" (74). The children are growing up neurotic, and in a few years, will be recycled into new Flans and Ouisas, complacent in their bourgeois norms and values but spiritually disconnected. The flashback ends in a litany of complaints:

Doug.	You never do anything for me.
Tess.	You've never done anything but tried to block me.
Ben.	I'm only this pathetic extension of your eighth-rate personality.
Doug.	Social Darwinism pushed beyond all limits.
Woody.	You gave away my pink shirt?
Tess.	You want me to be everything you weren't.
Doug.	You said drugs and looked at me. (74–75)

The children, through a process of elimination, trace down the culprit as Trent Conway, one of their former high school chums, now at MIT. Trent, in exchange for sex, introduced Paul to his address book, and acting as the American version of Henry Higgins, gave neophyte Paul, playing the role of Eliza Doolittle, a crash course in habits of the rich and famous. Trent coached Paul: "Rich people do something nice for you, you give them a pot of jam" (77). For three months, Trent went through his address book and told Paul tidbits about each family, which eventually was the means for Paul to gain access to their homes.

A short time after Paul had left the Kittredge household, he met Rick and Elizabeth, two lovers in their mid-twenties, in Central Park. Rick and Elizabeth were aspiring actors from Utah, temporarily waiting on tables before they could get their big chance at stardom. Paul claimed that his parents, the Kittredges, are wealthy art dealers who have abandoned him. Rick and Elizabeth, identifying with Paul as an outcast like themselves, invite him to live with them in their tenement loft. Paul, himself now acting as Henry Higgins, eventually teaches the two performers how rich people behave; this endears Paul to them because he has tapped into their dreams of being rich and famous. Elizabeth even asks Paul if her resemblance to Liv Ullmann will be a deterrent in her career (88). Paul later convinces Rick and Elizabeth that he has reconciled with his father but now needs money to meet him in Maine, where he is visiting Paul's grandparents. Rick and Elizabeth withdraw the money from their bank and give it to Paul. Paul then takes part of that money and treats Rick to a night of dancing at the Rainbow Room, culminating in a carriage ride and then sex between the two men. Rick, like Ouisa, cherishes the time spent with Paul, admitting, "It was the greatest night I ever had and before we got home he kissed me on the mouth and he vanished" (91). Rick, apparently confused about his sexuality, commits suicide by jumping off a building, leaving Elizabeth to press charges against Paul for stealing their money.

Paul telephones the Kittredges, who urge him to turn himself in to the police. Questioned about why he would bring a hustler back to the room when the Kittredges extended their hospitality to him as well as their trust, Paul responds, "I was so happy. I wanted to add sex to it. Don't you do that?" (108). Paul is implying that he valued the experience—the vitality of meaningful contact with others. When Paul asks Ouisa if she ever adds sex to her relationship and she says no, this middle-aged sterility, such as is found in Edward Albee's impotent protagonists, indicates the overt effects of the modern neurosis. Ouisa begins to accept Paul's individuality and chooses to defer going to an auction at Sotheby's in order to take Paul to the police where, she says, "They will treat you with dignity" (114). However, when Ouisa and Flan arrive at the Waverly Theater to meet Paul, the police had already dragged him, kicking and screaming, into a squad car. Ouisa and Flan are helpless to bail Paul out because they do not even know his real name and thus cannot identify him for the authorities.

On the surface level, *Six Degrees of Separation* documents the pathology of middle- and upper-class modern urban life in the United States. Guare depicts a life of fatuity in which anecdote has replaced worthwhile experience. In his essay, "Radical Chic," Tom Wolfe described how wealthy Leonard Bernstein invited revolutionary members of the Black Panther Party to soirées at his thirteen-room penthouse on Park Avenue. Attendees included celebrities from all walks of life who had a liberal penchant for fetishizing the downtrodden. Full of liberal guilt, the Bernsteins and their compatriots made a desperate effort to hire white servants for these "occasions" with the Panthers. The trend, endemic to the upper classes, is described as "nostalgie de la boue," a romanticizing of "primitive souls."[29] The fashionable Radical Chic movement thus favored minorities who were exotic and romantic—the stuff of which anecdotes are made. Wolfe clarified how this attitude typifies modern American society: "Radical Chic, after all, is only radical in style; in its heart it is part of Society and its traditions."[30]

Flan and Ouisa participate in their own version of Radical Chic. Money colors their politics. When Flan mentions Gorbachev's support for the striking coal miners in the Ukraine, Ouisa's only thought is the "chic" strangely mixed with the lower classes: "The phrase— striking coal miners—I see all these very striking coal miners modelling fall fashions—" (11). The people's revolt in Russia and Poland—"Follow Follow Follow"—is equated with a song in *The Fantasticks* (11). Geoffrey's condescending promise of a trip to the Okavango Swamp to repay the Kittredges for their hospitality intimates the elite's quaint attraction with what is perceived to be the primitive.

Thus, when Paul enters, Radical Chic comes into all of its glory as the upper class engages in liberal guilt to help the literally wounded black man. As Julie Salamon has noted, Paul becomes the perfect black for the Kittredges to fetishize: Ivy League, polite, a celebrity, and the son of a man who is himself an anecdote, the "barrier breaker of the fifties and sixties" (24).[31] Paul's upbringing in Europe, his polished education, and his fine ancestry make him much more exotic and less of a threat. He even admits, "I don't feel American. I don't even feel black" (30). The Kittredges are not the only ones duped by Paul's "celebrity status." Kitty and Larkin's encounter with Paul is reduced to the proud announcement, "We are going to be in the movie of *Cats*" (55). Dr. Fine was also seduced by the lure of the movies: "And this kid's father—the bravery of his films—had given me a direction, a confidence" (64). Dr. Fine says he now has the opportunity to rub shoulders with the son of a Hollywood legend, "Somebody who had really forged ahead and made new paths for blacks just by the strength of his own talent" (64). Paul's con game also affects those who aspire to the values of Radical Chic. Trent Conway, who keeps written records of the lives of the rich and famous, fetishizes Paul to the extent that the latter becomes a sex object and uses the MIT student to gain valuable information about the argot of the wealthy. Finally, Rick and Elizabeth, with star-struck visions of performing Shakespeare and Chekhov on stages all over the world, are conned by Paul's admission that his father is a millionaire. Paul persuades Rick and Elizabeth to give him money for an alleged trip to Maine by insinuating that he is close to the rich and famous and is thus worthy of being trusted. Paul entices the two aspiring actors by implying that his assistance from the wealthy will one day lead to their own stardom:

> But I am going to give you the money to put on a showcase of any play you want and you'll be in it and agents will come see you and you'll be seen and you'll be started. And when you win your Oscars—both of you—you'll look in the camera and thank me—(88–89)

Although on the surface Guare explores the concept of Radical Chic, the leitmotif of the play involves the fragmentation of the psyche and our efforts to connect with self and others in a society where we are constantly alienated. Ouisa mentions the spiritual connection that potentially unites us all: "I read somewhere that everybody on this planet is separated by only six other people. Six degrees of separation" (81).[32] However, one must find the right six people to make the connection. Most individuals in modern society are alienated to the extent that separation and division have become the norm. Guare stated, "For me, the play is all about the Kandinsky."[33] The painting by Kandinsky is the image that opens (3) and closes the play (120). The stage directions indicate, "*One side is geometric and somber. The other side is wild and vivid*" (4). Flan reduces the painting to "A burst of color asked to carry so much" (14). The Kandinsky represents color without structure, a condition that characterizes the lives of Ouisa and Flan, and to a certain extent, defines the personae of Geoffrey, Kitty, Larkin, and Dr. Fine as well; Ouisa, for example, realizes "There is color in my life, but I'm not aware of any structure"

(118). Color also becomes a metaphor for the race-based problems of separation inherent in the play. Furthermore, as Frank Rich mentions, like the Kandinsky, Ouisa, Flan, and their colleagues are two-faced, double-sided.[34] The spiritual needs of the psyche do not match up with our superficial desire for celebrity. For example, Ouisa and Flan agreed that *Cats* was, as Tess reminds them, "an all-time low in a lifetime of theater-going" (72), but the chance to be part of the film version is the carrot that lingers in their infatuation with Paul. Larkin, who asserts that Flan, Ouisa, and Dr. Fine are all financially successful, cannot understand why Paul's celebrity status intrigued them so much: "We let him in our lives. I run a foundation. You're a dealer. You're a doctor. You'd think we'd be satisfied with our achievements" (68). Sadly, instead of finding the links in the degrees of separation, Ouisa admits, "It seems the common thread linking us all is an overwhelming need to be in the movie of *Cats*" (68).

In *Six Degrees of Separation*, alienation and isolation are the norm rather than spiritual connectiveness. Parents do not know their children, heterosexuals are alienated from homosexuals, whites are separated from blacks, and the wealthy do not understand the less fortunate. Guare depicts a bifurcated society in which the emotional and intellectual vitality of individual consciousness is reduced to fragmentation and a neurotic obsession with celebrity status. Individuals are divorced from each other, and thus families, classes, and races are also further divided. Of course, the spiritual connection is lost in the modern world; the image of man touching the hand of God in the Sistine Chapel, which Paul longs to see, is, as Ouisa views it, in need of cleaning (101).

This modern estrangement has allowed us to wear the mask of the con artist to hide our real feelings while taking advantage of others. Paul gains access to houses in order to find the family that he lacks; he is searching for an identity and yearns to be loved, wanted, and appreciated. He seeks contact in a society out of touch with the spiritual and with no passion for individuality. He explains to Ouisa why he sought her advice and comfort:

> No, I only visited you. I didn't like the first people so much. They went out and just left me alone. I didn't like the doctor. He was too eager to please. And he left me alone. But you. You and your husband. We all stayed together. (99)

When Paul is asked what he wanted from the Kittredges, he states, "everlasting friendship" (99). However, Paul, like many of us, is more outwardly interested in rubbing shoulders with the rich and famous, and thus his envy of celebrity forced him to assume the guise of con artist. Similarly, Flan and Ouisa, whose children are alienated from them, reached out to Paul as the ideal son they would love to have as part of their family. On the surface, however, Ouisa and Flan are con artists just like Paul, only their scams involve Cezannes and Kandinskys. Their seduction of Geoffrey is a fine demonstration of the con game fully at work. Like Paul, Flan and Ouisa have learned the art of the deal: figure out what the client wants and then deliver it. Trent Conway fully realizes that the wealthy participate in the con game as well: "Hand to mouth on a higher plateau" (77). The only difference is that people at the bottom of the social stratum have further to go as they aspire to this plateau.

Although Paul is a con man who has borrowed ideas from others, his appearance becomes the catalyst for Ouisa's transformation by the end of the play. Paul the catalyst is similar to the role that Mildred Douglas plays in O'Neill's *The Hairy Ape*. In O'Neill's play, Yank pursues a quest for identity to determine if he "belongs" in the modern world. At first, Yank is in his element as the powerful stoker, at ease in his role as the fire that powers the ship's engines. Even when Paddy mocks Yank's choice to belong to the primitive and animalistic world of the grimy stokehole, Yank, although he internalizes Paddy's remarks, sloughs off any indication that he cannot "connect" with the men and machines around him. However, when Mildred Douglas penetrates the bowels of the ship, appearing to Yank as a ghost in white, he is shocked out of his complacency and pursues a quest to determine his identity. Paul is the Mildred Douglas of *Six Degrees of Separation*. Ouisa and Flan were perfectly content to entertain Geoffrey for the evening in what amounted to just another con game. Paul became the impetus for Ouisa and Flan to become aware of life lived in ignorant bliss.

Paul helps Ouisa understand how estranged modern society has become and how empty her own life is without the vitality of imagination. Paul's first indication of his understanding of the modern *angoisse* is revealed when he mentions his passion for Holden Caulfield, the protagonist in Salinger's *The Catcher in the Rye*. Paul describes Caulfield as a young man suffering from emotional and intellectual paralysis; although Caulfield mocks the phoniness around him, his insight forces him to become divorced from others. To Paul, Salinger's novel reflects the death of the imagination. He tells Flan and Ouisa, "The imagination has moved out of the realm of being our link, our most personal link, with our inner lives and the world outside that world—this world we share" (34). Paul is lamenting the lack of passion in a society where habit, convenience, and style have replaced meaningful human connections. The "world we share" that he speaks of refers to the spiritual commitment necessary to find the "six degrees of communication" that unite humanity. Paul is trying to explain his existence to Flan and Ouisa: he is an effective con man because he is merely mirroring American values and falling prey to the myth of the American Dream as we know it. This type of society, where human connections are fleeting and imagination is nonexistent, gets what it deserves: hustlers, con men, and impostors. Values are distorted: art is sold mainly for profit in private homes and in public at places like Sotheby's, *Cats* achieves theatrical prominence, and intimate experience is devalued in favor of cocktail-party anecdote. Even Salinger's art is distorted by those who turn the message around to suit their own whims: Mark David Chapman and John Hinckley use the novel as a defense for the shootings of John Lennon and Ronald Reagan, respectively. Paul understands that to connect with others, we must first come to grips with our selves, our imaginations. He states, "I believe the imagination is another phrase for what is most uniquely *us*" (34). Ouisa begins to understand the need to connect with others by using our imaginations to hold onto a purity of experience that may be alive, vibrant, and poignant rather than to substitute it for disposable anecdotal information. Paul realizes that the imagination is what prevents the American Dream from disintegrating into a nightmare: "It's there to sort out your nightmare, to show you the exit from the maze of your nightmare, to transform the nightmare into dreams that become your bedrock. It we don't listen to that voice, it dies. It shrivels. It vanishes" (62–63). And during the initial run of *Six Degrees* at Lincoln Center, Guare echoed Paul's comments when he hinted to an interviewer why the play has become significant to a contemporary New York audience: "We're all on top of each other. My concerns are about the imagination and how we live in this city. We can't go on living like this, where the ideals are so high and the opposite of what ideals are, the bedrock, is so weak."[35]

Although the Kittredges are wealthy and seem to have everything to make them feel comfortable, they learn that material things do not suffice when there is no connection with self and others. Again, Guare demonstrates that the lives of the rich and famous are often spiritually hollow at the core—certainly nothing to emulate. Although Flan and Ouisa are appalled that Paul took advantage of them, his presence made the couple suddenly feel alive. They become aware of the artificiality of life devoid of experience where meaningful emotional connections are reduced to constantly changing identities. In this sense, *Six Degrees of Separation* has much in common with director Paul Mazursky's screenplay for *Down and Out in Beverly Hills*. In that film, homeless Jerry Baskin imposes himself on wealthy Dave Whiteman's family in Beverly Hills. Dave rescues Jerry from suicide when the latter attempts to drown in the Whitemans' pool. Dave invites Jerry to stay in his house until he recovers; Jerry, intuitively understanding that he has found a sucker in upperclass white liberals, takes advantage of the situation and "reluctantly" agrees to stay. The Whitemans are attracted to Jerry for various reasons. Dave, who is a successful businessman enamored with Radical Chic, is fascinated by Jerry's devil-may-care attitude, which has enabled him to drop out of the "rat race." Barbara Whiteman, who compensates for her sexless marriage by seeking self-gratification through shopping, aerobics, meditation, and yoga, reaches Nirvana when Jerry gives her a deep massage followed by sex. Jerry also has a profound effect on the Whiteman children: he accepts Max's punk lifestyle and brings Jenny, the snobbish and anorexic Sarah Lawrence student, down to earth. The Whitemans' maid becomes aware of class consciousness through books Jerry lends her, and even Matisse, the canine who is counselled by a dog psychiatrist, is less temperamental around Jerry. Irascible and prickly, Jerry eventually become a nuisance, demanding better quality food and accommodations while making no attempt to leave the mansion. When Jerry does wear out his welcome and returns to the streets, the Whitemans realize that he was not merely an anecdote but instead provided them with meaningful experience, which is priceless. After finding Jerry roaming the streets, the Whitemans bring him back home.

When Ouisa speaks with Paul on the telephone near the end of the play, he declares, "You don't sound happy" (107). Paul realizes that, even with all of their wealth, the Kittredges' lives are empty. Paul provided the Kittredges the chance to connect emotionally with another human being. Paul, like Jerry in *Down and Out in Beverly Hills*, became the catalyst for the release of the imagination, allowing authenticity to replace artificiality. Ouisa tries to get her husband to understand that high culture is not merely wealth and conspicuous consumption but rather a community of lives that connect spiritually despite differences in race, gender, or class. Ouisa realizes that although it only requires six people to connect all humanity, most of us are unable to find the right six people to make the connection, and thus we remain separated. Paul, someone who cared about the Kittredges, provided a meaningful connection for Ouisa. David Román notes, "Moreover, Paul's humanity must be available to her on some level even if he is neither the son of Sidney Poitier nor her children's class-mate."[36] In a dehumanizing society where artifice and phoniness are the norm, Paul, despite the fact that he duped the Kittredges, re-flected a strong desire to bond with them as family. In a sick society where most people are two-faced like the Kandinsky and contact is bogus and fleeting, reduced primarily to disposable anecdotes, Ouisa desperately wants to hold onto the experience. She explains her feel-ings to Flan at the end of the play: "But it was an experience. I will not turn him into an anecdote. How do we fit what happened to us into life without turning it into an anecdote with no teeth and a punch line you'll mouth over and over for years to come" (117). As she ex-plores the existential angst troubling her, Ouisa's dilemma concerns the modern identity in a fraudulent society: "But it was an experi-ence. How do we keep the experience?" (118). Through the same sort of redemptive spirit that we witnessed in the tetralogy, Ouisa, willing to forgive Paul for his transgressions, will find the means to locate the right six people in the chain that will lead to an authen-tic spiritual connection. Guare expects his middle- and upper-class audience of theatergoers to identify with Ouisa and learn from the epiphany she experiences at the end of the play.

Guare's brilliant achievement in *Six Degrees of Separation* is a result of his ability to take black comedy to another level, mixing farce and pathos. As the Kandinsky turns at the beginning of the play, we real-ize the sarcasm of the duplicity of con artists Flan and Ouisa during their soirée with Geoffrey. Paul's con game develops into farce when he is discovered with a male prostitute. The scene of a naked, ag-gressive hustler chasing Flan and Ouisa around their apartment is as demonstrative as any sick behavior represented in classical farce from Molière to the Marx Brothers. Moreover, the vision of a young black man who stabs himself to gain access to the apartments of the well-to-do and then charms them with knowledge acquired through others represents the modern neurosis at its best. Guare's black com-edy is most effective here as the humorous turns to pain, despair, and horror when the Kittredges discover that they and their colleagues have been duped. As in classical farce or black comedy, the audience laughs but is also disgusted when the comic becomes frighteningly real and thus rather terrifying. As the play moves from the absurdly comic and pathetically disorienting crass materialistic world of the art of the deal to the unexpected pathos of Ouisa's epiphany about the potential of shared humanity, Guare's black comedy comes into its own by depicting modern society as a neurotic circus and simultaneously a vale of tears. *Six Degrees of Separation*, then, reflects the pinnacle of success with a genre that liberates through laughter yet forces the audience to engage seriously in an examination of their own humanity in a grotesque world.

9

The Later Plays

BETWEEN 1979 AND 1992, GUARE COMPLETED FOUR SHORT PLAYS and two full-length dramas, excluding the tetralogy and *Six Degrees of Separation*. Although these are not his best-known plays, they do probe the modern neuroses through black comedy and thus must be considered seriously.

In Fireworks Lie Secret Codes, the first of these plays, was one of ten dramas about holidays that producer Jon Jory commissioned as a festival celebration. Other playwrights contributing to the festival included Ray Aranha (*New Year's*), Tom Eyen (*Independence Day*), Oliver Hailey (*I Can't Find It Anywhere*), Israel Horovitz (*The Great Labor Day Classic*), Preston Jones (*June-Teenth*), Marsha Norman (*Merry Christmas*), Megan Terry (*Fireworks*), Douglas Turner Ward (*Redeemer*), and Lanford Wilson (*Bar Play*). These ten dramas were initially staged as part of the Actors Theatre of Louisville's Festival of New American Plays ("Holidays") on 26 January 1979, at the Victor Jory Theatre.[1] Michael Hankins directed a fine ensemble of six versatile performers who played all of the roles. *In Fireworks Lie Secret Codes* was later staged in a different version for a one-act play festival under artistic direction of Edward Albee at the Mitzi E. Newhouse Theater in Lincoln Center.[2] Directed by Guare himself, *In Fireworks Lie Secret Codes* opened on 5 March 1981 with two other plays staged by the Lincoln Center Theater Company: Jeffrey Sweet's *Stops Along the Way* and Percy Granger's *Vivien*. The cast for Guare's play included William Newman (Number 1), Kathleen Widdoes (Number 2), James Woods (Number 3), Barbra Andres (Number 4), and Graham Beckel (Number 5).

In Fireworks Lie Secret Codes occurs on the Fourth of July when five sophisticated New Yorkers have gathered on the terrace of a penthouse to watch the Macy's fireworks display. Characters 1, 3, and 5 are men; 2 and 4 are women. Their lack of individual names suggests anonymity, as is often expressed in expressionist drama such as Elmer Rice's *The Adding Machine*, particularly reminiscent of scene 3 in the play in which Mr. Zero meets other nameless automatons like himself at a party. In Guare's drama, all the characters are Americans except Number 3, who is British. Guare's stage directions indicate, "*Everyone is enthralled.*"[3] With every burst of fireworks that explodes into arrays of colorful streams, someone is reminded of the more glamorous and glorious past events in their lives in much the same manner that Marcel Proust used the *madeleine* in the tea to unlock the buried memories of the unconscious in *Du côte de chez Swann*. Number 1 is reminded of the time when the tall ships sailed up the Hudson River. He recalls, "People in New York were happy for a year after that" (145). Number 1 notes that even when the urban mire of being stuck in an elevator or subway becomes too overbearing, he reminisces about the tall ships, enabling him to quash the modern *angoisse*, albeit momentarily. Number 2 is so enamored with the fireworks that she suggests that the host ask the guests to return for a future celebration: "We could have quilting parties and sewing bees" (147). Number 2 begins to fantasize about utopias. The fireworks have triggered her imagination to the extent that the urban anonymity of a penthouse world of granite and steel is now transformed into the open space of farmland. She muses, "Kansas or Oz. Oz or Kansas. With me, it's always been Kansas or Oz. But here tonight this roof—the eternal dilemma finally and irrevocably resolved. Everything here. I'd never have to leave" (147). Several of the characters reminisce about wonderful holidays they have experienced, including the International Fireworks Exhibition during Bastille Day (149), the Christmas show at the Music Hall (149–50), Christmas in Bethlehem (150–51), and a special Memorial Day for the English gentleman (153).

However, as the evening wears on, the "oohs" and "aahs," exclamations resulting from the onlookers in awe of the beauty of the fireworks, now degenerate into the modern neuroses we have come to expect in a Guare comedy. The clever veneer of the urban elite is soon replaced by horror stories about life in the contemporary metropolis. Numbers 3 and 5 recount that their Memorial Day escapade was marred by a woman on the subway who protested that she had been sexually harassed; unfortunately, an innocent Chinese man was accused of committing the offense, resulting in a wildly absurd fracas between the crazed woman and the Chinese gentleman, who was forced to use his newspaper in self-defense. Number 3's story is tinged with references to Molière, Buster Keaton, Feydeau, and Noel Coward, implicitly comparing the incident to farce. Number 3 explains how this type of farce moves into the realm of dark comedy, much in the same manner of the structure of *Six Degrees of Separation*:

"People back to the newspapers of their native language. Some people still laughing. Others no longer laughing. But the laughter had purified nothing. Our laughter had only helped anguish move into anecdote" (156).

As the fireworks display wanes and the alcohol begins to take effect, the conversation is infused with more stories of melancholy and despair. The tales of urban affluence are as short-lived as the fireworks. Number 5 remembers a bus ride in Kensington where two women were talking about their friend's suicide attempt. Number 5 believes that this conversation reflects ordinary events rather than "an hysterical day like a holiday" when fantasies are more likely to develop (157). Through the secret codes of the fireworks, the English gentleman gradually understands that life in America is over for him. He plans to return to England, noting, "I just find it difficult to survive on the days that are not holidays" (157). Number 2 suddenly realizes that she has lived one third of her life in New York City (159). Number 5, now faced with the reality that his roommate is abandoning him for England, is left deserted and in distress (158). And Number 4 is alarmed that her decision to move to New Jersey, described as "the worst state in the union" where poisonous nuclear gases inundate everyone (149), is a disaster waiting to happen. In essence, Guare, confined by the one-act play structure and the holiday theme that set the parameters for which he was initially asked to conform, still managed to craftily move the play from what seems to be a trivial subject on the surface to a more subtle exploration of the dark comedy underlying the modern *angoisse*.

In 1985, Anne Cattaneo, dramaturge for the Acting Company, a national repertory theater on tour for the John F. Kennedy Center, commissioned a dozen playwrights to adapt Chekhov's short stories for the stage. Seven of the twelve playwrights who were asked agreed to work on the project. Guare adapted Chekhov's "A Joke," from a translation by Marian Fell, into a one-act play, *The Talking Dog*. The seven adaptations premiered as "Orchards," at the Krannert Center for the Performing Arts in Champaign-Urbana, Illinois, on 19 September 1985. Other playwrights contributing to the evening's program included Maria Irene Fornes, Spalding Gray, David Mamet, Wendy Wasserstein, Michael Weller, and Samm-Art Williams. Robert Falls directed, Louis Rosen composed the music, Laura Crow created the costumes, and Adrianne Lobel designed the sets.[4]

Chekhov's short story, "A Joke," written in first person, concerns a young couple sledding down a high summit. The nameless young man initially has to coax his partner, Nadia, to brave the mountain.

During the ride on the sled, with his arms around her, they slide down the hill while the young man whispers, "I love you, Nadia."[5] The young man wonders how he had the courage to speak his mind and consequently has doubts that he did: "Had I really uttered those four words, or had she only fancied she heard them in the tumult of the wind?" (121). Nadia also cannot believe how frank her companion had been and would like to make sure she was hearing correctly, for until now, he had made no gesture of love to her. Each time they slide down the hill, the young man says "I love you, Nadia." The young girl is so confused that she believes she heard the wind instead and cannot determine what is real. The same scenario continues day after day. However, when spring arrives and the snow melts, the mystery ends. Eventually, the young man goes to St. Petersburg, and Nadia marries but never forgets the fond memory of how they coasted together in bliss.

Guare changes the situation to the more contemporary idea of hang-gliding rather than sledding and moves the locale to the Cat-skills. At first, the young nameless woman, in her twenties, is reluctant to hang-glide with her male counterpart, a sort of parody of Erica Jong's novel, *Fear of Flying*. The young man, however, is persistent, encouraging the woman to develop a sense of adventure. He coaxes her, saying, "We have to give ourselves tests of courage all the time to grow, to know we're progressing."[6] During their flight in the air, the young man whispers to her, "I. Love. You" (168). Upon landing, the woman is ecstatic from the hang-gliding yet confused and intrigued by what she thought she heard. They go up again several times, and the young man, soaring through the air with her, repeats the same words. The young woman wonders if Nature is speaking through the wind. Rather than express his true feelings for the woman, the young man puts doubts in her mind by relating a story about his friend who trained her dog to growl (hence the title of the play), making a sound that resembled "Hello/I/Love/You" (172). Later, the young man transfers to another city, and the woman eventually marries a fellow whom the young man describes as "some nerd" (174). The young man realizes the lost opportunity to express his love to her but rationalizes it by stating that he would just as soon live alone than with someone who could not "take a joke" (174). To Guare, the tale accentuates the difference between the real and the ephemeral. The mythology is in the moment; lost opportunities in the past will forever color the future. The imagination must never be stifled. Like Bunny in *The House of Blue Leaves*, Betty Yearn in *Landscape of the Body*, Sally in *Atlantic City*, and Gussie at the end of *Lydie Breeze*, who follow their instincts, thus allowing them to dream, the young man should have expressed his love directly to the girl when he had the opportunity. Otherwise, life merely becomes a series of useless anecdotes instead of the truth determined through viable experience.

Guare, busy with the New York theatrical debut of *Lydie Breeze* in February 1982, told the press that he was working on a political farce set in Miami.[7] Guare's original intention was to work on a screenplay, tentatively titled *Moon Under Miami*, for a film that was to costar John Belushi and Dan Ackroyd; when Belushi died in March 1982 of a drug overdose, Guare abandoned the project temporarily. After allowing sufficient time for Belushi's ghost to be put to rest, Guare began adapting the screenplay for the stage with the hope that Louis Malle would eventually direct it. The first version of *Moon Under Miami* was presented at the Williamstown Theater Festival in Williamstown, Massachusetts, during August 1987. This three-hour production was directed by Larry Sloan and featured James Belushi, John's brother, as Shelley. Guare had set the play in a Florida hotel during a presidential election.

In April 1989, the revised version of the play, *Moon Over Miami*, premiered at the Yale Repertory Theatre, which was under artistic direction of Lloyd Richards. Andrei Belgrader directed the play, Lawrence Yerman composed the music, and Judy Gallen designed the sets. The twenty-seven-member cast included Oliver Platt (Otis), Susan Kellermann (Giselle), Stanley Tucci (Shelley), Laurel Cronin (Fran), Sam Stoneburner (Bentine), and Julie Hagerty (Corleen). The New York press did not descend upon Yale University to cover this production. However, Frank Rich, writing in the *New York Times*, welcomed the fact that Guare abandoned "the sober classical style" of the Lydie Breeze trilogy and praised Guare's wit, while noting that *Moon Over Miami* "frequently seems more burdened than liberated by the author's far-flung inventiveness, as if five or six plays were constantly fighting for the author's attention."[8] Guare then turned his attention to *Six Degrees of Separation*, returned to *Moon Over Miami*, worked on *Four Baboons Adoring the Sun*, then went back to *Moon*, planned a film biography of Gershwin, and then, after a spring 1993 workshop production staged by students at the Juilliard School of the Performing Arts (where Guare taught), again revised the play in 1994—a total of twelve drafts written since 1987. For the definitive version of the play, *Moon Under Miami*, Guare made revisions to reduce the number of characters and cut its nearly three hours of playing time to one hour and fifty minutes. The premiere was on 30 April 1995, at the Organic Theatre of the Remains Theater in Chicago. Neel Keller directed, artist Red Grooms designed exquisite sets of cartoonlike pop scenery, and Jeremy Kahn supervised the musical numbers. Coverage of this production was virtually nonexistent in the New York media; however, Richard Christiansen reviewed the play for the *Chicago Tribune*. Although recognizing the zany farcical quality of the production, Christiansen perceived the drama as an awkward attempt at hip art, rather plodding, confusing, rash, and too undisciplined for his tastes.[9] The $180,000 production unfortunately closed on 21 May, three weeks earlier than had been anticipated.[10]

Moon Under Miami was begun as a parody of the ABSCAM scandal that began in February 1978 and ran through the early 1980s.[11] Miami now replaces New York as a microcosm of greed, fraudulence, and corruption—a lawless East Coast frontier town that epitomizes the decadence of modern American society. Miami, a resort town catering to corrupt politicians and sleazy gangsters, resembles the "old" Atlantic City that Lou remembered as a mecca for hoodlums in their glory years. In Guare's play, one has difficulty distinguishing the politicians, the mobsters, and the FBI agents, who are all cut from the same tainted cloth. Written after Guare had completed the first part of the tetralogy, *Moon Under Miami*, like *Lydie Breeze*, which dealt partly with political corruption in the Gilded Age, is about the misuse and abuse of political power in the latter part of the twentieth century. In an interview with John Harrop published in 1987, Guare acknowledged how the ABSCAM scandal became the impetus for his exploration of how idealism is replaced by corruption: "*Moon Over Miami* is about the problems of politics, of being a politician in America today. How can you be a politician and stay pure? What does the process do to your ideals?"[12] If *Lydie Breeze* depicts the loss of idealism and the concomitant rise of greed associated with political influence at the end of the nineteenth century, *Moon Under Miami* would be well served as the fourth part of the tetralogy, tracing the same sort of corruption almost one hundred years later.

However, the form of *Moon Under Miami* is unlike the realism of the tetralogy. With *Moon Under Miami*, Guare returned to the zany, fast-paced black comedy that he began with in *Marco Polo Sings a Solo* and eventually adapted so successfully in *Rich and Famous* and *Landscape of the Body*. Employing wit, one-liners, sexual innuendo, biting sarcasm, and topical humor, *Moon Under Miami* can be compared to a frenetic Marx Brothers musical comedy. The play is also reminiscent of French farce. Before the premiere of the play in Chicago, Guare stated, "I wanted to reflect what was happening on our political scene and thought it demanded really brutal farce."[13] Like *Rich and Famous* and *Landscape of the Body, Moon Under Miami* is filled with musical numbers that Guare wrote, including several songs by a trio of mermaids who function as a chorus to reiterate the action; the play's length and its two-act structure, however, make it more closely resemble *Landscape of the Body* than the former play.

Moon Under Miami begins in the purity of Alaska where FBI Special Agent Otis Presby is investigating the influx of heroin that has been killing Eskimos. The trail of corruption leads him to the Boom Boom Room of the Fountaine Moon Hotel in Miami where lewd songstress Fran Farkus entertains the elite, including Alaska's own congressman, Reggie Kayak. With help from fellow FBI agents Belden and Wilcox, Otis investigates Shelley Slutsky, the source of the drug supply for Kayak. Hialeah's own congressman, Osvaldo Munoz, and Rhode Island's Honorable Wayne Bentine are also seen frequenting the Boom Boom Room. Apparently, Slutsky is in the business of paying congressmen for political favors, and the FBI wants to entrap him in the act; the politicians, all too eager to use the money for advertising in order to get reelected, are glad to do business with gangsters like Slutsky. After Slutsky shoots Congressman Kayak, the FBI arrests him. Slutsky, however, convinces the FBI that he is merely "a simple pimp panderer procurer drug dealing serial killer pervert,"[14] but that a much better catch would be Congressman Munoz.

Act 2 begins with Shelly assisting the FBI in setting up a wiretap and videotape of Munoz attempting to sell the wealthy Sheik of Akbahran U.S. citizenship. In return for his help, Shelley expects the FBI to release his femme fatale girlfriend, Giselle St. Just, from custody where she is charged as an illegal alien. Otis, torn over having to work with a criminal and even more absurd, in love with Slutsky's wife, Corleen, reluctantly agrees to participate in the setup. He poses as the sheik so the FBI can videotape the congressman offering citizenship for money and then is asked to marry Giselle so she can obtain U.S. citizenship. Meanwhile, a hurricane is sweeping the Everglades, destroying virtually everything in its path, much like the apocalyptic lightning bolts of *Marco Polo Sings a Solo*. The denouement follows at a frantic pace as Fran Farkus reveals herself to be J. Edgar Hoover, the icon of FBI legend. When Otis leaps at Shelley, blaming him for Corleen's death due to a drug overdose, he is shot by the gangster. Congressman Munoz dies while helping the boat people flee Fidel Castro. Shelley decides to run for political office; ahead in the polls, the gangster is already taking bribes, promising the sheik all marketing rights to the next war, Gulf Storm 2. His campaign office will now be the notorious Boom Boom Room run by none other than Fran Farkus herself.

The measuring stick at the center of this corrupt universe is Shelley Slutsky, whose last name, a combination of slushy and slut, suggests sleaze. The first words that he speaks in the play reveal his persona: "Who do you have to fuck to get a drink in this joint?" (98). Decked out in tropic shirts, gold chains, and linen jackets, Shelley is the personification of a materialistic lifestyle at any cost even if it means selling his soul. His businesses include investments, loan-sharking, money laundering, and general extortion; when Slutsky finds a sucker with money, such as the sheik, he will sell him anything, even U.S. citizenship. Slutsky has no conscience and could care little whether or not the drugs destined for Eskimos turn them into zombies as long as he gets his fair share of the money. Shelley even has no qualms about using Giselle, an art connoisseur, to purchase stolen art in order to launder drug money. He also gives money to congressmen for political favors, such as his plans for a new football team to play in the Moondome, all paid for by government funding acquired through the offices of Osvaldo Munoz. And his dope-selling profits help to finance the reelection campaign of Reggie Kayak. In his spare time, Shelley even sells condensed versions of the Bible that omit the more depressing events, such as Jesus's death. One of his favorite activities is selling fake permissions for boat people to enter the United States and then dumping them after relieving the dupes of their money. Thus, when Shelley faces prison, he falls back on money as the ultimate answer to the problem: "I cannot be put behind bars! It is medically impossible for me to be held! I want my lawyer! I can pay any amount of fucking bail you set up. I have *Cash*!" (117). The irony is that Shelley becomes the ideal FBI agent when he is sworn in to aid in the entrapment of a congressman! The result of his honesty is that when Congressman Munoz dies, Shelley, the opportunist, sees his chance to fill his shoes by running for political office. Shelley, already filling his campaign coffers by bribing the sheik to invest in America through a promise of marketing rights during the next Persian Gulf war, is, as Giselle admits, the icon of this corrupt society: "He is Miami" (147).

Shelley Slutsky's favorite hangout is the Boom Boom Room, where he is provided solace through the entertainment of his mother, the saucy aged platinum blond, Fran Farkus, whose character has evolved in Guare's canon via her predecessors—songwriter Artie Shaughnessy and crooner Robert Goulet in *Atlantic City*. Foul-mouthed Fran would appear to be the perfect role model for a lowlife gangster like

Shelley. She sings hilariously raunchy torch songs for tourists and celebrities vacationing in Miami: "I go to Hawaii / When I want a good lei / Now we're in Miami / Going down at the Moon!" (96). Fran is not afraid to offend anyone with her tasteless language: "Missed the toilet last night / Shit all over the floor / Cleaned it up with my toothbrush / Don't brush my teeth much anymore" (99). Fran's sexual innuendo implies that she is nothing more than a slut who plays musical chairs with sex partners. She entices the men in the audience at the start of her routines: "Nothing could be finer / Than your tongue in my vagina in the / morning / Nothing could be sweeter / Than my lips around your peter in the dawning" (110) and "So stay in Hawaii / If all you wants a lei / Or else come to Miami / And park your carcass / On top of Fran Farkus" (96). Fran describes Shelley as one of the regulars who "gets more ass than a toilet seat" (98), and Giselle, his "classy" girlfriend, as someone who, "If she had every dick that's been stuck in her sticking out of her, she'd look like a porcupine" (98).

Fran, Shelley, and Giselle form the perfect welcoming committee at the Boom Boom Room, where congressmen get the chance to fraternize with raunchy gangsters, femme fatales, and lewd torch singers: the ideal setting for Guare's vicious satire on politics. Fran reveals, "We get all the politicians in here. Reagan was in here. He's a doll. We danced. He kept circling to the right. He sang in my ear. (*Sings*:) 'Seventy-six hormones did the trick for me / Nancy's feeling just like a bride to be'" (97). One of the regular customers is Congressman Osvaldo S. Munoz, who is up for reelection. Munoz, who needs votes from the Jewish and Cuban communities in Miami, claims to be a Juban—half Jewish and half Cuban. Although Munoz has the worst attendance record of any congressman in the House, this matters little to him as long as he can get reelected. He is mainly concerned about how his image will be projected in the commercials he plans to run for his reelection campaign. Trailing in the polls by "only ninety-two points," Munoz tells Shelley and Giselle that he has the image that will take him to victory: "I can win. Do you like my new hairdo? Softer. And my new wardrobe? Forceful colors. My problem is I was wearing too much taupe. Confienza! Give me the trust" (103–4). He begs Shelley to lend him money for his campaign. Munoz, in short, prostitutes himself and is no different from Fran Farkus or Shelley Slutsky; he is even willing to spend millions so he can get a job that pays one hundred thirty-five thousand dollars (but with plenty of perks). He reminds Shelley that they are old friends: "Oh, Shelley, let's drop some acid and pick up some chicks for old times' sake and drive up to Disney World" (104). Munoz is confused about his role as a politician, and although he ostensibly goes out of his way to help the boat people, it is nothing more than a promotional ploy. Instead he is totally ego-driven: "I am magnificent! If I lose, I will sue the people of Miami. They deny me my constitutional right to be a congressman" (105). His primary focus is to get reelected, and if that means selling citizenships to Arab sheiks so he can add to his campaign coffers, Munoz is more than eager to do so. He sees himself as omnipotent, above the law: "I am the god of Miami. I got fucking *halos* shining out of me" (130). When Munoz is caught taking bribes, he pleads his case: "You realize how hard it is to take bribes? You have to call up all the people, remind them over and over" (145). His only hope to get reelected is to take the sheik's money, charter a plane to Cuba, and personally capture Fidel Castro, thus freeing the boat people. Munoz believes that his efforts will have a noble result: "The people of Miami will coronate me" (145).

The other congressmen who frequent the Boom Boom Room are no better than Munoz and will sell their souls to get reelected. Reggie Kayak, the congressman from Alaska, admits to Shelley, "I betrayed my own tribe, my own people, to do business with you" (98). Reggie has no reservations about selling heroin to his constituents in order to finance his campaign. He feels qualmish, not because of any moral code that he is breaking, but because lowlife Shelley may back out of the deal, thus leaving Reggie without a clue as to how to get reelected. Distinguished Congressman Wayne Bentine from Rhode Island also appears as a lounge lizard in the Boom Boom Room. However, when Fran introduces him to the audience, he immediately takes refuge as a pillar of the community, calling the songstress "absolutely disgusting" and insinuating that he inadvertently wandered into the wrong place. After all, he is chairman of the House Ethics Committee and must play the role accordingly. Guare later exposes him as a hypocrite who will do whatever is necessary to get reelected. Bentine is candid about his political aspirations: "I need money! That's why this World Hunger Conference means so much to me. I'm trying to make the people aware of the issues, to let them see I'm valuable. Anything to get re-elected!" (140). The Arab sheik, who has a penchant for giving congressmen gifts to get fighter planes that he needs, can do business with Bentine. Like Congressman Kayak, who was accustomed to accepting attaché cases filled with money from his benefactor (Shelley), Bentine, in a parody of the AB-SCAM scandal, will soon be receiving an attaché case from the Sheik of Akbahran.

In this zany black comedy, one finds it difficult to distinguish between the hoodlums and the government agents. FBI Special Agent Walt Wilcox and Deputy Agent Belden are remarkably adept at the fine points of entrapment: wiretapping, videotaping, bribery, disguise, and making deals with informants. In act 1, Wilcox and Belden are in the Boom Boom Room hoping to catch Congressman Kayak buying drugs from Shelley. Wilcox and Belden fit right into the sleaze of the Boom Boom Room. Wilcox seems more interested in Fran Farkus's musical talents than in his job and even urges the waiter to get him a table closer to the act so he can ogle her better (100). Wilcox's comments hint that his mind is in the gutter as he writes down tidbits from Fran's song: "Big man small dick. No. Big dick small man. If I could only meet her" (103). When Otis tries to make an arrest, Wilcox intervenes, pleading, "The show is still on. Can't we wait till—" (110). At one point during the investigation, Wilcox asks to employ prostitutes who had worked with him on a case, but when informed that it has been twenty years since the FBI used them, he laments, "Shit. They were wonderful girls" (134). Wilcox, the playboy, has no moral conscience about his sexual escapades. When he learns that his wife was lost in the hurricane, his response is "I'm free!" (145) as he embraces Fran, the slut. Furthermore, Guare's sarcastic humor makes it obvious that Wilcox has affinities for the gangsters, always remembering Shelley's name but constantly forgetting the name of his fellow FBI agent, Otis Presby, who is mistakenly referred to by Wilcox as Grimsby (124), Presley (128), Pitsby (129), Mosby (134), Kitsby (138), or Hugsby (140).

Guare's black comedy becomes darker as the FBI agents mirror the gangsters they are trying to entrap, thus forcing the audience to laugh at the satire but, at the same time, react with a certain disgust or horror at the truth of the resemblance. Shelley Slutsky, who murdered a congressman, winds up working alongside Wilcox and Belden as their accomplice. With Otis they set up a two-way mirror to videotape, wiretap, and don disguises (Belden even poses as a French maid) to entrap a congressman. Shelley cuts a deal with the FBI agents for his assistance: he wants them to free his girlfriend, Giselle, who is being held as an illegal alien. Wilcox offers his justification for agreeing to Shelley's request, arguing that Giselle is technically not an illegal alien: "That label only applies to dark people who travel on rafts. Not to white people of elegance like Giselle" (126). Wilcox even goes so far as to make Shelley an official FBI agent; and when the sheik asks if it is easy to get sworn into service, Wilcox responds, "No! These days we're having so much better luck with amateurs. Let me swear you all in! Corleen! Giselle! Your Excellency! Everybody! Raise your right hand—" (137). One of Wilcox's last deeds is to try and get Giselle citizenship via marriage to an American. Wilcox, acting as a minister, performs a quick ceremony making Giselle's marriage to Otis official, using a ring that he lifted from a dead congressman as the wedding band. In Guare's dark comedy, hoodlums act as FBI agents who act as ministers: the world is comic but also pathetically disturbing.

Special Agent Otis Presby is Guare's prototypical idealist in search of the purity of the American Dream. He inhabits the quiet, barren landscape of Alaska, a microcosm of beauty and truth where the peace of living near icebergs and caribou is never interrupted by gangsters, corrupt politicians, or obscene songstresses. Alaska, then, replaces Nantucket as the alternative to neurotic Miami, which substitutes for New York. However, the purity of the landscape has been tainted when Congressman Kayak inundates the wilderness with drugs, thus bringing Otis down to Miami to investigate. After Kayak is murdered by Shelley, Otis, the idealist, becomes inextricably drawn to the FBI's plan to entrap congressmen, even though he constantly dreams of wrapping up the case and returning to idyllic Alaska. Yet Otis is committed to finishing the job and saving the citizens of Alaska. He tells Wilcox, "If you could see the eyes of those corpses on ice floes clutching needles, dead of an overdose of snow. I hate how they desecrate the name of the purest element on earth" (111). Otis is invigorated by the glory days of the FBI when J. Edgar Hoover proudly led his team of government agents on missions to gun down enemies of the people, such as John Dillinger. Now Otis must cooperate with jaded cynics, such as Wilcox, who have been working so closely with gangsters that they have become indistinguishable from them.

During his investigation of Kayak's murder, Otis meets Corleen, a nurse in her twenties who is married to Shelley. Otis is attracted to Corleen's humanism: she cares for the wounded and is a connoisseur of the arts. Corleen has founded the Everglades Light Opera Association in order to enrich and enliven the denizens of the Everglades, including the drug pushers. She explains, "The Everglades is a lot more than ten thousand islands. I'm trying to bring culture into these people's lives. I'm trying to keep the tiny shreds of their souls alive" (115). Corleen says she is attracted to he-men, like Jesus, her role model. Otis enamors himself to Corleen when he plays upon her nurturing spirit and depicts Alaska as the home of the Savior: "Suppose you're driving along and you see someone stranded on the side of the road, if it's more than 20 degrees below zero, it's against the law not to stop and help that person. I love a land where it's a crime not to help someone" (115). He also impresses her by displaying his range of singing talent, which includes an Elvis rendition followed by a ballad—all good enough to convince Corleen that he has the qualifications to be in the Everglades Light Opera Association, which now consists of two members.

During the sting operation, Otis is forced to demean himself by posing as a sheik to entrap Congressman Munoz. In addition, he must witness the swearing in of a murderer, Shelley, as his fellow FBI agent, and the release from prison of Giselle, an illegal alien; even worse, Otis is asked to marry Giselle to make her legal. Otis calls on the spirit of J. Edgar Hoover, pleading with him to understand that his cooperation with a criminal is on behalf of the interests of the federal government. Otis merely would like to wind up the case and then return to Alaska with nurse Corleen to devote time to healing, particularly to "see how nature has healed the oil spill" (136).

The definitive moment when the gangsters, the FBI agents, and the idyllic lovers discover their raison d'être occurs as Fran Farkus reveals herself to be J. Edgar Hoover, the icon of moral conduct. Hoover admits that she joined the Bureau (which was its name before the organization became the FBI) as a female secretary; one day, she came to work as a man, took the name Hoover from a vacuum cleaner, and was suddenly giving orders. Eventually, she captured John Dillinger, which ultimately led to her power and authority. In 1972, she faked her death in order to find the child she had given up to pursue her career. Shelley, sworn in also as an FBI agent, is now in the same league as his mother; more significantly, they can relate to each other as sleazy lowlifes. Shelley had even admitted earlier, "The Boom Boom Room is the only place I've ever known warmth, ever known love, that ever gave me oxygen" (137). Shelley, who acknowledges that he has never known family (137), is now at home, which is Guare's sarcastic way of establishing the affinity between hoodlum and government agent. And when Shelley goes one step further by deciding to run for political office and adopting the Boom Boom Room as his campaign headquarters under the tutelage of his mother, the connection between gangsters and congressmen is cemented. For the FBI, the joke is on them, for their icon, the person who created their code of conduct and defined the responsibilities of this elite federal agency, is revealed to be nothing more than a foul-mouthed tart. Otis is also affected by the transformation, especially when the Colossus, Hoover's image, exhorts him to return the tape that contains incriminating evidence about Reggie Kayak's murder and Congressman Munoz's entrapment. Otis pleads, "I came into the bureau to do good. Shouldn't I bring Shelley to justice?" (144). Fran / Hoover, realizing that nepotism is stronger than good deeds, responds, "Wrong, Agent Presby. Politics. Everything is politics. Give me the tape" (144).

After Corleen dies from a drug overdose and Otis is killed when he is shot by Shelley, these two idealists appear on an iceberg in idyllic Alaska. Meanwhile, Fran engages Shelley, Wilcox, Giselle, the Sheik, and the Mermaids in a song that seems to bind them to the spirit of sleaze: "'Missed the toilet last night . . .'" (148). The stage directions indicate, "*Otis is lost, desperate*" (148), seemingly out of place in the neurotic, corrupt world in which he briefly made contact. He prefers the silence of the icebergs, a world of introspection where the self seeks to identify the voices within (148). Otis and Corleen embrace passionately and vow to keep the culture alive through their efforts to rehearse for the Aurora Borealis Light Opera Company, albeit with a cast of two. The spiritual connections have a chance to flourish in this environment, but the idyllic purity is drowned out by the more pervasive litany that ends the play: "So stay in Hawaii / If all you want's a lei / Or else come to Miami / And park your carcass / On top of Fran Farkus / And let's all go down at the Moon" (149). The dominant image of Fran / Hoover inundates the stage and seems to leave us with the impression that the idyllic love duet shared by Otis and Corleen is only fleeting.

The last full-length play that Guare wrote in the early 1990s, *Four Baboons Adoring the Sun*, was originally intended as a libretto for a Leonard Bernstein opera. The first version of *Four Baboons Adoring the Sun* was published in *Antaeus* in Spring 1991, which is ostensibly a variant of the play that Guare sent to British director Sir Peter Hall in London during October of that year.[15] After three days of discussion with him in London, Guare seemed convinced that their aims coincided and that Hall would feel comfortable directing it, especially since he had extensive experience staging opera and classical drama. Hall also seemed to understand Guare's popular appeal to modern audiences, stating, "His plays, with their combination of direct audience address, sudden time shifts, and vivid metaphorical emblems, rely on the sensibility of an age conditioned by the jump cuts and dissolves of the cinema."[16] Guare fleshed out the material to stretch to a playing time of one hour and twenty minutes without an intermission, again to create lots of energy on stage and an atmosphere of zeal, even panic, to keep the action flowing. He changed the Messenger from a choric representative of an eighteenth-century baroque Italian court to Eros, a scantily clad singer representing the voice of chaos. Guare, perhaps through the suggestions of Hall, who previously had staged myths, also added several sections of incantatory dialogue and rhythmic language to the revised version of the play.

The production required careful timing and preparation. Stephen Edwards, who had worked with Hall earlier, composed more than twenty short songs and an electronic score for the musical interludes interspersed throughout the play. Sound designer Paul Arditti choreographed Nature's various rumblings through sound effects that changed pitch, depending upon rain, wind, and volcanic activity. Tony Walton designed the sets, which included a mountain range, an airport, a volcano, tons of sand representing an archaeological site, and the sculpture that gives credence to the title of the play. Richard Pilbrow arranged the lighting while Willa Kim designed the costumes.

Four Baboons Adoring the Sun premiered at the Vivian Beaumont Theater in Lincoln Center under Hall's direction on 18 March 1992. The cast included Stockard Channing (Penny), James Naughton (Philip), Eugene Perry (Eros), Wil Horneff (Wayne), and Angela Goethals (Halcy). The play featured nine children, only one of which, Goethals, had any notable previous stage experience. Guare was taking a major gamble, for any experienced theater impresario realizes that when that many children are on a Broadway stage, the potential for disaster is real. Furthermore, the form of the play, a long one-acter without intermission yet replete with a musical chorus, flash-forwards and sudden time changes, direct audience address, stichomythic dialogue, the wit of modern comedy, and the pathos of classical Greek tragedy, proved more than challenging for critics who usually prefer plays to be presented in a more recognizable structure. Director Hall understood that Guare's intentions might be somewhat too ambitious: "The play was truly an attempt to write a modern Greek tragedy combining all the instruments of the theater."[17]

Unfortunately, most critics refused to make a serious effort to understand Guare's intentions and were also in disagreement about the quality of the production. Virtually all of the critics acknowledged that Hall was responsible for maintaining the crisp pace Guare had intended and for creating a lavish production. Walton was praised for immaculate sets that became conversation pieces, and critics, for the most part, admired Edwards's score, although it was rather depressing at times. The acting, however, was depicted in the press as uneven. For example, John Simon (*New York*) described Channing's performance as eager and effervescent,[18] Edith Oliver (*New Yorker*) referred to it as glowing and exquisite,[19] Richard Hornby (*Hudson Review*) deemed it charming and energetic,[20] while Thomas M. Disch (*Nation*) argued that she and Naughton lacked sufficient erotic energy in their roles.[21] The supporting cast was viewed as more problematic. Stefan Kanfer (*New Leader*) singled out Angela Goethals as the highlight of the cast;[22] Hornby disagreed, citing her performance, as well as Horneff's, as wooden.[23] Lloyd Rose (*Washington Post*) stated that the children's acting was unimpressive,[24] and John Simon was bothered by their squeaky voices.[25] Finally, several critics were disturbed by Eros, who looked to them somewhat like a male go-go dancer; Robert Brustein (*New Republic*), for example, noted, "Eros, representing pagan sexual freedom, turns the play into a Cliff Notes version of D. H. Lawrence's *Sea and Sardinia.*"[26]

The critics were also divided over Guare's script, although the vast majority of them received it negatively. Only a few critics offered any serious and thoughtful assessment of Guare's drama. Jack Kroll (*Newsweek*), with reservations about the abrupt suicide at the end of the play, nevertheless commended Guare for blending the harrowing and the hilarious in a courageous effort that attempted to do too much yet met the challenge.[27] Jeremy Gerard (*Variety*) characterized the play as a stylistic exercise with "ineluctable emotional power."[28] Frank Rich (*New York Times*), in his poignant and thoughtful essay, became Guare's most eloquent defender as he lauded Guare for his spare, incantatory, and often witty dialogue associated with the myth and dreams of a transcendent quest for a reason to continue living in a fraudulent world.[29] David Richards (*New York Times*) and Edith Oliver offered neutral reviews—they praised the production as evocative but were disappointed in Guare's flimsy script.[30] Gerald Weales (*Commonweal*) and John Beaufort (*Christian Science Monitor*) complained that the play was too pretentious,[31] Disch argued that it was boring and unpoetic,[32] and Kanfer thought the plot was telegraphed.[33] The charge of obscurity, seemingly forever plaguing Guare, was again brought up here by Beaufort, Rose, Simon, Edwin Wilson (*Wall Street Journal*), and Linda Winer (*New York Newsday*);[34] in particular, Hornby and Wilson agreed that Wayne's suicide seemed arbitrary and preposterous, especially since the two child lovers were not fully developed enough for their motivations to be grasped by the audience.[35] Echoing the charge of obscurity was Howard Kissel (*Daily News*), who viewed Guare's attempt to parody baroque Italian opera as "bizarre and irrational."[36] Brustein insisted that the play was rushed into production too soon and required several more drafts.[37]

Nevertheless, the play received enough support for a Tony Award nomination as Best Play of 1992.[38]

Four Baboons Adoring the Sun begins in Sicily where recently married Philip and Penny McKenzie, both in their early forties, are awaiting the arrival of their children (he has four, she five), who are flying from New York. Philip and Penny are archaeologists working on a dig at La Muculufa. They met as college students studying archaeology twenty years earlier and soon started a romance. However, after the tryst ended, they eventually went their separate ways. Penny left archaeology and married Mel, a congressman; she assumed the duties of housewife, settling in to mundane middle-aged life as the wife of a distinguished politician: "I'm a very good wife. I give the support. I shake the hands. Mel runs for Congress? Sure! I raise the money."[39] Despite the fact that Mel was a fine breadwinner, he cheated on Penny, leaving her with doubts about the efficacy of their lives together: "I love him. Our kids. The most *wonderful* kids. I'm happy. I hate my life" (30). Her daughter, Halcy, aged thirteen, began to take drugs. Penny ultimately blamed her husband for their deteriorating marriage. She tells her children, "Your daddy hurt me. He was unfaithful. He put his career over everything" (52). Philip meanwhile stayed in the profession and became head of the archaeology department at the University of California at San Luis Obispo. His wife, Jeanne, was promiscuous, cheated on him, and became dependent upon liquor and drugs. Wayne, Philip's thirteen-year-old son, got involved with motorcycles and alcohol. Philip later admitted to Penny, "I hate my life. I feel like some mutilated Greek statue sitting at a desk. No arms. No face. No legs. No phallus" (30). To compensate for his feelings of inadequacy, Philip had affairs with other women, including a tryst with a colleague in his department. He feels particularly guilty about the effects of his deteriorating marriage on his children, admitting to Penny, "They don't know anything about love. They've never seen love. All they knew about adults with me and Jeanne was hate and fury and rage and homicide" (39)

When Philip came to New York to give a lecture about Sicily at the Met, Penny by chance happened to be in the audience. After Philip's lecture, he accompanied Penny for a drink at a hotel across the street, and they commiserated about their lackluster existences. They discovered that they shared an intrinsic need for a better life. Penny lamented, "The values. The emptiness. The promise they'll all be on crack. I want my kids to have a life" (31). Philip and Penny understood the need to divorce themselves from the fraudulence of an American Dream that has gone awry and instead try to recapture a sense of identity through the imagination. Philip urges Penny to transcend the mundane and seek the idyllic: "Is there a moment when all our lives are *mythic*? Are touched by grace—by God—and we start life? Is it now?" (31). The image recalls the touching of man's hands to God in the Sistine Chapel—Ouisa's search for meaningful experience in a neurotic society. Penny poses the existential dilemma plaguing all of Guare's characters in their search for Being: "We don't know who we truly are" (31). Penny and Philip cemented their spiritual union by having sex in the hotel bedroom. A year later, they got their divorces and married in Paris. The newlyweds now await the arrival of their children, whom they have not seen in ten weeks.

Penny and Philip have divorced their spouses in order to evade the neuroticism of modern urban life and thus tap into their imaginative selves through their art. Penny's life with the congressman was bland. Mel lacked her imaginative vision; she complained that he was not an Etruscan (30), which, in Guare's metaphor, means that he was not compatible with his wife's idyllic dreams.[40] Penny's life in the metropolis consisted of stultifying routine and acceptance of the horrors associated with modern life, including adultery and drug abuse. By escaping to the idyllic world of Sicily, now serving the same function that Nantucket held in the tetralogy, Penny retreats to the mythic world of art. She is thus more in tune with self and others, revealing, in an aside to the audience, "I belonged to the world" (23). Penny, like Alan Strang in Peter Shaffer's *Equus*, is in search of godhead through a concerted effort to grasp the instinctual impulses of a pagan culture.[41]

Philip also has escaped the mundane world of academia and a deteriorating domestic situation in order to forge a new identity with a long-lost love in what he hopes will be a mythical Eden. Philip would like to annihilate the past and instead live in an idyllic mythical world with his new sweetheart. He explains to Penny how he plans to live in "Universe B," which he associates with the purity of childhood:

> No past. Everything free. Mythic. No wonder everything is different for these little monsters. They live in a universe that's constantly brand new. No rules. All adults try to get back to that world. But you can only do it by falling in love. (21)

Philip, like Penny, was alienated in modern society, unable to connect with self or others. Through Penny, he hopes to rekindle the love of youth, thus stirring his imagination. Moreover, his stultifying academic life will now be injected with a new sense of vigor as

California gives way to exotic Sicily and the theory of archaeology is replaced with practice. The reins of family and profession are cast aside since Philip will now be able to love freely while remaining close to his art.

Penny and Philip want to create an idealistic society where their children are also sheltered from the *angoisse* and anomie of contemporary life—a modern-day Aipotu, Sicilian style. They fly their nine children to Sicily with the hopes of creating a nuclear family far removed from the neuroses of New York and California (either coast of the United States is fraught with its own tensions) and now newly infused with love and artistic freedom. Penny views the children as traveling from the twentieth century into a mythic land: "Philip! *We've* done it! Now the kids are about to escape the twentieth century!" (6). Penny and Philip, like Lydie Breeze, Joshua Hickman, Amos Mason, and Dan Grady, hope to form a utopian community of their own. Penny explains to Philip the idyllic vision that she has for their children: "I want them to be thrilled by Sicily. I want them to see Sicily through our eyes. To see its grandeur—its majesty" (13). When the children arrive from New York, they draw mythical names from a bag; in essence, Penny hopes they will adopt new personae and become fully immersed in the myth and magic of a novel culture and a fresh way of life. They pile into a van to get a tour of their mythic surroundings. Philip, the tour guide, carefully selects what he wants the children to see, making sure the scenery does not interfere with the purity of his idealistic vision: "Everything started here. This is where the gods came on holiday. Don't look at the petro-chemical plants—" (16). Philip and Penny want so much to make their dreams happen that they are thrilled when they discover that the children are conforming to their fantasies of a united household. Philip exclaims, "They *like* each other" (18), and Penny echoes, "They get along! Thank you, gods!" (18). Penny, like Lydie Breeze, initially sees her experiment in utopian living as a big success, especially in the way that once-alienated individuals now have become a coherent unit soon to be immersed in a vibrant, imaginative spirit. She expresses this excitement to her children: "You can laugh at those silly myths in that stupid book. People transformed into trees. Into birds. But we have become transformed. We have become a family and families become civilizations. You are not the same kids who got on that plane in America last night. You are transformed" (46).

The image that inspires the McKenzies to pursue their utopian dreams is a nineteenth-dynasty sculpture that they discovered in the Louvre. The sculpture depicted four baboons whose eyes had been burnt out gazing at the sun, their god. Although the baboons were blinded, their eyes suggested joy at coming face to face with their deity. The baboons had been newly transformed through this vision of the immortal. Penny and Philip are searching for god by opening their eyes to their own imaginative vision.

In Guare's black comedy, archaeology, which is a means to unearth the past and also is the profession that led Penny and Philip to the Louvre to experience the image that gave meaning to their lives, instead becomes a tool for the newlyweds to bury their pasts. By choosing to commit to a life of art through archaeology, Penny and Philip focus on an idealistic vision of the future but hope to put the past behind them in their private lives. In Guare's theater, particularly in the tetralogy, we have seen that trying to bury the past leads to disaster. As is true of many of Ibsen's plays, characters who try to evade the past learn that they cannot and are always much worse off until they discover that heredity and environment always will affect their lives. Mrs. Alving, for example, may attempt to open an orphanage to eradicate the memory of her husband's vices and how they affected Oswald's upbringing; however, the shrine burns down. Similarly, in Guare's play, when the expedition goes awry, we realize how he ironically employs archaeology as a metaphor to reveal the impact of the past on individuals trying to escape from it.

The utopian visions of Penny and Philip slowly self-destruct throughout the play. The idyllic community of Nantucket in the tetralogy recalled images of Prospero and Caliban from *The Tempest*; in *Four Baboons Adoring the Sun*, Eros is reminiscent of spritelike Ariel in appearance. Eros is also Guare's Greek chorus forecasting the gloom and doom that awaits the idealists. Director Peter Hall described Eros's role in the play: "But Guare had set this comic world of high optimism and easy solutions into a dark world of chaotic life forces. These were represented by Eros, and he would be the only singer" (x).[42] Eros is a realist, the only character in the drama without illusions. His first words in the play reveal his foresight and common sense: "The start of another perfect day / Something will go wrong" (3). Like the witches in *Macbeth* or the chorus in Greek tragedy, Eros acts as a seer rather than as the cause of the action. He admits, "I do not control things / I simply urge them along" (3). He fully understands that sometimes lust conflicts with the idyllic notion of everlasting love, and as we eventually see in the relationship between Wayne and Halcy, lust can be disastrous. Moreover, he mocks the attempt made by Penny and Philip to bury their pasts: "Is this the moment / You think you're gifted / To see the present / Annihilate the past?" (22). Disaster, previously seen in Guare's plays in the form of lightning bolts and hurricanes, is now transformed into a volcanic eruption. Eros forecasts the apocalyptic immediately before the earthquake does its damage: "Rocks split / Earth shakes / Ground moves / Air burns" (50). In essence, Eros predicts the earth separating, which, as David Richards has indicated, suggests a natural rift—in this instance, one that contributes to destroying idyllic relationships.[43]

As is typical in Guare's dramas, the utopian dreams and fantasies of an idyllic life free from the anomie of modern civilization that creates alienation and leaves individuals unable to connect soon degenerate into brutal reality. After the children arrive in Sicily and are given mythical names, the first indication that life will not be as ideal as Philip and Penny have envisioned occurs when Wayne chooses Icarus as his pseudonym. Halcy, after reading Penny's book about mythology, remarks, "But it says here the sun melted his wings and Icarus crashed into the sea and died. Every one of these stories ends horribly" (15). Soon, the purity of the love between Penny and Philip becomes tainted as Halcy and Wayne reveal that they have listened in on intimate telephone conversations between the two archaeologists. The two thirteen-year-olds imitate their parents. When Wayne and Halcy are discovered in bed together, Wayne's response is "Love is the only reality. Love is all" (35); both children are so impressed that Penny and Philip abandoned everything for love that Wayne stops drinking and Halcy abandons her drugs. Guare's comedy turns dark: instead of romance, we witness underage sex between two thirteen-year-olds and shame between Penny and Philip as a result of their love being scandalized. In addition, instead of creating family unity, Penny and Philip discover that their children view their new nuclear family as chaotic. Sarah asks Penny, "You broke up our family for pots?" (25). Furthermore, when Jane wonders, "Is it true you lied to us when you said you went to a college reunion and you really went off with Philip?" (25), she intimates that the children consider the relationship between their parents to be disingenuous.

The drama moves closer to the abyss when Penny and Philip refuse permission for Halcy and Wayne to spend the night together. Through their prying, Wayne and Halcy discover Philip's affair with Wanda Hess, thus driving a wedge between the newlyweds, who were still enjoying the early stages of marital bliss. The nuclear family slowly begins to disintegrate as Philip and Penny accuse each other's offspring of deviant behavior, producing a negative influence on the sanctity of the family:

| Philip. | Halcy, you leave my son alone! Do you have drugs? What are you selling to my boy?! |
| Penny. | My daughter is hardly a drug pusher! Your alcoholic son can't keep it in his pants long enough to get through puberty! (56) |

Philip then raises his hand to Penny. Violence is typical of what occurs in Guare's plays when the modern neurosis reaches its peak. Penny lashes out at her husband: "Don't you come near me. I see why Jeanne had to take drugs. And drink. Jeanne was terrified of you!" (56). This macabre degeneration from the purity of love to the madness of violence helps us to understand Peter Hall's critical assessment of Guare's intentions when writing the drama: "It's trying to be a big play dealing with the idea that people like to fall in love because it returns them to the simple directness of childhood—but also dealing with the sickening, farcical nature of violence."[44]

Philip and Penny gradually become more aware of the destruction of their idyllic dreams. Their honeymoon is now over:

| Penny. | And Wayne and Halcy want to be us? |
| Philip. | Good Christ, they're us and we've become Mel and Jeanne. It's just like home. (57) |

Wayne and Halcy soon wander away from their parents, their stripped-off clothes leaving a trail to follow; the children are wound up in the heat of lust. Philip, in horror, begins to see the irony of dreams gone awry: "Instead of our getting into the kids' world, we had dragged the kids into our world. For all our ideals, we had passed only our fever on to our children" (60). Wayne, ironically following the wishes of his parents, becomes Icarus as he plunges off a cliff; however, in the brutal reality of modern society, the result is suicide rather than melted wings. The stage directions indicate that the comedy has turned into revulsion or horror: "*Eros descends triumphantly into the earth, Wayne's body in his arms*" (64). Guare twists the knife a bit more as Penny learns that her idyllic notion of bringing the two families together will never materialize: "We got back to the dig. There was a fax. My kids' father was getting married. Mel wanted his children at the wedding" (64). And Halcy is certainly traumatized by the ordeal of watching Wayne commit suicide after they had made love. An ideal moment of perfection has been turned into a travesty for her. She buries for Penny any idyllic notion that the family could ever be united after this trauma:

I loved him. I'll never get over this. I'll live to be a hundred years old and never get over that I didn't take his hand. I had one chance to be a goddess. Now all I'll be the rest of my life is this. Like everyone else. I hate this. Mom. I hate this. Me. I hate my life. I hate life. (67)

At the end of the play, Philip returns to the university with the children, but Penny stays in Sicily with Peter and Halcy. Penny, like Bunny Flingus, Gussie Hickman, Sally, or Betty Yearn, is a dreamer, an idealist who pursues the fantasy, the mythology of the imagination, until the bitter end despite enormous odds. Penny is another of Guare's starry-eyed romantics who demands a better life for herself and pursues a transcendent quest for a spiritual connection in a world where separation and isolation are the norm. In the denouement, Eros urges Penny to follow her idyllic dreams and seek spiritual vitality in spite of the fact that there will be tremendous obstacles along the way: "Open your eyes / And Adore the Sun / Find your true god / And Adore the Sun" (71). Penny looks up, opens her eyes, and makes the palms-up gesture reminiscent of the statue of the four baboons whose eyes were burnt out after they had found their god. Penny is wedded to the mythology.

Guare's brief one-act drama, *New York Actor*, was first performed at the American Repertory Theater in Cambridge, Massachusetts, during April 1992. The first New York production of the play occurred on 1 February 1993, at the New York Public Library for its Performing Arts Reading Room Series. For these performances, Neel Keeler directed a cast that included John Vickery (Craig), Jerry Stiller (Nat), Marion Seldes (Eileen), and André Gregory (Critic).

New York Actor takes place in Joe Allen's theater bar in Manhattan where stage performers Nat, Barry, and Eileen have gathered to welcome Craig, one of their own, back to New York. Craig has given up his television work in California to return to New York to star in *The Locksmith*, the play that was a smash hit in London and has now transferred to Broadway. At the beginning of Guare's drama, these actors gaze wide-eyed at the theater posters lining the walls of the restaurant-bar, thereby reinforcing the notion that they rub shoulders with the elite in a profession that is nothing short of noble and dignified.

In *New York Actor*, Guare virtually acts as a surgeon meticulously slicing away the veneer to strip characters of their masks, ultimately revealing the fraudulence of their lives. Guare has respect for actors and is not merely criticizing their profession; instead, he uses acting as a metaphor for the artificiality associated with modern life in an urban metropolis. Through Guare's deeply rooted sarcastic comedy, he exposes the modern neuroses of a fraudulent American society. Ego forces Nat, Eileen, and Barry to wear the mask and pose as big-time celebrities seeking fame and fortune. Eileen and Barry lay their claim to fame for a ten-second television commercial they filmed about NU-TRIX Bran cereal, guaranteed not to give anyone cancer. Craig calls the performance "great," and Nat compliments the couple for helping to save lives.[45] Eileen swears Barry looked like a bank president on television, while Barry, in turn, compares Eileen to Katharine Hepburn. Craig assures them that when the commercial goes nationwide, they will make a lot of money (178). Nat also has a commercial in the works: he is doing one on athlete's foot (the third toe, actually), but he realizes, "it can't all be *The Oresteia*" (178). Barry also reveals that he was once in the running to do a voiceover for a Volvo commercial. Barry even won an Obie, but he acknowledges it was "An ensemble Obie. The whole cast got the Obie" (182). They all agree that a New York actor is something special, a giant among mortals, a "teller of truths" (181), someone who rubs shoulders with the likes of Marlon Brando, Montgomery Clift, George C. Scott, Jimmy Dean, and other performers who made it big to go on to play Broadway. Eileen is so enamored with her persona as a New York actress that she admits, "I've never been to London. Always afraid to leave New York. Always afraid the big call would come and I'd miss it" (180). When Nat discovers that the producers of *The Locksmith* cast the play in Los Angeles and ignored the talent in New York, he feels that they neglected the best performers in the world: "They skipped New York? Fuck 'em" (180). Craig tells him not to worry, for an actor in California must be pleasant and likable at all times, constantly wearing the mask. Nat thus rationalizes the glory of being a New York actor rather than a Hollywood star: "That's why I could never make it out there. I'm not likable. I like that about me" (181).

The fact that Craig is the icon that these would-be celebrities most admire and respect as one who has made it big in Hollywood indicates their fraudulence and how isolated they are from the truth. He has just finished starring in the television series, *Lawyer From Another Planet*, which sounds gauche to any person with taste but is nothing short of wonderful to these New York actors. Craig compares what he is doing in pitiful Los Angeles television roles to the artistry of Laurence Olivier:

> It's like what Laurence Olivier said. "If acting decides to embrace you and take you to its heart, it will hurl you up there among the gods. It

will change your wooden clogs overnight and replace them with glass slippers." I'm not saying I'm Sir Larry—(180)

When his television series was cancelled, Craig did what was only natural: he crashed his Volvo into a guardrail on the freeway. The day before he left Los Angeles, Craig was promised the part of Richard Nixon's hairdresser. However, he had to turn down this very demanding artistic engagement because he realized he already was the greatest thing he could be: a New York actor! Craig, unfortunately, has kept a secret from his friends throughout his life: he has never played Broadway. He confides in his comrades, "I'd wake up in the middle of the night and say my life is worthless because I never played Broadway" (182). Craig believes that his Broadway role in *The Locksmith* will change his life for the better, forever removing the albatross around his neck. Nat even hints that the play has a good chance to be a Tony winner (179). Sammy enters, ecstatic that he has just had a great audition. He says, "I think I got the part! This new English play! They're replacing the guy who's doing the Locksmith. Some L.A. actor" (184). In Guare's black comedy, as soon as someone receives a taste of the idyllic possibilities of a life of glitz and glamor, reality intervenes to take it away from them. After Craig telephones home, the truth is confirmed: "There's a message on my machine to call the producers" (186). Craig, the once-likable actor, becomes violent, insulting Sammy and then storming out of the theater bar, but not before he exposes the glamorous life of the New York actor: "I can't go back to L.A. But how will I stay here in New York? Out there I tried to kill myself. Maybe that's the answer. Why not! Why not!" (187).

When the new critic for the *New York Times* enters the theater bar with his wife, the New York actors are disturbed by his presence. Barry speaks for the group: "What the world needs now. More reviews" (183). Nat musters the courage to go to the critic's table and thank him for a review that he wrote in a weekly magazine six years ago commending Nat's work in *Tomorrow's Meadow*. At first, the critic mistakes the "star" for a waiter. When Nat mentions *Tomorrow's Meadow*, the critic wonders, "Is that a horse?" (183). Nat's glowing words of admiration for the critic represent his hypocrisy and duplicity: "I just heard your good news and wanted to tell you it's great news for the theater community having more reviews and how everyone admires you and what an addition and privilege you are" (184). Nat's hypocrisy is a prime example of how behind the veneer of artistry lies the more fundamental need to get ahead through fame and eventual fortune. He insists on flattering the critic in order to leave a lasting impression on him, hoping that one day the critic may return the favor: "Your judgments are synonyms for perspicacity and insight into the craft of where we theater artists are striving and it's a great day for the New York theater and I speak for all of us personally looking forward to reading you and if you some Tuesday find yourself writing a column about 'Down Memory Lane,' about performances you've admired over recent years—Nat Boyle!" (184). However, it soon becomes clear that the only image the critic will remember about Nat Boyle will be how he stole his wife's purse right from under their noses. Eileen and Barry, usually extroverted stage stars, are forced to hide their faces under napkins to avoid being associated with Nat. When confronted with the charge, Nat insists that his name is Pat Doyle instead, suggesting that the critic must have the wrong man. Nat, the critic, and the critic's wife wind up punching and wrestling each other to the floor. As we have seen earlier, in Guare's twisted dark comedy, violence is often the culmination of frustration among individuals who fool themselves into believing their fantasies are larger than life. At the end of the play, out-of-towners enter the theater bar and declare, "This place is adorable!" (188), echoing the comments of the hypocritical New York actors at the beginning of the drama. In short, the fraudulence is endemic to our culture, and to make matters worse, it is cyclical and thus difficult to break.

In 1997, Anne Cattaneo, dramaturge of the Acting Company, commissioned Guare and six other playwrights to focus on carefully selected sonnets of Shakespeare she had chosen as the inspiration for an evening of playlets about love and sex. Beginning with the last of the sonnets—153 and 154—Guare, incorporating material from Jacobus de Voragine's *The Golden Legend*, drew his inspiration to create the one-act play, *The General of Hot Desire*. The evening's entertainment, deemed "Love's Fire," included plays by Eric Bogosian (*Bitter Sauce*), Ntozake Shange (*Hydraulics Phat Like Mean*), Marsha Norman (*140*), Tony Kushner (*Terminating, or Lass Meine Schmerzen Nicht Verloren Sein, or Ambivalence*), William Finn (*Painting You*), and Wendy Wasserstein (*Waiting for Philip Glass*); Guare's play terminated the performance. "Love's Fire" premiered at the Guthrie Theater Lab in Minneapolis on 7 January 1998 under direction by Mark Lamos, then toured the United States and London before its New York debut at the Joseph Papp Public Theater in June 1998.[46]

Guare may have begun with sonnets 153 and 154, but he soon abandons the notion of using them as bulwarks for his own ideas. Sonnet 153 indicates that the poet's ultimate cure for love—his mistress's eyes—is the only way to quench his love; Cupid's torch may be put out by the bathwaters, but the poet's fire will not be reignited except through the eyes of his lover. Sonnet 154 omits any reference to Cupid but remains as a variation on the theme expressed in sonnet 153 in which passion wins out over chastity. As Guare read the sonnets aloud with the Acting Company, the creation of the play became a collaborative effort; in short, the play went through various drafts as the ensemble continued to explore the meaning of sonnets 153 and 154.

The General of Hot Desire begins as two members of the Acting Company (Erika Rolfsrud and James Farmer) recite sonnets 153 and 154, respectively. Subsequently, the remaining members of the troupe (Daniel Pearce, Hamish Linklater, Heather Robison, Lisa Tharps, Stephen DeRosa, and Jason Alan Carvell) bring out their Cliff Notes and university paperback editions of Shakespeare to clarify the meaning of the two sonnets as a starting point for their performance piece. When Jason notes that Cupid is the general of hot desire in sonnet 153, Daniel states that the initials spell God, with a silent "h" thrown in. The improvisational method of discovery leads the actors to Cupid and Diana, the goddess; to Diana the woman; to the First Woman; and then to Eve banished from the Garden of Eden by God. The performers work through the Genesis story of Adam and Eve and the first death, represented by the Cain and Abel myth. The "scene" transforms into the biblical tale of Solomon and Sheba in much the same manner as the Open Theater composed *The Serpent* by using biblical myths to parallel the violence in modern life. Civilizations prosper, people make music and paint pictures, even write poetry (sonnets)—always in hopes of getting God's attention. In essence, Guare's play describes the quest for the imaginative vision throughout history. The quest is equated with the longing to return to the Garden of Eden. However, the imaginative vision is often difficult to obtain. As the actors wrestle with the shape of *The General of Hot Desire*, the audience begins to understand Guare's own dilemma in the act of creating a play that he was commissioned to write but with which he was perhaps not totally comfortable. Although the actors shape the play collaboratively, they leave the stage arguing vehemently over the meaning of the text and its relevance. Guare is implying that the shape of art is always fraught with problems of creation, of "genesis," so to speak. In short, Guare has taken two Shakespearean sonnets about love and turned the task of creating a play about them into humanity's quest for creation, which albeit must end not in harmony or love, but more likely in success tinged with a sense of disarray.

In these late plays, Guare demonstrates that the purity of a quest for the imaginative vision may still linger despite the fact that contemporary society is inundated with greed, hypocrisy, and deceit. When Guare acts as a seer where no salvific alternative is suggested, the drama becomes particularly caustic while the black comedy grows much darker and more sarcastic. By experimenting with the form of the play and by creating panic on stage when he abandons the conventions of the theater, Guare has expanded his artistic talents despite the fact that his plays have become somewhat more inaccessible to certain types of audiences. However, when one takes the time to examine these late plays more carefully, one discovers that the charge that he is a difficult playwright to pin down is untrue; the motifs are merely more unrecognizable only because Guare has become unusually clever and subtle.

10

Conclusion

Guare's message, masked in black comedy or farce and often diluted by his overtly conscious need to break the fourth-wall conventions of the theater, frequently becomes enigmatic. However, when one casts aside these very real barriers that Guare presents, one discovers that the themes and motifs that he explores in his plays coincide with many of the significant philosophical issues examined by playwrights such as Beckett, O'Neill, Albee, Pinter, Ibsen, Chekhov, Stoppard, and Miller.

The existential dilemma that Guare poses is how individuals can possess a sense of dignity and humanism in a world that is essentially fraudulent. Guare, like Wilson, Albee, and Mamet, is a sociologist of the contemporary theater. As such, he strips the veneer of modern American society to indicate its vacuity. He views it as a sterile universe where anecdote replaces worthwhile experience and where the very real dangers of the mundane and the bland, represented by ubiquitous commercialization, have turned people into automatons. As in the theater of the absurd, Guare depicts civilization decaying as a result of its alienation, isolation, and lack of spiritual connection. Relationships disintegrate, individuals do not connect with self or others, and people seem to have lost a passion for life. Guare's protagonists are essentially neurotic, desperately in search of an identity and a sense of dignity in a vicious, ruthless, corrupt society—a morally and spiritually bankrupt world.

The idealistic vision of America's founding fathers has been eroded in favor of the more mundane, yet preferable, goal of avoiding humiliation and trying to maintain a sense of importance in a cruel, chaotic society. The once noble and lofty values of friendship, family relationships, and spiritual connections have given way to power, greed, ambition, and wealth. Thus, the idealistic visions of the nineteenth century, exemplified in the Lydie Breeze tetralogy, have been replaced by the new American Dream, which is essentially the lure of the glitz and glamor of fame and fortune.

Guare evokes the revolutionary spirit of the founding fathers who based their ethos on the chance to dream and to use imaginative vision. Guare's theater honors the imagination and opposes the bland. He admires individuals who pursue their dreams of a better life, who seek to establish a utopian community, and who realize the need to search for a deeper meaning in life. Those who learn from the past instead of fictionalizing it and those who understand the importance of forgiveness will be better able to fulfill their dreams and connect with self and others. However, individuals who become immersed in the myth of celebrity will find that their dreams are merely artificial, and Guare shows that they frequently become prisoners trapped in the warped fantasies that others have created for them. When their outlandish dreams cannot be realized, individuals who have invested their lives in pursuit of such superficial facades find themselves immersed in anomie and *angoisse*, often culminating in violence as a means of escape. Although we must realize that our utopian dreams usually will dissipate due to brutal reality, Guare asserts that one must always strive for the pursuit of the imaginative vision as a means to liberate ourselves from the mundane.

Guare's message, then, has profound sociological and philosophical implications with regard to the search for dignity amidst the neuroticism and anomie of modern civilization. So why is it that Guare's ideas, which, as we have seen, are shared by many of the finest modern and contemporary playwrights, have been described as enigmatic? The key to unravelling Guare's theater is understanding how his motifs are intrinsically intertwined with the form and structure of his dramas. As we have seen, Guare depicts the quest for identity and dignity in the modern world as residing in the liberation of the imagination. The individual must be allowed to dream, fantasize, even mythologize about making meaningful connections free both from the "narcotizing" power of commercialization that hypes the glitz and glamor of celebrity status and from our own superficial desires of fame, power, and greed. Guare's theater literally becomes a place to liberate our imaginations. In other words, in Guare's plays, form matches content: he consciously structures his plays to break down fourth-wall conventions of the theater. On the surface, his dramas may appear to be unstructured; instead, Guare deliberately organizes plays that abandon kitchen-sink realism to engage, challenge, and invigorate the audience's creative and imaginative vision. Guare's model is the fast-paced musical comedies he so admires and the vaudeville theater of his ancestors. His use of songs, musical accompaniment, blackouts, fade-ins and fade-outs, flash-forwards, flashbacks, long monologues, transformational techniques, abrupt changes in lighting, direct audience address, and the shock value of having the audience experience incongruous stage effects, such as hurricanes, volcanoes, lightning, and earthquakes at the least likely moments, all serve to free us from the complacency of conventional theater that often stifles the imagination. Moreover, Guare's metatheatrical stage effects that engage the audience more directly in the action go further in breaking down the fourth-wall boundaries. Finally, the structure of Guare's plays, which appears to be chaotic, often formulated without even the traditional intermission, is primarily designed to maintain a sense of panic onstage and keep the audience's imagination thoroughly stimulated and active without chance of egress. Thus, in the tetralogy, when Guare limits his use of experimental stage techniques and imitates the masters of the modern realist theater, he takes the Guare out of Guare; those plays are soundly constructed but are not his forte.

Guare is at his best liberating our imaginative vision through black comedy and farce, dramatic structures that work by taking the familiar and rendering it absurd, pathetic, and ultimately, terrifying. Guare employs the zany, fast pace of farce to suggest that our modern lives are neurotic and chaotic. Our healthy fantasies are shown to be somewhat synonymous with the cruelty of sick behavior. Farce and black comedy thus liberate the audience's imaginative vision by challenging the assumption that life in the latter part of the twentieth century reflects normative behavior. Black comedy and farce knock down the facade to allow us to see the hypocrisy of our modern neuroses as simultaneously a vale of tears and a circus. Guare's theater becomes even more enigmatic because the dual nature of black comedy as humor that forms the foundation of our painful, fearful, and even revolting awareness of bitter reality is what makes his plays unique. Thus, in contrast to the reaction achieved from spectators watching, for example, a play by Albee, Wilson, or Mamet, the response to a Guare play is usually more frustrating due to the paradoxical effect of the black comedy.

What, then, is Guare's place in contemporary American drama? With his goal to liberate our imaginations through experimental theater techniques and black comedy, Guare will never be considered a mainstream playwright. The somewhat offensive and caustic nature of his plays will forever limit his audience and make him less accessible than most other late twentieth-century American dramatists who are not as disconcerting. Nonetheless, Guare is perhaps one of the most successful innovators of the contemporary American stage, and his sense of humor is particularly apropos for a highly intelligent, and perhaps a bit cynical or jaded, literary audience. Finally, with his acute understanding of the modern consciousness, Guare has joined the ranks of the great American dramatists of the twentieth century who have made significant cultural contributions in engaging the audience to understand the joy and pain behind their own existences.

Notes

CHAPTER 1. INTRODUCTION

1. Gautam Dasgupta, "John Guare," in *American Playwrights: A Critical Survey*, vol. 1, ed. Bonnie Marranca and Gautam Dasgupta (New York: Drama Book Specialists, 1981), 42.

2. Lloyd Rose, "A New American Master," *Atlantic Monthly*, March 1984, 121.

3. Tad Friend, "The Guare Facts," *Vogue*, March 1992, 328.

4. John L. DiGaetani, *A Search for a Postmodern Theater: Interviews With Contemporary Playwrights*, Contributions in Drama and Theatre Studies, no. 41 (Westport, Conn.: Greenwood Press, 1991), 109.

5. Ibid. Guare is intrigued by the *possibility* of the dream matching reality. In "Setting the Scene," Guare writes about the ideal family that is able to connect emotionally with reality and the present. Guare affectionately describes Inger and Oz Elliott's family life: "They have an enormous family of children and grandchildren and husbands and wives and friends that they have incorporated into the fabric of their lives. Their houses in New York and Connecticut bring all their worlds together and have long served as the scene for some extraordinarily comfortable evenings. Delightful Christmas Eve dinners. Birthdays. The fiftieth wedding anniversary party for Inger's parents. Graduations. Marriages." See "Setting the Scene," *House & Garden*, November 1990, 72. Guare also wrote about artist Chuck Close, who suffered from paralysis due to a blood clot that lodged within an artery in his neck, disrupting the blood flow and damaging his spinal cord. Guare obviously admires Chuck Close, who persevered despite his paralysis and is able "to connect." Guare wondered, "Is Chuck a Zen master? No, he's too matter-of-fact and cheery for that. He's just practical. I think he might be the most realistic and accepting person I've ever met." See John Guare, *Chuck Close: Life and Work, 1988–1995* (New York and London: Thames and Hudson, 1995), 40. In short, Guare admires people who can "connect" but realizes that most of us are not like Chuck Close or the Elliotts.

This notion of the need to create a childhoodlike dream world despite the inevitability of the modern angst is the focus of Guare's critique of Eugene O'Neill's *Ah, Wilderness*. Guare asserts that O'Neill had to build the illusionary past of *Ah, Wilderness* in order to destroy it in his three mature plays: *The Iceman Cometh, Moon for the Misbegotten*, and *Long Day's Journey Into Night*. Guare equates O'Neill's vision in *Ah, Wilderness* with America's need to be sold a dream childhood just to be able to go on:

> It is the nuttiest genealogy. Eugene O'Neill creates Richard Miller, who spawns Andy Hardy, who begets Henry Aldrich, and Ozzie and Harriet beget Beaver Cleaver and the Brady Bunch and the Partridge Family and *Father Knows Best* and Donna Reed.

See John Guare, "The Cheerful Past That O'Neill Had to Invent," *New York Times*, 25 March 1998, sec. 2, 5.

6. Henry Hewes, "Theater in '71," *Saturday Review*, 12 June 1971, 14.

7. For example, see David Savran, *In Their Own Words: Contemporary American Playwrights* (New York: Theatre Communications Group, 1988), 88; John Guare, "Preface," in *The War Against the Kitchen Sink*, vol. 1 (Lyme, N.H.: Smith and Kraus, 1996), vi; and DiGaetani, *A Search for a Postmodern Theater: Interviews With Contemporary Playwrights*, 107.

8. Friend, "The Guare Facts," 328.

9. John Guare, "Introduction," in *The House of Blue Leaves and Two Other Plays* (New York and Scarborough: Plume, 1987), 5.

10. Harold Clurman, "Theatre," *Nation*, 1 March 1971, 285.

11. DiGaetani, *A Search for a Postmodern Theater: Interviews With Contemporary Playwrights*, 109.

12. Samuel J. Bernstein, *The Strands Entwined: A New Direction in American Drama* (Boston: Northeastern University Press, 1980), 55.

13. Friend, "The Guare Facts," 329. Guare, like Andy Warhol, finds the concept of fifteen minutes of fame intriguing. For example, in his article on the Broadway success of the rock musical *Rent*, Guare is particularly fascinated by the fact that Jonathan Larson, the thirty-five-year-old composer of the smash hit, died from an aortic aneurysm after attending the final dress rehearsal of the show he had worked on for five years. In his review of the musical, Guare notes, "Roger, the doomed hero, wants to write one great song—'one blaze of glory,' he calls it—before he dies. The joy of *Rent* is that Jonathan Larson did it." See Guare, "Smash!" *Vogue*, May 1996, 347.

14. John Harrop, "'Ibsen Translated by Lewis Carroll': The Theatre of John Guare," *New Theatre Quarterly* 10 (1987): 152. This penchant for growing up glamorous, surrounded by celebrities, is the subject of Guare's fascination with Brooke Hayward's memoir, *Haywire*, and her husband Peter Duchin's *Ghost of a Chance*, which traces his charmed life as the son of the famed bandleader Eddy Duchin. See John Guare, "King of Swing," *Harper's Bazaar*, June 1996, 74–75.

15. Daryl Chin, "From Popular to Pop: The Arts in/of Commerce," *Performing Arts Journal* 37 (1991): 9.

16. Ruth Goetz, "John Guare," *Dramatics*, May 1983, 28.

17. Louis Malle, "Foreword," in *Three Exposures: Plays by John Guare* (San Diego and New York: Harcourt Brace Jovanovich, 1982), viii.

18. Steven Drukman, "In Guare's Art, Zero Degrees of Separation," *New York Times*, 11 April 1999, sec. 2, 7.

19. Frances Herridge, "*Bosoms*—What's in a Title?" *New York Post*, 27 April 1979, 44.

20. John Lahr, "Introduction to *Cop-Out*," in *The Great American Life Show: 9 Plays From the Avant-Garde Theater*, ed. John Lahr and Jonathan Price (New York: Bantam, 1974), 264.

21. Friend, "The Guare Facts," 329.

22. Savran, *In Their Own Words: Contemporary American Playwrights*, 98.

23. Linda Winer, "*Atlantic City* Pays Off for Guare," *Daily News*, 15 May 1981, "Manhattan" section, 2.

24. Hal Hinson, "Ordinary Absurdity," *Washington Post*, 17 June 1984, C7.

25. DiGaetani, *A Search for a Postmodern Theater: Interviews With Contemporary Playwrights*, 110.

26. Lawrence Christon, "World According to Guare," *Los Angeles Times*, 9 October 1984, sec. 6, 1.

27. Richard Christiansen, "A Chicago Premiere," *Chicago Tribune*, 11 March 1979, sec. 6, 4.

28. Guare, "Preface," x.

29. See DiGaetani, *A Search for a Postmodern Theater: Interviews With Contemporary Playwrights*, 107.

30. Hinson, "Ordinary Absurdity," C7.

31. Fran Weil, "Guare's Too Busy for Success," *Boston Herald American*, 22 November 1979, WD5.

32. John Guare, "From Atlantic Beach to Broadway, A Playwright Grows in New York," in *Playwrights, Lyricists, Composers on Theater*, ed. Otis L. Guernsey, Jr. (New York: Dodd, Mead & Company, 1974), 12.

33. William Harris, "For John Guare a Return to Roots in the Comic Style," *New York Times*, 10 June 1990, sec. 2, 8.

34. Robert Berkvist, "John Guare Stirs Up a *Breeze*," *New York Times*, 21 February 1982, sec. 2, 5.

35. John Guare, "Foreword to the 1978 Edition," *From Ibsen's Workshop*, trans. A.G. Chater, ed. William Archer (New York: Da Capo Press, 1978), unpaginated.

36. Ibid., unpaginated.

37. Drukman, "In Guare's Art, Zero Degrees of Separation," sec. 2, 24. Guare also paid homage to Wilder's art when he agreed to write the Introduction to Wilder's collected short plays. See Guare, "Introduction," in *The Collected Short Plays of Thornton Wilder*, vol. 1, ed. Donald Gallup and A. Tappan Wilder (New York: Theatre Communications Group, 1997), xv–xxvii.

38. In addition to Guare's admiration for Aeschylus, Chekhov, Williams, Ibsen, Barry (the glamorous wish-fulfillment worlds of *Holiday* and *The Philadelphia Story*), Orton, Calderón de la Barca, Anouilh, Dürrenmatt, Feydeau, Strindberg, and Pinter, he cites musicals as having a profound effect on his views about theater. When asked what were his favorite plays, Guare mentioned Aeschylus's *The Oresteia* (the first "family" play), Calderón's *Life Is a Dream* (the Edwin Honig translation), and Mozart and Da Ponte's *Don Giovanni*, which represents the ideal musical. With regard to *Don Giovanni*, Guare noted, "The music and libretto transform the audience into a brilliant, daring, intelligent creature leaping effortlessly from one seemingly contradictory mood to another and able to weave all the parts into one emotional whole." See Robert Anderson, "A Playwright's Choice of 'Perfect' Plays," *New York Times*, 14 January 1979, sec. 2, 1, 10.

39. Anne Cattaneo, "John Guare: The Art of Theater," *Paris Review* 34, no. 125 (1992): 99.

40. Guare, "Preface," vii.

41. Cattaneo, "John Guare: The Art of Theater," 102.

42. Ross Wetzsteon, "The Coming of Age of John Guare," *New York*, 22 February 1982, 36.

43. Guare, "Preface," xii.

44. Guare, "Introduction," 7.

45. Sandra Schmidt, "Zeroing In (Farce) on Right Now (Craziness)," *Los Angeles Times*, 16 January 1972, "Calendar," 26.

46. Farce is a frequently misunderstood form of drama. Although it is often associated with fast action, contrived plots, outrageous comedy, and slapstick, farce

is found in many high comedies. Several of the plays of Aristophanes, Shakespeare, Molière, Sheridan, Wilde, and Shaw contain elements of farce. Indeed, many so-called high comedies include farcical elements. Eric Bentley has argued that farce's therapeutic value can relieve the inhibitions and frustrations of our modern world. See Bentley, "The Psychology of Farce," in *Let's Get a Divorce! and Other Plays*, ed. Eric Bentley (New York: Hill and Wang, 1958), vii–xx. Moreover, a surprising number of high comedies may be trivial because of the comic devices employed, such as pratfalls, puns, or horseplay, whereas low comedies, such as farces, may provide insight into the intricate nature of modern civilization and serve as effective devices for social criticism.

47.   Schmidt, "Zeroing In (Farce) on Right Now (Craziness)," 26.

48.   Patricia Bosworth, "Yes for a Young Man's Fantasies," *New York Times*, 7 March 1971, sec. 2, 12.

49.   Cattaneo, "John Guare: The Art of Theater," 85.

50.   Not all of Guare's plays are tragicomedies or black comedies. His trilogy (*Lydie Breeze, Gardenia,* and *Women and Water*) explores America's heritage in the nineteenth century. Obviously, he realized that farcical tragicomedy would not be suitable for this type of drama, especially since Guare was trying to search for his own roots by emulating the masters of classical modernism, such as O'Neill, Chekhov, Strindberg, and Ibsen. Thus, these three plays, each combining elements of realism and melodrama, are exceptions in Guare's canon. Although Guare's reputation will never rest upon his trilogy, writing these plays taught him more about his heritage as a playwright and allowed him to expand his talents in other directions.

51.   Northrop Frye, Sheridan Baker, and George Perkins, eds., *The Harper Handbook to Literature* (New York: Harper & Row, 1985), 75.

52.   Wolfgang Kayser, *The Grotesque in Art and Literature*, trans. Ulrich Weisstein (Bloomington: Indiana University Press, 1963). See especially pp. 19–47, 179–189.

53.   Jackson R. Bryer, ed., *The Playwright's Art: Conversations With Contemporary American Dramatists* (New Brunswick, N.J.: Rutgers University Press, 1995), 83.

54.   Philip Thomson, *The Grotesque*, The Critical Idiom, no. 24 (London: Methuen, 1972), 63.

55.   Ibid., 59.

56.   Jack Kroll, "Laugh When It Hurts," *Newsweek*, 14 May 1979, 86.

57.   Wetzsteon, "The Coming of Age of John Guare," 37.

58.   Cattaneo, "John Guare: The Art of Theater," 74. Bill Grady's ability to discover new talent may be a bit exaggerated. He once wrote of newcomer Fred Astaire, "Can't act. Can't sing. Slightly bald. Can dance a little." See Geordie Greig, "Centre Stage and Staying There," *Sunday Times*, 31 May 1992, sec. 7, 11.

59.   Bosworth, "Yes for a Young Man's Fantasies," sec. 2, 12.

60.   Ibid.

61.   Greig, "Centre Stage and Staying There," sec. 7, 11.

62.   Although Guare has written that his young friend's name was Bobby Shlomm, in an interview that he conducted with Kevin Kelly, Guare used the name Boris Shlomm several times. See Kevin Kelly, "Guare: Stagestruck and Successful," *Boston Globe*, 23 November 1979, 31.

63.   Kelly, "Guare: Stagestruck and Successful," 31.

64.   Guare, "Preface," vi.

65.   Savran, *In Their Own Words: Contemporary American Playwrights*, 89.

66.   Goetz, "John Guare," 6.

67. Kroll, "Laugh When It Hurts," 86.

68. Cattaneo, "John Guare: The Art of Theater," 75.

69. This date is probably correct, although several biographical précis list 1961 as his graduation date. In the earlier interviews with Guare during the 1970s, he cites 1960 as the graduation date, which leads one to believe that this is accurate. In 1971, Guare told Jerry Tallmer that he spent three years working on his masters degree, and since 1963 has never been questioned as the year Guare received his M.F.A. from Yale, 1960 would be the year of his graduation from Georgetown. See Tallmer, "Huck Finn Strikes Back," *New York Post Magazine*, 26 February 1971, 3. However, in 1971, Guare must have told Patricia Bosworth that he graduated in 1961, for she reported it that way in her article. See Bosworth, "Yes for a Young Man's Fantasies," sec. 2, 12. One should note that these sources list 1961 as the graduation date: "Guare, John," in *Contemporary Authors*, vols. 73–76, ed. Frances Carol Locher (Detroit: Gale Research Company, 1978), 259; "Guare, John," in *Contemporary Theatre, Film, and Television*, vol. 8, ed. Owen O'Donnell (Detroit: Gale Research Company, 1990), 175; Susan Salter, "Guare, John," in *Contemporary Authors*, New Revision Series, vol. 21, ed. Deborah A. Straub (Detroit: Gale Research Company, 1987), 163; and "Guare, John," in *Who's Who in America, 1997*, vol. 1 (New Providence, N.J.: Reed Elsevier, 1996), 1700.

70. Cattaneo, "John Guare: The Art of Theater," 87.

71. Ibid., 88.

72. Bosworth, "Yes for a Young Man's Fantasies," sec. 2, 12.

73. Cattaneo, "John Guare: The Art of Theater," 89.

74. Ibid., 88.

75. Oddly enough, this project was continued eighteen years later, in 1986, albeit without Sondheim, who was unavailable. Guare, Robbins, and Bernstein worked on the musical for six months before it was given five performances as a workshop in Lincoln Center. Although the group disbanded their collaborative effort to work on individual projects, Guare learned from Jerome Robbins, whom Guare says, "has an understanding of energy on stage—a play's unit of energy." See DiGaetani, *A Search for a Postmodern Theater: Interviews With Contemporary Playwrights*, 107.

76. Guare takes his craft as a playwright seriously and is often obsessive about his work. His wife has stated, "It takes him years to get over a failure: it ages him." See Friend, "The Guare Facts," 329. Guare insists, "It's important that a playwright always have another play in the works when he finishes one. If the first is a flop, it's very hard to work up the energy to begin another." See Constance Gorfinkle, "John Guare/ Surviving Broadway and Heavy Subjects With Humor," *Patriot Ledger*, 20 November 1979, 11. In his early years, Guare's strategy in dealing with plays that were failures was to flee from the scene, but, in his later years, he has turned to his next project instead. He prefers not to read reviews, allowing his wife to do so and then summarize them for him.

77. For a copy of the script, see Milos Forman, John Guare, Jean-Claude Carrière, and John Klein, *Taking Off* (New York: New American Library, 1971).

78. Derek Jewell, "Perfect Lady," *Sunday Times*, 29 April 1973, 38.

79. See Clive Barnes, "*Gentlemen of Verona* Rocks in Park," *New York Times*, 29 July 1971, 40; Clive Barnes, "Stage: *Two Gentlemen of Verona*," *New York Times*, 2 December 1971, 65; Martin Gottfried, "The Theatre," *Women's Wear Daily*, 3 December 1971, 12; Irma Pascal Heldman, "Shakespeare as a Soul Delight," *Wall Street Journal*, 3 December 1971, 12; Hobe, "Show on Broadway," *Variety*, 8 December 1971,

48; Walter Kerr, "Simply Carefree, Simply Wonderful," *New York Times*, 12 December 1971, sec. 2, 3, 22; Jack Kroll, "Avon Rock," *Newsweek*, 13 April 1971, 114; Peter Schjeldaht, "An Up-to-Date and Sexy *Verona*," *New York Times*, 8 August 1971, sec. 2, 1, 16; Douglas Watt, "With *Two Gents* Joy and Love," *Daily News*, 2 December 1971, 114; and Richard Watts, "Happy Days in Old Verona," *New York Post*, 2 December 1971, 55. John Simon's review of the Central Park production was mixed. He praised the cleverness of Guare's lyrics and the enthusiastic cast but declared that the staging ranged from resourceful to cluttered; his overall assessment was that the play is "an above-average varsity show." See Simon, *Uneasy Stages* (New York: Random House, 1975), 363–364. The only dissenting opinion was T. E. Kalem's review in *Time*. Kalem complained that Papp demolished Shakespeare's play, turning it into a vehicle for modern audiences that want distractions in the form of rock music, silly props, and lofty sentimentality. See Kalem, "Cultural Vandalism," *Time*, 13 December 1971, 48.

80.   See John Barber, "Buoyant Spirits of Multi-racial Musical," *Daily Telegraph*, 27 April 1973, 14; Ronald Hayman, "Mel Shapiro's Verona," *Times*, 26 April 1973, 14; and Irving Wardle, "*Two Gentlemen of Verona*," *Times*, 27 April 1973, 9. For a neutral review, see Harold Hobson, "Stars in Their Glory," *Sunday Times*, 29 April 1973, 35. Michael Billington referred to Shakespeare's play as "worthless," reduced to babbling incoherence by this adaptation. He was upset that the production had what he believed was no direction and reflected merely glittering tinsel acting as camouflage. See Billington, "*Two Gentlemen of Verona* at the Phoenix," *Guardian*, 27 April 1973, 14.

81.   Charles Michener, "The Bard of Jackson Heights," *New York*, 24–31 December 1990, 85.

82.   Cattaneo, "John Guare: The Art of Theater," 80.

83.   Christon, "World According to Guare," sec. 6, 1.

84.   Guare demonstrated his gratitude towards Joseph Papp a couple of years later when he wrote the playlet *Take a Dream* for Papp's surprise party at the Delacorte Theatre in Central Park. In that play, Guare took the role of Bernard Gersten, Papp's alter ego.

85.   For more details about their marriage, see "His & Hers," *House & Garden*, April 1988, 121–27, 210.

86.   Cattaneo, "John Guare: The Art of Theater," 93.

87.   Larry Sloan of the Goodman Theater staff conceived of the idea and staged the production on a small, bare platform stage. The evening's entertainment, which ran approximately one and three-quarters hours, included music by Jan Warner and performances by Kevin C. Anderson, William Dick, Nancy Giles, and Megan Mullally. The title, *Hey, Stay a While*, is derived from a line in *Landscape of the Body*. For more information on this production, see Richard Christiansen, "*Stay* a Joyous Celebration of John Guare's Wondrous Works," *Chicago Tribune*, 28 February 1984, sec. 5, 7.

88.   The other contributors included playwrights Edward Albee, Christopher Durang, Amlin Gray, Romulus Linney, Jean-Claude van Itallie, and fiction writer Joyce Carol Oates. For a review of the performance, see Alvin Klein, "A Sinful Pastiche at McCarter Theatre," *New York Times*, 3 February 1985, sec. 11, 17.

89.   The other plays included *A Dopey Fairy Tale* (Michael Weller), *Drowning* (Maria Irene Fornes), *Eve of the Trial* (Samm-Art Williams), *The Man in a Case* (Wendy Wasserstein), *Rivkala's Ring* (Spalding Gray), and *Vint* (David Mamet). For a review

of this production, see Mel Gussow, "Theater: *Orchards*, 7 One-Acts," *New York Times*, 23 April 1986, C15.

90.   David Hampton has led an intriguing life as a con man. He was born in Buffalo, New York, in 1964, the eldest of three children; his father, an attorney, refuses to talk about his son. Star-struck and unhappy with the parochial climate in Buffalo, Hampton left the city at age seventeen to seek his fortune as an artist in New York. He supported himself by working in an ice cream shop and in a bookstore before returning home briefly in 1982. In May 1982, he ventured out to California and was arrested in San Francisco for taking a vehicle without the owner's consent. Those charges were later dropped. He returned to his hometown and enrolled in classes at SUNY-Buffalo. Hampton was arrested there for stealing from another student's dorm room and for breaking a window on campus. He pleaded guilty to criminal trespass and paid restitution. Banned from campus, he was arrested again when he unlawfully entered a dormitory. For this offense, Hampton served six months in prison.

During summer 1983, Hampton returned to New York and began loitering on the Columbia University campus. Claiming to be a friend of a local gay rights activist, Hampton used that con game to persuade students to let him stay in their dorms. After Hampton was accused of stealing from the students, Columbia University administrators banned him from campus. One evening during 1983, Hampton and a friend were trying to get into Studio 54. Unable to gain entry, Hampton's friend decided to pose as Gregory Peck's son while Hampton assumed the identity of Sidney Poitier's son. They were ushered in as celebrities; no one knew that Sidney Poitier has no son.

All of a sudden, David Hampton had a new persona. At times, he would enter a restaurant and tell the manager that he was there to meet his father, Sidney Poitier. After eating the meal, "David Poitier" would lament that his father must have been detained on business. The restaurant manager would pick up the tab for the dinner. One evening, when he needed lodging, Hampton called on actress Melanie Griffith; although she was not at home, actor Gary Sinise was temporarily occupying her residence. Hampton claimed that, as Sidney Poitier's son, he was a friend of Griffith's and had just missed his plane to Los Angeles. He regretted that his luggage was on board the plane, so he was now without lodging and amenities. Sinise let him stay overnight, bought him breakfast the next day, and gave him some spending money.

While Hampton was at Connecticut College soon after this incident with Sinise, he gained access to the address book of Robert Stammers, a student Hampton met there. The book contained names and addresses of parents whose children went to Andover College with Stammers. Hampton began by calling on John Jay Iselin, then president of New York's public television station (WNET), and his wife Lea in late September 1983. He claimed to be David Poitier, a friend of their daughter Josie, who was a student at Andover. Supposedly arriving in New York to meet his father, who was starting rehearsals for a film version of *Dreamgirls*, "Poitier" claimed to have had his money and belongings stolen, including his term paper. The Iselins took him in for the weekend, fed him, and gave him $20. On 2 October, Hampton pulled the same stunt with Osborn Elliott and his wife Inger; the only difference was that Oz Elliott paid him $50 instead of the $20 he previously received. After taking him in for the night, the Elliotts found the "celebrity" in bed with another man the following morning. The Elliotts were astounded and threw David out of the house without successfully getting their money back (Hampton even had the gall to ask for more money to purchase flowers for Inger).

Once the police began investigating Hampton when the Elliotts reported the fraud to them, they found that he had conned at least eleven other people into giving him money, including a Manhattan urologist and a young couple who forked over $350. Hampton was arrested on 18 October 1983. Discovering that he had a criminal record that included charges of burglary, illegal entry, and grand larceny, the State Supreme Court ordered him to pay restitution of $4,490 to the hosts from which he had stolen. Hampton did not pay off his debt and refused to stay away from New York, even after the judge banned him from the city. When he failed to pay for a limousine he had rented to check into an exclusive hotel, he was arrested again. The judge sentenced him to a term of eighteen months to four years in prison. He served his time in Dannemora State Prison from 10 January 1985 to 6 October 1986. Three months after his release, Hampton, now in Amherst, New York, was caught using someone's credit card to rent a limousine to go to Toronto. Charges were reduced to service of ninety days for disorderly conduct.

Hampton spent the next several years travelling to Florida, London, Rome, Paris, Ibiza, and West Hollywood before he returned to New York in summer 1989. Hampton then began hanging out on the New York University campus as a freeloader whose claim to fame was the authorship of *Six Degrees of Separation*. Again, Hampton tried to cajole students into providing accommodations for him. Security guards eventually escorted him off the campus. On 10 October, Hampton got into an altercation when he refused to pay a cab driver for transporting him. The taxi driver charged that Hampton pulled out a small black handgun. In his first court date to resolve the dispute with the cab driver, Hampton failed to appear. He later told the judge that he had been hospitalized after a traffic accident. When the judge asked for proof, Hampton provided what later turned out to be phony ambulance records. On 10 December 1991, the judge sentenced him to three years' probation, five days of community service, and a fine of $500.

For more information about Hampton's notorious career, see Jeanie Kasindorf, "Six Degrees of Impersonation," *New York*, 25 March 1991, 40–46; Joyce Wadler, "His Story Is a Hit on Broadway, but This Con Man Is in Trouble Again," *People Weekly*, 18 March 1991, 99–100; Alex Witchel, "Impersonator Wants to Portray Still Others, This Time, on Stage," *New York Times*, 31 July 1990, C13–C14; and Alex Witchel, "The Life of Fakery and Delusion in John Guare's *Six Degrees*," *New York Times*, 21 June 1990, C17, C20.

91. Kasindorf, "Six Degrees of Impersonation," 45.

92. Ibid., 46.

93. "Judge Tells Con Man to Avoid Playwright," *New York Times*, 7 May 1991, B9.

94. Jacques Steinberg, "Jury Acquits Man of One Count in the Harassment of Playwright," *New York Times*, 2 October 1992, B3.

95. David Richards, "Critics, Happiness and Sex: 2 Playwrights' Views," *Washington Sunday Star*, 16 January 1972, C5.

96. Henry Hewes, "The Playwright as Voyager," *Saturday Review World*, 20 November 1973, 48.

97. Savran, *In Their Own Words: Contemporary American Playwrights*, 92.

98. Cattaneo, "John Guare: The Art of Theater," 98.

99. Bryer, ed., *The Playwright's Art: Conversations With Contemporary American Dramatists*, 74.

Chapter 2. Early Plays, 1966–1969

1. John Guare, *Something I'll Tell You Tuesday and The Loveliest Afternoon of the Year* (New York: Dramatists Play Service, 1967), 4.

2. Ibid.

3. Ibid.

4. John Guare, *Something I'll Tell You Tuesday,* in *Four Baboons Adoring the Sun and Other Plays* (New York: Vintage Books, 1993), 76. All subsequent citations are from this edition and are included within parentheses in the text.

5. Scott Giantvalley, "John Guare," in *Critical Survey of Drama*, vol. 2, English Language Series, ed. Frank N. Magill (Englewood Cliffs, N.J.: Salem Press, 1985), 862.

6. Gautam Dasgupta, "John Guare," in *American Playwrights: A Critical Survey*, vol. 1, ed. Bonnie Marranca and Gautam Dasgupta (New York: Drama Book Specialists, 1981), 42.

7. John Guare, *The Loveliest Afternoon of the Year,* in *Four Baboons Adoring the Sun and Other Plays* (New York: Vintage Books, 1993), 93. All subsequent citations are from this edition and are included within parentheses in the text.

8. Dasgupta, "John Guare," 43.

9. Anne Cattaneo, "John Guare: The Art of Theater," *Paris Review* 34, no. 125 (Winter 1992): 88.

10. See Albert Poland and Bruce Mailman, eds., *The Off Off Broadway Book: Plays, People, Theatre* (Indianapolis: Bobbs-Merrill, 1977).

11. John Harrop, "*NTQ* Checklist No. 3: John Guare," *New Theatre Quarterly* 10 (1987): 164.

12. John Guare, *Kissing Sweet and A Day for Surprises* (New York: Dramatists Play Service, 1971), 18–19. All subsequent citations from either of these two plays are from this edition and are included within parentheses in the text.

13. See Humm, "Off-Broadway Reviews," *Variety*, 1 May 1968, 72; Robert F. Shepard, "Theater: *Red Cross* and *Muzeeka*," *New York Times*, 29 April 1968, 47; and John Simon, "The Stage," *Commonweal*, 14 June 1968, 382, 384.

14. Shepard, "Theater: *Red Cross* and *Muzeeka*," 47.

15. Humm, "Off-Broadway Reviews," 72.

16. Simon, "The Stage," 384.

17. Edith Oliver, "Theater," *New Yorker*, 11 May 1968, 91–92.

18. Giantvalley, "John Guare," 862.

19. Cattaneo, "John Guare: The Art of Theater," 91.

20. Gautam Dasgupta believes the opening scene, the ode to a penny, is an allusion to Brecht's *The Threepenny Opera*. He also is convinced that Guare's play presents a Marxist dialectic, as Argue's name suggests, and "antithetical social and political issues are presented as arguments." I assert that the Brechtian elements are confined to the alienation effects and to the overall epic structure of the play; I have difficulty discerning a well-established dialectic of any sort here. See Dasgupta, "John Guare," 45.

21. John Guare, *Three Plays by John Guare: Cop-Out, Muzeeka, Home Fires* (New York: Grove Press, 1970), 52. All subsequent citations from these three plays are from this edition and are included within parentheses in the text.

22. Patricia Bosworth, "Yes for a Young Man's Fantasies," *New York Times*, 7 March 1971, sec. 2, 12.

23.   See John Chapman, "Play Critic Cops Out," *Daily News*, 8 April 1969, 54; Richard P. Cooke, "The Theater: Talent for Small Things," *Wall Street Journal*, 9 April 1969, 18; Martin Gottfried, "Theatre: *Cop-Out*," *Women's Wear Daily*, 8 April 1969, sec. 1, 47; and Hobe, "Show on Broadway," *Variety*, 9 April 1969, 78.

24.   Hobe, "Show on Broadway," 78.

25.   Chapman, "Play Critic Cops Out," 54.

26.   Cooke, "The Theater: Talent for Small Things," 18.

27.   Gottfried, "Theatre: *Cop-Out*," sec. 1, 47.

28.   Brendan Gill, "Theater: Pranks," *New Yorker*, 19 April 1969, 98.

29.   Clive Barnes, "Theater: Guare's Humorous *Cop-Out*," *New York Times*, 8 April 1969, 42

30.   Cattaneo, "John Guare: The Art of Theater," 91.

31.   Brendan Gill, writing in the *New Yorker*, complained about Guare's warped sense of humor that would force the audience to make a detour around the body and blamed director Melvin Bernhardt for not intervening. See Gill, "Theater: Pranks," 98.

32.   John Lahr, "Introduction to *Cop-Out*," in *The Great American Life Show: 9 Plays From the Avant-Garde Theater*, ed. John Lahr and Jonathan Price (New York: Bantam, 1974), 263.

CHAPTER 3. *THE HOUSE OF BLUE LEAVES*

1.   John Guare, "Introduction," in *The House of Blue Leaves and Two Other Plays*, by John Guare (New York and Scarborough: Plume, 1987), 6.

2.   Patricia Bosworth, "Yes for a Young Man's Fantasies," *New York Times*, 7 March 1971, sec. 2, 12.

3.   Ibid.

4.   John Guare, "Preface," in *The War Against the Kitchen Sink*, vol. 1, Contemporary Playwrights Series (Lyme, N.H.: Smith and Kraus, 1996), x.

5.   For more information about the early search for a cast and director, see Warren Lyons, "No More Crying the *Blue Leaves* Blues," *New York Times*, 25 July 1971, sec. 2, 1, 5.

6.   Jackson R. Bryer, ed., *The Playwright's Art: Conversations With Contemporary American Dramatists* (New Brunswick, N.J.: Rutgers University Press, 1995), 76.

7.   The favorable reviews include Clive Barnes, "Theater: John Guare's *House of Blue Leaves* Opens," *New York Times*, 11 February 1971, 54; James Davis, "*House of Blue Leaves* a Brilliant New Play," *Daily News*, 11 February 1971, 108; Henry Hewes, "Under the Rainbow," *Saturday Review*, 20 March 1971, 10; Walter Kerr, "The Most Striking New American Play," *New York Times*, 4 April 1971, sec. 2, 3; Edith Oliver, "The Theatre: Off Broadway," *New Yorker*, 20 February 1971, 90; and Sege, "Off-Broadway Reviews," *Variety*, 24 February 1971, 58.

8.   Barnes, "Theater: John Guare's *House of Blue Leaves* Opens," 54 and Sege, "Off-Broadway Reviews," 58.

9.   Oliver, "The Theatre: Off Broadway," 90.

10.   Davis, "*House of Blue Leaves* a Brilliant New Play," 108; Hewes, "Under the Rainbow," 10; and Kerr, "The Most Striking New American Play," sec. 2, 3.

11.   Catharine Hughes, "New York," *Plays and Players*, July 1971, 54–55.

12. Richard Watts, "The Day the Pope Was Here," *New York Post*, 11 February 1971, 75.

13. John Simon, "The Sorcerer and His Apprentices," *New York*, 1 March 1971, 58.

14. Harold Clurman, "Theatre," *Nation*, 1 March 1971, 285–286.

15. Jack Kroll, "Theater," *Newsweek*, 1 March 1971, 66–67.

16. Martin Gottfried, "The Theatre," *Women's Wear Daily*, 11 February 1971, 12.

17. Julius Novick, "Very Funny—Or a Long Sick Joke?" *New York Times*, 21 February 1971, sec. 2, 9. Walter Kerr, whose review in the *New York Times* appeared a month and a half after Novick's critique, agreed with his colleague Barnes in the latter's assessment of the play.

18. Bosworth, "Yes for a Young Man's Fantasies," sec. 2, 1, 12.

19. See Mel Gussow, "Revisiting a Realm of Broken Dreams," *New York Times*, 6 April 1986, sec. 2, 3, 16; William A. Henry, "Irreverence: *The House of Blue Leaves*," *Time*, 31 March 1986, 77; Janet Hobhouse, "Theater: Oh, What a Funny Hell," *Vogue*, July 1986, 38; Jack Kroll, "Swoosie Goes Bananas," *Newsweek*, 19 May 1986, 77; Michael Malone, "Theater," *Nation*, 7 June 1986, 798–800; Edith Oliver, "Off Broadway: Old and Improved," *New Yorker*, 31 March 1986, 66–67; Frank Rich, "John Guare's *House of Blue Leaves*," *New York Times*, 20 March 1986, C21; John Simon, "Crazed Husbands, Crazy Wives," *New York*, 31 March 1986, 72, 77–78; and Edwin Wilson, "Theater: A Smash Revival," *Wall Street Journal*, 9 April 1986, 31.

20. Only a few reviewers expressed negative criticism about the play. Humm, the critic for *Variety*, claimed that the farce was effective even with the extraneous slapstick but complained about John Mahoney's performance and felt that the play seemed more "tired" than it did in 1971. Leo Sauvage (*New Leader*) was neutral in his assessment, arguing that the production was superior to the original staging fifteen years earlier but that Guare's humor was too bizarre to be convincing. Paul J. McCarren's review in *America* praised Zaks's direction, which veiled what McCarren believed were implausible coincidences, beleaguered setups, and typed characters. Finally, Robert Brustein, writing in the *New Republic*, stated that Guare, who mixed one-liners with droll characters and whimsical situations, attempted to ingratiate himself with the audience by writing "an eager-to-please middlebrow commodity" that could be recycled as a television situation comedy. See Humm, "*The House of Blue Leaves*," *Variety*, 26 March 1986, 98; Leo Sauvage, "Tragic Misalliances," *New Leader*, 5–19 May 1986, 21–22; Paul J. McCarren, "Play the Thing," *America*, 2–9 August 1986, 52, 58; and Robert Brustein, "A Shaggy Dog Story," *New Republic*, 5 May 1986, 27–30.

21. Although *The House of Blue Leaves* was a revival in 1986, it was considered for Tony nominations for the first time. The 1971 production was ineligible to receive any Tony nominations because it was produced off Broadway. In 1986, the play was staged in a Tony-eligible theater (Vivian Beaumont). Initially, the revival was to be considered merely for best reproduction, a much less prestigious award. However, the producers prevailed in convincing the drama critics that the play should be eligible for appropriate Tony nominations.

22. A couple of the more notable productions include the American Conservatory Theater's (ACT) 1972 staging of the play as the opening for its seventh season in San Francisco and Mel Shapiro's 1988 direction of a mostly Hispanic cast at the Coconut Grove Playhouse in Miami. For reviews of these two productions, see Dan Sullivan, "ACT Opens S. F. Season With *Leaves*," *Los Angeles Times*, 8 November 1972,

sec. 4, 1, 21 and John Nordheimer, "In the New Miami, a Theater Adapts," *New York Times*, 9 April 1988, 13.

23. John Guare, "Author's Note," in *Marco Polo Sings a Solo*, by John Guare (New York: Dramatists Play Service, 1977), 4.

24. Steven H. Gale, "Guare, John (Edward)," in *Contemporary Dramatists*, 4th ed., ed. D. L. Kirkpatrick (Chicago and London: St. James Press, 1988), 219.

25. Guare, "Introduction," 3–4.

26. Much of the play is autobiographical. In the "Introduction" to the play, Guare wrote, "My father worked for the New York Stock Exchange, but he called it a zoo and Artie in the play is a zoo-keeper." See Guare, "Introduction," 6.

27. John Guare, *The House of Blue Leaves and Two Other Plays* (New York and Scarborough: Plume, 1987), 30. All subsequent citations are from this edition and are included within parentheses in the text.

28. Samuel J. Bernstein, *The Strands Entwined: A New Direction in American Drama* (Boston: Northeastern University Press, 1980), 48.

29. Suzanne Dieckman, "John Guare," in *Dictionary of Literary Biography*, vol. 7, pt. 1, ed. John MacNicholas (Detroit: Gale Research Company, 1981), 245.

30. Samuel G. Freedman, "*Blue Leaves* Is Back and Guare's in the Pink," *New York Times*, 16 March 1986, sec. 2, 16.

31. John L. DiGaetani, *A Search for a Postmodern Theater: Interviews With Contemporary Playwrights*, Contributions in Drama and Theatre Studies, no. 41 (Westport, Conn.: Greenwood Press, 1991), 109.

32. Gautam Dasgupta, "John Guare," in *American Playwrights: A Critical Survey*, vol. 1, ed. Bonnie Marranca and Gautam Dasgupta (New York: Drama Book Specialists, 1981), 47.

33. Ruby Cohn, "Camp, Cruelty, Colloquialism," in *Comic Relief: Humor in Contemporary American Literature*, ed. Sarah Blacher Cohen (Urbana: University of Illinois Press, 1978), 288.

34. Bernstein, *The Strands Entwined: A New Direction in American Drama*, 48.

35. Clurman, "Theatre," 285.

36. Bernstein, *The Strands Entwined: A New Direction in American Drama*, 56–57.

CHAPTER 4. *MARCO POLO SINGS A SOLO* AND *RICH AND FAMOUS*

1. See Anne Cattaneo, "John Guare: The Art of Theater," *Paris Review* 34, no. 125 (1992): 95.

2. Jackson R. Bryer, ed., *The Playwright's Art: Conversations With Contemporary American Dramatists* (New Brunswick, N.J.: Rutgers University Press, 1995), 83.

3. Ibid., 84.

4. Several of the biographical précis on Guare erroneously report that the Nantucket premiere occurred in 1976.

5. Positive reviews of *Marco Polo Sings a Solo* included Richard Eder, "The Destination Matters Less Than the Journey," *New York Times*, 20 February 1977, sec. 2, 3, 12; Michael Feingold, "John Guare's Freeze-Dried Despair," *Village Voice*, 14 February 1977, 43; and Edith Oliver, "Off Broadway: 1999 and All That," *New Yorker*, 14 February 1977, 53–54.

6. Negative reviews of the play were the following: Clive Barnes, "*Marco Polo Sings a Solo*, a Play by John Guare, Opens at the Public," *New York Times*, 7 February

1977, 30; Gerald Clarke, "Fissionable Confusion," *Time*, 21 February 1977, 57; Martin Gottfried, "Marco Polo's Sinking Solo," *New York Post*, 7 February 1977, 15; Howard Kissel, "*Marco Polo Sings a Solo*," *Women's Wear Daily*, 8 February 1977, 18; Alan Rich, "Cast Away by a Very Usual Destiny in the Gray Slush of February," *New York*, 21 February 1977, 62; Douglas Watt, "Solo With Marco Polo," *Daily News*, 7 February 1977, 21; and Ross Wetzsteon, "New York," *Plays and Players*, June 1977, 37–38.

7. Eder, "The Destination Matters Less Than the Journey," 3.

8. Oliver, "Off Broadway: 1999 and All That," 53–54.

9. Feingold, "John Guare's Freeze-Dried Despair," 43.

10. Jack Kroll, "Slapshtik," *Newsweek*, 14 February 1977, 66, 69.

11. See Barnes, "*Marco Polo Sings a Solo*, a Play by John Guare, Opens at the Public," 30; Clarke, "Fissionable Confusion," 57; and Rich, "Cast Away by a Very Usual Destiny in the Gray Slush of February," 62.

12. Kissel, "*Marco Polo Sings a Solo*," 18

13. Watt, "Solo With Marco Polo," 21.

14. Wetzsteon, "New York," 37–38.

15. Gottfried, "Marco Polo's Sinking Solo," 15.

16. Donald Lyons, "Theater: Human Tragedy," *Wall Street Journal*, 30 September 1998, A16.

17. Peter Marks, "Alienation on an Iceberg Where Anger Is Warmth," *New York Times*, 28 September 1998, sec. E, 1, 3.

18. John Simon, "Revival Instinct," *New York*, 12 October 1998, 86–87.

19. John Lahr, "Ice Follies," *New Yorker*, 12 October 1998, 98.

20. John Guare, "Author's Note," in *Marco Polo Sings a Solo*, by John Guare (New York: Dramatists Play Service, 1977), 4.

21. Ibid.

22. John Guare, *Marco Polo Sings a Solo*, in *The War Against the Kitchen Sink*, vol. 1, Contemporary Playwrights Series (Lyme, N.H.: Smith and Kraus, 1996), 83. All subsequent citations are from this edition and are included within parentheses in the text.

23. Lusty McBride's presence is not felt very strongly in the play. He is a weakly developed character who appears only occasionally on stage. Most of what we learn about him is derived from his wife's long monologue, not from his stage actions or from what he tells the audience.

24. Guare, "Author's Note," 4.

25. Lahr, "Ice Follies," 98.

26. Ibid.

27. The reviews were positive. See Michael Feingold, "Are the Lean Years Over?," *Village Voice*, 22 August 1974, 67, 70; William Leonard, "*Rich* Is a Smashing 'Little' Show," *Chicago Tribune*, 26 July 1974, sec. 2, 2; and Bill Marvel, "Dear Mrs. Guare: Send the Sweater Parcel Post; I Wear Size 42, Large," *National Observer*, 10 August 1974, 16.

28. See Feingold, "Are the Lean Years Over?," 70 and Leonard, "Rich Is a Smashing 'Little' Show," sec. 2, 2.

29. Feingold, "Are the Lean Years Over?," 70.

30. Terry Curtis Fox, "John Guare: At Long Last, *Landscape*," *Village Voice*, 15 August 1977, 34.

31. See Clive Barnes, "*Rich and Famous*, Play About Writer, Opens," *New York Times*, 20 February 1976, 15; Catharine Hughes, "*Rich and Famous*," *America*, 13

March 1976, 208; Jack Kroll, "Promises, Promises," *Newsweek*, 1 March 1976, 57; and Edith Oliver, "Off Broadway," *New Yorker*, 1 March 1976, 76–77.

32. Barnes, *"Rich and Famous*, Play About Writer, Opens," 15.

33. See Oliver, "Off Broadway," 77; Kroll, "Promises, Promises," 57; and Hughes, *"Rich and Famous,"* 208.

34. Michael Feingold, "Two Playwrights Clowning Around," *New York Times*, 29 February 1976, sec. 2, 5.

35. Christopher Sharp, *"Rich and Famous,"* *Women's Wear Daily*, 20 February 1976, 12.

36. Stanley Kauffmann, "Off-Broadway Offerings," *New Republic*, 13 March 1976, 28–29; Alan Rich, "'Tis Pity She's No Whore," *New York*, 8 March 1976, 77; and Ross Wetzsteon, "New York Round-up," *Plays and Players*, July 1976, 39–41.

37. R. Z. Sheppard, "Fear of Flopping," *Time*, 1 March 1976, 51.

38. Martin Gottfried, "Another Off-Broadway Phony," *New York Post*, 20 February 1976, 10.

39. *Rich and Famous* has had successful productions outside of New York, where the atmosphere is more relaxed and the critics are less offended and somewhat more amused about Guare's satire of the Broadway show business world. For example, Kim Friedman directed a strong production of the play at the Coronot Theater in Los Angeles during June 1982. For a review of these performances, see Dan Sullivan, "Author Bing Ringling's 3-Ring Opening Night," *Los Angeles Times*, 22 June 1982, "Calendar," 1, 5.

40. Douglas Watt, "Empty Show-Biz Allegory," *Daily News*, 20 February 1976, 48 and Harold Clurman, "Theatre," *Nation*, 13 March 1976, 318.

41. John Guare, "Production Notes," in *Rich and Famous*, by John Guare (New York: Dramatists Play Service, 1977), 6.

42. John Guare, *Rich and Famous*, in *The War Against the Kitchen Sink*, vol. 1, Contemporary Playwrights Series (Lyme, N.H.: Smith and Kraus, 1996), 154. All subsequent citations are from this edition and are included within parentheses in the text.

43. Suzanne Dieckman, "John Guare," in *Dictionary of Literary Biography*, vol. 7, pt. 1, ed. John MacNicholas (Detroit: Gale Research Company, 1981), 245.

44. Guare, "Production Notes," 6.

45. Mel Shapiro, "Frequently Asked Questions on Playing Guare," in John Guare, *The War Against the Kitchen Sink*, vol. 1, Contemporary Playwrights Series (Lyme, N.H.: Smith and Kraus, 1996), 189.

CHAPTER 5. *LANDSCAPE OF THE BODY* AND *BOSOMS AND NEGLECT*

1. Terry Curtis Fox, "John Guare: At Long Last, *Landscape*," *Village Voice*, 15 August 1977, 34.

2. Anne Cattaneo, "John Guare: The Art of Theater," *Paris Review* 34, no. 125 (1992): 96.

3. Linda Winer, "Guare's 'Oddball' Comedy Is Unwieldy but Refreshing," *Chicago Tribune*, 12 July 1977, sec. 2, 11.

4. Edith Oliver, "Off Broadway: Betty and Bert in New York," *New Yorker*, 24 October 1977, 144–145.

5. Alvin Klein, "Two Views: John Guare's *Landscape of the Body*," *New York Theatre Review*, 21 December 1977, 21.

6. Walter Kerr, "Two Failures—One Noble, One Tedious," *New York Times*, 23 October 1977, sec. 2, 5, 16.

7. Jack Kroll, "Cracked Mirror," *Newsweek*, 24 October 1977, 86.

8. Harold Clurman, "Theatre," *Nation*, 12 November 1977, 504–6.

9. John Simon, "Strindberg Agonistes," *New York*, 31 October 1977, 94.

10. Richard Eder, "Stage: Guare Play Misses Its Target," *New York Times*, 13 October 1977, C17.

11. Mel Gussow, "Stage: Guare's *Landscape Revived*," *New York Times*, 9 May 1984, C22.

12. Clive Barnes, "There Is Life in the *Body*," *New York Post*, 11 May 1984, 24.

13. Edith Oliver, "The Theatre: Off Broadway," *New Yorker*, 21 May 1984, 98.

14. John Simon, "Bangs and Whimpers," *New York*, 21 May 1984, 104–6.

15. *Landscape of the Body* will not work onstage if theater companies disregard the poetry and pathos in the play. Such was the case with director James C. Nicola's production at the Studio Theatre in Washington, D.C., during January and February 1986. Nicola staged the play as a pop rock musical version of *A Clockwork Orange*, which buried Guare's zany sense of humor and instead stressed the text's abrasive and grotesque sadism. For a review of this production, see David Richards, "Guare's Bleak *Landscape*," *Washington Post*, 17 January 1986, C3.

16. Holly Hill, "John Guare Talks About *Landscape . . .* ," *New York Theatre Review*, 21 December 1977, 21.

17. Gautam Dasgupta, "John Guare," in *American Playwrights: A Critical Survey*, vol. 1, ed. Bonnie Marranca and Gautam Dasgupta (New York: Drama Book Specialists, 1981), 51.

18. Hill, "John Guare Talks About *Landscape . . .* ," 21.

19. John Guare, *Landscape of the Body*, in *The House of Blue Leaves and Two Other Plays*, by John Guare (New York and Scarborough: Plume, 1987), 164. All subsequent citations are from this edition and are included within parentheses in the text.

20. John Harrop, "'Ibsen Translated by Lewis Carroll': The Theatre of John Guare," *New Theatre Quarterly* 10 (1987): 152.

21. Shirley Knight, who played Betty in the 1977 production at the Public Theater in New York, mentioned that the shampooing scene was being considered for deletion from the play. Guare, however, insisted that the scene remain intact. Knight explained Guare's rationale: "It's partly symbolism. I want to get my life out of my hair." See Angela Taylor, "Nightly, Shirley Has the Cleanest Hair on Stage," *New York Times*, 20 October 1977, C17.

22. Guare visited the luncheonette and saw the four teenagers fawning over their watches; later that week, a cyclist on a speed bicycle knocked him down. The words spoken by the cyclist in the play are virtually verbatim what he said to Guare as he was lying on the street trying to recover from the accident. Guare recalls, "The collision must have unlocked some buried fantasy because I went home and wrote the play very quickly." See Cattaneo, "John Guare: The Art of Theater," 96.

23. Gussow, "Stage: Guare's *Landscape Revived*," C22.

24. The stories that Joanne tells are tales that Guare had read about and wanted to incorporate at the appropriate opportunity somewhere in one of his plays.

25. Hill, "John Guare Talks About *Landscape. . .* ," 21.

26. Richard Christiansen, "A Chicago Premiere," *Chicago Tribune*, 11 March 1979, sec. 6, 4.

27. Richard Christiansen, "Stunning Flood of Words in Guare Premiere Here," *Chicago Tribune,* 2 March 1979, sec. 4, 2.

28. Howard Kissel, *"Bosoms and Neglect," Women's Wear Daily,* 4 May 1979, 58.

29. Martin Gottfried, "Theater: An Unmerry Month of May," *Saturday Review,* 7 July 1979, 40.

30. Terry Curtis Fox, "Premature Burial," *Village Voice,* 14 May 1979, 95–97.

31. Jack Kroll, "Laugh When It Hurts," *Newsweek,* 14 May 1979, 85.

32. Edwin Wilson, "A Play That Tries to Get by on Cleverness," *Wall Street Journal,* 4 May 1979, 15.

33. Hobe, "Shows on Broadway, " *Variety,* 9 May 1979, 550.

34. Douglas Watt, "This Is Too Tough to Take to Our Bosom," *Daily News,* 4 May 1979, 5 and Richard Eder, "Theater: *Bosoms and Neglect,*" *New York Times,* 4 May 1979, C3.

35. Walter Kerr, "Three Plays, One 'A Treasure,'" *New York Times,* 13 May 1979, sec. 2, 5, 24.

36. Brendan Gill, "The Theatre: Family Troubles," *New Yorker,* 14 May 1979, 83–84.

37. Clive Barnes, "The 'Neglect' Is in John Guare's Plot," *New York Post,* 4 May 1979, 43.

38. John Simon, "Theater: Folie à Deux," *New York,* 21 May 1979, 76–78.

39. Virginia Lucier, *"Bosoms* Playwright Well Pleased," *Middlesex News,* 21 November 1979, 8A.

40. Kevin Kelly, "Bitter, Bruising . . . and Funny," *Boston Globe,* 29 October 1979, 24.

41. Mel Gussow, "Theater: Guare's *Bosoms and Neglect* at Yale Rep," *New York Times,* 14 October 1979, 63. For another review of this production, see Joan Fleckenstein, Review of *Bosoms and Neglect, Theatre Journal* 32, no. 2 (1980): 259–61.

42. For a review of this production, see Bernard Weiner, "A Splendid West Coast Premiere of *Bosoms,*" *San Francisco Chronicle,* 5 February 1980, 48.

43. Dan Sullivan, "A Playful Festival at Stratford," *Los Angeles Times,* 31 August 1980, "Calendar," 1, 51. For an additional review of *Bosoms and Neglect* at Stratford, see Mark Czarnecki, "Memory as a Loaded Gun," *Macleans,* 4 August 1980, 46.

44. For more information about the Atlanta and Los Angeles productions, see these reviews, respectively: Scott Cain, "Imaginary's Latest Is Funny, Odd," *Atlanta Journal,* 22 January 1981, 9B and Lawrence Christon, "More Uneasy Laughter From Guare," *Los Angeles Times,* 7 February 1986, "Calendar," 18.

45. See Mel Gussow, "Stage: John Guare's *Bosoms and Neglect,*" *New York Times,* 13 April 1986, 66 and Edith Oliver, "Off Broadway," *New Yorker,* 21 April 1986, 107–9.

46. For example, see Vincent Canby, "In *Cabaret,* Evolution Repositions the Stars," *New York Times,* 10 January 1999, sec. 2, pt. 1, 7, 24 and Peter Marks, "Mother Love It Isn't: Analyzing Attachments," *New York Times,* 15 December 1998, sec. E, 3. Marks's review was neutral, claiming that the play's forte is that Henny grounds the production in "psychological reality," albeit one that makes it difficult to mask the hyperbolic repartee and the fact that Guare does not make us care about any of these characters.

47. Jackson R. Bryer, ed., *The Playwright's Art: Conversations With Contemporary American Dramatists* (New Brunswick, N.J.: Rutgers University Press, 1995), 82.

48. Don Shewey, "The Playwright's Revenge: John Guare 10, Critics 0," *Boston Phoenix,* 27 November 1979, sec. 3, 11.

49. Kroll, "Laugh When It Hurts," 86.

50. John Guare, *Bosoms and Neglect*, in *The House of Blue Leaves and Two Other Plays*, by John Guare (New York and Scarborough: Plume, 1987), 177. All subsequent citations are from this edition and are included within parentheses in the text.

51. Frances Herridge, "*Bosoms*—What's in a Title?" *New York Post*, 27 April 1979, 44.

52. Harrop, "'Ibsen Translated by Lewis Carroll': The Theatre of John Guare," 154.

CHAPTER 6. *ATLANTIC CITY*

1. Ross Wetzsteon, "The Coming of Age of John Guare," *New York*, 22 February 1982, 36.

2. Linda Winer, "*Atlantic City* Pays Off for John Guare," *Daily News*, 15 May 1981, "Manhattan," 2.

3. For more information on how Guare developed his first impressions about the framework of the screenplay, see Guare, "John Guare on Louis Malle," *New Yorker*, 21 March 1994, 137.

4. Wetzsteon, "The Coming of Age of John Guare," 36.

5. Anne Cattaneo, "John Guare: The Art of Theater," *Paris Review* 34, no. 125 (1992): 102.

6. An astute student of Guare's work may be able to catch a glimpse of Adele Chatfield-Taylor, later to be Guare's wife, as a flower girl in the movie.

7. For details about Guare's work on the set, see Bonnie Marranca and Gautam Dasgupta, eds., *Conversations on Art and Performance* (Baltimore and London: Johns Hopkins University Press, 1999), 262–66.

8. Cattaneo, "John Guare: The Art of Theater," 101.

9. For a review of the screening of the film in Venice, see Mosk, "*Atlantic City, U.S.A.*," *Variety*, 3 September 1980, 25.

10. Robert Berkvist, "John Guare Stirs Up a *Breeze*," *New York Times*, 21 February 1982, sec. 2, 5.

11. Guare has implied that the film was ideal for Malle. As a child, Malle worked with Jacques Cousteau exploring underseas terrain. Throughout his life, Malle loved exploring new terrain, using the camera as a pickax. Guare stated, "We went to Atlantic City, and it seemed an eminently pickaxable place. All these people coming from Las Vegas, pushing other people out, everything being torn down." See Chris Chase, "At the Movies," *New York Times*, 29 May 1981, C8.

12. Winer, "*Atlantic City* Pays Off for John Guare," 2.

13. Vincent Canby, "Screen: *Atlantic City*, Louis Malle Ghost Story," *New York Times*, 3 April 1981, C15.

14. Pauline Kael, "The Current Cinema," *New Yorker*, 6 April 1981, 157.

15. "Utopian" is probably an appropriate word to describe Lou's vision. When Guare wrote the screenplay for *Atlantic City*, he was fully immersed in the tetralogy, having recently completed *Lydie Breeze*. The *Atlantic City* project was actually a break in his work on nineteenth-century American utopianism.

16. Kael, "The Current Cinema," 157.

17. Guare revealed that Grace was modelled on his father's brother's wife (Aunt Peggy), who came to New York to compete in a Mary Pickford lookalike contest. See Winer, "*Atlantic City* Pays Off for John Guare," 2.

18.   The producers of the film wanted to cut these lines, claiming that because the Atlantic Ocean does not change, the words were meaningless. Guare and Malle, however, realized the significance of retaining the evocative language.

19.   Guare does not regard the scene as kinky but instead perceives Sally to be a chaste goddess who happens to work at an oyster bar and smears herself with lemons only to cut the smell of the seafood. See John L. DiGaetani, *A Search for a Postmodern Theater: Interviews With Contemporary Playwrights*, Contributions in Drama and Theatre Studies, no. 41 (Westport, Conn.: Greenwood Press, 1991), 110.

20.   Kael, "The Current Cinema," 160.

21.   Lloyd Rose, "A New American Master," *Atlantic Monthly*, March 1984, 122.

Chapter 7. The Tetralogy

1.   Robert Berkvist, "John Guare Stirs Up a *Breeze*," *New York Times*, 21 February 1982, sec. 2, 4.

2.   Hal Hinson, "Ordinary Absurdity," *Washington Post*, 17 June 1984, C7.

3.   Ibid.

4.   See Lawrence Christon, "World According to Guare," *Los Angeles Times*, 9 October 1984, sec. 6, 1.

5.   Ibid., sec. 6, 6.

6.   Hinson, "Ordinary Absurdity," C7.

7.   Berkvist, "John Guare Stirs Up a *Breeze*," sec. 2, 5.

8.   John Guare, "Behind the Creative Curtain," *Washington Post*, 1 December 1985, G2.

9.   See Guare's comments in his interview with John Harrop, "'Living in That Dark Room': The Playwright and His Audience," *New Theatre Quarterly* 10 (1987): 156.

10.   Scott Haller, "Malle's American Connection," *Saturday Review*, June 1982, 19.

11.   Berkvist, "John Guare Stirs Up a *Breeze*," sec. 2, 4.

12.   During his interview with Hal Hinson, published in June 1984, Guare mentioned that he was in the middle of writing *Bulfinch's Mythology*. See Hinson, "Ordinary Absurdity," C1.

13.   David Savran, ed., *In Their Own Words: Contemporary American Playwrights* (New York: Theatre Communications Group, 1988), 90.

14.   For a hint of the play's original length, see Constance Gorfinkle, "John Guare/Surviving Broadway and Heavy Subjects With Humor," *Patriot Ledger*, 20 November 1979, 11. One week after his remarks to Gorfinkle, at a press luncheon in Boston to promote *Bosoms and Neglect*, Guare mentioned that *Lydie Breeze* included "lots of characters." See Don Shewey, "The Playwright's Revenge: John Guare 10, Critics 0," *Boston Phoenix*, 27 November 1979, sec. 3, 11.

15.   See Howard Kissel, "*Lydie Breeze*," *Women's Wear Daily*, 26 February 1982, 25; Jack Kroll, "Yankee Doodle Deadly," *Newsweek*, 8 March 1982, 94; and Edith Oliver,"The Theatre: Off Broadway," *New Yorker*, 8 March 1982, 96, 98.

16.   Oliver, "The Theatre: Off Broadway," 96.

17.   Kissel, "*Lydie Breeze*," 25.

18. Kroll, "Yankee Doodle Deadly," 94.

19. T. E. Kalem, "Sick Souls," *Time*, 8 March 1982, 86.

20. Clive Barnes, "Becalmed Without Hope of a Breeze," *New York Post*, 26 February 1982, 41.

21. Rex Reed, "*Lydie Breeze* Is Just a Lot of Hot Air," *Daily News*, 26 February 1982, "Friday," 3, 14.

22. Richard Gilman, "Theater," *Nation*, 3 April 1982, 409–10.

23. Robert Brustein, "Unsound Breeze From the Sound," *New Republic*, 24 March 1982, 26–28.

24. Douglas Watt, "*Lydie Breeze*," *Daily News*, 26 February 1982, "Friday," 5, 14.

25. Allan Wallach, "Symbols Clash in *Lydie Breeze*," *Newsday*, 14 March 1982, pt. 2, 13.

26. Humm, "*Lydie Breeze*," *Variety*, 3 March 1982, 90.

27. John Simon, "Malle De Guare," *New York*, 8 March 1982, 81–82.

28. Ibid., 81; Brustein, "Unsound Breeze From the Sound," 27; and Reed, "*Lydie Breeze* Is Just a Lot of Hot Air," 3.

29. For a review of this production, see David Richards, "Marching to Utopia," *Washington Post*, 31 May 1984, B1, B9.

30. For a review of this production, see Steve Vineberg, "*Lydie Breeze*," *Theatre Journal* 38, no. 4 (1986): 487–88. Vineberg's assessment of Steppenwolf's staging includes a caveat: the disappointing tête-à-tête between Joshua Hickman and Jeremiah Grady. Vineberg states that James Noah, in the role of Joshua, played the part "as a crusty, old drunk who has stopped caring about everything." Vineberg notes, "The sole quality that emerged in his long scene with Jeremiah was inebriation, and his whole performance read as one long shrug."

31. Ross Wetzsteon, "The Coming of Age of John Guare," *New York*, 27 February 1982, 37. By "so many Annies around," Guare, of course, was referring to the title of the popular Broadway play; he might also have been thinking of *Annie Get Your Gun*, the Irving Berlin musical.

There seems to be some confusion about whether Annie Breeze was Guare's grandmother or great-grandmother, for in several other interviews, Guare contradicts himself on this matter. For example, he told Terry Curtis Fox that Annie was his grandmother's name. See Fox, "John Guare: At Long Last, *Landscape*," *Village Voice*, 15 August 1977, 34. However, during Virginia Lucier's conversation with Guare, he mentioned that Annie was his great-grandmother. See Lucier, "*Bosoms* Playwright Well Pleased," *Middlesex News*, 21 November 1979, 9A.

32. Savran, *In Their Own Words: Contemporary American Playwrights*, 97.

33. Critics have long contended that Ibsen's late plays resemble Chekhov's dramas, particularly his last four plays: *The Sea Gull*, *Uncle Vanya*, *Three Sisters*, and *The Cherry Orchard*. Probably the major difference is that Ibsen's language in his later plays is much more highly poetically charged and somewhat more heavy-handed than Chekhov's diction (certainly more so than in Chekhov's last three plays).

34. The reference to *The Tempest* is obvious when one considers *Gardenia*. In act 1, scene 4, Lydie Breeze, Dan, Amos, and Joshua argue about who shall play Prospero in a production of *The Tempest* they fantasize about staging. At this point, Joshua hints that he may heave his manuscript into the sea and begin all over again.

35. Lloyd Rose, "A New American Master," *Atlantic Monthly*, March 1984, 122.

36.   Whitman's poem appears later in the tetralogy. *Gardenia* opens with Joshua reading "On the Beach at Night Alone" to Lydie Breeze in 1875, twenty years before the events occur in *Lydie Breeze.* Thus, Guare, in beginning the second play where the first part of the tetralogy ends, highlighted the poem's significance. In addition, in act 1 of *Women and Water,* Joshua introduces Lydie and Amos to the poem during their initial meeting in 1864.

37.   John Guare, "Behind the Creative Curtain," *Washington Post,* 1 December 1985, G2.

38.   Wetzsteon, "The Coming of Age of John Guare," 37.

39.   In this sense, the tetralogy is similar to *Atlantic City,* the screenplay that Guare had completed in 1980 when he was revising *Lydie Breeze.* In other words, *Atlantic City* is also concerned with how, in the midst of one's loss of dignity in the modern wasteland, a person comes to terms with what one often perceives is an idyllic past. Furthermore, like *Lydie Breeze, Atlantic City* (both directed by Malle) is about how an individual finds peace and heals oneself while maintaining a sense of dignity.

40.   In any analysis of *Lydie Breeze,* one must understand that although we have *Gardenia* and *Women and Water* as historical reference points, Guare probably did not have such details when he wrote the first part of the tetralogy. There is no evidence to suggest that Guare knew how he was going to frame the historical events occurring between 1861 and 1895, nor are we certain that he had any intention of pursuing the genealogy beyond the writing of *Lydie Breeze.* Thus, any attempt to discuss *Lydie Breeze* in context with the earlier history chronicled in *Gardenia* and *Women and Water* would be misleading.

41.   John Guare, *Lydie Breeze* (New York: Dramatists Play Service, 1982), 24. All subsequent citations are from this edition and are included within parentheses in the text.

42.   Robert F. Gross, "Life in a Silken Net: Mourning the Beloved Monstrous in *Lydie Breeze," Journal of Dramatic Theory and Criticism* 9, no. 1 (1994): 23.

43.   Lydie Hickman is the name that will be used to distinguish mother (Lydie Breeze) from daughter, although the free love of the commune makes the family's lineage questionable.

44.   Savran, *In Their Own Words: Contemporary American Playwrights,* 91.

45.   Gross, "Life in a Silken Net: Mourning the Beloved Monstrous in *Lydie Breeze,"* 24.

46.   Savran, *In Their Own Words: Contemporary American Playwrights,* 91.

47.   Guare is quite accurate with the historical details. Oscar Wilde's name would have been all over the news at this time because his trial on sodomy charges brought forth by the Marquis of Queensbury occurred in 1895. The Marquis of Queensbury, attempting to quash Wilde's friendship with his son, Lord Alfred Douglas, managed to get Wilde sent to jail for two years.

48.   Gross, "Life in a Silken Net: Mourning the Beloved Monstrous in *Lydie Breeze,"* 29.

49.   Ibid., 34.

50.   Guare stated that the Lucian-Gussie relationship at the end of the play was not planned, although he admitted that Gussie's surprise departure was based upon an event that happened to his great aunt. See Savran, *In Their Own Words: Contemporary American Playwrights,* 97.

51.   The situation parallels Bunny Flingus's abrupt departure for California with Billy Einhorn, leaving Artie at home in what appears to be drab reality.

52.   See Clive Barnes, "Essence of *Gardenia*," *New York Post*, 29 April 1982, 28; Howard Kissel, "*Gardenia*," *Women's Wear Daily*, 30 April 1982, 48; Jack Kroll, "Nantucket Gothic," *Newsweek*, 10 May 1982, 89; Edith Oliver, "The Theatre: Off Broadway," *New Yorker*, 10 May 1982, 148, 151; and Douglas Watt, "Pre-*Lydie*, A Vital Drama," *Daily News*, 29 April 1982, 71.

53.   Walter Kerr, "John Guare: A Distant Way of Doing Things," *New York Times*, 2 May 1982, sec. 2, 5, 9.

54.   Robert Brustein, "Back at the Starting Point," *New Republic*, 19 May 1982, 24–25.

55.   Frank Rich, "Stage: Guare's *Gardenia* Antedates His *Lydie*," *New York Times*, 29 April 1982, C20.

56.   John Simon, "Of Gardens, Gardenias, and Garbage," *New York*, 10 May 1982, 75–76.

57.   For a review of this production, see Richards, "Marching to Utopia," B1, B9.

58.   For a review of the 1984 Los Angeles Actors' Theater production of *Gardenia*, see Dan Sullivan, "Lydie and Admirers Move on in *Gardenia*," *Los Angeles Times*, 22 October 1984, "Calendar," 1, 6.

59.   John Guare, *Gardenia* (New York: Dramatists Play Service, 1982), 15. All subsequent citations are from this edition and are included within parentheses in the text.

60.   Kroll, "Nantucket Gothic," 89.

61.   Dennis Carroll, "Not-Quite Mainstream Male Playwrights: Guare, Durang and Rabe," in *Contemporary American Theatre*, ed. Bruce King (New York: St. Martin's Press, 1991), 47.

62.   Savran, *In Their Own Words: Contemporary American Playwrights*, 91.

63.   Gross, "Life in a Silken Net: Mourning the Beloved Monstrous in *Lydie Breeze*," 24–25.

64.   For a review of this production, see Dan Sullivan, "LAAT, Guare Launch a 4-Part Saga," *Los Angeles Times*, 15 October 1984, sec. 6, 1, 4.

65.   Edwin Wilson, "Roll Over Chekhov: Sellars Stages *Seagull*," *Wall Street Journal*, 31 December 1985, 6.

66.   Richard Christiansen, "*Women and Water* Full of Energy," *Chicago Tribune*, 20 December 1985, sec. 5, 2.

67.   David Richards, "The More the Murkier," *Washington Post*, 6 December 1985, C1, C12.

68.   Joe Brown, "Windy *Women and Water*," *Washington Post*, 6 December 1985, "Weekend," 15.

69.   Mel Gussow, "The Stage: Guare Chronicle, *Women and Water*," *New York Times*, 8 December 1985, 102.

70.   Guare, "Behind the Creative Curtain," G2.

71.   Jackson R. Bryer, ed., *The Playwright's Art: Conversations With Contemporary American Dramatists* (New Brunswick, N.J.: Rutgers University Press, 1995), 80.

72.   John Guare, "Author's Notes," in *Women and Water* (New York: Dramatists Play Service, 1990), 5. All subsequent citations are from this edition and are included within parentheses in the text.

73.   Guare, "Behind the Creative Curtain," G2.

74.   Savran, *In Their Own Words: Contemporary American Playwrights*, 91.

CHAPTER 8. *SIX DEGREES OF SEPARATION*

1.　Jackson R. Bryer, ed., *The Playwright's Art: Conversations With Contemporary American Dramatists* (New Brunswick, N.J.: Rutgers University Press, 1995), 81.

2.　John Guare, "Production Notes," in *Six Degrees of Separation*, 2nd ed. (New York: Vintage Books, 1994), xi–xii. All subsequent citations are from this edition and are included within parentheses in the text.

3.　David Patrick Stearns, "Confronting Chaos in Dazzling *Degrees*," *USA Today*, 19 June 1990, 4D and James S. Torrens, "Six Degrees, Earth and Sky," *America*, 23 February 1991, 212.

4.　John Simon, "Open for Inventory," *New York*, 25 June 1990, 58.

5.　John Beaufort, "Lies, Money and Fantasy From John Guare," *Christian Science Monitor*, 26 June 1990, 11.

6.　Melanie Kirkpatrick, "Guare Comedy Premieres; Weill-Lerner Revival," *Wall Street Journal*, 19 June 1990, A18.

7.　Humm, "Off-Broadway Reviews," *Variety*, 20 June 1990, 68.

8.　Frank Rich, "The Schisms of the City, Comically and Tragically," *New York Times*, 15 June 1990, C1.

9.　Paik, "*Six Degrees of Separation*," *Variety*, 12 November 1990, 68.

10.　See Clive Barnes, "Duped to the nth Degree," *New York Post*, 15 June 1990, 22; Robert Brustein, "End-of-Season Notes," *New Republic*, 9–16 July 1990, 33–34; William A. Henry III, "Con Game," *Time*, 25 June 1990, 77; Howard Kissel, "*Separation* Gets It All Together," *Daily News*, 9 November 1990, 45, 60; Mimi Kramer, "Landscape of the Psyche," *New Yorker*, 25 June 1990, 71–72; Jack Kroll, "The Con Games People Play," *Newsweek*, 25 June 1990, 54; and David Richards, "Destiny's Dizzy Spin," *Washington Post*, 12 July 1990, B1, B10.

11.　Gerald Weales, "Degrees of Difference," *Commonweal*, 11 January 1991, 17–18.

12.　Thomas M. Disch, "Theater," *Nation*, 17 December 1990, 782–84.

13.　Guare had already won New York Drama Critics' Circle Awards for *The House of Blue Leaves* and *Two Gentlemen of Verona*. *Six Degrees of Separation* received thirteen of nineteen first-ballot votes by the critics selecting the award winners.

14.　For example, see James Campbell, "Radical Cheek," *Times Literary Supplement*, 26 June 1992, 19; Jeremy Kingston, "Conners Conned," *Times*, 15 August 1992, "Weekend," 5; Benedict Nightingale, "Questions From a Dark Stranger," *Times*, 20 June 1992, "Weekend Times," 5; and John Peter, "Reality Take Two," *Sunday Times*, 21 June 1992, sec. 7, 6–7.

15.　For reviews of the touring production, see, for example, Dick Lochte, "A Real Three-Ringer," *Los Angeles*, December 1992, 146–51 and Lloyd Rose, "Laughing Till It Hurts," *Washington Post*, 18 March 1993, D1, D8.

16.　See Rose, "Laughing Till It Hurts," D8.

17.　For reviews of some of the less publicized regional productions of the play in the United States, see Leonard Hughes, "*Six Degrees*: A Daring, Dark Comedy," *Washington Post*, 19 January 1995, Va-2; Leonard Hughes, "*Six Degrees of Separation* Shows Cedar Lane Director's Sure Hand," *Washington Post*, 5 October 1995, "Md. Weekly," 3; Alvin Klein, "Guare's *Six Degrees* at the Schoolhouse," *New York Times*, 21 November 1993, sec. 13—"Westchester," 10; and Whitney Smith, "Playhouse Cast Gives *Degrees* Adept Turn," *Commercial Appeal*, 30 April 1994, C1, C4.

18. Richard David Story, "Six Degrees of Preparation," *New York*, 7 June 1993, 40.

19. Guare was even able to get several of his friends into the film. Chuck Close, Kitty Carlisle Hart, Peter Duchin, and Brooke Hayward have bit roles. Guare's wife is also cast as an extra.

20. For more information about the film's genesis and its production, see Story, "Six Degrees of Preparation," 38–43.

21. For example, see Janet Maslin, "John Guare's *Six Degrees* on Art and Life Stories, Real and Fake," *New York Times*, 8 December 1993, C17, C20 and Julie Salamon, "A Young Con Artist, Old Men on Ice, and a Weird Lady," *Wall Street Journal*, 9 December 1993, A14.

22. Guare may have had his wife in mind when he wrote the role of Ouisa. In any event, when Stockard Channing acted Ouisa, she played it as Guare's wife, Adele. See Channing's comment in John Guare, "Lady Macbeth of Mobile," *New York*, 21 April 1997, 34. If Channing identifies Ouisa with Guare's wife, then we might assume that Guare has much in common with Flan. However, André Bishop, the artistic director for Lincoln Center during its staging of the original production, made this interesting observation: "I thing John really identifies with the Courtney Vance character (Paul, the chameleon con man); he's a real outsider who knocked on that door and has been accepted." See Tad Friend, "The Guare Facts," *Vogue*, March 1992, 329.

23. Peter, "Reality Take Two," 6.

24. Guare, of course, laughs at his infatuation with celebrities. In an article written for the *New York Times*, Guare recalled an invitation that he and his wife received to the White House. Apparently, Adele had asked President Clinton if he would hand out Rome Prizes to honor artists, scholars, composers, and writers who had distinguished themselves nationwide. When President Clinton graciously agreed to do so, Guare and his wife, the President of the American Academy of Rome, were invited to the ceremony, held in the East Wing of the White House. Upon returning to New York City, Guare could not resist the temptation to let his friends know of his brief moment of rubbing shoulders with the President. He good naturedly wrote, "I prayed for people to ask me where we had stayed; it's a hard fact to cram into casual conversation." See John Guare, "My Night in the Lincoln Bedroom," *New York Times*, 2 March 1997, sec. 4, 15.

25. Campbell, "Radical Cheek," 19.

26. The Dallas Theater Center was charged with a Class C misdemeanor for operating a sexually oriented business when a complaint was filed because of the inclusion of nudity during their staging of the play.

27. The reaction from Ouisa and Flan is typical of any middle- or upper-class couple who have learned that their trust has been betrayed. For a guest to leave the apartment, pick up a male hustler on the street, and then return with a stranger violates decency and hospitality. John Clum, however, believed the chaos developed because of Paul's sexual preferences, ill-perceived as part of the Kittredges' homophobia. See John M. Clum, *Acting Gay: Male Homosexuality in Modern Drama* (New York: Columbia University Press, 1992), 18–22. According to Clum, the play's popularity may even be due to the titillation of male nudity on stage, much like in Peter Shaffer's *Equus* (22). Clum, in an afterthought that he places in parentheses, judges the play through Guare's depiction of gay males: "That Rick feels compelled to kill himself puts *Six Degrees of Separation* back into the dramatic conventions of dramas of

the forties and fifties" (22). Equally ludicrous is David Román's assertion that Paul as a gay black man causes audience turmoil. Román's reading reduces the play to a "spectacle of difference," a study of racial attitudes among the middle and upper classes in the United States:

> That Paul is the only non-white character in the play further facilitates such a reading. This chaos is construed at one point or another by all the characters in the play. He is described as "this fucking black kid crack addict," "a black fraud," continually associated with drugs, urban crime, and AIDS (Ouisa to Paul: "Are you suicidal? Do you have AIDS? Are you infected?"). . . . It is Paul and not the white hustler whose sexuality is never clear, who becomes the site of white liberal anxieties.

See David Román, "*Fierce Love* and Fierce Response: Intervening in the Cultural Politics of Race, Sexuality, and AIDS," in *Critical Essays: Gay and Lesbian Writers of Color,* ed. Emmanuel S. Nelson (Binghamton, N.Y.: Haworth Press, 1993), 200–201. Guare is more interested in reproducing David Hampton's story as an example of how anecdote has replaced imagination in our lives rather than in promoting any sort of political or social agenda; Clum and Román, of course, have their own agendas to promote.

28.   Jennifer Gillan argues that the reaction that the Kittredges have toward Paul "dramatizes the shifting of blame for social and economic exploitation and general societal decay onto a 'deviant' individual." Comparing *Six Degrees of Separation* with the mentality of Reagan-era films such as *Rambo* that sought to represent the men of the 1980s as aggressive and determined icons capable of defending the state against those who have threatened or damaged the American Dream (e.g., people of color, blacks, or gays), Gillan views the underlying motif of the play as an exploration of the need to return to the normalcy of a time when middle-class iconicity was not challenged. In short, the threat that Paul poses to the Kittredges as a self-made American risk taker usurps the Kittredges as legitimate heirs while simultaneously calling attention to their own illegitimate business dealings. Rather than being fearful of Paul's sexuality, as Clum and Román infer, Paul, Gillan insists, becomes part of that "abject population" that threatens the good life for white Anglo-Saxon Protestants who long to return to the nostalgia of the "incontestable inequality" of former years. See Gillan, "Staging a Staged Crisis in Masculinity: Race and Masculinity in *Six Degrees of Separation,*" *American Drama* 9, no. 2 (2000): 50–73.

29.   Tom Wolfe, *Radical Chic & Mau-mauing the Flak Catchers* (New York: Farrar, Straus and Giroux, 1970), 32.

30.   Ibid., 91.

31.   Salamon, "A Young Con Artist, Old Men on Ice, and a Weird Lady," A14.

32.   During an interview with David Finkle, Guare explained the genesis of the title for the play: "I was reading about Marconi. He connected the world by wire, and it became a statistical problem, a question of how many stations you'd have to go to [in order to] find anybody on the planet. It was something like 5.82 stations. Five-point-eight-two is not a great number." See David Finkle, "Guare Necessities," *InTheater,* 25 December 1998, 32.

33.   Campbell, "Radical Cheek," 19.

34.   Frank Rich, "A Guidebook to the Soul of a City in Confusion," *New York Times,* 1 July 1990, sec. 2, 7.

35.   William Harris, "For John Guare a Return to Roots in the Comic Style," *New York Times,* 10 June 1990, sec. 2, 8.

36. Román, "*Fierce Love* and Fierce Response: Intervening in the Cultural Politics of Race, Sexuality, and AIDS," 198.

CHAPTER 9. THE LATER PLAYS

1. For reviews of this production, see William Mootz, "*Holidays* Is a Big Production That Succeeds Thanks to Many," *Louisville Courier-Journal*, 27 January 1979, B6 and Dudley Saunders, "Versatile ATL Actors Shine in *Holidays*," *Louisville Times*, 27 January 1979, "Scene," 23.

2. The one-act play festival was minimally reviewed in the press. See John Beaufort, "The One-Act Play Festival," *Christian Science Monitor*, Eastern Edition, 11 March 1981, 18; Mel Gussow, "Theater: Festival of One-Acters," *New York Times*, 6 March 1981, C5; Humm, "One-Act Play Festival," *Variety*, 18 March 1981, 310; and Edith Oliver, "Off-Broadway," *New Yorker*, 16 March 1981, 62, 65–66. I*n Fireworks Lie Secret Codes* was described as "fragmented" (Gussow), "frail" (Oliver), "an artificial trifle" (Beaufort), and "disappointingly trivial" (Humm).

3. John Guare, *In Fireworks Lie Secret Codes*, in *Four Baboons Adoring the Sun and Other Plays* (New York: Vintage Books, 1993), 145. All subsequent citations are from this edition and are included within parentheses in the text.

4. For a review of the performances presented at the Lucille Lortel Theater in New York City at the conclusion of the national tour of these seven short plays, see Mel Gussow, "Theater: *Orchards*, 7 One-Acts," *New York Times*, 23 April 1986, C15.

5. Anton Chekhov, "A Joke," trans. Marian Fell, in *Orchards* (New York: Alfred A. Knopf, 1986), 121. All subsequent citations are from this edition and are included within parentheses in the text.

6. John Guare, *The Talking Dog*, in *Four Baboons Adoring the Sun and Other Plays* (New York: Vintage Books, 1993), 164. All subsequent citations are from this edition and are included within parentheses in the text.

7. See Robert Berkvist, "John Guare Stirs Up a *Breeze*," *New York Times*, 21 February 1982, sec. 2, 5.

8. Frank Rich, "An Overstuffed and Uninhibited John Guare," *New York Times*, 24 February 1989, C3.

9. Richard Christiansen, "Dim and Dimmer," *Chicago Tribune*, 1 May 1995, "ArtsPlus," 1.

10. The Remains Theater undertook the production as a gamble, hoping to rejuvenate their financially troubled theater company through public interest in a new work from one of America's most successful contemporary playwrights.

11. The ABSCAM scandal erupted when evidence was revealed that the FBI secretly taped meetings with public officials, including congressmen, who offered bribes to undercover agents posing as Arab sheiks. Thus, "Arab Scam" became known as ABSCAM. In exchange for money, which ranged up to fifty thousand dollars, undercover agents promised immigration aid, help with financial investments, permission for Arab businessmen to reside in the United States, and information about how to profit from gambling operations in Atlantic City. Seven congressmen were indicted and then found guilty of bribery and conspiracy charges. After they leaked news about the investigation as early as February 1980, several FBI agents were disciplined.

12. John Harrop, "'Living in That Dark Room': The Playwright and His Audience," *New Theatre Quarterly* 10 (1987): 157.

13. Alan G. Artner, "New *Moon* Rising," *Chicago Tribune*, 23 April 1995, sec. 13, 5.

14. John Guare, *Moon Under Miami*, in *The War Against the Kitchen Sink*, vol. 1 (Lyme, N.H.: Smith and Kraus, 1996), 118. All subsequent citations are from this edition and are included within parentheses in the text.

15. See John Guare, *"Four Baboons Adoring the Sun,"* *Antaeus* 66 (Spring 1991): 115–40.

16. Sir Peter Hall, "Preface," in *Four Baboons Adoring the Sun and Other Plays* (New York: Vintage Books, 1993), ix.

17. Ibid., xi.

18. John Simon, "The Guary Apes," *New York*, 30 March 1992, 87.

19. Edith Oliver, "The Theatre: At the Dig," *New Yorker*, 30 March 1992, 69.

20. Richard Hornby, "Historical Drama," *Hudson Review* 45, no. 2 (1992): 297.

21. Thomas M. Disch, "Theater," *Nation*, 20 April 1992, 536.

22. Stefan Kanfer, "On Stage: Fantastic Voyages," *New Leader*, 23 March 1992, 21.

23. Hornby, "Historical Drama," 297.

24. Lloyd Rose, "Guare's *Baboons*: Poetry in Ruins," *Washington Post*, 19 March 1993, C2.

25. Simon, "The Guary Apes," 87.

26. Robert Brustein, "Opinions," *New Republic*, 11 May 1992, 32.

27. Jack Kroll, "Broadway Mind-Stretchers," *Newsweek*, 30 March 1992, 65.

28. Jeremy Gerard, *"Four Baboons Adoring the Sun,"* *Variety*, 23 March 1992, 112.

29. Frank Rich, "Desperate for a Reason to Live," *New York Times*, 19 March 1992, C15, C20.

30. David Richards, "One Touch of Eros, and Worlds Divide," *New York Times*, 29 March 1992, sec. 2, 5, 14–15 and Oliver, "The Theatre: At the Dig," 69.

31. Gerald Weales, "Go Ahead, Shoot: *Death and the Maiden* and *Baboons*," *Commonweal*, 8 May 1992, 21 and John Beaufort, "New York Stage Brims With Quirky Dramas," *Christian Science Monitor*, 3 April 1992, 13.

32. Disch, "Theater," 535.

33. Kanfer, "On Stage: Fantastic Voyages," 21.

34. Beaufort, "New York Stage Brims With Quirky Dramas," 13; Rose, "Guare's *Baboons*: Poetry in Ruins," C1, C2; Simon, "The Guary Apes," 87; Edwin Wilson, "New Plays by Ariel Dorfman and John Guare," *Wall Street Journal*, 24 March 1992, A14; and Linda Winer, "Mom, Dad, Kids and a God or Two," *New York Newsday*, Nassau Edition, 19 March 1992, 59, 67.

35. Hornby, "Historical Drama," 297 and Wilson, "New Plays by Ariel Dorfman and John Guare," A14.

36. Howard Kissel, "Going for Baroque," *Daily News*, 19 March 1992, 41.

37. Brustein, "Openings," 32.

38. Other reviews of the play, although short and rather uninspiring, include Clive Barnes, "Family Gets Lust in Itself," *New York Post*, 19 March 1992, 27; William A. Henry III, "Give My Regards to Malibu," *Time*, 30 March 1992, 61; and Doug Watt, "Keeping a 'Death' Watch on B'way Plays," *Daily News*, 27 March 1992, 53.

39. John Guare, *Four Baboons Adoring the Sun*, in *Four Baboons Adoring the Sun*

and Other Plays (New York: Vintage Books, 1993), 30. All subsequent citations are from this edition and are included within parentheses in the text.

40. Penny's comment that Mel "Just does not possess one drop of Etruscan blood" (30) reminds us of Guare's 1965 entry in his journal, written in Rome during his visit to the Etruscan Museum, stating that he wished he had been born an Etruscan. This vision was significant in Argue's quest for identity in *Muzeeka* and certainly motivates Penny in a play set in Sicily, not far from Rome.

41. In Shaffer's *The Royal Hunt of the Sun*, the Incan king, Atahuallpa, is representative of an atavistic sense of Being established through the myths and rituals of a primitive culture. An Apollonian-Dionysian dialectic between the banal world of conformity and the innovative genius associated with the life of the imagination is also the major conflict in Shaffer's *Amadeus*, which, strangely enough, was directed by Peter Hall at the Olivier Theatre in London during late 1979.

42. Guare, of course, wrote the play as a fast-paced dark comedy, but music, as is typical of his plays, played a major role. Guare probably realized that allowing nine children to perform musical numbers could be disastrous. Thus, by creating Eros, Guare understood that the theater company would be able to hire a professional singer to perform all the musical numbers, thus removing the burden from the children, as well as from Stockard Channing (whom Guare most likely had in mind for the role of Penny) and James Naughton.

43. Richards, "One Touch of Eros, and Worlds Divide," 5.

44. Tad Friend, "The Guare Facts," *Vogue*, March 1992, 328.

45. John Guare, *New York Actor*, in *Four Baboons Adoring the Sun and Other Plays* (New York: Vintage Books, 1993), 178. All subsequent citations are from this edition and are included within parentheses in the text.

46. For a review of this production, see Ben Brantley, "How Aged These Sonnets, but They Doth Speak Fresh," *New York Times*, 23 June 1998, sec. E, 1, 3.

Bibliography

Works by John Guare

"Author's Note." In *Marco Polo Sings a Solo*. New York: Dramatists Play Service, 1977. 4.

"Author's Notes." In *Women and Water*. New York: Dramatists Play Service, 1990. 3–5.

"Behind the Creative Curtain." *Washington Post*, 1 December 1985, G1–G2.

"Broadway 2003: The New Generation Arrives." *New Yorker*, 31 May 1993, 168.

"The Cheerful Past That O'Neill Had to Invent." *New York Times*, 25 March 1998, sec. 2, 5.

Chuck Close: Life and Work, 1988–1995. New York and London: Thames and Hudson, 1995.

"Close: Encounters of an Incredible Kind." *Interview*, November 1995, 80–83.

Cop-Out. In *The Great American Life Show: 9 Plays From the Avant-Garde Theater*, edited by John Lahr and Jonathan Price, 265–96. New York: Bantam, 1974.

Cop-Out. In *Off-Broadway Plays*. Vol. 1, edited by Charles Marovitz, 163–89. Harmondsworth: Penguin, 1970.

A Day for Surprises. In *The Best Short Plays 1970*, edited by Stanley Richards, 287–94. Philadelphia and New York: Chilton Book Company, 1970.

"Foreword to the 1978 Edition." In Henrik Ibsen, *From Ibsen's Workshop*, edited by William Archer and translated by A. G. Chater, unpaginated. New York: Da Capo Press, 1978.

"Four Baboons Adoring the Sun." *Antaeus* 66 (Spring 1991): 115–40.

Four Baboons Adoring the Sun and Other Plays. New York: Vintage Books, 1993.

"From Atlantic Beach to Broadway, a Playwright Grows in New York." In *Playwrights, Lyricists, Composers on Theater*, edited by Otis L. Guernsey, Jr., 8–12. New York: Dodd, Mead & Company, 1974.

Gardenia. New York: Dramatists Play Service, 1982.

The General of Hot Desire. In *Love's Fire*. New York: William Morrow & Co., 1998. 93–116.

"His & Hers." *House & Garden*, April 1988, 122–27, 210.

The House of Blue Leaves. In *The Best Plays of 1970–1971*, edited by Otis L. Guernsey, Jr., 215–34. New York: Dodd, Mead & Company, 1971.

The House of Blue Leaves. In *Best American Plays*, Seventh Series 1967–1973, edited by Clive Barnes, 313–36. New York: Crown Publishers, 1987.

The House of Blue Leaves and Two Other Plays: Landscape of the Body and Bosoms and Neglect. New York and Scarborough: Plume, 1987.

"Introduction." In Dawn Powell, *The Locusts Have No King.* New York: Yarrow Press, 1990. vii–xi.

"Introduction." In James McMullan, *The Theater Posters of James McMullan.* New York: Penguin Studio, 1998. x–xiii.

"Introduction." In John Guare, T*he House of Blue Leaves and Two Other Plays: Landscape of the Body and Bosoms and Neglect.* New York and Scarborough: Plume, 1987. 3–8.

"Introduction." In Thornton Wilder, *The Collected Short Plays of Thornton Wilder.* Vol. 1, edited by Donald Gallup and A. Tappan Wilder, xv–xxvii. New York: Theatre Communications Group, 1997.

"John Guare on Louis Malle." *New Yorker,* 21 March 1994, 137.

"King of Swing." *Harper's Bazaar,* June 1996, 74–75.

Kissing Sweet and A Day for Surprises. New York: Dramatists Play Service, 1971.

"Lady Macbeth of Mobile." *New York,* 21 April 1997, 32–34.

The Loveliest Afternoon of the Year. In *The Off Off Broadway Book: The Plays, People, Theatre,* edited by Albert Poland and Bruce Mailman, 175–79. Indianapolis: Bobbs-Merrill, 1972.

Lydie Breeze. New York: Dramatists Play Service, 1982.

Marco Polo Sings a Solo. New York: Dramatists Play Service, 1977.

Muzeeka. In *Off-Broadway Plays.* Vol. 1, edited by Charles Marovitz, 135–61. Harmondsworth: Penguin, 1970.

Muzeeka. In *Showcase I,* edited by John Lahr, 183–220. New York: Grove Press, 1969.

"My Dinner With Donald, and Other Happenings." *New York Times,* 25 January 1998, sec. 15, 26.

"My Night in the Lincoln Bedroom." *New York Times,* 2 March 1997, sec. 4, 15.

"Preface." In John Guare, *The War Against the Kitchen Sink.* Vol. 1. Lyme, N.H.: Smith and Kraus, 1996. vi–xii.

"Preface to the Plume Edition." In John Guare, T*he House of Blue Leaves and Two Other Plays: Landscape of the Body and Bosoms and Neglect.* New York and Scarborough: Plume, 1987. vii–xiii.

"Production Note." In *Six Degrees of Separation.* 2nd ed. New York: Vintage Books, 1994. xi–xiii.

"Production Notes." In *Rich and Famous.* New York: Dramatists Play Service, 1977. 6.

"Production Notes." In *Women and Water.* New York: Dramatists Play Service, 1990. 5–7.

Rich and Famous. New York: Dramatists Play Service, 1977.

"Setting the Scene." *House & Garden,* November 1990, 72, 74.

Six Degrees of Separation. 2nd ed. New York: Vintage Books, 1994.

"Smash!" *Vogue,* May 1996, 305, 347.

Something I'll Tell You Tuesday. In *The Off Off Broadway Book: The Plays, People, Theatre,* edited by Albert Poland and Bruce Mailman, 168–74. Indianapolis: Bobbs-Merrill, 1972.

Something I'll Tell You Tuesday and The Loveliest Afternoon of the Year. New York: Dramatists Play Service, 1967.

Three Exposures: Plays by John Guare. San Diego and New York: Harcourt Brace Jovanovich, 1982.

Three Plays by John Guare: Cop-Out, Muzeeka, Home Fires. New York: Grove Press, 1970.

The War Against the Kitchen Sink. Vol. 1. Contemporary American Playwrights Series. Lyme, N.H.: Smith and Kraus, 1996.

Women and Water. New York: Dramatists Play Service, 1990.

SECONDARY SOURCES

"American Productions Win Awards in London." *New York Times*, 20 April 1993, C14.

Anderson, Robert. "A Playwright's Choice of 'Perfect' Plays." *New York Times*, 14 January 1979, sec. 2, 1, 10.

Anderson, Susan Heller. "Chronicle." *New York Times*, 26 March 1991, B20.

Artner, Alan. "New *Moon* Rising." *Chicago Tribune*, 23 April 1995, sec. 13, 5, 22.

Barber, John. "Buoyant Spirits of Multi-racial Musical." *Daily Telegraph*, 27 April 1973, 14.

Barnes, Clive. "Becalmed Without Hope of a Breeze." *New York Post*, 26 February 1982, 41.

———. "Duped to the nth Degree." *New York Post*, 15 June 1990, 22.

———. "Essence of *Gardenia*." *New York Post*, 29 April 1982, 28.

———. "Family Gets Lust in Itself." *New York Post*, 19 March 1992, 27.

———. "*Gentlemen of Verona* Rocks in Park." *New York Times*, 29 July 1971, 40.

———. "*Marco Polo Sings a Solo*, a Play by John Guare, Opens at the Public." *New York Times*, 7 February 1977, 30.

———. "The 'Neglect' Is in John Guare's Plot." *New York Post*, 4 May 1979, 43.

———. "*Rich and Famous*, Play About Writer, Opens." *New York Times*, 20 February 1976, 15.

———. "Stage: *Two Gentlemen of Verona*." *New York Times*, 2 December 1971, 65.

———. "Theater: Guare's Humorous *Cop-Out*." *New York Times*, 8 April 1969, 42.

———. "Theater: John Guare's *House of Blue Leaves* Opens." *New York Times*, 11 February 1971, 54.

———. "There Is Life in the *Body*." *New York Post*, 11 May 1984, 24.

Beaufort, John. "Lies, Money and Fantasy From John Guare." *Christian Science Monitor*, 26 June 1990, 11.

———. "New York Stage Brims With Quirky Dramas." *Christian Science Monitor*, 3 April 1992, 13.

———. "The One-Act Play Festival." *Christian Science Monitor*, Eastern Edition, 11 March 1981, 18.

Bennetts, Leslie. "Dramatists Pay Tribute to Givers of Dreams." *New York Times*, 17 December 1985, C24.

————. "The Duality in *House of Blue Leaves*." *New York Times*, 9 April 1986, C19.

————. "Plays by Guare and Fugard Are Ruled Eligible for Tonys." *New York Times*, 2 May 1986, C9.

————. "Singing and Dancing Debuts, of Sorts." *New York Times*, 14 October 1982, C18.

Bentley, Eric. "The Psychology of Farce." In *Let's Get a Divorce! and Other Plays*, edited by Eric Bentley, vii–xx. New York: Hill and Wang, 1958.

Berkvist, Robert. "John Guare Stirs up a *Breeze*." *New York Times*, 21 February 1982, sec. 2, 4–5.

Bernstein, Samuel J. *The Strands Entwined: A New Direction in American Drama*. Boston: Northeastern University Press, 1980.

Billington, Michael. "*Two Gentlemen of Verona* at the Phoenix." *Guardian*, 27 April 1973, 14.

"*Blue Leaves* to Close." *New York Times*, 12 March 1987, C19.

Bonin, Jane. *Major Themes in Prize-Winning American Drama*. Metuchen, N.J.: Scarecrow Press, 1975.

Bosworth, Patricia. "Yes for a Young Man's Fantasies." *New York Times*, 7 March 1971, sec. 2, 1, 12.

Boyum, Joy Gould. "Small-Town Squalor; High-Tech Glamour." *Wall Street Journal*, 3 April 1981, 21.

Brantley, Ben. "How Aged These Sonnets, but They Doth Speak Fresh." *New York Times*, 23 June 1998, sec. E, 1, 3.

"Broadway to Get Papp Production." *New York Times*, 27 September 1971, 42.

Brown, Joe. "Windy *Women and Water*." *Washington Post*, 6 December 1985, "Weekend," 15.

Brustein, Robert. "Back at the Starting Post." *New Republic*, 19 May 1982, 24–25.

————. "End-of-Season Notes." *New Republic*, 9–16 July 1990, 33–34, 36.

————. "Opinions." *New Republic*, 11 May 1992, 31–33.

————. "A Shaggy Dog Story." *New Republic*, 5 May 1986, 27–30.

————. *Who Needs Theatre: Dramatic Opinions*. New York: Atlantic Monthly Press, 1987.

————. "Unsound Breeze From the Sound." *New Republic*, 24 March 1982, 26–28.

Bryer, Jackson R., ed. *The Playwright's Art: Conversations With Contemporary American Dramatists*. New Brunswick, N.J.: Rutgers University Press, 1995.

Buckley, Tom. "At the Movies." *New York Times*, 7 December 1979, C12.

Cain, Scott. "Imaginary's Latest Is Funny, Odd." *Atlanta Journal*, 22 January 1981, 9B.

Campbell, James. "Radical Cheek." *Times Literary Supplement*, 26 June 1992, 19.

Canby, Vincent. "In *Cabaret*, Evolution Repositions the Stars." *New York Times*, 10 January 1999, sec. 2, pt. 1, 7, 24.

————. "Screen: *Atlantic City*, Louis Malle Ghost Story." *New York Times*, 3 April 1981, C15.

Carroll, Dennis. "Guare, John (Edward)." In *International Directory of Theatre*. Vol. 2: Playwrights, edited by Mark Hawkins-Dady, 432–34. Detroit: St. James Press, 1994.

————. "Not-Quite Mainstream Male Playwrights: Guare, Durang and Rabe." In

Contemporary American Theatre, edited by Bruce King, 41–61. New York: St. Martin's Press, 1991.

Cattaneo, Anne. "John Guare: The Art of Theater." *Paris Review* 34, no. 125 (1992): 69–103.

Chapman, John. "Play Critic Cops Out." *Daily News,* 8 April 1969, 54.

Chase, Chris. "At the Movies." *New York Times,* 3 April 1981, C6.

———. "At the Movies." *New York Times,* 29 May 1981, C8.

Chekhov, Anton. "A Joke." In *Orchards.* Trans. Marian Fell, 120–24. New York: Alfred A. Knopf, 1986.

Chin, Daryl. "From Popular to Pop: The Arts in/of Commerce." *Performing Arts Journal* 37 (1991): 5–20.

Christiansen, Richard. "A Chicago Premiere." *Chicago Tribune,* 11 March 1979, sec. 6, 4–5.

———. "Dim and Dimmer." *Chicago Tribune,* 1 May 1995, "ArtsPlus," 1.

———. "Quick Exit." *Chicago Tribune,* 11 May 1995, sec. 5, 11C.

———. "*Stay* a Joyous Celebration of John Guare's Wondrous Works." *Chicago Tribune,* 28 February 1984, sec. 5, 7.

———. "Stunning Flood of Words in Guare Premiere Here." *Chicago Tribune,* 2 March 1979, sec. 4, 2.

———. "*Women and Water* Full of Energy." *Chicago Tribune,* 20 December 1985, sec. 5, 2.

Christon, Lawrence. "More Uneasy Laughter From Guare." *Los Angeles Times,* 7 February 1986, "Calendar," 18.

———. "World According to Guare." *Los Angeles Times,* 9 October 1984, sec. 6, 1, 6.

"Chronicle." *New York Times,* 24 September 1992, B8.

Clarke, Gerald. "Fissionable Confusion." *Time,* 21 February 1977, 57.

Clum, John M. *Acting Gay: Male Homosexuality in Modern Drama.* New York: Columbia University Press, 1992.

Clurman, Harold. "Theatre." *Nation,* 1 March 1971, 285–86.

———. "Theatre." *Nation,* 13 March 1976, 318.

———. "Theatre." *Nation,* 12 November 1977, 504–6.

Cohn, Ruby. "Camp, Cruelty, Colloquialism." In *Comic Relief: Humor in Contemporary American Literature,* edited by Sarah Blacher Cohen, 281–303. Urbana: University of Illinois Press, 1978.

———. *New American Dramatists: 1960–1980.* New York: Grove Press, 1982.

Collins, Glenn. "Damages Again Denied in *Six Degrees* Lawsuit." *New York Times,* 19 July 1993, C13.

"Commencements." *New York Times,* 25 May 1987, 22.

Conjunctions: 25, The New American Theater. Ed. John Guare. Annandale-on-Hudson, N.Y.: Bard College, 1995.

Cooke, Richard P. "The Theater: Talent for Small Things." *Wall Street Journal,* 9 April 1969, 18.

Corry, John. "Broadway." *New York Times,* 10 December 1976, C2.

Cruice, Valerie. "On the Road With Marlo Thomas." *New York Times*, 14 February 1993, sec. 13, "Connecticut Weekly," 10–11.

Czarnecki, Mark. "Memory as a Loaded Gun." *Macleans*, 4 August 1980, 46.

Davis, James. "*House of Blue Leaves* a Brilliant New Play." *Daily News*, 11 February 1971, 108.

Davis, Peter G. "Erotic *Psyché*." *New York*, 27 October 1997, 130–31.

Dieckman, Suzanne. "John Guare." In *Dictionary of Literary Biography*. Vol. 7, pt. 1, edited by John MacNicholas, 243–47. Detroit: Gale Research Company, 1981.

DiGaetani, John L. *A Search for a Postmodern Theater: Interviews With Contemporary Playwrights*. Contributions in Drama and Theatre Studies, no. 41. Westport, Conn: Greenwood Press, 1991.

Disch, Thomas M. "Theater." *Nation*, 17 December 1990, 782–84.

———. "Theater." *Nation*, 20 April 1992, 533–36.

Drukman, Steven. "In Guare's Art, Zero Degrees of Separation." *New York Times*, 11 April 1999, sec. 2, 7, 24.

Dugger, Celia. "Playing Close to the Bone in *Six Degrees*." *New York Times*, 5 December 1993, sec. 2, 32.

Eder, Richard. "The Destination Matters Less Than the Journey." *New York Times*, 20 February 1977, sec. 2, 3, 12.

———. "Stage: Guare Play Misses Its Target." *New York Times*, 13 October 1977, C17.

———. "Theater: *Bosoms and Neglect*." *New York Times*, 4 May 1979, C3.

"Fantasy Island on the Hudson." *New York Times*, 12 December 1993, sec. 9, 3.

Feingold, Michael. "Are the Lean Years Over?" *Village Voice*, 22 August 1974, 67, 70.

———. "John Guare's Freeze-Dried Despair." *Village Voice*, 14 February 1977, 43.

———. "Two Playwrights Clowning Around." *New York Times*, 29 February 1976, sec. 2, 5.

Finkle, David. "Guare Necessities." *InTheater*, 28 December 1998, 30–33.

Fleckenstein, Joan. Review of *Bosoms and Neglect*. *Theatre Journal* 32, no. 2 (1980): 259–61.

Forman, Milos; John Guare; Jean-Claude Carrière; and John Klein. *Taking Off*. New York: New American Library, 1971.

Fox, Terry Curtis. "John Guare: At Long Last, *Landscape*." *Village Voice*, 15 August 1977, 34–35.

———. "Premature Burial." *Village Voice*, 14 May 1979, 95–97.

Frank, Leah D. "*House of Blue Leaves*, Tragicomedy." *New York Times*, 15 November 1987, sec. 21, 29.

Freedman, Samuel G. "*Blue Leaves* Is Back and Guare's in the Pink." *New York Times*, 16 March 1986, sec. 2, 1, 16.

Friend, Tad. "The Guare Facts." *Vogue*, March 1992, 327–29.

Frye, Northrop; Sheridan Baker; and George Perkins, eds. *The Harper Handbook to Literature*. New York: Harper & Row, 1985.

"Funky Shakespeare?" *Radio Times*, 26 April 1973, 5

Gale, Steven H. "Guare, John (Edward)." In *Contemporary Dramatists*. 4th ed., edited by D.L. Kirkpatrick, 218–21. Chicago and London: St. James Press, 1988.

Gerard, Jeremy. "*Four Baboons Adoring the Sun.*" *Variety*, 23 March 1992, 112.

———. "Two Master Lyricists Talk Shop at the Y." *New York Times*, 28 March 1987, 11.

Giantvalley, Scott. "John Guare." In *Critical Survey of Drama*. Vol. 2. English Language Series, edited by Frank N. Magill, 857–64. Englewood Cliffs, N.J.: Salem Press, 1985.

Gill, Brendan. "The Theatre: Family Troubles." *New Yorker*, 14 May 1979, 83–84.

———. "Theater: Pranks." *New Yorker*, 19 April 1969, 98.

Gillan, Jennifer. "Staging a Staged Crisis in Masculinity: Race and Masculinity in *Six Degrees of Separation.*" *American Drama* 9, no. 2 (2000): 50–73.

Gilman, Richard. "Theater." *Nation*, 3 April 1982, 409–10.

Goetz, Ruth. "John Guare." *Dramatics*, May 1983, 5–6, 28–30.

Gorfinkle, Constance. "John Guare/Surviving Broadway and Heavy Subjects With Humor." *Patriot Ledger*, 20 November 1979, 11.

Gottfried, Martin. "Another Off-Broadway Phony." *New York Post*, 20 February 1976, 10.

———. "*Cop-Out.*" *Women's Wear Daily*, 8 April 1969, 47.

———. "Marco Polo's Sinking Solo." *New York Post*, 7 February 1977, 15.

———. "Theater: An Unmerry Month of May." *Saturday Review*, 7 July 1979, 40.

———. "The Theatre." *Women's Wear Daily*, 11 February 1971, 12.

———. "The Theatre." *Women's Wear Daily*, 3 December 1971, 12.

Greig, Geordie. "Centre Stage and Staying There." *Sunday Times*, 31 May 1992, sec. 7, 11.

Grimes, William. "Ruling in *Six Degrees* Suit." *New York Times*, 30 April 1992, C13.

Gross, Robert F. "Life in a Silken Net: Mourning the Beloved Monstrous in *Lydie Breeze.*" *Journal of Dramatic Theory and Criticism* 9, no. 1 (1994): 21–42.

"Guare, John." In *Celebrity Register*, edited by Earl Blackwell, 213. New York: Simon and Schuster, 1973.

"Guare, John." In *Contemporary Authors*. Vol. 73–76, edited by Frances Carol Locher, 259–60. Detroit: Gale Research Company, 1978.

"Guare, John." In *Contemporary Theatre, Film, and Television*. Vol. 8, edited by Owen O'Donnell, 175–76. Detroit: Gale Research Company, 1990.

"Guare, John." In *Current Biography Yearbook—1982*, edited by Charles Moritz, 133–36. New York: H. W. Wilson Company, 1983.

"Guare, John." In *Notable Names in the American Theatre*, edited by Raymond D. McGill, 791. Clifton, N.J.: James T. White & Company, 1976.

"Guare, John." In *The Oxford Companion to the Theatre*. 4th ed., edited by Phyllis Hartnoll, 360. Oxford: Oxford University Press, 1983.

"Guare, John." In *Who's Who in America*. Vol. 1, 1700. New Providence, N.J.: Reed Elsevier, 1997.

"Guare, John (Edward)." In *World Authors, 1970–1975*. Wilson Authors Series, edited by John Wakeman, 323–26. New York: H. W. Wilson Company, 1980.

Gussow, Mel. "Broadway Again Blooms on Nantucket." *New York Times*, 9 July 1973, 41.

———. "Chasing Serendipity in New York City." *New York Times*, 20 May 1993, C1, C10.

———. "Revisiting a Realm of Broken Dreams." *New York Times*, 6 April 1986, sec. 2, 3, 16.

———. "*Six Degrees* and *Rogers* Honored by Critics Circle." *New York Times*, 14 May 1991, C14.

———. "Stage: A New Look at 7 Deadly Sins." *New York Times*, 3 February 1985, 55.

———. "The Stage: Guare Chronicle, *Women and Water*." *New York Times*, 8 December 1985, 102.

———. "Stage: Guare's *Landscape* Revived." *New York Times*, 9 May 1984, C22.

———. "Stage: John Guare's *Bosoms and Neglect*." *New York Times*, 13 April 1986, 66.

———. "Theater: Festival of One-Acters." *New York Times*, 6 March 1981, C5.

———. "Theater: Guare's *Bosoms and Neglect* at Yale Rep." *New York Times*, 14 October 1979, 63.

———. "Theater: *Orchards*, 7 One-Acts." *New York Times*, 23 April 1986, C15.

Hall, Sir Peter. "Preface." In *Four Baboons Adoring the Sun and Other Plays*. New York: Vintage Books, 1993. ix–xii.

Haller, Scott. "Louis Malle Hits the Big Time." *Saturday Review*, June 1982, 16–19.

———. "Malle's American Connection." *Saturday Review*, June 1982, 19.

Harford, Margaret. "Forum to Offer New Play Series." *Los Angeles Times*, 10 September 1967, "Calendar," 23.

Harris, William. "For John Guare a Return to Roots in the Comic Style." *New York Times*, 10 June 1990, sec. 2, 7–8.

Harrop, John. "'Ibsen Translated by Lewis Carroll': The Theatre of John Guare." *New Theatre Quarterly* 10 (1987): 150–54.

———. "'Living in That Dark Room': The Playwright and His Audience." *New Theatre Quarterly* 10 (1987): 155–59.

———. "*NTQ* Checklist No. 3: John Guare." *New Theatre Quarterly* 10 (1987): 160–73.

Hayman, Ronald. "Mel Shapiro's Verona." *Times*, 26 April 1973, 14.

Heldman, Irma Pascal. "Shakespeare as a Soul Delight." *Wall Street Journal*, 3 December 1971, 12.

Henry, William A., III. "Con Game." *Time*, 25 June 1990, 77.

———. "Give My Regards to Malibu." *Time*, 30 March 1992, 60–61.

———. "Irreverence: *The House of Blue Leaves*." *Time*, 31 March 1986, 77.

Herridge, Frances. "*Bosoms*—What's in a Title?" *New York Post*, 27 April 1979, 44.

Hewes, Henry. "The Playwright as Voyager." *Saturday Review World*, 20 November 1973, 48.

———. "Theater in '71." *Saturday Review*, 12 June 1971, 14–19.

———. "Under the Rainbow." *Saturday Review*, 20 March 1971, 10.

Hill, Holly. "John Guare Talks About *Landscape*. . . ." *New York Theatre Review*, 21 December 1977, 21.

Hinson, Hal. "Ordinary Absurdity." *Washington Post*, 17 June 1984, C1, C7.

Hobe. "Show on Broadway." *Variety*, 8 December 1971, 48.

———. "Show on Broadway." *Variety*, 9 May 1979, 550.

———. "Show on B'way." *Variety*, 9 April 1969, 78.

Hobhouse, Janet. "Theater: Oh, What a Funny Hell." *Vogue*, July 1986, 38.

Hobson, Harold. "Stars in Their Glory." *Sunday Times*, 29 April 1973, 35.

Hornby, Richard. "Historical Drama." *Hudson Review* 45, no. 2 (1992): 293–300.

Hughes, Catharine. "New York." *Plays and Players*, July 1971, 54–55, 59.

———. "*Rich and Famous.*" *America*, 13 March 1976, 208.

Hughes, Leonard. "A Laudable *House of Blue Leaves.*" *Washington Post*, 13 May 1993, "D.C.," 5.

———. "*Six Degrees*: A Daring, Dark Comedy," *Washington Post*, 19 January 1995, "Va," 2.

———. "*Six Degrees of Separation* Shows Cedar Lane Director's Sure Hand." *Washington Post*, 5 October 1995, "Md Weekly," 3.

Humm. "*The House of Blue Leaves.*" *Variety*, 26 March 1986, 98.

———. "*Lydie Breeze.*" *Variety*, 3 March 1982, 90.

———. "Off-Broadway Reviews." *Variety*, 1 May 1968, 72.

———. "Off-Broadway Reviews." *Variety*, 20 June 1990, 68.

———. "One-Act Play Festival." *Variety*, 8 March 1981, 310.

Isherwood, Charles. "*Lake Hollywood.*" *Variety*, 3–9 May 1999, 95–6.

Jewell, Derek. "Perfect Lady." *Sunday Times*, 29 April 1973, 38.

"John Guare." In *Contemporary Literary Criticism*. Vol. 67, edited by Roger Matuz, 77–90. Detroit: Gale Research Company, 1992.

"John Guare." In *National Playwrights Directory*. 2nd ed., edited by Phyllis Johnson Kaye, 156–57. Waterford, Conn: Eugene O'Neill Theater Center, 1981.

"Judge Tells Con Man to Avoid Playwright." *New York Times*, 7 May 1991, B9.

Kael, Pauline. "The Current Cinema." *New Yorker*, 6 April 1981, 154, 157–58, 160, 163–66.

———. *Taking It All in.* New York: Holt, Rinehart and Winston, 1984.

Kalem, T. E. "Cultural Vandalism." *Time*, 13 December 1971, 48.

Kanfer, Stefan. "On Stage: Fantastic Voyages." *New Leader*, 23 March 1992, 20–21.

Kasindorf, Jeanie. "Six Degrees of Impersonation." *New York*, 25 March 1991, 40–46.

Kayser, Wolfgang. *The Grotesque in Art and Literature.* Trans. Ulrich Weisstein. Bloomington: Indiana University Press, 1963.

Kauffmann, Stanley. "Off-Broadway Offerings." *New Republic*, 13 March 1976, 28–29.

Kelly, Kevin. "Bitter, Bruising . . . and Funny." *Boston Globe*, 29 October 1979, 24.

———. "Guare: Stagestruck and Successful." *Boston Globe*, 23 November 1979, 31.

Kerr, Walter. "John Guare: A Distant Way of Doing Things." *New York Times*, 2 May 1982, sec. 2, 5, 9.

———. "Language Alone Isn't Drama." *New York Times*, 6 March 1977, sec. 2, 3, 26.

———. "The Most Striking New American Play." *New York Times*, 4 April 1971, sec. 2, 3.

———. "Simply Carefree, Simply Wonderful." *New York Times*, 12 December 1971, sec. 2, 3, 22.

———. "Three New Plays, One 'A Treasure.'" *New York Times*, 13 May 1979, sec. 2, 5, 24.

———. "Two Failures—One Noble, One Tedious." *New York Times*, 23 October 1977, sec. 2, 5, 16.

Kingston, Jeremy. "Conners Conned." *Times*, 15 August 1992, "Weekend," 5.

Kirkpatrick, Melanie. "Guare Comedy Premieres; Weill-Lerner Revival." *Wall Street Journal*, 19 June 1990, A18.

Kissel, Howard. "*Bosoms and Neglect*." *Women's Wear Daily*, 4 May 1979, 58.

———. "*Gardenia*." *Women's Wear Daily*, 30 April 1982, 48.

———. "Going for Baroque." *Daily News*, 19 March 1992, 41.

———. "*Lydie Breeze*." *Women's Wear Daily*, 26 February 1982, 25.

———. "*Marco Polo Sings a Solo*." *Women's Wear Daily*, 8 February 1977, 18.

———. "*Separation* Gets It All Together." *Daily News*, 9 November 1990, 45, 60.

Klein, Alvin. "Guare's *Six Degrees* at the Schoolhouse." *New York Times*, 21 November 1993, sec. 13, "Westchester," 10.

———. "A Sinful Pastiche at McCarter Theatre," *New York Times*, 3 February 1985, sec. 11, 17.

———. "Two Views: John Guare's *Landscape of the Body*." *New York Theatre Review*, 21 December 1977, 21.

Kramer, Mimi. "Interlude 1990: *Six Degrees of Separation*." 31 May 1993, 114.

———. "Landscape of the Psyche." *New Yorker*, 25 June 1990, 71–72.

Krebs, Albin. "A Triply Rewarding Day for John Guare." *New York Times*, 21 May 1981, C22.

Kroll, Jack. "Avon Rock." *Newsweek*, 13 April 1971, 114.

———. "Broadway Mind-Stretchers." *Newsweek*, 30 March 1992, 65.

———. "The Con Games People Play." *Newsweek*, 25 June 1990, 54.

———. "Cracked Mirror." *Newsweek*, 24 October 1977, 86.

———. "Laugh When It Hurts." *Newsweek*, 14 May 1979, 85–86.

———. "Nantucket Gothic." *Newsweek*, 10 May 1982, 89.

———. "Promises, Promises." *Newsweek*, 1 March 1976, 57.

———. "Slapshtik." *Newsweek*, 14 February 1977, 66, 69.

———. "Swoosie Goes Bananas." *Newsweek*, 19 May 1986, 77.

———. "Theater." *Newsweek*, 1 March 1971, 66–67.

———. "Yankee Doodle Deadly." *Newsweek*, 8 March 1982, 94.

Lahr, John. "Ice Follies." *New Yorker*, 12 October 1998, 97–98.

———. "John Guare." In *Showcase* I, edited by John Lahr, 185–87. New York: Grove Press, 1969.

———. *Up Against the Fourth Wall: Essays on Modern Theater*. New York: Grove Press, 1970.

Leiter, Samuel L. *Ten Seasons: New York Theatre in the Seventies*. Contributions in Drama and Theatre Studies, no. 21. New York and Westport, Conn: Greenwood Press, 1986.

Leonard, William. "*Rich* Is a Smashing 'Little' Show." *Chicago Tribune*, 26 July 1974, sec. 2, 2.

Lochte, Dick. "A Real Three-Ringer." *Los Angeles*, December 1992, 146–51.

Lucier, Virginia. "*Bosoms* Playwright Well Pleased." *Middlesex News*, 21 November 1979, 8A-9A.

"Lunch." *Lear's*, January 1994, 10–11.

Lyman, Rick. "On Stage and Off." *New York Times*, 12 December 1977, sec. E, 5.

———. "On Stage and Off." *New York Times*, 15 May 1998, sec. E, 2.

Lyons, Donald. "Theater: Human Tragedy." *Wall Street Journal*, 30 September 1998, A16.

Lyons, Warren. "No More Crying the *Blue Leaves* Blues." *New York Times*, 25 July 1971, sec. 2, 1, 5.

McCarren, Paul J. "Play the Thing." *America*, 2–9 August 1986, 52, 58.

McDowell, Edwin. "American Academy Medals Given to Cowley and Soyer." *New York Times*, 21 May 1981, sec. 3, 14.

McKinley, Jesse. "On Stage and Off." *New York Times*, 15 September 1998, sec. E, 2.

Malle, Louis. "Foreword." In John Guare, *Three Exposures: Plays by John Guare*, vii–viii. San Diego and New York: Harcourt Brace Jovanovich, 1982.

Malone, Michael. "Theater." *Nation*, 7 June 1986, 798–800.

Marks, Peter. "Alienation on an Iceberg Where Anger Is Warmth." *New York Times*, 28 September 1998, sec. E, 1, 3.

———. "Mother Love It Isn't: Analyzing Attachments." *New York Times*, 15 December 1998, sec. E, 3.

Markus, Thomas B. "Guare, John." In *Contemporary Dramatists*. 3d ed., edited by James Vinson, 330–32. New York: St. Martin's Press, 1982.

Marranca, Bonnie and Gautam Dasgupta. *American Playwrights: A Critical Survey*. Vol. 1. New York: Drama Book Specialists, 1981.

Marranca, Bonnie and Gautam Dasgupta, eds. *Conversations on Art and Performance*. Baltimore and London: Johns Hopkins University Press, 1999.

Martin, Judith. "The Trashy Hope of *Atlantic City*." *Washington Post*, 17 April 1981, "Weekend," 19.

Marvel, Bill. "Dear Mrs. Guare: Send the Sweater Parcel Post; I Wear Size 42, Large." *National Observer*, 10 August 1974, 16.

Maslin, Janet. "Critics Vote *Reds*, Burt Lancaster the Best of '81." *New York Times*, 21 December 1981, C7.

———. "John Guare's *Six Degrees* on Art and Life Stories, Real and Fake." *New York Times*, 8 December 1993, C17, C20.

Michener, Charles. "The Bard of Jackson Heights." *New York*, 24–31 December 1990, 84–85.

Miller, Terry. "Guare, John (Edward)." In *McGraw-Hill Encyclopedia of World Drama*. 2nd ed. Vol. 2, edited by Stanley Hochman, 427–29. New York: McGraw-Hill, 1984.

Mootz, William. "*Holidays* Is a Big Production That Succeeds Thanks to Many." *Louisville Courier Journal*, 27 January 1979, B6.

Morrow, Lee Alan. *The Tony Award Book: Four Decades of Great American Theater*. New York: Abbeville Press, 1987.

Mosk. *"Atlantic City, U.S.A."* *Variety*, 3 September 1980, 25.

Nightingale, Benedict. "Questions From a Dark Stranger." *Times*, 20 June 1992, "Weekend Times," 5.

Nordheimer, John. "In the New Miami, a Theater Adapts." *New York Times*, 9 April 1988, 13.

Novick, Julius. "Very Funny—or a Long Sick Joke?" *New York Times*, 21 February 1971, sec. 2, 9.

Oliver, Edith. "Off Broadway." *New Yorker*, 1 March 1976, 76–77.

———. "Off Broadway." *New Yorker*, 21 April 1986, 107–9.

———. "Off Broadway." *New Yorker*, 16 March 1981, 62, 65–66.

———. "Off Broadway: Betty and Bert in New York." *New Yorker*, 24 October 1977, 144–45.

———. "Off Broadway: Lightweight." *New Yorker*, 21 April 1986, 108–9.

———. "Off Broadway: 1999 and All That." *New Yorker*, 14 February 1977, 53–54.

———. "Off Broadway: Old and Improved." *New Yorker*, 31 March 1986, 66–67.

———. "Theatre." *New Yorker*, 11 May 1968, 83–92.

———. "The Theatre: At the Dig." *New Yorker*, 30 March 1992, 69.

———. "The Theatre: Off Broadway." *New Yorker*, 20 February 1971, 90.

———. "The Theatre: Off Broadway." *New Yorker*, 10 May 1982, 148, 151.

———. "The Theatre: Off Broadway." *New Yorker*, 21 May 1984, 98.

Orr, John. "Paranoia and Celebrity in American Dramatic Writing: 1970–1990." In *The Theatrical Gamut: Notes for a Post-Beckettian Stage*, edited by Enoch Brater, 141–58. Ann Arbor: University of Michigan Press, 1995.

Paik. *"Six Degrees of Separation."* *Variety*, 12 November 1990, 68.

Peter, John. "Reality Take Two." *Sunday Times*, 21 June 1992, sec. 7, 6–7.

Plimpton, George. "Hanging Out." *Esquire*, September 1991, 102, 104, 106, 108.

Plunka, Gene A. "The Black Comedy of John Guare: *Six Degrees of Separation*." *Essays in Theatre/Etudes théâtrales* 17, no. 2 (1999): 165–76.

———. "The Black Comedy of Urban Neurosis: John Guare's *The House of Blue Leaves*." *Studies in the Humanities* 25, nos. 1–2 (1998): 38–52.

———. "Freud and the Psychology of Neurosis: John Guare's *Bosoms and Neglect*." *Papers on Language and Literature* 36, no. 1 (2000): 93–108.

Pogrebin, Robin. "Vigilant Guardians Keep *Kiss Me, Kate* True to Its Roots." *New York Times*, 7 December 1999, sec. E, 1, 8.

Poland, Albert and Bruce Mailman, eds. *The Off Off Broadway Book: The Plays, People, Theatre*. Indianapolis: Bobbs-Merrill, 1972.

"Police Cite Nude Scene in Acclaimed Play." *New York Times*, 4 November 1993, A15.

Reed, Rex. "*Lydie Breeze* Is Just a Lot of Hot Air." *Daily News*, 26 February 1982, "Friday," 3, 14.

Reif, Rita. "To Fake It Well on the Set, It Pays to Be Genuine." *New York Times*, 16 May 1993, sec. 2, 26.

Rich, Alan. "Cast Away by a Very Usual Destiny in the Gray Slush of February." *New York*, 21 February 1977, 62.

———. "'Tis Pity She's No Whore." *New York*, 8 March 1976, 77.

Rich, Frank. "Desperate for a Reason to Live." *New York Times*, 19 March 1992, C15, C20.

———. "A Guidebook to the Soul of a City in Confusion." *New York Times*, 1 July 1990, sec. 2, 1, 7.

———. "An Overstuffed and Uninhibited John Guare." *New York Times*, 24 February 1989, C3.

———. "The Schisms of the City, Comically and Tragically." *New York Times*, 15 June 1990, C1, C3.

———. "*Six Degrees* Reopens, Larger but Still Intimate." *New York Times*, 9 November 1990, C5.

———. "Stage: Guare's *Gardenia* Antedates His *Lydie*." *New York Times*, 29 April 1982, C20.

———. "Theater: John Guare's *House of Blue Leaves*." *New York Times*, 20 March 1986, C21.

Richards, David. "Critics, Happiness and Sex: 2 Playwrights' Views." *Washington Sunday Star*, 16 January 1972, C5.

———. "Destiny's Dizzy Spin." *Washington Post*, 12 July 1990, B1, B10.

———. "Guare's Bleak *Landscape*." *Washington Post*, 17 January 1986, C3.

———. "Marching to Utopia." *Washington Post*, 31 May 1984, B1, B9.

———. "The More the Murkier." *Washington Post*, 6 December 1985, C1, C12.

———. "One Touch of Eros, and Worlds Divide." *New York Times*, 29 March 1992, sec. 2, 5, 14–15.

Robertson, Nan. "*Blue Leaves* Moving up to Beaumont." *New York Times*, 1 April 1986, C16.

Román, David. "*Fierce Love* and Fierce Response: Intervening in the Cultural Politics of Race, Sexuality, and AIDS." In *Critical Essays: Gay and Lesbian Writers of Color*, edited by Emmanuel S. Nelson, 195–219. Binghamton, N.Y.: Haworth Press, 1993.

Rose, Lloyd. "Guare's *Baboons*: Poetry in Ruins." *Washington Post*, 19 March 1992, C1-C2.

———. "Laughing Till It Hurts." *Washington Post*, 18 March 1993, D1, D8.

———. "A New American Master." *Atlantic Monthly*, March 1984, 120–24.

Salamon, Julie. "A Young Con Artist, Old Men on Ice, and a Weird Lady." *Wall Street Journal*, 9 December 1993, A14.

Salter, Susan. "Guare, John." In *Contemporary Authors*, New Revision Series. Vol. 21, edited by Deborah A. Straub, 163–66. Detroit: Gale Research Company, 1987.

Saunders, Dudley. "Versatile ATL Actors Shine in *Holidays*." *Louisville Times*, 27 January 1979, "Scene," 23.

Sauvage, Leo. "Tragic Misalliances." *New Leader*, 5–19 May 1986, 21–22.

Savran, David, ed. *In Their Own Words: Contemporary American Playwrights*. New York: Theatre Communications Group, 1988.

Schjeldahl, Peter. "An Up-to-Date and Sexy *Verona*." *New York Times*, 8 August 1971, sec. 2, 1, 16.

Schmidt, Sandra. "Zeroing in (Farce) on Right Now (Craziness)." *Los Angeles Times*, 16 January 1972, "Calendar," 26.

Sege. "Off-Broadway Reviews." *Variety*, 24 February 1971, 58.

Sharp, Christopher. "*Rich and Famous*." *Women's Wear Daily*, 20 February 1986, 12.

Shepard, Richard F. "Friends of Papp Produce a Party." *New York Times*, 23 June 1978, C4.

———. "Theater: *Red Cross* and *Muzeeka*." *New York Times*, 29 April 1968, 47.

———. "They Put *Verona* on Broadway Map." *New York Times*, 3 December 1971, 30.

Sheppard, R. Z. "Fear of Flopping." *Time*, 1 March 1976, 51.

Shewey, Don. "Chekhov's Stories Through the Eyes of Seven Playwrights." *New York Times*, 25 August 1985, sec. 2, 4, 26.

———. "The Playwright's Revenge: John Guare 10, Critics 0." *Boston Phoenix*, 27 November 1979, sec. 3, 5, 11.

Simon, John. "Bangs and Whimpers." *New York*, 21 May 1984, 104–6.

———. "Crazed Husbands, Crazy Wives." *New York*, 31 March 1986, 72, 77–78.

———. "The Guary Apes." *New York*, 30 March 1992, 87–88.

———. "Malle De Guare." *New York*, 8 March 1982, 81–82.

———. "Of Gardens, Gardenias, and Garbage." *New York*, 10 May 1982, 75–76.

———. "Open for Inventory." *New York*, 25 June 1990, 58–60.

———. "Revival Instinct." *New York*, 12 October 1998, 86–87.

———. "The Sorcerer and His Apprentices." *New York*, 1 March 1971, 58.

———. "Strindberg Agonistes." *New York*, 31 October 1977, 93–95.

———. "The Stage." *Commonweal*, 14 June 1968, 382, 384.

———. "Theater: Folie à Deux." *New York*, 21 May 1979, 76–78.

———. *Uneasy Stages*. New York: Random House, 1975.

Smith, Whitney. "Playhouse Cast Gives *Degrees* Adept Turn." *Commercial Appeal*, 30 April 1994, C1, C4.

Stearns, David Patrick. "Confronting Chaos in Dazzling *Degrees*." *USA Today*, 19 June 1990, 4D.

Steinberg, Jacques. "Jury Acquits Man of One Count in the Harassment of Playwright." *New York Times*, 2 October 1992, B3.

Stevens, Andrea. "Aspects of Love: Seven Playwrights on the Sonnets." *New York Times*, 31 May 1998, sec. 2, 4, 16.

Story, Richard David. "Six Degrees of Preparation." *New York*, 7 June 1993, 38–43.

Stuart, Jan. "Stars & Strife Forever." *American Theatre*, April 1985, 12–19.

Sullivan, Dan. "ACT Opens S.F. Season With *Leaves*." *Los Angeles Times*, 8 November 1972, sec. 4, 1, 21.

———. "Author Bing Ringling's 3-Ring Opening Night." *Los Angeles Times*, 22 June 1982, "Calendar," 1, 5.

———. "*Blue Leaves* a Polished American Dream Machine." *Los Angeles Times*, 30 January 1972, "Calendar," 34.

———. "LAAT, Guare Launch a 4-Part Saga." *Los Angeles Times*, 15 October 1984, pt. 6, 1, 4.

———. "*Lydie* and Admirers Move on in *Gardenia*." *Los Angeles Times*, 22 October 1984, "Calendar," 1, 6.

———. "A Playful Festival at Stratford." *Los Angeles Times*, 31 August 1980, "Calendar," 1, 51.

Tallmer, Jerry. "Huck Finn Strikes Back." *New York Post*, 26 February 1971, "Magazine," 3.

Taylor, Angela. "Nightly, Shirley Has the Cleanest Hair on Stage." *New York Times*, 20 October 1977, C17.

"10 to Write Plays for an N.E.T. Special." *New York Times*, 19 June 1969, 91.

Thomas, Kevin. "*Atlantic City*: A Jackpot of Dreams From Malle." *Los Angeles Times*, 5 April 1981, "Calendar," 29.

Thomson, Philip. *The Grotesque*. The Critical Idiom, no. 24. London: Methuen, 1972.

Tommasini, Anthony. "Spelling Out the Musical Tale of *Psyché*." *New York Times*, 5 October 1997, sec. 2, 33, 35.

Torrens, James S. "Six Degrees, Earth and Sky." *America*, 23 February 1991, 212–13.

Van Gelder, Lawrence. "This Week." *New York Times*, 15 June 1998, sec. E, 1.

"*Verona* to Tour City's Parks and Playgrounds." *New York Times*, 6 August 1971, 15.

Vineberg, Steve. Review of *Lydie Breeze*. *Theatre Journal* 38, no. 4 (1986): 487–88.

Wadler, Joyce. "His Story Is a Hit on Broadway, but This Con Man Is in Trouble Again." *People Weekly*, 18 March 1991, 99–100.

Wallach, Allan. "Symbols Clash in *Lydie Breeze*." *Newsday*, 14 March 1982, pt. 2, 13.

Wardle, Irving. "*Two Gentlemen of Verona*." *Times*, 27 April 1973, 9.

Watt, Douglas. "Empty Show-Biz Allegory." *Daily News*, 20 February 1976, 48.

———. "Keeping a 'Death' Watch on B'way Plays." *Daily News*, 27 March 1992, 53.

———. "*Lydie Breeze*." *Daily News*, 26 February 1982, "Friday," 5, 14.

———. "Pre-*Lydie*, a Vital Drama." *Daily News*, 29 April 1982, 71.

———. "Solo With Marco Polo." *Daily News*, 7 February 1977, 21.

———. "This Is Too Tough to Take to Our Bosom." *Daily News*, 4 May 1979, 5.

———. "With *Two Gents*, Joy and Love." *Daily News*, 2 December 1971, 114.

Watts, Richard. "The Day the Pope Was Here." *New York Post*, 11 February 1971, 75.

———. "Happy Days in Old Verona." *New York Post*, 2 December 1971, 55.

Weales, Gerald. "Degrees of Difference." *Commonweal*, 11 January 1991, 17–18.

———. "Go Ahead, Shoot: *Death and the Maiden* and *Baboons*." *Commonweal*, 8 May 1992, 21.

Weil, Fran. "Guare's Too Busy for Success." *Boston Herald American*, 22 November 1979, WD5.

Weiner, Bernard. "A Splendid West Coast Premiere of *Bosoms*." *San Francisco Chronicle*, 5 February 1980, 48.

Wetzsteon, Ross. "The Coming of Age of John Guare." *New York*, 22 February 1982, 35–39.

———. "New York." *Plays and Players*, June 1977, 37–38.

———. "New York Round-up." *Plays and Players*, July 1976, 39–41.

Who's Who in the Theatre. 17th ed. Vol. 1: Biographies, edited by Ian Herbert, 283. Detroit: Gale Research Company, 1981.

Wilmeth, Don B. "John Guare." In *American Playwrights Since 1945: A Guide to Scholarship, Criticism and Performance*, edited by Philip C. Kolin, 142–54. Westport, Conn: Greenwood Press, 1989.

Wilson, Edwin. "New Plays by Ariel Dorfman and John Guare." *Wall Street Journal*, 24 March 1992, A14.

———. "A Play That Tries to Get by on Cleverness." *Wall Street Journal*, 4 May 1979, 15.

———. "Retreat From Intelligence in U.S. Theater." *Wall Street Journal*, 5 September 1980, 19.

———. "Roll Over, Chekhov: Sellars Stages *Seagull*." *Wall Street Journal*, 31 December 1985, 6.

———. "Theater: A Smash Revival." *Wall Street Journal*, 9 April 1986, 31.

Winer, Laurie. "Playwright John Guare: Nice Guys Can Finish First." *Wall Street Journal*, 15 May 1986, 25.

Winer, Linda. "*Atlantic City* Pays Off for John Guare." *Daily News*, 15 May 1981, "Manhattan," 1–2.

———. "Guare's 'Oddball' Comedy Is Unwieldy but Refreshing." *Chicago Tribune*, 12 July 1977, sec. 2, 11.

———. "Mom, Dad, Kids and a God or Two." *New York Newsday*, Nassau Edition, 19 March 1992, 59, 67.

Witchel, Alex. "Impersonator Wants to Portray Still Others, This Time, Onstage." *New York Times*, 31 July 1990, C13, C14.

———. "The Life of Fakery and Delusion in John Guare's *Six Degrees*." *New York Times*, 21 June 1990, C17, C20.

Wolf, Matt. "A Father Figure Leads Nine Children Into *Four Baboons*." *New York Times*, 15 March 1992, sec. 2, 5, 34.

———. "Manhattan Chill and Thrill Comes to Town." *Sunday Times Magazine*, 3 May 1992, 52.

———. "Reborn at the Heart of a Play." *Times*, 8 June 1992, "Life and Times," 3.

Wolfe, Tom. *Radical Chic & Mau-mauing the Flak Catchers*. New York: Farrar, Straus and Giroux, 1970.

Zimmerman, David A. "Six Degrees of Distinction: Connection, Contagion, and the Aesthetics of Anything." *Arizona Quarterly* 55, no. 3 (1999): 106–133.

Index

Abraham, F. Murray, 113
Academy Award, 11, 35, 140
Academy Festival Theatre, 34, 99, 112–13
Ackerman, Nicholas, 40
Ackroyd, Dan, 37, 207
Acting Company, 38, 42, 205, 228–29
Actors Equity, 71
Actors Theatre, 35, 203
Adding Machine, The (Rice), 203
Aeschylus, 102, 237n. 38
Ah, Wilderness (O'Neill), 235n. 5
Albee, Barr, Wilder Workshop, 29
Albee, Edward, 11, 29, 36, 41, 194, 203, 231, 233, 240n. 88
Aldredge, Theoni V., 89, 100
Alladin, Opal, 90
Allen, Jonelle, 33
Allport, Christopher, 177
Amadeus (Shaffer), 261n. 41
America Hurrah (van Itallie), 60
American Academy and Institute of Arts and Letters, 35, 36, 39
American Academy of Rome, 257n. 24
American Conservatory Theater, 245n. 22
American Place Theater, 37, 151–52
American Repertory Theater, 42, 225
American Shakespeare Festival, 25
Anderson, Kevin C., 240n. 87
Andres, Barbra, 203
Anka, Paul, 142
Anna Christie (O'Neill), 155
Annie Breeze, 153
Annie Get Your Gun, 24–25, 252n. 31
Anouilh, Jean, 237n. 38
Antoinette Perry "Tony" Award, 11, 33, 38, 39, 42, 74, 186, 218, 227, 245n. 21
Aranha, Ray, 203

Arditti, Paul, 217
Arena Stage, 37, 177–78, 179
Aristophanes, 238n. 46
Aristotle, 53
Arnold, Benedict, 95
Arrick, Larry, 126, 127
Astaire, Fred, 238n. 58
Atherton, William, 71, 100
Atlantic City, 11, 16, 33, 35, 37, 151, 206, 210, 251n. 15; as black comedy, 142, 147; and fantasy fulfillment, 141–47; genesis of, 35, 138–39; and mythmaking, 142–47; and the passage of time, 141; screening of, 140; setting of, 140–41; and the tetralogy, 254n. 39
Atlantic City, U.S.A., 140
Atlantic Theater Company, 178–79
Auden, W. H., 35
Au revoir les enfants, 138
Award of Merit, 35, 36

Baitz, Jon Robin, 14
Baker, David Aaron, 127
Baker, Ian, 39, 189
Bancroft, Anne, 70
Barbican Center, 42
Baron, Suzanne, 140
Bar Play (Wilson), 203
Barry, Philip, 26, 237n. 38
Basement Theatre, 51
Bauer, Richard, 113
Beatty, Warren, 27
Beau Geste (Wren), 24
Beckel, Graham, 203
Beckett, Samuel, 179, 191, 231
Belgrader, Andrei, 207
Bell, Alexander Graham, 107
Bellini, Vincenzo, 144

Belushi, James, 207
Belushi, John, 37, 207
Benedict, Paul, 89
Bennett, Michael, 150
Berkeley Stage Company, 127
Berlin, Irving, 76, 253n. 31
Berlind, Roger S., 151
Bernhardt, Melvin, 53, 58, 71, 244n. 31
Bernstein, Leonard, 31, 42, 195, 216, 239n. 75
Besch, Betty Ann, 30, 53, 71
Bevan, Ernest, 27
Beyond the Horizon (O'Neill), 155–56, 180
Biggs, Casey, 178
Big Kiss, 36
Big Lebowski, The (Coen Brothers), 21
Bishop, André, 257n. 22
Bishop, Kelly, 187
Bitter Sauce (Bogosian), 228
Bogart, Humphrey, 61
Bogosian, Eric, 228
Bolger, Ray, 25
Bolt, Robert, 114
Bosoms and Neglect, 13, 18, 35, 48, 111, 140, 150–51, 252n. 14; as autobiography, 128; as black comedy, 112, 127–29, 133–34, 136–37; and fantasy lives, 129–37; genesis of, 124; and meaningful spiritual connection, 128–37; and neglect, indifference, isolation, 128–37; productions of, 34–35, 124–27; reviews of, 124–27, 250n. 46; setting of, 127; structure of, 127–28; and violence, 129, 133, 135
Brandenstein, Patrizia von, 39, 189
Brando, Marlon, 82, 226
Brecht, Bertolt, 31, 53–54, 102, 115, 189, 243n. 20
British Academy Award, 140
Brown, Kenneth, 30
Bulfinch's Mythology, 37, 151, 252n. 12
Burke, R. J., 169
Bush, Geoffrey, 53
Bushnell, Bill, 177

Caffe Cino, 28, 30, 45, 50
Calderón de la Barca, Pedro, 237n. 38
Camus, Albert, 51
Cannes Film Festival, 33
Cantor, Eddie, 23
Capone, Al, 139

Carlin, Lynn, 33
Carnegie, Andrew, 162, 171
Carousel, 103
Carrière, Jean-Claude, 32
Carroll, Beeson, 89–90
Carroll, Lewis, 51
Carson, Johnny, 57, 84–85, 119
Carvell, Jason Alan, 229
Castro, Fidel, 212
Catcher in the Rye, The (Salinger), 191, 198
Cats, 191–92, 196–97, 199
Cattaneo, Anne, 21, 38, 50, 54, 140, 205, 228
Cezanne, Paul, 190, 198
Chaikin, Joseph, 60
Chaillet, Ned, 178
Channing, Stockard, 38, 39, 42, 73, 186–88, 217–18, 257n. 22, and 24, 241n. 42
Chaplin, Charlie, 104
Chapman, Mark David, 199
Charles Playhouse, 126
Chatfield-Taylor, Adele, 13, 36, 128, 251n. 6, 257n. 22
Chekhov, Anton, 20, 25, 50, 96, 102, 141, 191, 196, 231, 237n. 38, 253n. 33; compared with Guare, 13–14; Guare's adaptation of, 38, 205–6; as model for Guare's theater, 37, 74, 78, 87, 150, 154, 170, 179–80, 185, 238n. 50
Cherry Orchard, The (Chekhov), 14, 25, 141, 253n. 33
Christie, Agatha, 116, 123
Cino, Joe, 28
Cleopatra, 82
Clift, Montgomery, 226
Clinton, William, 257n. 24
Clockwork Orange, A (Burgess), 249n. 15
Close, Chuck, 41, 235n. 5, 257n. 19
Coconut Grove Playhouse, 245n. 22
Coen Brothers, 21
Cohan, George M., 24
Collins, Wilkie, 149
Conroy, Jarlath, 169
Converse, Frank, 71
Cooper, Gary, 93
Cop-Out, 37, 45, 66, 68, 71, 99; and celebrity status, 62; compared with *Home Fires*, 63; critical reception of, 31; genesis of, 31, 58; as parody of detective films, 61; and the power

of the media, 6; productions of, 31, 58–59; reality vs. mythmaking in, 60–62; reviews of, 59; and the search for connection in modern society, 60–62; structure of, 59–60
Copple, Mary, 114
Coronot Theatre, 248n. 39
Cort Theatre, 31, 58
Cousteau, Jacques, 251n. 11
Coward, Noel, 204
Cronin, Laurel, 207
Crosby, Bing, 102
Cross, Ben, 151
Crow, Laura, 113, 205
Cunningham, John, 39, 186, 188
Cyrano de Bergerac (Rostand), 188
Cyrus Pierce Theater, 34, 89

Dallas Theater Center, 257n. 26
Dance of Death (Strindberg), 21
Dante's Inferno, 102
Da Ponte, Lorenzo, 237n. 38
Davidson, Gordon, 53
Davis, Clifton, 33
Davison, Bruce, 39, 188
Day, Dennis, 107
Day, Doris, 82, 85
Day for Surprises, A, 31; and the imaginative vision, 52; and lack of contact in society, 51–52; productions of, 37, 50–51
Dean, James, 109, 226
Debuskey, Merle, 40
Dee, Sandra, 81–82
Delacorte Theatre, 33, 240n. 84
De Mille, Cecil B., 179
DeRosa, Stephen, 229
Desire Under the Elms (O'Neill), 155
Dick, William, 240n. 87
Dickens, Charles, 115
Did You Write My Name in the Snow?, 27, 28
Dillinger, John, 214–15
Distinguished Achievement in the American Theatre Award, 41
Doll House, A (Ibsen), 93, 96
Don Giovanni (Mozart), 237n. 38
Doolittle Theater, 39
Dopey Fairy Tale, A (Weller), 240n. 89
Douglas, Lord Alfred, 254n. 47
Down and Out in Beverly Hills, 200
Drama Desk Award, 11, 33

Dramatists Guild Council, 32, 41
Dreamgirls, 241n. 90
Dreiser, Theodore, 35
Drowning (Fornes), 240n. 89
Duchin, Eddy, 236n. 14
Duchin, Peter, 236n. 14, 257n. 19
Du côte de chez Swann (Proust), 204
Durang, Christopher, 240n. 88
Dürrenmatt, Friedrich, 237n. 38

Eagels, Jeanne, 23
Edwards, Stephen, 217
Eigsti, Karl, 71
Eliot, George, 149
Eliot, T. S., 191
Elliott, Inger, 235n. 5, 241–42n. 90
Elliott, Osborn, 40, 235n. 5, 241–42n. 90
Emerson, Ralph Waldo, 157, 167
Equus (Shaffer), 220, 257n. 27
Erdman, Jean, 33
Estelle Newman Public Theater, 34, 100
Esthétique du Mal (Stevens), 123
Eugene O'Neill Memorial Theatre, 30, 31, 34, 52–53, 58
Eugene O'Neill Memorial Theatre Playwrights' Conference, 31, 52, 70
Eugene O'Neill Theatre Center, 29, 30, 32
Eve of the Trial (Williams), 240n. 89
Everett, Tom, 177
Exception and the Rule, The (Brecht), 31
Eyen, Tom, 203

Fagadau, Michel, 73
Faith Healer (Friel), 125, 205
Falls, Robert, 38
Fantasticks, The, 195
Fargo (Coen Brothers), 21
Farmer, James, 229
Father Knows Best, 51, 235n. 5
Faulkner, William, 151
Faustus in Hell, 38
Fear of Flying (Jong), 205
Feiffer, Jules, 126
Festival of New American Plays, 35, 203
Feydeau, Georges, 21, 32, 70, 102, 147, 204, 237n. 38
Fields, W. C., 24, 62
Fingerhut, Arden, 100
Finn, William, 228
Finneran, Katie, 127

Fire Within, The, 138
Fireworks (Terry), 203
Fisher, Eddie, 38
Flanagan, Robert, 178
Flaubert, Gustav (27),
Flea in Her Ear, A (Feydeau), 21
Florek, Dann, 114
Forman, Milos, 32–33
Fornes, Maria Irene, 205, 240n. 89
Forster, E. M., 13, 134
Four Baboons Adoring the Sun, 207; and
    black comedy, 223–24; drafts of, 216;
    form of, 217; and the fraudulence
    of the American Dream, 219–25;
    and the idyllic, 220–25; and the
    imaginative spirit, 219–25; and the
    neuroticism of modern life, 220–25;
    productions of, 42, 217; reviews of,
    189, 217–18; and violence in, 224
Franck, César, 42
Frankenstein (Shelley), 154, 162
Freud, Sigmund, 191
Friedman, Kim, 248n. 39
Funicello, Annette, 82
Fun War, The, 53

Gallen, Judy, 207
Gallo, Paul, 73, 186
Garbo, Greta, 104
Gardenia, 37, 73, 151, 153, 179–81, 238n.
    50, 253n. 34, 254n. 36, and 40, 255n.
    58; genesis of, 37; loss of idealism
    in, 170–77; productions of, 153,
    169–70, 177; reviews of, 169–70; and
    self-destruction, 172–73; and spiritual
    disintegration, 173; structure of, 170,
    177
Gardner, William, 112
Garson, Barbara, 30
Garson, Greer, 82
Gassner, John, 20, 27
Gaynor, Mitzi, 82
Gegenhuber, John, 178
General of Hot Desire, The, 42; and
    humanity's quest for creation, 229–
    30; productions of, 228; and the quest
    for the imaginative vision, 229–30;
    source of, 228–29
George M. Cohan Review, 24
Gershwin, George, 42
Gershwin, Ira, 42, 207

Gersten, Bernard, 40, 41, 73, 124, 126,
    186, 240n. 84
Ghandi, Indira, 104
Ghosts (Ibsen), 124, 141, 154, 156–57
Giles, Nancy, 240n. 87
Gillette, Anita, 100
Girl of the Garrison, 23
Gluttony, 38
Goethals, Angela, 217–18
Goethe, Johann Wolfgang von, 38
Golden Cherub, The, 27
Golden Lion Award, 35, 140
Goodman, Robyn, 114
Goodman Theater, 34, 37, 73, 124,
    240n. 87
Gorbachev, Mikhail, 195
Gould, Harold, 32, 71–72
Gould, Jay, 171
Goulet, Robert, 140, 210
Grable, Betty, 139, 142
Grady, Bill, 69, 238n. 58
Grady, Helen Clare, 23
Grady, Jere, 23
Grady, Jimmy, 23
Granger, Percy, 203
Grant, Ulysses S., 171, 173, 178
Gray, Amlin, 240n. 88
Gray, Spalding, 205, 240n. 89
Great Labor Day Classic, The (Horovitz),
    203
Greenwood, Jane, 71
Gregory, André, 42, 225
Grey, Joel, 89
Griffith, Melanie, 241n. 90
Grooms, Red, 208
Guare, John Edward, 23
Guess Who's Coming to Dinner, 191
Guthrie Theater Lab, 42, 228
Guthrie, Tyrone, 20

Hackman, Gene, 70
Hagerty, Julie, 207
Hailey, Oliver, 203
Hair, 33
Hairy Ape, The (O'Neill), 198
Hall, Sir Peter, 42, 216–17, 222, 224,
    261n. 41
Hamlet (Shakespeare), 103
Hamlisch, Marvin, 42
Hammer, Mark, 178
Hampton, David, 39–41, 241–42n. 90,
    258n. 27

Handke, Peter, 126
Hankins, Michael, 203
Hare, David, 188
Harper, Wally, 113
Hart, Kitty Carlisle, 257n. 19
Havel, Václav, 32
Hawking, Judith, 90
Hawthorne, Nathaniel, 155
Hayward, Brooke, 236n. 14, 257n. 19
Hayworth, Rita, 118
Hearst, William Randolph, 161–62, 167–68
Helmond, Katherine, 32, 71
Hemingway, Ernest, 35
Henry, Buck, 33
Hepburn, Katharine, 226
Herrmann, Edward, 169
Hewitt, Tom, 178
Hey, Stay a While, 37, 240n. 87
Hinckley, John, 199
Holiday (Barry), 237n. 38
Holliday, Polly, 90
Homecoming, The (Pinter), 29
Home Fires, 68, 71; and celebrity status, 65–66; and class consciousness, 63–66; compared with *Cop-Out*, 63; genesis of, 58; and lost American heritage, 66; productions of, 31, 58–59; reviews of, 59; and the search for identity, 65–66; structure of, 63
Hoover, J. Edgar, 209, 214–16
Hope, Bob, 57, 84–85
Horneff, Wil, 217–18
Horovitz, Israel, 203
Houghton, James, 16
House of Blue Leaves, The, 11, 14, 23, 33, 34, 35, 39, 53, 89, 91, 108, 113, 127, 186, 206, 245n. 21, 256n. 13; and black comedy, 79–80; Catholicism and show business, 78, 83–84; and celebrity worship, 75–87; and the debunking of the American Dream, 74–87; form of, 74; genesis of, 29, 30, 32, 69–71; and lack of spiritual connections in modern society, 81–83, 87; productions of, 32, 38, 71–74, 245n. 22; reviews of, 71–72, 73–74, 245n. 20; setting of, 75; songs in, 26
House of Love, 38
House of the Seven Gables, The (Hawthorne), 155
Howells, William Dean, 171–76

Huckleberry Finn (Twain), 69
Hudson, Rock, 82, 85
Huffman, David, 170, 177
Hughes, Allan Lee, 177
Hull Warriner Award, 39
Hurt, Mary Beth, 39, 188
Hydraulics Phat Like Mean (Shange), 228

Ibsen, Henrik, 20, 89, 124, 141, 222, 231, 237n. 38, 253n. 33; as model for change in *Marco Polo Sings a Solo*, 93; as model for the tetralogy, 37, 149–50, 153–55, 170, 179–80, 185, 238n. 50
I Can't Find It Anywhere (Hailey), 203
Iceman Cometh, The (O'Neill), 235n. 5
Iliad, The (Homer), 104
Imaginary Theatre, 127
Importance of Being Earnest, The (Wilde), 26
Independence Day (Eyen), 203
In Fireworks Lie Secret Codes, and black comedy, 204–5; and the imaginative vision, 204; and the modern neurosis, 204–5; productions of, 35, 203; reviews of, 259n. 2
Inge, William, 29
Interview (van Itallie), 60
Iselin, John Jay, 241n. 90

Jackson, Anne, 70, 89
Jackson, Nagle, 38
James, Henry, 18, 149
Jewison, Norman, 188
John F. Kennedy Center, 205
John Gabriel Borkman (Ibsen), 154
John Paul II, Pope, 74
Johnson, Lyndon, 84, 94
"Joke, A" (Chekhov), 38, 205–6
Jolson, Al, 24
Jones, Preston, 203
Jones, Quincy, 188
Jong, Erica, 206
Jory, Jon, 35, 203
Joseph Jefferson Award, 34
Joseph Papp Public Theater, 42, 89, 113, 124, 138, 228, 249n. 21
Joy, Robert, 140, 143, 144, 151
Juilliard School of the Performing Arts, 207
Julia, Raul, 33
June-Teenth (Jones), 203
Jury Prize, 33

Kahn, Jeremy, 208
Kahn, Madeleine, 89
Kaiser, Russ, 45
Kandinsky, Wassily, 196–98, 201
Kavanaugh, Richard, 127
Kaye, Danny, 69
Keaton, Buster, 204
Keller, Neel, 207, 225
Kellermann, Susan, 207
Kelly, Gene, 69
Kennedy, Jacqueline, 83, 84–85
Kim, Willa, 151, 217
Kimbrough, Charles, 99
Kissing Sweet, 45, 66; and the media
    and loss of imagination, 68; the
    power of the media on perceptions
    of self, 67–68; productions of, 32, 66;
    structure of, 66–67; synopsis of, 67
Kiss Me Kate, 42
Klein, John, 32
Knight, Shirley, 113, 249n. 21
Koenig, Jack, 90
Krannert Center, 38, 205
Kurtz, Marcia Jean, 53
Kurtz, Swoosie, 38, 39, 73–74, 187
Kushner, Tony, 228

Lacombe, Lucien, 138
Lady From the Sea, The (Ibsen), 153–54
Lahti, Christine, 114
Lake Hollywood, 42
Lamos, Mark, 42, 228
Lancaster, Burt, 139–40, 142
Landscape of the Body, 43, 111, 124, 136,
    138, 206, 240n. 87; as black comedy,
    112, 116–17, 119–21, 137, 208–9;
    genesis of, 112–13, 115; and idyllic
    life, 118; life as enigmatic and based
    upon chance in, 116–18, 120, 123–24;
    productions of, 34, 113–14, 249n. 15;
    reviews of, 113–14; setting of, 115;
    and spiritual connection, 116–124;
    structure of, 115
Lange, Jessica, 188
Langella, Frank, 151
Lansky, Meyer, 142
Larson, Jonathan, 236n. 13
Laurie, Piper, 89
Lavin, Linda, 58–59, 99
Lawrence, D. H., 218
Lean, David, 114
Leary, Timothy, 57

Leaves of Grass (Whitman), 155
Lee, Robert E., 178
Legrand, Michel, 142
Lehner, Edward H., 41
Leibman, Ron, 58–59, 99, 100
Lennon, John, 36, 199
Leonard, John, 178
Lester, Adrian, 188
Lewis, Bobby, 30
Life Is a Dream (Calderón), 237n. 38
Lincoln Center Theater Company, 35,
    41, 203
Linklater, Hamish, 229
Linney, Romulus, 240n. 88
Little Eyolf (Ibsen), 154
Lloyd, Phyllida, 39, 188
Lobel, Adrianne, 205
Logan, Joshua, 25
Long, William Ivey, 186
Longacre Theatre, 35, 124
Long Day's Journey Into Night (O'Neill),
    235n. 5
Look Back in Anger (Osborne), 27
Loquasto, Santo, 113, 169, 175
Lord of the Rings (Tolkien), 191
Loren, Sophia, 73
Los Angeles Actors' Theater, 37, 170,
    177, 255n. 58
Los Angeles Drama Critics' Circle
    Award, 73
Los Angeles Film Critics' Award, 11, 35,
    140
Lott, Plummer, 40
Loveliest Afternoon of the Year, The, 43, 45;
    and absurdities of life, 50; alienation
    and isolation in, 49; black comedy in,
    49–50; form of, 50; genesis of, 30, 45;
    and lack of spiritual connection in
    life, 50; productions of, 37, 45; and
    violence, 50
Love's Fire, 42
Luciano, Lucky, 142
Lucille Lortel Theater, 38, 259n. 4
Lum, Alvin, 33
Lydie Breeze, 16, 124, 127–28, 169, 171,
    175, 177, 179–80, 206, 207, 208, 238n.
    50, 251n. 15, 252n. 14, 254n. 36,
    254n. 39; and the dissipation of the
    American Dream, 156–69; drafts of,
    153; exploring the past, 156–69; and
    forgiveness to destroy the curse of the
    past, 164–69; form of, 170; genesis of,

37, 149–51,153, 54n. 40; and idealism, 156–60; productions of, 151–53, 170; reviews of, 152–53; and the search for spiritual connection, 156–69; sources of, 153–56

Lyons, Warren, 30, 53, 70–71

Macbeth (Shakespeare), 222
McCarter Theatre, 38
McCarthy, Eugene, 57
McCrane, Paul, 113
McDaniel, James, 39, 186–87
MacDermot, Galt, 33
McKellen, Ian, 39, 188
McKinney, John, 177
McKnight, Fuzzy, 107
McLaren, Hollis, 140, 144
McLuhan, Marshall, 68
Madame Bovary (Flaubert), 24
Mahoney, John, 38, 73–74, 245n. 20
Mailer, Norman, 109
Make Room for Daddy, 51
Makovsky, Judianna, 189
Malle, Louis, 16, 35, 37, 138–41, 151–52, 156, 179, 207, 251n. 11, 252n. 18, 254n. 39
Mamet, David, 11, 73, 205, 231, 233, 240n. 89
Manhattan Theater Club, 37, 153, 169
Man in a Case, The (Wasserstein), 240n. 89
Marconi, Guglielmo, 258n. 32
Marco Polo Sings a Solo, 43, 88, 112, 115, 151, 208; and the apocalypse, 92, 94, 97, 209; comparisons to *Rich and Famous*, 110–11; genesis of, 88; and the glorification of ego, 89–99; as an obscure play, 91; productions of, 34, 89–90, 127; reviews of, 89–91; setting of, 92
Mark Taper Forum, 31, 53
Marlowe, Christopher, 38
Martin, Nicholas, 127
Martin, Steve, 188
Marty (Chayefsky), 21
Marx Brothers, 126, 201, 208
Marx, Groucho, 62, 122
Masur, Kurt, 42
Maxwell, Roberta, 151
Mazursky, Paul, 200
MCA, 28
Meara, Anne, 32, 71–72, 127

Melfi, Leonard, 29
Mercer, Marian, 124
Merman, Ethel, 24
Merry Christmas (Norman), 203
Method acting, 20
Metro-Goldwyn-Mayer (MGM), 24, 28, 40–41, 69, 188
Midler, Bette, 36
Miller, Arthur, 11, 41, 72, 231
Miller, Craig, 169
Miss Julie (Strindberg), 159
Mitzi E. Newhouse Theater, 38, 39, 73, 186–87, 203
Molière, 25, 38, 102, 201, 204, 238n. 46
Monroe, Marilyn, 62, 109
Moon for the Misbegotten (O'Neill), 235n. 5
Moon Over Miami, drafts of, 207; genesis of, 37; productions of, 207; reviews of, 207
Moon Under Miami, 42, 207; and the abuse of political power, 208–16; and the apocalypse, 209; as black comedy, 208–16; and corruption in modern society, 210–16; form of, 208–9; productions of, 207–8; reviews of, 208; as satire of politics, 211–16
Mosher, Gregory, 73, 124, 186
Mostel, Zero, 31
Mourning Becomes Electra (O'Neill), 155–56
Mozart, Wolfgang Amadeus, 25, 237n. 38
Mullaly, Megan, 240n. 87
Murmur of the Heart, 138
Muzeeka, 45, 261n. 40; and celebrity status, 57; and conformity, 54–55, 58; genesis of, 31, 52, 54; and lack of imagination in modern society, 55, 58; and lack of spiritual contact in modern society, 56; productions of, 31, 52–53; reviews of, 53; structure of, 53–54
Mwine, Ntare, 188
My Dinner With Andre, 138, 179

Nantucket Stage Company, 34, 84
National Endowment of the Arts, 36
National Society of Film Critics' Award, 35, 140
National Theatre (London), 21, 27

National Theatre (Washington, D.C.), 39

Naughton, James, 42, 217–18, 241n. 42

New Generation Prize, 140

Newman, Paul, 93

Newman, Thomas, 177

Newman, William, 203

New Playwrights Theatre, 153, 170, 177

New Theatre for Now Series, 31, 53

New Year's (Aranha), 203

New York Actor, as black comedy, 227; and celebrity worship, 225–28; and fraudulence in modern life, 225–28; productions of, 42, 225; and violence in modern society, 228

New York Drama Critics' Circle Award, 11, 32, 33, 39, 73, 187, 256n. 13

New York Film Critics' Circle Award, 11, 35, 140

New York Landmarks Preservation Foundation, 36

New York Philharmonic, 42

New York Shakespeare Festival, 34, 89, 113

Nicola, James C., 153, 177, 249n. 15

Nixon, Cynthia, 151

Nixon, Richard, 62, 226

Noah, James, 252n. 30

Norma (Bellini), 144

Norman, Marsha, 203, 228

Norris, Bruce, 90

Oates, Joyce Carol, 240n. 88

Obie Award, 11, 31, 32, 39, 53, 73, 226

O'Brien, Laurie, 170, 177

O'Casey, Sean, 26

Odyssey, The (Homer), 104

Odyssey Theatre, 127

Oedipus the King (Sophocles), 154

Oenslager, Donald, 27

Old Toll House, The, 23

Oliver, Jason, 177

Olivier Best Play Award, 11, 39, 188

Olivier, Laurence, 21, 29, 32, 70, 226–27

Olivier Theatre, 261n. 41

O'Neill, Eugene, 11, 37, 150, 155, 180, 185, 198, 231, 235n. 5, 238n. 50

Open Space Theatre, 53

Open Theater, 60, 66, 229

Optimism, or the Adventures of Candide (Voltaire), 34

Orchards: A Chekhov Evening, 38

Oresteia, The, (Aeschylus), 226

Orton, Joe, 237n. 38

Osborne, John, 27

Othello (Shakespeare), 29

Our Town (Wilder), 20

Outer Critics' Circle Award, 11, 32, 73

Page, Geraldine, 70

Painting You (Finn), 228

Papp, Joseph, 33, 89, 100, 113, 240n. 79, 240n. 84

Parone, Edward, 53

Pasquin, John, 34, 113

Pathé, 40

Pawn Ticket 210, 23

Pearce, Daniel, 229

Peck, Gregory, 241n. 90

PEN, 38

Perry, Eugene, 42, 217

Perry Street Theatre, 127

Philadelphia Story, The (Barry), 237n. 38

Phoenix Theatre, 34

Piccoli, Michel, 140, 145

Pickford, Mary, 251n. 17

Pilbrow, Richard, 217

Pinter, Harold, 29, 53–54, 60, 231, 237n. 38

Platt, Oliver, 207

Play by Brecht, 31

Plenty (Hare), 188

Plough and the Stars, The (O'Casey), 26

Plymouth Theater, 38, 73

Poe, Edgar Allan, 155, 157–58, 166–67

Poitier, Sidney, 40, 191–92, 201, 241n. 91

Ponti, Carlo, 35, 73

Pope, Peggy, 53

Porter, Katherine Anne, 27

Potter, Madeleine, 151

Pretty Baby, 138, 140

Proust, Marcel, 51, 204

Provincetown Playhouse, 31, 53

Psyché, 42

Public Theater. *See* Joseph Papp Public Theater.

Python, Monty, 90

Quintero, Jose, 30, 70

Racine, Jean, 102

Rain, 23

Raisin in the Sun (Hellman), 20

Rambo, 258n. 28

Reagan, Ronald, 37, 199, 211, 258n. 28

Red Cross (Shepard), 53

Reddin, Keith, 19

Redeemer (Ward), 203

Reed, Rondi, 153

Reid, Kate, 124–25, 127, 139–40, 142

Reisz, Karel, 37, 169

Remains Theater, 42, 207, 259n. 10

Rent (Larson), 236n. 13

Rhodes, Billy, 24

Rice, Elmer, 203

Rich and Famous, 88, as autobiography, 108; as black comedy, 104–11, 208–9; compared with *Marco Polo Sings a Solo*, 110–11; and egotism, 103–6; and infatuation with celebrity status, 101–11, 116; and lack of spiritual connection, 102, 105, 108–9; and life as fantasy, 103, 108–10; productions of, 34, 99, 248n. 39; reviews of, 99–101; structure of, 101; and violence, 108

Richards, Lloyd, 30, 126, 207

Rilke, Rainer Maria, 134

Rimbaud, Arthur, 102

Rivkala's Ring (Gray), 240n. 89

Robards, Jason, 70, 151

Robbins, Jerome, 31, 239n. 75

Robison, Heather, 229

Robman, Steven, 126

Rockefeller, John Davison, 171

Rogers, Will, 24

Rolfsrud, Erika, 229

Rooney, Mickey, 70

Rose, Lloyd, 153, 177

Rosen, Louis, 205

Rosmersholm (Ibsen), 154

Roth, Ann, 169

Rothman, Carole, 114

Roven, Glen, 151–52, 169

Roxanne, 188

Royal Court Theatre, 39, 188, 191

Royal Hunt of the Sun, The (Shaffer), 261n. 41

Rudd, Paul, 124–25

Russia House, The, 188

St. James Theater, 33

Salinger, J. D., 191, 198–99

Sarandon, Susan, 138–40, 144

Schacter, Stephen, 178

Schepisi, Fred, 39, 188–89

Schneider, Alan, 30

Scott, George C., 226

Schultz, Dutch, 142

Scorsese, Martin, 42

Sea and Sardinia (Lawrence), 218

Sea Gull, The (Chekhov), 253n. 33

Second Stage, 114

Seldes, Marion, 42, 225

Serpent, The (van Itallie), 229

Shaffer, Peter, 41, 220, 257n. 27, 261n. 41

Shakespeare, William, 25, 33, 42, 154, 196, 228–29, 238n. 46, 240n. 79, 249n. 80

Shange, Ntozake, 228

Shapiro, Mel, 32, 33, 34, 71–72, 89–90, 99, 100, 110, 124–25, 127, 245n. 22

Shaw, George Bernard, 238n. 46

Shawhan, April, 127

She Conqs to Stooper, 26

Shelley, Mary, 154, 163

Shelley, Paul, 188

Shepard, Sam, 29, 30, 53

Sheridan, Richard Brinsley, 238n. 46

Shlomm, Bobby, 25, 238n. 62

Shubert Theater, 27

Siegel, Bugsy, 143, 146

Signature Theatre, 16, 90, 127

Simmons, Gregory, 187

Sinatra, Frank, 58

Singing in the Rain, 26

Sinise, Gary, 114, 241n. 90

Six Degrees of Separation, 11, 18, 39–41, 203, 207, 256n. 13, 257n. 27; alienation and isolation in, 197–202; as black comedy, 201–2, 204; and celebrity status, 191–92, 194–97; con artistry in, 190–202; and David Hampton, 39–41, 242n. 90; film version, 39, 188–89; and meaningful contact vs. anecdote, 194–202; productions of, 39, 186–86; reviews of, 187–88; source of, 39–40; and spiritual connection in modern society, 193–202; staging of, 186–87; structure of, 189–90

Skin of Our Teeth, The (Wilder), 90, 141

Slater, Christian, 114

Sloan, Larry, 207, 240n. 87

Smith, Kate, 85

Smith, Will, 39, 188–89

Snyder, Dan, 100
Somer, Josef, 151
Something I'll Tell You Tuesday, form
    of, 46; genesis of, 30; and lack of
    spiritual connection in life, 47–49;
    and modern angoisse 47–49; and
    modern urban life, 46; productions
    of, 45; setting of, 45–46
Sondheim, Stephen, 31, 239n. 75
Sound of Music, The, 83, 103
South Pacific, 103
Spear, Cary Ann, 178
Spellman, Cardinal, 84–85
Spiegel, Sam, 34, 114
Spillane, Mickey, 61
Stanislavsky, Konstantin, 20, 26
Stapleton, Maureen, 70
Steppenwolf Theatre Company, 153,
    252n. 30
Stevens, Wallace, 123
Stewart, James, 24
Stiller, Ben, 38, 73
Stiller, Jerry, 33, 42, 225
Stone, Harold, 34
Stoneburner, Sam, 186, 207
Stoppard, Tom, 188, 231
Stops Along the Way (Sweet), 203
Straiges, Tony, 177
Strange Interlude (O'Neill), 156
Stratford Festival, 127
Streep, Meryl, 151
Streisand, Barbra, 188
Strindberg, August, 21, 32, 37, 70, 150,
    159, 237n. 38, 238n. 50
Studio Theatre, 249n. 15
Sullivan, Jeremiah, 71
Sutherland, Donald, 39, 188
Swanson, Gloria, 28
Sweet, Jeffrey, 203
Sweet Smell of Success, The, 42

Take a Dream, 240n. 84.
Taking Off, 32–33
Talking Dog, The, 38, 205–6; and lost
    opportunities, 206–7; the real vs. the
    ephemeral in, 206
Tamburlaine the Great (Marlowe), 20
Taylor, Elizabeth, 24, 38
Taymor, Julie, 178
Tedesco, John, 71
Tempest, The (Shakespeare), 154, 171,
    222, 253n. 34

Terminating, or Lass Meine Schmerzen
    Nicht Verloren Sein, or Ambivalence
    (Kushner), 228
Terry, Megan, 30, 203
Tetralogy, 201, 203, 208, 220, 222, 231,
    251n. 15, 254n. 36; as fall of American
    utopianism, 151–85; form of, 149–50;
    genesis of, 36, 148–50; and Guare's
    reputation, 185; shift from black
    comedy, 37, 233; sources of, 153–56
Tharps, Lisa, 229
Theatre Communications Group, 38
Théâtre de la Gaité-Montparnasse, 73
They Are Dying Out (Handke), 126
Thirties Girl, 26, 69
Thomas, Marlo, 39, 188
Threepenny Opera, The (Brecht), 243n.
    20
Three Sisters, The (Chekhov), 14, 25, 96,
    253n. 33
Tipton, Jennifer, 113, 151
Toadstool Boy, The, 26
Tom Sawyer (Mark Twain), 25
Tony Award. See Antoinette Perry
    "Tony" Award.
Tony Rome, 58
To Wally Pantoni, We Leave a Credenza, 29
Trinity Square Repertory Company, 126
Truck and Warehouse Theater, 32,
    71–72
Truman, Harry, 104
Tucci, Stanley, 207
Two Gentlemen of Verona, 11, 34, 37, 88,
    256n. 13; critical reception of, 33–34,
    240n. 79; music in, 33; productions
    of, 33; utopian visions in, 33
Tyrone Guthrie Theater, 32

Ullmann, Liv, 194
Uncle Vanya (Chekhov), 253n. 33
Universal Studios, 28, 32
Universe, 25

Vance, Courtney B., 39, 187, 257n. 22
van Itallie, Jean-Claude, 60, 240n. 88
Veblen, Thorstein, 91
Venice Film Festival, 35, 140
Verdon, Gwen, 70
Vickery, John, 225
Victor Jory Theatre, 203
Vietnam War, 15, 31, 53–58, 81, 94, 156,
    180

Vint (Mamet), 240n. 89
Vivian Beaumont Theater, 38, 39, 40, 42, 73, 187, 217, 245n. 21
Vivien (Granger), 203
Voltaire, 34
Voragine, Jacobus de, 228

Wager, Douglas C., 177–78
Waiting for Philip Glass (Wasserstein), 228
Walken, Christopher, 38, 73
Walken, Glenn, 71
Walker, David, 127
Wallach, Eli, 70
Walter McGinn/John Cazale Theater, 114
Walton, Tony, 38, 73, 186–87, 217
Ward, Douglas Turner, 203
Warhol, Andy, 15, 236n. 13
Warriner, Frederic, 33
Washington, George, 62
Washington One-Act Play Contest, 26
Wasserstein, Wendy, 205, 228
Waters, John, 90
Waterston, Sam, 37, 53, 169
Weaver, Sigourney, 89
Weller, Michael, 205, 240n. 89
Where's Charley?, 25
Where's Daddy? (Inge), 29
Whitman, Walt, 155, 158, 166–68, 171, 175, 177, 182, 254n. 36
Whoopie, 23
Who's Afraid of Virginia Woolf? (Albee), 29
Widdoes, Kathleen, 203

Wilde, Oscar, 26, 163, 238n. 46, 254n. 47
Wilder, Thornton, 20, 90, 141, 237n. 37
William Inge Theatre Festival, 41
Williams, JoBeth, 37, 169
Williams, Samm-Art, 205, 240n. 89
Williams, Tennessee, 11, 237n. 38
Williamstown Theater Festival, 37, 207
Wilson, August, 11, 41, 231, 233
Wilson, Lanford, 29, 203
Wilson, Mary Louise, 127
Winter Garden Theater, 20
Wisteria Trees, The (Logan), 25
Wolfe, Tom, 195
Women and Water, 151, 238n. 50, 254nn. 36 and 40; compared with *Lydie Breeze* and *Gardenia*, 185; difficulties in staging, 178–79; form of, 179–80; genesis of, 37; and learning from written history, 180–85; productions of, 170, 177–78; reviews of, 178; revisions of, 151, 177–78; sources of, 179–80; spiritual connections with self and others, 181–85
Woods, James, 37, 89, 169, 203
Wright, Orville, 107
Wright, Wilbur, 107
Wulp, John, 84, 113, 124–26, 128, 151, 153

Yale Repertory Theatre, 37, 126, 207
Yale University Theatre, 27
Yerman, Lawrence, 207

Zaks, Jerry, 38, 39, 73, 78, 186–88, 245n. 20